Optimizing AI and Machine Learning Solutions

Your ultimate guide to building high-impact ML/AI solutions

Mirza Rahim Baig

www.bpbonline.com

First Edition 2024
REPRINT 2025

ISBN: 978-93-55519-818

Distributors:

BPB PUBLICATIONS
20, Ansari Road, Darya Ganj
New Delhi-110002
Ph: 23254990/23254991

DECCAN AGENCIES
4-3-329, Bank Street,
Hyderabad-500195
Ph: 24756967/24756400

MICRO MEDIA
Shop No. 5, Mahendra Chambers,
150 DN Rd. Next to Capital Cinema,
V.T. (C.S.T.) Station, MUMBAI-400 001
Ph: 22078296/22078297

To View Complete BPB Publications Catalogue Scan the QR Code:

Published by Manish Jain for BPB Publications, 20 Ansari Road, Darya Ganj, New Delhi-110002 and Printed by him at Manipal Technologies, Manipal

www.bpbonline.com

Dedicated to

My lovely wife

About the Author

Since 2009, **Mirza Rahim Baig** has been exploring, practicing, learning, and teaching all things machine learning / artificial intelligence. He is a seasoned data science expert and renowned thought leader. Rahim is adept at solving complex business problems using AI / ML in a career spanning multiple domains and geographies. Numerous job titles aside, his focus has always been using data science to solve business problems and create high impact.

Rahim is also an author, a speaker and educator. In addition to this book, he has authored two well received books *The Deep Learning Workshop* and *Data Science for Marketing Analytics*. In all his titles, Rahim focuses on application and outcomes, and shares best practices derived from his experience. A key feature of his work is the approach of focusing not merely on model building but on the entire end-to-end solution building process. The explanations are easy to follow, even for non-technical learners, thanks to his style developed over years of teaching.

Rahim is a renowned subject matter expert in data science topics, having worked with most of the popular ed-tech platforms in designing courses and delivering content for master's level programs. He is a visiting faculty at NMIMS for MBA programs. In addition to having been published multiple times, Rahim speaks on various platforms about data science.

About the Reviewer

Sujit Pal is a Technology Research Director at Elsevier Health Markets, where he works as an applied researcher at the intersection of search and Machine Learning. His interests are in Information Retrieval, Natural Language Processing, Knowledge Graphs and Machine Learning, and more recently, Large Language Models and Generative AI. He has co-authored two books on Deep Learning and one on Graph-based Natural Language Processing.

Acknowledgement

In writing this book, my aim has been to benefit others with the little knowledge I have. However, it would be insincere to claim that all the insights and knowledge contained in these chapters originated solely from me. A lot comes from my incredible mentors and excellent teachers. What you find here are also their tremendous efforts reaching you through my words.

I would like to acknowledge the achievements of the open-source community. In the past few years, this community has democratized artificial intelligence and machine learning like never before, making state-of-the-art models accessible to anyone with an internet connection. We are truly witnessing a revolution and I am genuinely grateful for it.

I am also grateful to the team at BPB Publications for their guidance and patience throughout the journey of writing this book. Working with some extremely competent editors, reviewers, and technical experts was an enriching experience.

Finally, I would like to thank all the readers who have taken an interest in my book and for their support in making it a reality. Your encouragement has been invaluable.

Preface

Building High-impact Machine Learning / Artificial Intelligence solutions is intended for several types of readers:

- Data science developers (data analysts / scientists) who will create the data science solutions using data,
- Data science professionals who manage data science teams or data science projects,
- Aspiring data scientists who want to learn more than just the techniques,
- Anyone interested in learning the hows of building great solutions and the whys in making the multiple choices in data science solution building.

A key difference between this book and the others in the market is that this book provides a holistic view on data science problem solving. Throughout, the book keeps reminding that business impact and utility are paramount and reminds the learner to be pragmatic in their approach. The book approaches data science solution building using a principled framework. Machine learning model building is one of the many steps in the framework, and this book treats it accordingly. The book will teach what optimization means at each step. Whether it is problem formulation or hyper-parameter tuning for deep learning models, this book provides frameworks and case studies, with extensive hands-on wherever possible.

This book is not focused on the algorithms for building solutions and is not a replacement for algorithm focused books. The book will however provide you enough intuition, functional information, and references to help you make even complex deep learning models. Using this book you will create complex models without implementing the detailed mathematical operations yourself. Instead, you will use abstractions and helpful libraries wherever possible to create clean and simple code. In the later chapters, the book will even teach you how to use transfer learning for using readymade ML and AI models as a part of your solutions. You do not need extensive coding experience for machine learning, the book will guide you step-by-step and provide code and explanations.

With this book, you will be able to approach a ML/AI solution in a systematic way, optimizing each step of the solution building process. You will thus be able to create high impact, high value machine learning/artificial intelligence solutions – which is the ultimate goal of every data science professional.

Chapter 1: Optimizing a Machine Learning /Artificial Intelligence Solution – introduces some core concepts and sets up the foundation for our journey together in this book. It provides an overview of machine learning, followed by addressing the various practical challenges in machine learning. It introduces some key ideas which will be expanded on in the later chapters. It is crucial to distinguish between simply making a model and carefully designing an end-to-end solution to the business problem. A framework to approach such end-to-end solutions is introduced and the chapter will point to the chapters in the book that help you optimize the solution at each step highlighted in the framework, to ultimately develop a truly optimized machine learning/artificial intelligence solution.

Chapter 2: ML Problem Formulation: Setting the Right Objective – discusses perhaps the most important step in any data science project that involves machine learning problem formulation. A problem can be formulated in various ways employing different solutions: machine learning or not. Further, there are multiple possible ML approaches. Making these decisions is not a trivial matter. The chapter also highlights the important of aligning the model objective with the business objective for achieving maximum impact.

Chapter 3: Data Collection and Pre-processing – addresses a basic reality in the ML/AI space – that the sophistication level of the technique is irrelevant if the input data is poor. The chapter explains the various factors that influence the data collection process and how you should tackle associated problems. A principled approach is introduced that helps you optimize the entire pre-processing process as a pipeline, with the help of a case study.

Chapter 4: Model Evaluation and Debugging – teaches model evaluation in the context of solving business problems. Learn various considerations that make a model better than another. The chapter introduces metrics for model evaluation, classification, and regression problems. Learn a principled way to diagnose and debug models to identify the cause of poor performance, along with approaches to handle underfitting and overfitting.

Chapter 5: Imbalanced Machine Learning – shows how to tackle one of the most common and challenging problems in machine learning/artificial intelligence. The chapter explains how imbalance impacts model evaluation and teaches how to diagnose issues due to imbalance. Apart from introducing better metrics for evaluation, it also introduces multiple approaches to tackle imbalance. Learn using several types of under/over sampling techniques to balance the dataset better for a more optimized machine learning solution.

Chapter 6: Hyper-parameter Tuning – is dedicated to the process of finding the best set of *settings* for the model, i.e., hyper-parameters, to get the best generalized performance. The chapter covers the key considerations in defining *best* and proceeds to demonstrate multiple automated approaches to searching for the best hyper-parameters – from exhaustive methods like grid search to approaches like Randomized search.

Chapter 7: Parameter Optimization Algorithms – provides a good understanding of mathematical optimization, the core of machine learning/artificial intelligence models. The chapter contextualizes optimization for machine learning and discusses aspects that make optimization for machine learning unique. It then teaches a general, principled approach to solving optimization problems for classical machine learning and explains the variations developed for deep neural networks. The chapter helps you make important choices in optimization, like loss functions and optimization algorithms, to maximize the performance of the model.

Chapter 8: Optimizing Deep Learning Models – focuses on optimizing neural networks. Like with classical machine learning, hyper-parameter tuning is a key step for optimizing deep neural networks as well. The chapter focusses on the simple fully connected network architecture for these concepts and the accompanying case studies. In addition to automated hyper-parameter tuning for deep neural networks, the chapter will introduce several techniques to improve model performance, like data addition, data augmentation, ensembling, regularization, and injecting your domain knowledge via manual features.

Chapter 9: Optimizing Image Models – dives deeper by teaching optimization of deep learning models for image tasks. This chapter teaches concepts, architectures and parameters that are unique to Image models and then demonstrates how to optimize these using TensorFlow 2.0. The chapter discusses the design approach used in various popular model approaches and teaches you to implement your own versions of VGG and ResNet models. It teaches how to effective use regularization using multiple approaches - dropout, data augmentation, and the powerful batch normalization technique, ending with some general guidelines for designing deep learning models for image tasks.

Chapter 10: Optimizing Natural Language Processin Models – continues the deep learning deep dive by focusing on NLP models. The chapter introduces the peculiarities of natural language data and teaches handling them by appropriate text pre-processing and data representation (using embeddings). The chapter details the recurrent and architecture and the transformer architecture with hands on case studies. In addition to hyper-parameter tuning for NLP models, the chapter shares tricks like using 1D convolutions and pre-trained embeddings (a prelude to transfer learning).

Chapter 11: Transfer Learning – teaches you how to stand on the shoulders of giants and benefit from the excellent work done by the ML/AI community. The chapter explains the different types of transfer learning and how they are helpful in modern machine learning/artificial intelligence, highlighting both the benefits and limitations of it. The chapter demonstrates the usage of a SOTA model out of the box and eventually how to fine tune it for better performance. Transfer learning is slightly different for image processing and NLP tasks. The chapter will employ multiple SOTA models for both image and NLP tasks, employing popular libraries.

Code Bundle and Coloured Images

Please follow the link to download the
Code Bundle and the ***Coloured Images*** of the book:

https://rebrand.ly/zce3wew

The code bundle for the book is also hosted on GitHub at **https://github.com/bpbpublications/Optimizing-AI-and-Machine-Learning-Solutions**. In case there's an update to the code, it will be updated on the existing GitHub repository.

We have code bundles from our rich catalogue of books and videos available at **https://github.com/bpbpublications**. Check them out!

Errata

We take immense pride in our work at BPB Publications and follow best practices to ensure the accuracy of our content to provide with an indulging reading experience to our subscribers. Our readers are our mirrors, and we use their inputs to reflect and improve upon human errors, if any, that may have occurred during the publishing processes involved. To let us maintain the quality and help us reach out to any readers who might be having difficulties due to any unforeseen errors, please write to us at :

errata@bpbonline.com

Your support, suggestions and feedbacks are highly appreciated by the BPB Publications' Family.

Piracy

If you come across any illegal copies of our works in any form on the internet, we would be grateful if you would provide us with the location address or website name. Please contact us at **business@bpbonline.com** with a link to the material.

If you are interested in becoming an author

If there is a topic that you have expertise in, and you are interested in either writing or contributing to a book, please visit **www.bpbonline.com**. We have worked with thousands of developers and tech professionals, just like you, to help them share their insights with the global tech community. You can make a general application, apply for a specific hot topic that we are recruiting an author for, or submit your own idea.

Reviews

Please leave a review. Once you have read and used this book, why not leave a review on the site that you purchased it from? Potential readers can then see and use your unbiased opinion to make purchase decisions. We at BPB can understand what you think about our products, and our authors can see your feedback on their book. Thank you!

For more information about BPB, please visit **www.bpbonline.com**.

Join our book's Discord space

Join the book's Discord Workspace for Latest updates, Offers, Tech happenings around the world, New Release and Sessions with the Authors:

https://discord.bpbonline.com

Table of Contents

CHAPTER 1

Optimizing a Machine Learning /Artificial Intelligence Solution

Introduction

This chapter will provide an overview of **Machine Learning** (**ML**), followed by addressing the various practical challenges in machine learning. This chapter will introduce some key ideas which will be expanded on in the later chapters. We will make the crucial distinction between simply making a model and carefully designing an end-to-end solution to the business problem. We will learn about a framework to approach such end-to-end solutions learn what it means to optimize at each step, and ultimately develop a truly optimized machine learning/artificial intelligence solution.

Structure

In this chapter, we will cover the following topics:

- Case study
- Understanding machine learning
- Machine learning styles
- Challenges in ML/AI
    - o Poor formulation
    - o Invalid assumptions

  - Data availability and hygiene
  - Representative data (lack of)
  - Model scalability
  - Infeasible consumption
  - Misalignment with business objectives
- ML/AI models vs. end-to-end solutions
- CRISP-DM framework for solution development
- Optimization at each step of solution development
  - Business understanding
  - Data understanding
  - Data preparation
  - Model building
  - Evaluation
  - Deployment
- Conclusion

Objectives

In this chapter, we will take a good, holistic look at the field of machine learning. This chapter will introduce some key ideas which will be expanded on in the later chapters. We will make the crucial distinction between simply making a model and carefully designing an end-to-end solution to the business problem. We will learn about a framework to approach such end-to-end solutions and learn what it means to optimize at each step, and ultimately develop a truly optimized machine learning/artificial intelligence solution. The various examples and case studies in this chapter will make the ideas concrete.

Consider this chapter as the gateway – where you get an overview of the steps in creating high-impact, optimized machine learning/artificial intelligence solutions. Each of the steps/ideas we discuss in this chapter will be dealt with in detail in the chapters that follow.

Case study: Text deduplication for online fashion

Consider a data scientist working at the online fashion giant Azra Inc., to make the product detail page most helpful to the shopper. The product page contains detailed information about the product, including ratings, reviews, and questions that users ask about the product. The user questions section is of particular concern. There is a severe duplication of questions. Users are asking the same question with minor variations in language. For example, *Is the material durable*? can be considered a duplicate of *Is the shirt durable*? Due to this, a few common questions are suppressing the visibility of other useful questions and their answers, withholding useful information from users, and affecting product sales. The task for the data scientist is to use their ML / AI expertise to identify duplicate questions as shown in *Figure 1.1*:

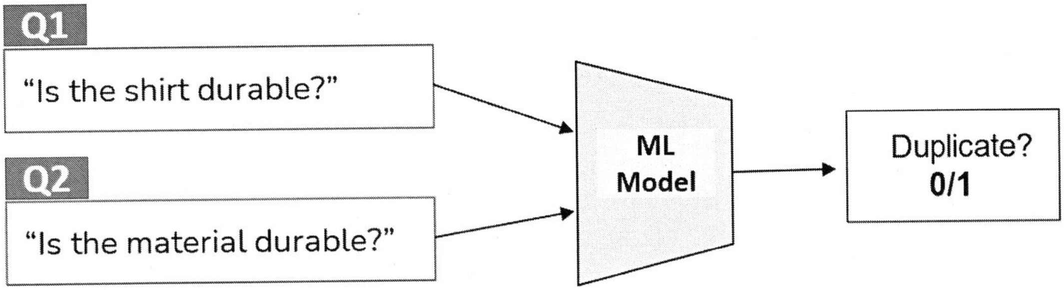

***Figure 1.1**: Deduplication using supervised classification*

The data scientist formulates this as a supervised classification problem, as illustrated in *Figure 1.1*, using a deep learning model for text classification. This makes intuitive sense as we expect deep learning methods to shine in such situations. Using the latest transformer architecture should solve this, right? Unfortunately, in this case, the project was stopped after about 3 months of effort. The reason was a lack of sufficient labeled data.

For the text deduplication task, using a transformer architecture would require at least a few thousand pairs of questions labeled. The problem is labeling tens of thousands of question pairs. Manual labeling would take time and solid guidelines for the labelers so that their labels are in agreement. This is an expensive and time-consuming approach. This logical approach failed because of a presumption of data availability. The solution that eventually worked used an unsupervised clustering approach. The lesson is that improper problem formulation and presumptions can spell disaster for a ML / AI solution.

For success in ML / AI solutions, there are various considerations and decisions at various steps that need to be optimized; this is why data science projects fail. Before we discuss those, let us take a step back. Let us establish the understanding of machine learning that we will employ throughout this book. It is imperative that we take a holistic look at what ML is and more importantly, what it is good for, and how to make it work.

Understanding machine learning

Our modern, data-driven world seeks to make decisions based on data insights to increasingly employ machines to perform repetitive tasks, drive cars, diagnose patients, allocate ads, recommend connections and songs, summarize news, etc. If data is oil in this new world, machine learning is the closest thing we have to the engine of this machinery.

Machine learning is the process that makes it possible to learn patterns from the provided data. The patterns learned by the machines can then be used to make some estimations/ predictions.

The outcome of the pattern learning process is often a mathematical model, capturing how the output relates to the input. The process of learning is also often referred to as model building or data mining. *Figure 1.2* illustrates this process. The historical data is input into the data mining/ model building process. The model-building process learns the patterns, which are expressed as a machine learning model. This model captures the relation between the inputs and the output and can therefore be employed to make estimations/ predictions. Depending on the technique employed, the model could be simpler and easily interpretable (e.g., a simple decision tree, or a linear regression equation), or a complex, hard-to-interpret from a deep neural network (complex series of matrix multiplications) that requires additional effort in post hoc explanations.

Note: Data mining is a broader term that encapsulates the entire process of building a machine learning solution from data, the end-to-end process. Model building is merely one part of this process. We will discuss this in detail later in the chapter in the section titled CRISP-DM Framework.

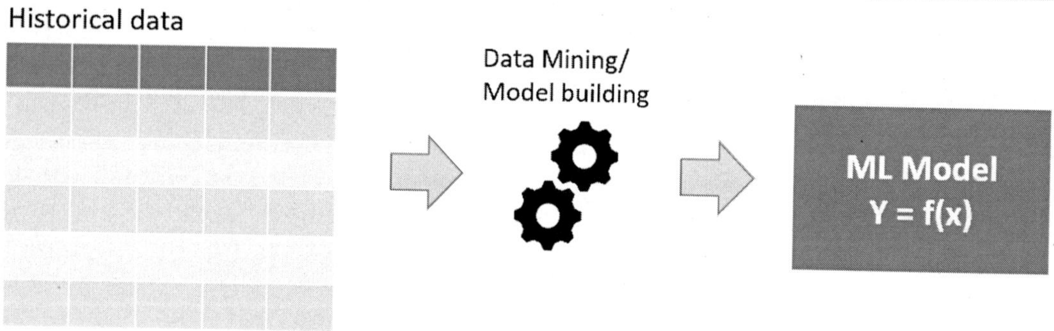

Figure 1.2: *Machines learning patterns from data*

Machine learning styles

Let us now learn how to make machines learn the relevant patterns. We will have to make several decisions. For instance, we need to decide if we want to provide feedback and if yes, how to do that. We must define the kind of estimations that the machine needs to make. We need to define whether the model would be used to make predictions for the future or to uncover some patterns to aid human decision-making. Also important is to define the kind of data we input into the model. The specific solution depends on these considerations, but over the decades we have arrived at broadly three different machine learning styles, as illustrated in *Figure 1.3*:

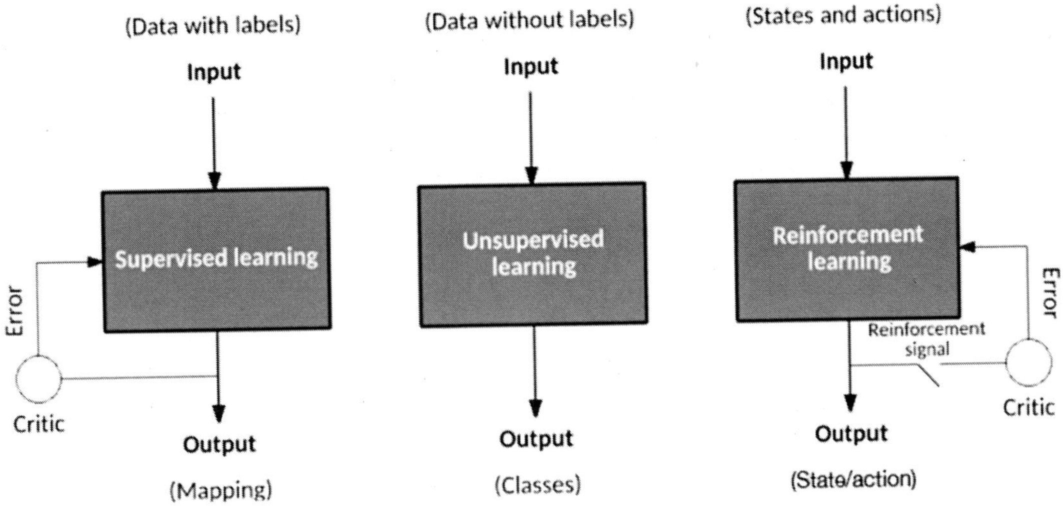

Figure 1.3: Machine learning styles

Supervised machine learning

A key feature of supervised machine learning is that the data provided to the model contains the target as well. The input data comprises the features and the target, as shown in *Figure 1.4*. The features contain the information that will be used to predict the target. For using the model in the future, the input features will be available to us and will be used to predict the target. The machine learning process learns to predict the target using the input features, as illustrated in *Figure 1.4*:

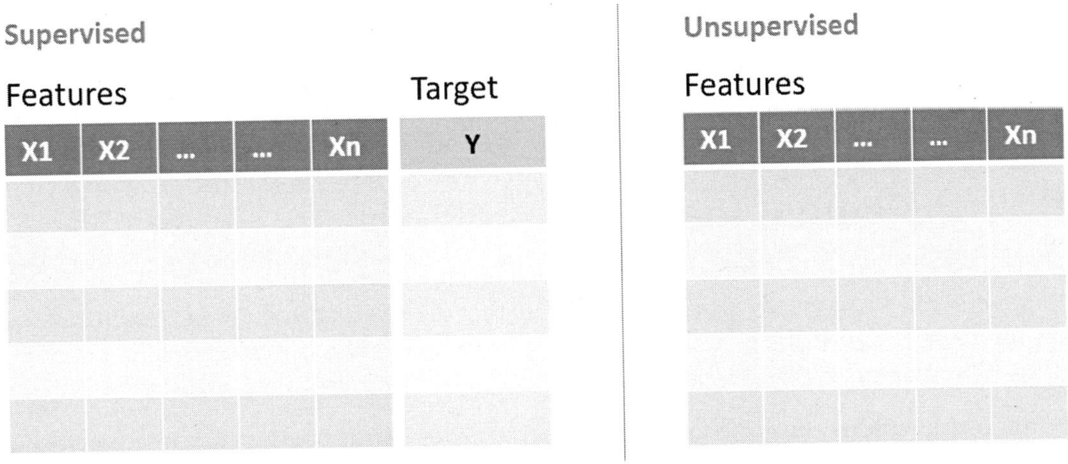

Figure 1.4: Input data for supervised vs. unsupervised ML

Figure 1.4 illustrates how the supervision is done. The modeling technique sees the true target values (often called labels) and their predictions, compares them using a notion of error, and updates the model until the difference between the true values and the predictions is minimized. Reliable, labeled data is a critical requirement for this style of machine learning. The learned model is then used to make predictions. For example, a supervised model for diagnosing lung cancer from X-rays would have been trained on several X-ray images as inputs, along with the true diagnosis (cancer/ no cancer) for each image for the machine learning process. The model could then be used to predict for any new X-ray, whether the patient has lung cancer or not.

The learning behavior is very different for unsupervised machine learning, as we shall see in the next section.

Unsupervised machine learning

Unsupervised machine learning, by contrast, does not have labels/ ground truth for the target to supervise the learning process. As shown in *Figure 1.4,* the data input to the process does not contain any information about the target. The machine usually learns some structural patterns in the data, typically condensing the information contained in the dataset.

One common utility of such a model is to organize data and divide it into similar groups (clusters). Some common applications are customer segmentation, image segmentation, association rule mining, etc. Another common use case is to reduce the data - dimensionality reduction - to make it more manageable while retaining most of the information contained. **Principal Component Analysis (PCA), Singular Value Decomposition (SVD), Non-Negative Matrix Factorization (NMF)**, and T-SNE are some popular examples of dimensionality reduction approaches.

None of these methods need a notion of the ground truth of the value they output. For unsupervised learning approaches, it is the human that must provide some guidance to the model to make the output useful (either by way of setting parameters or by way of iteration over the results). Let us now understand how reinforcement learning works.

Reinforcement learning

The reinforcement style of machine learning is different from the other two styles. It is somewhat like supervised learning in the sense that there is feedback/supervision, but the similarity ends there. The way the feedback is provided is also different. The most salient feature of this learning style is learning by trial and error.

In reinforcement learning, the agent (or the actor) tries various actions (choose between a given set of actions) in different states (or situations). The environment provides feedback to the agent, whether the move was a good one or not. Over several rounds of trial and error in various situations with feedback provided, the agent learns a good sequence of actions it must take to meet its objectives. Self-driving cars are an example where this learning style is preferable.

Many situations where the machine needs to decide the next best action based on the current situation can be formulated as reinforcement learning tasks. Perhaps a stock trading bot can be trained using reinforcement learning to optimize the portfolio and maximize investment performance. Reinforcement learning can also be used in recommendations where the state of the user, platform variables, and platform objectives can be considered to make the next best recommendation for the user.

Choosing the ML style

There are many cheat sheets available on the internet that tell you which machine learning style you should use for the task. Many of them are from reputed organizations. Further, there are cheat sheets that even tell you which technique is best for a certain situation. These cheat sheets provide recommendations along the lines of - If you are predicting a category and have more than N records, use an XGBoost classifier. This sounds massively helpful, prima facie.

We will soon discuss that the choice is not simple. *Chapter 2, ML Problem Formulation: Setting the Right Objective*, is dedicated to this topic. To begin with, choosing the right ML style is not obvious. The right technique is another choice and as you get involved in the solution-building process, you need to make plenty of choices to maximize the value of the solution. This is an art, not science, even if data science gurus out there mislead you into believing otherwise. Most chapters of this book meditate on these decisions and the trade-offs involved.

The bottom line - ML/AI solutions have often been looked at in an oversimplified and reduced manner, not respecting the complexities that building a solution usually entails. Such oversight is why many ML/AI solutions fail. Let us understand this aspect better and through the process discover various aspects of solving problems using ML/AI.

Challenges in ML/AI

It is no secret that many proposed ML/AI solutions do not see the light of day, i.e., successful deployment. Indeed, various studies have shown that about 70% of ML/AI projects fail to deliver any impact. At a very detailed level, it might seem like there was a specific, unique reason for each failure. Taking a step back and looking at the big picture, we can abstract all of them into one single reason which is the lack of optimization at each step of the solution development process.

We have not quite discussed this development process yet. We shall do so in the next section, providing a formal framework for developing a data science solution. We will also define what optimization means at each step of the process. To make the idea more concrete, we will look at some of the most common reasons why ML/AI solutions fail.

Poor formulation

By problem formulation, we refer to converting a business problem into a well-scoped, concrete data science problem. For example, the business might need the search results shown to the shopper on the e-commerce platform to be relevant to user interests and intent. This seems like a fairly well-articulated business problem. However, this is nowhere concrete enough as a data science problem. From a data science perspective, this could be formulated as a ranking problem wherein the items with the highest likelihood of being clicked by the user, in the context of the user journey, would be ranked better. These are entirely different articulations.

For example, a popular guided meditation and mindfulness application might be dealing with the problem of customer churn where users stop using the platform. The business objective could be to simply reduce customer churn, and as a result, retain more customers. The data science objectives could be many. Three common approaches are as follows:

- A classification problem of predicting whether the customer will churn, based on the characteristics of the customer along with their activity on the platform.
- A ranking/survival problem where the customers could be ranked on the likelihood of them churning and offering incentives (bonuses, vouchers, etc.) to the most valuable customers to retain them.
- A detailed analysis to identify the drivers of churn (e.g., top reasons why customers stop using the platform) and take corrective actions. This could be achieved by a well-designed user survey.

On further thinking, you might identify a few more data science problem formulations for this single business problem. Not all formulations are equal, as we already understand. Each formulation comes with specific requirements and trade-offs. Revisiting the text deduplication example, a different formulation could drastically change the data requirements and be the difference between success and failure.

A very detailed discussion of this topic, with various examples and trade-offs, is done in *Chapter 2, ML Problem Formulation: Setting the Right Objective*, which is dedicated to this topic.

Invalid/poor assumptions

The data science team at Azra Inc. is building a better click prediction model, to predict whether a user will click on a particular item. The idea is to provide higher visibility to items that are relevant to the customer. It results in a better customer experience. This seems like a fair approach. Let us take a moment to realize some of the big assumptions in this reasoning:

- The user only clicks on items that are relevant to the user intent. This assumption is hard to verify, primarily because the user intent is rarely known. The user might have come to buy a shoe but can very likely click on another item out of curiosity, without the intention of buying it.

- Customer interests do not change between the time the data was collected and the model would be deployed.
- Platform environment (newer fashion, styles, altogether new item categories, customer segment distribution) is similar enough.
- The biggest assumption is that more clicks by a user indicate a better customer experience.

Think and you would spot other assumptions in this reasoning. If these assumptions fail, the highest accuracy model would not solve the problem. One must be cognizant of the assumptions they make when designing a machine learning / artificial intelligence solution and validate them using data.

Data availability and hygiene

Let us revisit the text deduplication example for Azra Inc., the biggest assumption that the team made, was that several thousand labeled records would be available as training data for the model. This unmet need for data was enough to derail the solution. Consider another situation where the data scientist assumes that demographic data (e.g., gender, age) would be available for modeling. Various organizations and data protection laws in many countries now prohibit the use of such features. The features would have been very useful for the model, but unfortunately are not available. Again, data availability becomes the hurdle.

Any time a problem is designed to be solved using supervised learning, it is assumed that sufficient label data is available. There are assumptions made about the availability of various input features for modeling. There is this implicit assumption that the data available are reliable enough and the quality issues are manageable. Failure of any of these assumptions would lead you back to the drawing board.

Representative data (lack of)

Consider the case of detecting fraudulent transactions among credit card purchases. Typically, a very small proportion (usually less than 0.5%) of the transactions are truly fraudulent. Assuming that we have reliable, labeled data for the task, we go ahead using a supervised ML model for this task. A model you built could exhibit extremely high accuracy (99.5%) but might be completely useless for the task.

To understand why, consider a model that predicts all the transactions as not fraudulent. You can have 99.5% accuracy without detecting a single fraudulent transaction. This is common for fraud detection problems, where the classes have an imbalance i.e., one class (non-fraud) is present in the data far more than the other (fraud). Imbalanced data impacts the modeling process in two big ways:

- Model evaluation is tricky.
- Getting the model to handle imbalance is tricky.

A good solution must have a carefully considered model evaluation process and to ensure that the model learns enough from both classes to distinguish between them.

A very detailed discussion of these aspects is performed in *Chapter 5, Imbalanced Machine Learning*, which is dedicated to this topic.

Model scalability

For example, consider a situation where a data scientist develops a model that predicts for each shopper x item combination, whether the user would click on the item. The data scientists use several, extremely informative features for the model. They go through data like all the items the user has seen in the past 6 months, all the clicks in the past year, and so on. This is a massive amount of data that must be stored, retrieved, and processed by the model to predict the outcome for one user x item combination. The platform might have a million users each day and there might be a billion combinations that need predictions. Likely, these steps, i.e., storing the required data, retrieving, and processing at a high velocity are not supported by the infrastructure. It could also happen that the model worked well for one category of items but is not practical for all item categories. The solution does not scale.

This consideration applies to situations that are not one-time analyses to discover insights. For solutions that automate predictions, model scalability is an essential feature (not a good-to-have feature).

Infeasible consumption

An example of this failure is when the machine learning/AI solution was expected to aid decision-making and make clear, actionable recommendations for decision-makers. Instead, the solution only spits out probabilities of a class. The decision maker (end consumer) either does not know how to use these probabilities, finds it too tedious, or does not understand/trust the model. In all cases, the solution is not utilized and fails to deliver impact.

As an example, let us say that as a data scientist at Azra Inc., you have made a model that predicts whether a user will click on an item with high accuracy. The model predicts in 30 milliseconds. The engineering team rejects this solution as 30 milliseconds is too long. It would bring the platform's performance down. The team says that the prediction must be made in less than 5 milliseconds. You have ended up with a highly accurate model, but an infeasible solution.

There are multiple ways by which you can end up in this situation, which could be grouped into a single reason, that is, lack of optimization for end consumption/ deployment. The solution must respect the constraints of the environment in which it will be deployed. Whether it is a near real-time prediction model or a timely recommendation/insight for decision-makers.

Misalignment with business outcomes

We touched upon this aspect while discussing imbalanced data. The model evaluation metric (say, accuracy) might show great potential, but in practice, this could amount to a poor model that does not help solve the problem at all (or at an impractical cost). There could be several other ways in which the model evaluation could be flawed and therefore misleading. Consider the example of click prediction over search results on an e-commerce platform. A model evaluation method that focuses solely on accurately predicting clicks might rank cheaper (and low-quality) items over high-quality products with a higher price. If this solution is deployed, we might see an improvement in search **Click Through Rate (CTR)** in the short term. However, the lower quality of the items shown might put off customers, lower conversion (orders/visits), increase the return rate, and lower customer retention, negatively impacting the business in many ways.

The goals of the ML/AI model and the business must be aligned. This is easier said than done. It is extremely difficult to find one metric that captures business objectives and can serve as the model's objective. In such a situation, the model goal must be as close as possible (proxy) to the business objective. In case a direct proxy is not possible, the model objective must be close to some known driver of the business metric. As a good practice, the data scientist should first test out the model performance in live systems (A/B testing) on a small proportion of the audience. The solution must not harm business metrics in the form of guardrails set for the A/B experiment. Only then should the model be employed for the entire audience.

A more principled evaluation approach and various considerations will be discussed in detail in *Chapter 4, Model Evaluation and Debugging*.

The bottom line is that for a machine learning/artificial intelligence solution to be successful, the entire solution development process/lifecycle must be understood and optimized. Let us understand this process and an excellent framework in the next section.

ML / AI models vs. end-to-end solutions

Until recently, the output produced by a data science team used to be a predictive model. It could be the script with the predictive component specified (e.g., equation from linear regression). It could be a compressed model object (e.g., a pickle file) that expects the right input format and spits out predictions when used correctly. This would be the solution from the perspective of the data scientist, as illustrated in *Figure 1.5*. The data engineering team would work with these outputs to deploy the model, i.e., create the system that processes the data end to end and start to deliver value. Model development was considered the job of the data scientist, while model deployment was a task for the engineers.

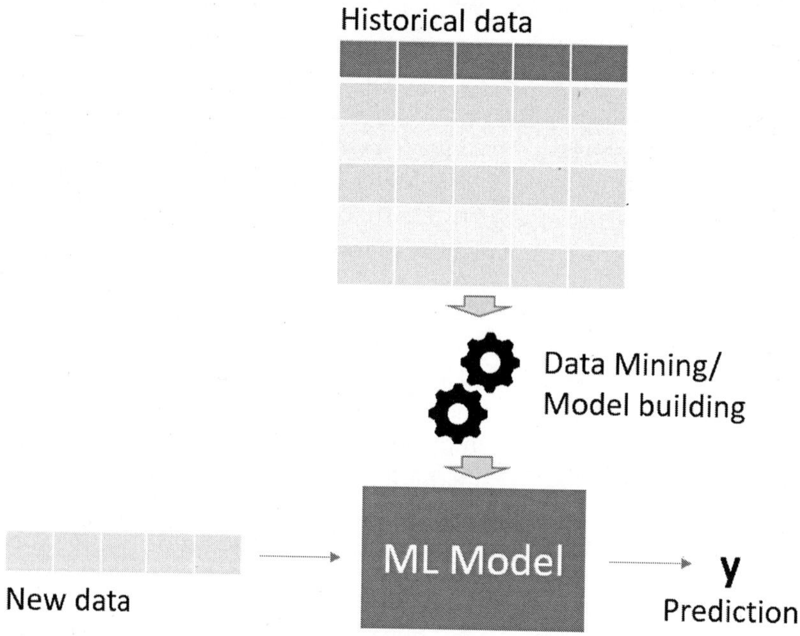

Figure 1.5: *Traditional view of ML solutions*

This arrangement had a dependency on engineering (the team that did not develop the model) to get value from the data mining process. This was suboptimal. It should be easy to expect that it would exacerbate many of the challenges around model deployment, consumption, and scalability. It is better if the team that creates the model also understands model consumption and makes sure the model is scalable. Similarly, the team that develops the model must ideally also understand well the business considerations and thereby generate maximum value from the model. This brings us to the natural conclusion that the team that develops the data science solution must understand and own the end-to-end process as shown in *Figure 1.6*:

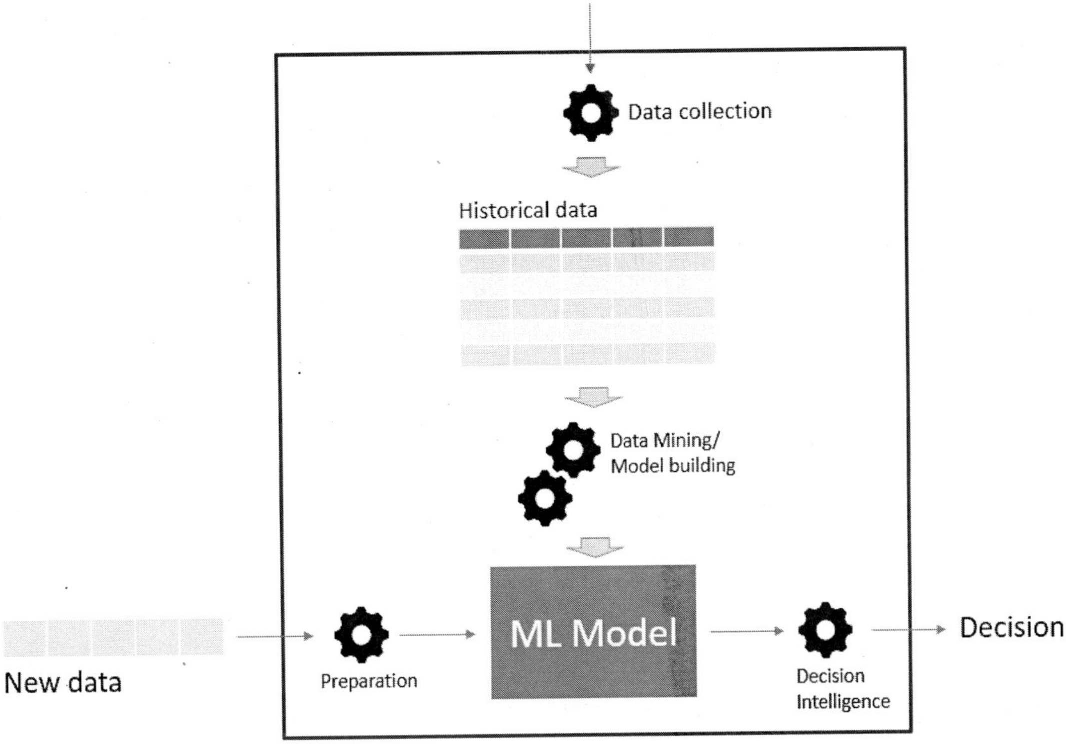

Figure 1.6: Data science solutions as end-to-end systems

The modern data scientist must therefore think not in terms of standalone models, but entire, end-to-end data science solutions, as illustrated in *Figure 1.6*. Let us now learn about a framework to approach this process.

CRISP-DM framework

We discussed earlier that the modern data scientist must think in terms of solutions that solve business problems, and not standalone models. A business problem often is not a static, standalone, one-time event. Business problems are usually complex, having many facets and nuances. The problems are not completely defined right at the beginning and often have no single endpoint that can be quickly achieved. Solving such problems requires dealing with a great amount of uncertainty and constant refinement of the approach with each new learning. After the problem has been sufficiently understood, creating the data science solution is a process that often requires iteration and a great deal of emphasis on end utility for the consumers. All this diligent effort might lead us merely to the first solution that sets the stage for future improvements. It may also lead us to learn some new information that could put us back at the drawing board, reviewing our assumptions and hypotheses, to create a different approach to the problem.

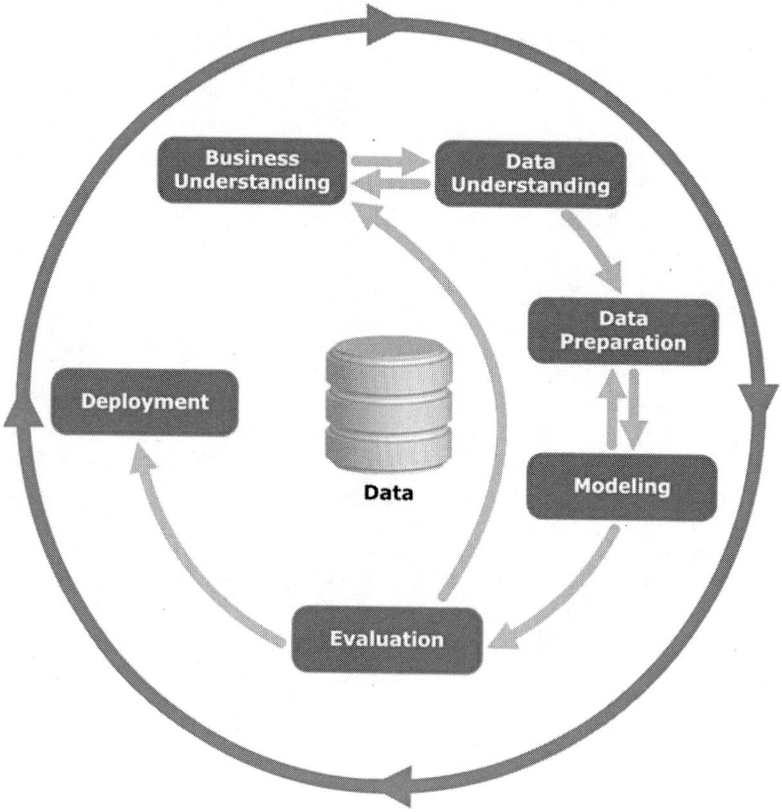

Figure 1.7: CRISP-DM framework

This iterative nature of problem-solving has been well captured in the Cross Industry Standard Process for Data Mining Framework also known as the CRISP-DM Framework. Illustrated in *Figure 1.7*, this framework applies to various types of problems and domains. It can be applied universally.

Optimization at each step of solution development

The CRIP-DM framework is a universal data mining framework that helps us build sound data science solutions. There are 6 steps in the framework, each capturing an important step of the solution building process. To build a high-impact data science solution, you must understand each step of the framework. To optimize the solution, you must optimize each step outlined in the CRISP-DM framework. Let us understand what optimization means at each step. To make the ideas more concrete, let us also learn what optimization would look like for the text deduplication case study for Azra Inc.

Business understanding

In this section, we will discuss the business problem. It is important to identify whether we are dealing with a single problem or a compositive of many smaller problems. We need to assess the urgency. We also need to assess if we can afford to perform research and take our time to build the solution. This is the step at which we formulate the business problem to solve – that is, convert a vague, high-level problem statement to a well-formulated and scoped, specific problem. At this stage, we do not decide on the modeling technique. Other questions need to be answered to design a solution. Are we building a prototype/ **Minimum Viable Product** (**MVP**) or are we building one solution designed to last for the long term? These decisions have a big impact on the solution that we ultimately develop.

We also need to define the consumption of the solution. We need to evaluate if it is enough to provide insight from the data science process in a well-designed dashboard. Alternatively, we need to be clear if it needs to be a system with multiple components. Each component could be a data science model. These components could be intelligently stitched together to form the necessary solution. These are additional considerations in developing the solution.

Business understanding also includes gaining an understanding of the nature of the problem at hand. The business teams or the data science teams usually have hypotheses about the problem and what can potentially solve it. These hypotheses could be of the nature: the problem lies within customer segment X i.e., trying to locate the problem. They could be of the type – *improving the return experience will help retain customers*, which attempts to capture actions that might solve the problem. Both types are hypotheses, nonetheless, and must be evaluated using data. An understanding is essential to begin deciding about the nature of the data that is needed to solve the problem.

We need to understand what optimization means at this step. Let us also revisit the text deduplication case study and try to define the optimization that we need at this step.

The optimization at this step is as follows:

- Choosing the right approach
- Identify the usage of the solution
- Design the entire system, components of the solution
- Identify constraints
- Identify key hypotheses

For the text de-duplication case study, it is as follows:

- The formulation as a supervised vs. Unsupervised problem
- Identify data requirements for the chosen formulation
- Design the system to make a prediction

- Design (as needed) a decision layer to flag duplicates
- Identify latency requirements and data storage/retrieval setup

Answering these questions does not end this process. *Figure 1.7* shows a back-and-forth between the *Business understanding* step and the *Data understanding* step. Let us understand the next step and get a better understanding of the dependency.

Data understanding

This crucial step is composed of three sub-steps:

1. Defining and collecting data
2. Exploring patterns in the data
3. Hypotheses validation and generation

The first step, that is, defining the right data to collect and analyze, has a significant impact on the efficiency of all the steps that follow. The hypotheses generated in the *Business understanding* step are the starting point for defining this data. Data collection can be an extremely time-consuming step, sometimes taking months to get the desired data. The needed data might not be recorded by the organization and might need to build the capabilities to track this data. In several cases, such data might need to be purchased from external vendors. The reader might have realized the importance and the impact of the *Business understanding* stage on this step. Bad decisions in the previous step can turn out to be quite expensive at this step.

Next, the collected data is explored to understand the various patterns contained in it. Exploration usually employs several data analysis techniques of varying complexities. The result of this exploration is a more informed approach to the problem. The various hypotheses that were generated in the *Business understanding* step are now validated/invalidated by such exploration. The data scientist might uncover several interesting patterns that generate new hypotheses that improve the overall understanding of the problem. Revelations at this step might put you back at the drawing board, reviewing your larger approach to solving the problem. Indeed, this is the back and forth between *Data understanding* and *Data preparation* steps, which was indicated in *Figure 1.7*. Let us understand what optimization means at this step. Let us also revisit the text deduplication case study and see how we could have optimized this step.

The optimization at this step is as follows:

- Identifying the right data
- Collecting data the right way
- Identifying specifics of the problem through data
- Validation of hypotheses
- Generation of new hypotheses
- Updating/refining collected data

For our text de-duplication case study, it is as follows:

- Understand domain-specific nuances (for example, questions are often about specific types of attributes of the item).
- Understand the nature of duplication – the kinds of similarities that exist in the questions. Identify clear duplicates (minor language variations) vs. logical duplicates (similar themed questions, for example, regarding delivery availability in city1 vs city2).
- Specifics of the language used in the data. Identify and item category-specific issues.
- Identifying non-standard usage of language (e.g., Roman Hindi mixed with English)

Data preparation

It is not enough that the data points are collected and explored and can be fed into the model. We must perform an important last step before modeling which is to prepare the data for modeling. This could mean a few things:

- Formatting the data for better working with intended algorithms.
- Deriving features from the data with the task at hand.
- Cleansing the data to remove unwanted artefacts etc.
- Handling issues like missing values.

It is important to note that this part of the solution building is rarely standard. It depends on the data collection process, the nature of the data, several domain-specific considerations, and the task at hand. This is the step where the skill of the practitioner makes a big difference and these are the bits that are part art, part science. There is no such thing as task-agnostic data preparation / pre-processing.

The optimization at this step is as follows:

- Task-oriented data manipulation
- Creating/deriving informative features
- Getting rid of redundancies to make modeling more efficient
- Data representation/formatting as per model requirements

All these actions should be reproducible, using pipelines that can smoothly repeat the processing for any new incoming data.

By this stage, you would have the Machine Learning style chosen. For example, a supervised learning approach is chosen for a fraud detection problem. The data preparation is done accordingly. The problem could also be approached in an unsupervised manner, as we will see in detail in *Chapter 2, ML Problem Formulation: Setting the Right Objective.* The key point is ML style is usually chosen by this stage, but it does not mean that we cannot go back, as we will briefly discuss in the next section.

For the text de-duplication case study, it is as follows:

- Data cleanup i.e., removal of unusable text content
- Creating numeric representations for each question text
- Adding features derived from domain knowledge (e.g., markers for specific text keywords).
- Creating a pipeline for an end-to-end transformation of the input text

Chapter 3, Data Collection and Pre-processing is dedicated to this topic.

Model building

We have arrived where we build the mathematical model that would capture the patterns in the data. For a prediction task, this model would capture the mathematical relationship between the inputs and the output that we want to predict. If the machine learning/ AI solution is the body, the model is the brain. By now, you must have realized that this model does not need to be excessively sophisticated to qualify as a model. It could be a simple pivot table in a dashboard that provides necessary insight, or rules derived from the data.

Perhaps the best advice to any data scientist at this stage of solution development is to understand and obey the constraints.

Following all the steps up to this stage, the data scientists would have realized various forms of constraints coming from various sources. There could be constraints on the transparency and interpretability of the model. In some cases, regulatory bodies might require interpretability and audit the model. Consumption of the model puts further constraints on what techniques can be even considered for the solution. Likewise, other considerations are offline vs. online prediction, near real-time vs. low-frequency predictions, latency requirements, data refresh requirements, etc. The data scientist must respect the constraints that the system and deployment environment bring, as they become the constraints on the solution they can develop.

The optimization at this step is as follows:

- Identify and obey constraints on the solution
- Developing model from scratch vs. transfer learning
- Choosing the optimal modeling technique
- Choosing the right architecture (especially for deep learning models)
- Hyper-parameter tuning to get the most out of the available data
- Data augmentation/balancing techniques

Model building is a core focus of this book and is discussed in almost all the chapters. Regarding some specific aspects, *Chapter 5, Imbalanced Machine Learning* teaches strategies to handle class imbalance. *Chapter 6, Hyper-parameter Tuning* teaches a principled way of tuning the model settings to get the maximum performance and derive the maximum value from the data. The other chapters teach how to approach model building.

For the text de-duplication case study, it is as follows:

- Choosing between transfer learning (the latest transformer-based model) and developing a solution from scratch
- Choosing the right deep learning architecture (recurrent networks vs. transformers)
- Hyper-parameter tuning for maximum accuracy

At this juncture, you might decide that the formulation might need to change due to the results you get. Revisiting the fraud detection example, you may have been approaching this as a supervised learning problem. After many approaches to supervised learning, you could decide that an unsupervised approach is worth trying. To do so, you need to go back to the previous step and prepare the data differently for unsupervised machine learning.

Evaluation

In practice, some parts of the evaluation must be addressed in the previous step. For example, choosing the best hyper-parameters for the modeling technique needs a good model to choose from the many options and optimize. The best model is not always the one with the highest accuracy, as we will discuss in detail in *Chapter 4, Model Evaluation and Debugging*. We discussed that the data science solution must obey several constraints. In this situation we have several candidate models that meet our requirements, the best model solves the (business) problem the best and provides the most value to its consumers.

Such an assessment necessitates a good way of model evaluation. Our assessment criteria must be close to the business outcome. If the model objective is not aligned with the business objective, you might end up with a solution that fails. In the model validation step, we ensure that we have an evaluation setup and can assess the generalized performance of the model. This performance can be linked to business outcomes.

The optimization at this stage is as follows:

- Evaluation of model outcomes and impact on business outcomes
- Build an evaluation pipeline for multiple competing solutions
- Choose the model that has the most business impact while respecting constraints/ requirements on the solution

For text deduplication case, consider the following:

- Evaluate the extent (for example, percentage) of duplicates detected by the model
- Choose the best model using this evaluation criterion
- Check if this meets business requirements

A more principled evaluation approach and various considerations will be discussed in detail in *Chapter 4, Evaluation and Debugging*.

Deployment

Depending on the nature of the solution, deployment can be a process of varying complexity. When the outcome of the data science solution is an actionable insight, deployment would entail communicating the insight in the most effective format. Even a smartly designed dashboard that provides necessary recommendations may suffice. For solutions that provide near real-time decisions, this would entail making an end-to-end process that quickly transforms the inputs, makes the prediction, and applies the necessary intelligence over the prediction to make a micro-decision.

Deployment is the last mile of the machine learning/AI solution, executing it well makes all the difference in the value that the solution delivers and the impact it creates. For example, an extremely high-accuracy model that uses the latest deep learning architecture could be rendered practically useless, if the consumption of its predictions is not optimally designed. In another situation, a simple model with lower accuracy could solve the business problem if it provides insight as a recommendation with a supporting explanation. A major part of this step is therefore optimizing for consumption.

Once the model is live (being used for its purpose), it must be monitored. Applications of monitoring include ensuring that the model's accuracy continues to be good on newer data, detecting data and concept drift (the model is still relevant, the nature of data has not changed), monitoring model latency, and ensuring good inference/ prediction time.

The optimization at this step is as follows:

- Creating a pipeline for end-to-end handling of the data and outputs
- Optimize the pipeline for the deployment environment
- Right communication of actionable insights
- Setup model performance monitoring with the right metrics

Note: Model performance monitoring is necessary for systems that make recurring predictions over an extended duration, for example, click prediction models on e-commerce platforms. Each situation needs to be carefully assessed, requiring a good understanding of the data, the technical setup, and the impact of the model on business metrics.

For the text deduplication case study, it is as follows:

- Creating a pipeline to evaluate every new user question
- Create a pipeline for end-to-end handling of the new input questions (text preprocessing, representation, flagging, categorization, action)
- Optimize for the efficient running of the above process
- Model monitoring setup and checking for data and concept drift

Conclusion

In this chapter, we discussed key ideas that are essential to understand when using data science to solve a problem. Many data science solutions fail. There are various reasons, which can be reduced and abstracted to one reason which is lack of optimization. By this, we do not refer to the mathematical model. Indeed, modern data scientists must differentiate between building a model and building an end-to-end machine learning/ AI solution.

The CRISM-DM framework is an excellent approach to developing data-based solutions that can be applied to all industries and domains. It starts with business understanding and ends at deployment. Optimizing the mathematical model is only a small part of optimizing the overall solution, and the solution must obey various constraints imposed on it - by business, by deployment requirements, and by regulatory authorities. A data science professional must understand each step and appreciate that optimizing a machine learning/ AI solution requires each step of the CRISM-DM framework to be optimized. With this understanding, we are one step closer to start delving into the details of each of the steps in the process of building an optimized solution.

In the next chapter, we will learn about setting the right objective to solve the business problem at hand and defining the formulation to get the best result and create maximum impact.

Join our book's Discord space

Chapter 2
ML Problem Formulation: Setting the Right Objective

Introduction

This chapter discusses perhaps the most important step in any data science project that involves machine learning problem formulation. A problem can be formulated in various ways employing different solutions: machine learning or not. Further, there are multiple possible ML approaches. Some problems can be solved as supervised classification problems, while others as clustering problems. Additionally, the dependent variables and the set of features are choices that significantly impact the performance of the machine-learning model. This chapter motivates the idea of setting the right objective for solving the business problem at hand; defining the formulation to get the best result. Finally, we will see that for a machine learning solution to create maximum impact, the model objective should be aligned with the business objective.

Structure

In the following chapter, we will discuss the following topics:

- Identifying a Machine Learning problem
- Choosing the ML style
- Problem 1: Fraud detection
- Problem 2: Predicting high-selling products

- Problem 3: Question de-duplication for an e-commerce website
- Blending the ML styles
  - For better accuracy
  - For dimensionality reduction
  - For better data representation
- Choosing the right dependent variable
- Business objective vs. ML objective

Objectives

In this chapter, we will discuss the first critical step in a machine learning/ artificial intelligence project – formulating the business problem as a machine learning problem. First, we will learn how to identify problems that are suitable for machine learning. Then, we will see whether a problem can be solved in multiple ways employing different ML approaches. We will see some thumb rules and then understand how these boundaries are blurry in real-world situations. We will also see how choosing the right dependent variable and features can set up a project for success. We will conclude this chapter with the idea that maximum impact is created when the model objective aligns with the business objective. At the end of this chapter, you will be able to identify the right formulation for your business problem and set up the machine learning/artificial intelligence endeavor for success.

Identifying a Machine Learning problem

In the Machine Learning approach to solving problems, we use data to make the model learn the patterns needed to make decisions/predictions. The promise of Machine learning is that it eliminates the need to manually encode your knowledge and domain understanding as a set of rules. You could feed thousands and even millions of data points to the model, and it, almost magically, figures out all it needs to make a prediction. Machine Learning approaches have gained such prominence that many data problems are straightaway considered ML problems, sometimes with great success, and sometimes with some hard lessons learnt. For any data science professional, it is imperative to understand that not all problems need to be solved as Machine Learning problems.

Machine Learning comes with its own set of requirements and challenges. The most common necessity of the popular ML approaches is a high(er) volume of training data that the machine needs to learn from to create a model. Additionally, building robust Machine Learning models is a time-consuming process involving multiple steps - fetching data, cleaning it up, other pre-processing and transformations, model building, evaluation, and scoring. While in some situations, the time and effort spent are worth the result, this is not always the case, especially considering that competing rule-based solutions might provide an acceptable result quicker with lesser effort.

Consider a new online job application portal, where users can submit their profiles in PDF format, following specific guidelines on the resume format. The portal would then automatically extract information from the resume such as contact information, job titles, graduation dates, and so on. Such a task falls in the category of *"information extraction"* tasks, an area of Natural Language Processing. Deep Learning-based models have shown great performance on such tasks, given adequate training data and time to train the data.

An alternative approach would be to use Regular Expressions – pattern-based text matching and extraction techniques. The modeller can define the pattern expected in a field to extract that information from the text. For example, if the phone numbers have a (few) consistent format(s), then the modellers can describe the pattern using Regular Expressions and extract the phone number with ease. Likewise, Regular Expressions can be used to extract other relevant pieces of information. Since the portal has guidelines on the resume format, we expect the patterns to be consistent across the resumes. This means that we can expect the Regular Expression-based solution to provide good results in a fraction of the time needed for a Machine Learning-based approach. ML-based solutions would be overkill in this situation, and a simple rule-based solution can do the job.

Consider another situation in which the online fast fashion giant Azra wishes to understand why its **Net Promoter Score** (**NPS**) has been reducing, that is, they wish to understand the factors that are negatively impacting customer satisfaction. Using Machine Learning, this can be solved using complex models. The features/predictors would include many user signals and their interactions with the platform and its products. We are talking about large volumes of data that would need to be collected and carefully synthesized into smart features to use in the model. Such activity typically takes several months. But there is an alternative: well-designed user surveys (or even talking to a few of the subject matter experts). Again, Machine Learning is not always the best solution for every problem and simpler approaches can provide pragmatic solutions to pressing business problems.

How do you decide if the problem at hand needs to be solved using Machine Learning? Here are some considerations:

- How much time do you have?
- Do you have data/enough data?
- Does it need high accuracy?
- Does the solution need to be scalable?
- Is it a **Minimum Viable Product** (**MVP**), or in other words, a first version that will be superseded?
- Is it a one-time fix or a long-term solution that needs to be maintained?

The ideal template for a Machine Learning solution is a problem where you have enough data, sufficient time, and higher accuracy requirements. For situations requiring immediate fixes and where high accuracy is not a requirement, rule-based approaches often suffice. Additionally, if the situation needs a stop-gap solution that will be eventually superseded by a thorough, sophisticated solution, this first attempt can very well be a rule-based solution. In this case, the solution is a long-term one, needing frequent retraining and maintenance, where the Machine Learning approach is ideal. Similarly, scalability requires employing Machine Learning techniques, as rule-based systems are difficult to maintain and even more difficult to scale.

With these guidelines, you should be able to decide if the problem at hand can be addressed using rule-based approaches, or if they indeed need a Machine Learning solution. In case you do need to take a Machine Learning approach, you need to choose the appropriate ML approach. Let us discuss that in the following section.

Choosing the ML style

We discussed some Machine Learning styles in the previous chapter. The implicit, simple decision process for choosing the appropriate style is shown in *Figure 2.1*. It captures the most popular guidelines for making such a choice:

	Supervised Learning	Unsupervised Learning	Reinforcement Learning
Definition	The machine learns from provided labeled data.	No labels are provided to the machine.	An agent interacts with the environment by performing actions and learns from errors and rewards.
Problem types	Classification, Regression	Clustering, Association, Dimensionality reduction	Optimal policy/ actions
Training	External supervision	No supervision	No supervision
Approach	Minimize error over training data.	Capture patterns/ structures in the data.	Trial and error to maximize reward.

***Figure 2.1**: Choosing a machine learning style*

Additionally, there are various thumb rules for choosing the specific formulation of the machine learning problem for a given task/situation:

- **Supervised**: If the target value is available
- **Classification**: If the target value is a category
- **Regression**: If the target value is a quantity
- **Unsupervised**: If the target label is not available
- **Clustering**: To group entities
- **Dimensionality reduction**: Distilling the information into a smaller set of features
- **Reinforcement learning**: To identify the best action in a situation

A note in the previous chapter said that the boundaries between the ML styles and the problem formulations can be blurry in some cases. Now, we expand that little note into a key idea; you can formulate the problem appropriately and choose between the various ML styles. Indeed, this formulation can make all the difference in the success of your data science project.

Pause and ponder: Consider the task of classifying an email as spam/non-spam. Which Machine Learning style is suitable for the task? Also, think about the requirements for the ML style to work.

An extremely important idea is that the boundaries between these formulations can often be blurry, which means that a problem can be solved using multiple Machine Learning styles. A problem that is usually thought of as a supervised classification problem can also be considered and solved as an unsupervised (clustering) problem. This choice of formulation can make all the difference in the success of your data science project. To make the idea more concrete, let us take a look at a few examples.

Problem 1: Fraud detection

Fraud is a problem that affects virtually all industries. In the e-commerce and the **Banking, Financial Services, and Insurance (BFSI)** sectors, this is a particularly big problem. In e-commerce alone, the losses due to payment fraud were around 20 billion USD in 2021. Auto insurance companies lose about 29 billion USD each year. In 2019, organizations globally lost more than 5 trillion USD to fraud. Clearly, fraud is a big problem and one that Machine Learning techniques have frequently been using to combat. Indeed, fraud detection is one of the most impactful use cases of Machine Learning. Interestingly, there are (at least) two prominent ML approaches for this.

Approach 1: Supervised classification

The obvious approach for detecting fraud is by treating it like a supervised classification task. The outcome/dependent variable is a binary indicator (0/1) of the transaction being fraudulent, which is predicted based on a lot of features related to the user and their behavior and the transaction itself. Indeed, this is the most popular formulation employed for fraud detection. This approach is successful, but also comes with a lot of challenges.

$$Pr\ (Y = 1) = f\ (user\ attributes, transaction\ attributes)$$

Fraud has a low incidence rate – which means that typically a very low proportion of customers/ transactions are fraudulent. For instance, only about 0.1% of credit card transactions are fraudulent - 1 in 1000 is a low incidence/ occurrence rate. The numbers vary by industry, but fraud transactions/users typically constitute <1% of all transactions/ users. In supervised Machine Learning terms, there is a heavy class imbalance - the majority class records (non-fraudulent) heavily outnumber the minority class records (fraudulent). Such heavy imbalance is always problematic since models have a hard time learning the patterns needed to discern the two classes, simply because the information and representation for fraudulent cases are too low to learn from. Getting satisfactory results from the supervised classification models is almost always challenging. Fortunately, there is another (very different) potential approach that deals with class imbalance better.

Approach 2: Unsupervised clustering

The idea is simple and powerful – fraudulent transactions/customers have specific behaviors that are very different from regular ones. As an example, fraudulent transactions are typically performed with accounts opened more recently, having more digits in the email address, preferring some payment methods and more commonly from certain locations. Additionally, the number of attempted transactions from the user, or the number of items in the transaction could be unusually high. If all this information were to be represented by data, and if clustering were to be performed properly - the fraudulent transactions would emerge as a separate cluster. Or these would appear as loose points far away from clusters belonging to regular, non-fraudulent transactions. As illustrated in *Figure 2.2*, all the tiny clusters and individual points are different from the bulk of the transactions and are therefore good candidates for fraudulent transactions.

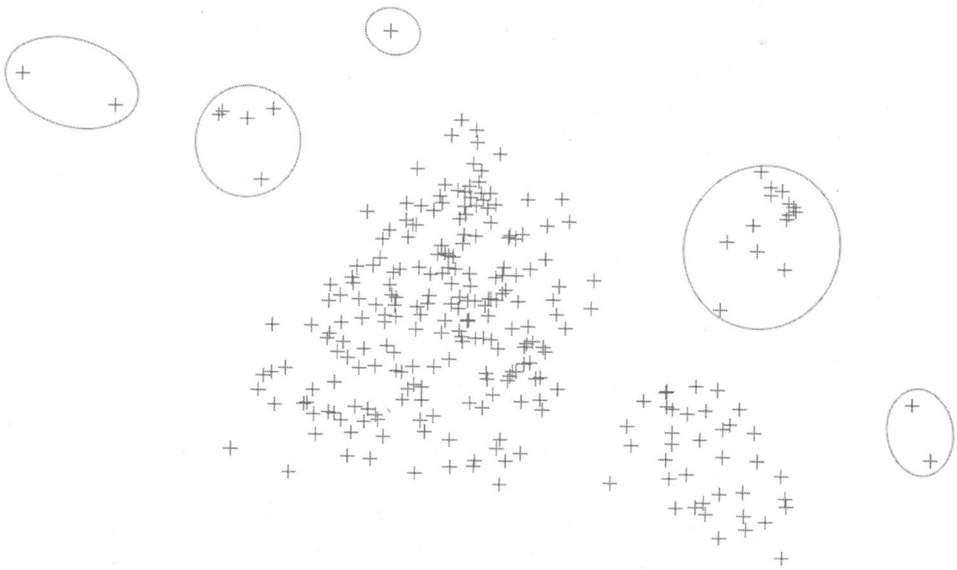

Figure 2.2: *Unsupervised approach to fraud detection*

As you may suspect, the unsupervised clustering approach does not naturally find class imbalance challenging. If the data contains features that are well discriminating between the fraudulent and the non-fraudulent transactions, clustering techniques would work well with imbalance. It is important to note that this does not naturally imply that the unsupervised approach performs markedly better. This just means that far less effort is needed to overcome the class imbalance issue, and an acceptable baseline can be achieved with less effort.

Which of the two approaches works better naturally depends on the specific situation and data. Regardless, we understood that the fraud detection problem can be tackled using more than one approach. Let us take a look at another problem that has more than one solution.

Problem 2: Predicting high-selling products

You are a Data Scientist at the online fashion giant, Azra. The task you are working on is identifying new items to merchandise/display on the home page of the Azra app. Only potentially high-sales items, among the top 10% by revenue, are to be displayed. The data you have is around attributes of the product – for example., color, brand, category, style, etc., using which you need to identify potentially high-selling (revenue) products.

Approach 1: Supervised Regression

You may already have figured out the obvious formulation - predict the sales (revenue) of the product based on its features that is; this is a Supervised Regression problem with revenue being the dependent/ outcome variable and product attributes being the features/ predictors.

$$Y\ (Revenue) = f\ (product\ attributes)$$

Pause and ponder: Do you need to predict the exact revenue of the product, or is it sufficient to predict that the product would be in the top 10%? Are these two different formulations?

Approach 2: Supervised Classification

This is a natural formulation of the task and by far the most popular approach. But consider this - you know that only the top 10% of revenue products would be allowed to be displayed. The precise value of the revenue of the product would not matter to you; you would not be doing much with it. Rather, the product being in the top 10% is of interest. This realization leads us to an alternative formulation to that of supervised classification. The dependent/ outcome variable would be an indicator of the product being in the top 10%.

$$Pr\ (Y = 1) = f\ (product\ attributes)$$

The benefit of this formulation is that precise prediction of the sales is irrelevant now. Revenues are generally hard to predict as they typically exhibit high variance from product to product. Therefore, model evaluation metrics for regression (example - R^2) would show lower values. While this is not an issue on its own, it is misleading as the modeller would be focusing on getting more precise, which does not matter as much. The classification formulation, on the other hand, is more aligned with the end objective, identifying the top 10% product and therefore naturally more effective.

Problem 3: Question de-duplication for an e-commerce website

This problem was posed as a thought experiment earlier in this section: let us try to answer it now. Imagine that you are a Data Scientist working at the online fashion giant Azra, in the Product Page team. The product page contains detailed information about the product, including ratings and reviews provided by customers, and questions that the users asked about the product. There seems to be severe duplication of the questions on the product pages users seem to be asking the same question with minor variations in language. For example, *"Is the material durable?"* can be considered a duplicate of *"Is the shirt durable?"*. This is a problem as a few popular questions would suppress the visibility of other useful questions and their answers, withholding useful information from the users and affecting the sale of the products. Your task is to identify questions that are duplicates.

Approach 1: Supervised classification using Deep Learning

Recurrent Neural Networks and more recently Transformer-based architectures have shown tremendous success in text classification tasks. Indeed, Deep Learning methods provide state-of-the-art results on most text-related tasks. Therefore, the first formulation is a supervised classification problem. Concretely, you could take pairs of questions and run them by a model which predicts whether the pair is just a duplicated question, as illustrated in *Figure 2.3:*

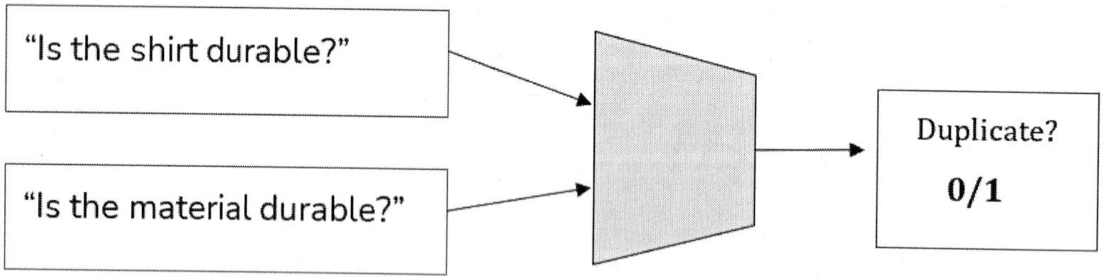

Figure 2.3: *Deduplication using supervised classification.*

This makes intuitive sense as we expect Deep Learning methods to shine in such situations if we have enough labelled data. Deep Learning methods are extremely data-hungry and need large volumes of data to be effective. For a text deduplication task like ours, we would need at least a few thousand pairs of questions labelled. The problem is that labelling tens of thousands of question pairs is not easy. Theoretically, the labelling can be done manually, but this would take numerous man-hours and some solid guidelines for the labellers so that their labels are in agreement. Clearly, it might take a long time possibly several weeks to prepare such training data from scratch. We note that the supervised classification approach has promise, but we presumed the availability of a lot of data for this formulation. Fortunately, an alternative approach of unsupervised clustering can save the day.

Approach 2: Unsupervised clustering of questions

Unsupervised clustering does not need any labelled data. This formulation, therefore, immediately does away with the need for labelling tens of thousands of pairs of questions. This formulation is simple conceptually - perform clustering on the questions. If the clustering is performed well (with appropriate distance measures applied), we expect duplicate questions to form very tight clusters. In the ideal case, we expect as many clusters as there are unique questions in the data. This simple approach is extremely powerful and perhaps the only feasible solution for our situation.

To conclude this section, a Machine Learning problem can usually be formulated in multiple ways. The obvious go-to formulation may have requirements that we might be able to meet and may not be feasible. The alternative formulations may not be obvious or intuitive initially but could be much more practical for your situation. It is therefore essential that the smart Data Scientist be aware of multiple formulations for a given task and be able to identify the right formulation for the task. This choice can very well make all the difference in the success of the Machine Learning project. But do we always have to choose between the formulations? Or is there a way we can benefit from the strengths of the various formulations? Let us now discuss a key idea – the blending of Machine Learning styles.

Blending ML styles

We saw that there are problems that can be solved using multiple approaches and that which approach performs better is dependent on the situation. Each approach may have some drawbacks/benefits, and there may be some cases in the data where one algorithm works better than the other. Here is a seemingly wild idea - why not combine different Machine Learning styles? If you could do this well somehow, the combined approach would be better than the individual approaches - one approach potentially overcoming the drawbacks of the other. The good news is that such a 'blending' of approaches can be done.

For better accuracy

Let us revisit the Fraud detection problem that we discussed in the previous section. We understood that heavy class imbalance is a problem for a purely supervised approach, but the unsupervised approach does not struggle with this problem as much. Also, recall that in the unsupervised approach, we obtained some clusters that we suspected to be outliers and further analysis was needed to identify the fraud cases. Therefore, either approach has a drawback. Consider this - what if we created some clusters using the unsupervised approach, and used these clusters as features for the supervised classification model?

Outcome	Features		
Fraud (y)	**User features**	**Transaction features**	**Cluster**

Table 2.1: *Using unsupervised cluster as a feature for a supervised model*

Table 2.1 shows how this can be achieved very simply - the unsupervised cluster assignments for the instances are simply included as a predictor in the training data for the classification model. The benefit of this approach is that the new feature, *Cluster,* is extremely informative and can help the supervised model perform better despite the heavy class imbalance. The problem of having features dominated by the information from the majority class is reduced by adding this new feature. Overall, we arrive at a blended solution that will likely work better than the individual approaches.

For dimensionality reduction

Blending supervised and unsupervised approaches also help when dealing with high-dimensional data (lots of features) and many training records. Predictive modelling with several hundred (if not thousands) predictors is a common situation in the **Banking, Financial Services, and Insurance** (**BFSI**) domain. Even with a few hundred thousand records, a model using a thousand predictors becomes unwieldy to the extent of being impractical.

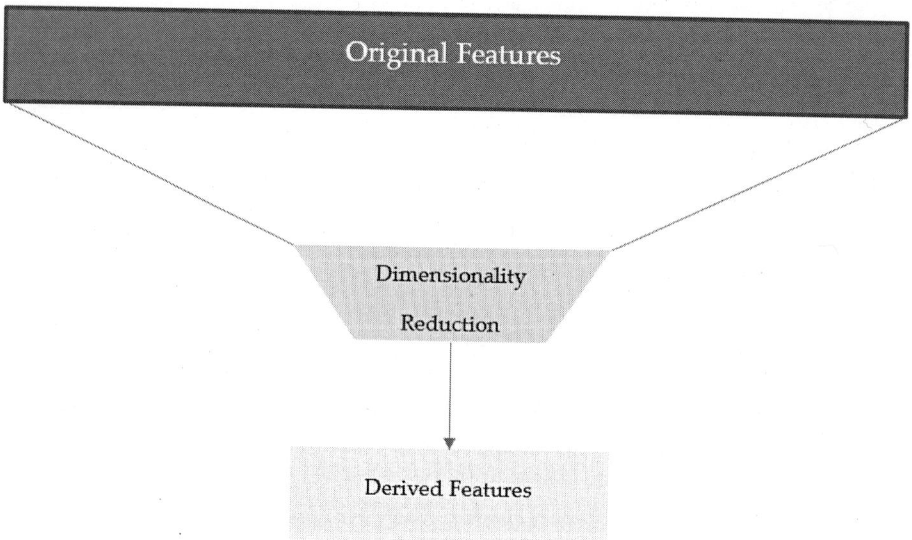

Figure 2.4: *Dimensionality reduction techniques in action*

A common strategy is to use dimensionality reduction techniques like **Principal Component Analysis (PCA)** and **Singular Value Decomposition (SVD)**. In both approaches (PCA and SVD), the original features are used to derive new *dimensions* or *components*. These new components are linear combinations of the original features that capture most of the information contained in the dataset. Typically, a very low number of dimensions capture the information contained in a thousand features. Indeed, it is common that 50 dimensions capture most of the information contained in about a thousand original features. This is a serious reduction in dimensionality - from about 1,000 to 50 - and improves the speed of the model by leaps. This is yet another example where blending approaches can give us significant gains in efficiency.

For better data representation

Most of the modern **Natural Language Processing (NLP)** tasks employs a similar combination of unsupervised and supervised learning approaches. Before 2013, the prevalent approach to represent text was using term frequencies - each text record would be represented by several thousand features/columns (one for each word found in the entire training data, about 10,000 columns wasn't rare). In 2013, *Mikolov et. al.* proposed scalable *word embeddings* (low-dimension vectors) which quickly became the most common approach to representing text data These embeddings help in the following two ways:

1. Dimensionality reduction: The size of the embedding for a term is much small (usually between 50 and 300).
2. Better representation capturing 'meaning': These embeddings are derived in a way that they represent *concepts* and it has been demonstrated that these embeddings capture many relationships between words

The derivation of the embeddings mostly did not care about the labels in the data (for example word2vec algorithm, the most popular by far) and was therefore *unsupervised* in that sense. Reducing the feature set from 10,000 relatively *dumb* frequencies to about 100 smart features that capture meaning: It is a major benefit that was possible by blending approaches.

We now understand and appreciate that Machine Learning problems can be solved using multiple formulations, each having its own benefits and drawbacks. We also saw that we need not always choose between competing formulations. Instead, we could blend multiple approaches in different ways and derive tremendous value from the data. Let us now turn our attention to another aspect of problem formulation - the choice of the dependent variable.

Choosing the right dependent variable

In the section, *Problem 2: Predicting high-selling products,* we saw that we can also tweak the choice of the dependent/outcome variable. The outcome variable could have been the revenue of the product (in the obvious formulation), but we decided that we could instead model whether the product would be in the top 10% of products. This choice changed the formulation from a Regression to a Classification problem. More importantly, the second formulation prevented us from focusing on chasing precise revenue predictions and instead got us focused on the outcome that aligned very well with the business objective. Clearly, choosing the right dependent variable is an important decision that affects the effectiveness of the solution.

Consider another situation: as a Data Scientist in the search team at the popular online fashion platform Azra, your goal is to improve the relevance of the search results. A better ranking will surface more relevant products higher up in the results, helping the shoppers find what they are looking for more easily. You are sure about this being a supervised learning problem, and you have tons of historical data to model on. The key question is: what should the dependent variable be? Let us first think about our options and take inspiration from current approaches in the industry.

An extremely popular formulation is that of predicting a click on the search results. A search is successful if any of the top N (a predetermined number) results is clicked. Therefore, the dependent variable Y is:

0: if none of the top N results was clicked on

1: if any of the top N results were clicked on

Note that this formulation does not care about the position of the click. A search where the last item, say 40th, is clicked is treated to be equally successful as a search where the topmost item was clicked on by the user. Does this make sense? One might argue that the click position is extremely relevant - a higher click position (rank 1 is the highest position) indicates a better search result set.

This brings us to another formulation; treating the problem as a ranking problem. Note that this is still a supervised learning approach. But instead of focusing on just a click, we try to get the click in the topmost result. In such a formulation, the dependent variable could simply be the click position and a lower value is better. A model that minimizes this value would surface more relevant items at the top and can arguably be more suitable for our objective.

Note that such formulation choices are common for recommender systems - both formulations, viz. ranking vs. click prediction, are commonly employed in the industry.

It is therefore essential that we reflect on the choice of the dependent variable. While often there is a natural choice that works well, there could be situations where you choose a dependent variable more in line with the task at hand.

Business objective vs. ML objective

Let us continue with the search relevance example we discussed in the previous section. The goal of the data science project was to improve the relevance of the search results. We discussed a couple of choices for the dependent variable and discussed that we could treat this as a click prediction problem or a ranking problem. In both formulations, the primary objective was getting the user to click on an item.

It is well known in the e-commerce industry that lower-priced items gather more clicks. Consider a search ranking algorithm that always surfaces very cheap items at the top. What would be your expectations around the click-through rate (Searches with Clicks/ Total Searches) for such an algorithm? Of course, it would lead to more clicks (as users click on cheaper items). Does this mean that such an algorithm is better for the platform?

The answer is *no*. Surfacing cheaper items at the top will mostly lead to more clicks and improve the click-through rate metric. However, there could be a few drawbacks of such an approach:

- The overall revenue for the platform could drop simply because the average selling price could drop.
- Lower quality items on top (cheaper items could be lower quality items) could harm the platform's perception.
- Lower quality items may lead to higher returns and therefore not just revenue loss but also reverse logistics costs.
- Surfacing cheaper items, without caring about the distance from the shopper, may lead to increased logistics costs and reduce profitability for the company.
- Overall conversion (purchases/visits) may drop as after clicking, the product details for lower quality items and their reviews may discourage shoppers from buying.
- Essentially, there are various, potentially competing objectives for a task like ranking. An approach that solely focuses on the click-through rate of the search may, and probably will, negatively impact the other objectives of the business. It is therefore imperative that the objectives of the Machine Learning modelling process mirror closely the objectives of the business.

For our example, it would help to model instead a metric that blends click-through rates and monetary value (or some other objectives). An example could be to maximize the estimated revenue from a click. Such a metric marries the probability of a click with the revenue coming from the click and helps balance two objectives. Even if you do not utilize such a blended metric, it would be a good idea to track metrics corresponding to the other business objectives. After all, the goal is to solve a business problem, and any acceptable solution should improve things rather than harm them.

Conclusion

ML has tremendous promise and adds great value by solving several business problems. However, not all problems need ML – many can be solved using much simpler rule-based approaches. We discussed some considerations to enable you to decide. Next, we discussed the various ML styles that a practitioner can choose from and saw that the lines between the styles can be blurry. Using examples from several domains, we saw that problems can have multiple formulations with different ML styles. The smart Data Scientist must be able to identify the right formulation for the task. This choice can very well make all the difference in the success of the ML project.

We then saw that blending ML styles is a powerful approach. There are several motivations for doing so - dimensionality reduction, better accuracy, better data representation – and combining supervised and unsupervised learning approaches is a common practice that yields great benefits. Choosing the right dependent variable is also a part of the formulation, and we saw that this choice can not only greatly simplify the modelling process, but also help obtain better outcomes. Finally, we saw that to add true value, the objective of the Machine Learning project should be well aligned with the business objective.

In the next chapter, we will learn the next crucial step in the data science solution-building process – data pre-processing. We will learn how to process data to refine it to best grade before modeling to derive maximum value from it.

Join our book's Discord space

CHAPTER 3
Data Collection and Pre-processing

Introduction

Garbage in, garbage out; you may have heard this adage before regarding the effectiveness of systems. This is true for machine learning processes as well. Regardless of the sophistication level of the machine learning technique, using poor data leads to poor results. With the popularity of data-hungry deep learning methods, AI and machine learning systems require more and more data. But better data beats more data each time, so understanding how to get the data right is critical.

In this chapter, we will learn more about the data understanding and data preparation steps of the CRISP-DM framework. It is essential to understand the various factors that influence the data collection process and how you should tackle associated problems. We will take a look at the entire pre-processing process as a pipeline, for which we can employ a principled approach. With the help of a case study, we will learn about the various details of the pipeline and implement them hands-on.

Structure

In this chapter, we will cover:

- Building a machine learning solution
- The case study

- The pre-processing process
    - Step 1: Gather data + basic checks + corrections
    - Step 2: Separate into train and test datasets
    - Step 3: Outlier treatment
    - Step 4: Missing value treatment
    - Step 5: Categorical feature handling
    - Step 6: Transformation of numeric features
- Case study steps review

Objectives

In this chapter, we learn how to process data to refine it to the best grade before modeling. We will first learn about the various factors that can influence the data and your understanding of it. We will learn about various possible issues with data and how to identify and handle them. We will introduce a principled approach to data pre-processing that can be applied to different solutions. We will learn the ways to avoid common pitfalls (like data leakage) and learn extremely useful data cleanup approaches. We will then see how to manipulate the features in the data (feature engineering), focusing on the task at hand. We will take a holistic look at the *data pre-processing pipeline*. We will apply all these concepts in a real-world case study.

By the end of this chapter, you will be able to master the process of data understanding and data preparation. You will be able to identify peculiarities of the domain and the data and approach the problem accordingly. You will be able to perform extensive data cleanup to enhance the quality of the data. You will also be able to make various transformations on the data to get the maximum performance from your machine learning/artificial intelligence solution.

Building a machine learning solution

Building a machine learning-based solution is not merely the technical exercise of fitting the model to the data. The solution building starts with business understanding, which guides the solution design and the steps afterwards. Unless done correctly, it can jeopardize the entire machine learning solution. Understanding the data and data preparation are the next two steps. Data understanding involves exploration of the data and understanding the patterns. Using this understanding, the data can be best prepared to extract maximum value from it and build the best machine learning solution. It is only after these steps that we approach the modelling part, the evaluation, and the deployment steps. The entire process is encapsulated in the **Cross-Industry Standard Process for Data Mining (CRISP-DM)** framework as shown in *Figure 3.1*:

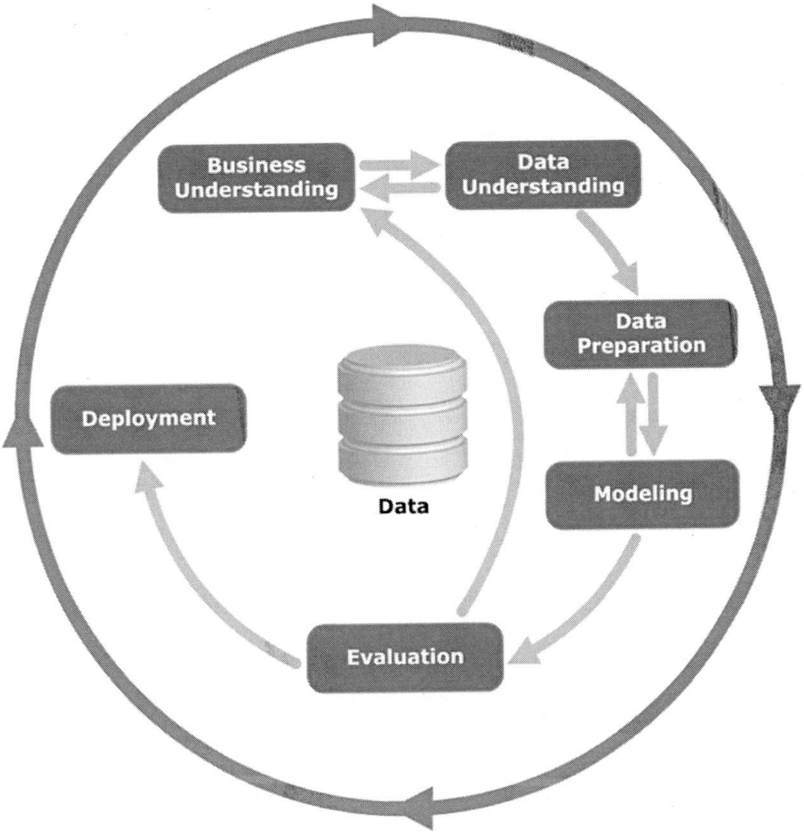

Figure 3.1: CRISP-DM framework

The takeaway is that the model fitting part is one of the many steps in the process. The understanding and preparation steps can be called *pre-processing*. The model fitting process is more technical and parts of it can be standardized, or even automated if the pre-processing has been done right. The pre-processing part, on the other hand, is rarely standard, it depends on the data collection process, the nature of the data, some domain-specific considerations, and the task at hand. Pre-processing is where the practitioner's skill makes a big difference; these are the bits that are part art and part science. Let us understand how each aspect influences the pre-processing process.

The data collection process

How has the data been collected? Are you collating data from multiple disparate systems, involving complex joins using different criteria? or are you consuming well-curated data from a single table that has been standardized and its quality established? In the first case, having missing values for multiple fields would not be surprising. Understanding the root cause of a missing value may take effort and discussions with the engineering teams. In the latter case, the reasons for missing values would be well studied, and you would know how to interpret missing values.

The nature of the data

Let us think about surveys. Can you think of any peculiarities of data generated from survey responses? For one, survey data is understood to contain *volunteer bias* meaning it usually does not represent all users. Another peculiar phenomenon is the *halo effect*. A user who had a bad experience with one aspect of the product usually rates all aspects poorly, and likewise for users with great experience with one aspect. Third, often there are some questions the user might not be comfortable responding honestly to. So, the user either skips the question or adds some dishonest value (potentially useless for your task). The data scientist working on the survey data must understand these peculiarities of the data to create any valuable solution from it. Similarly, transaction data from an e-commerce platform may not have these challenges but may have its peculiarities.

Domain-specific aspects

Consider that your dataset contains the field *age* and in a sample, you encounter a value of 300. Should this surprise you? You may have encountered a relatively young tree's data if the data is about sequoia trees. A value of 6,000 would be surprising. Now, let us say that you are working with data for humans. 300 should be surprising but only if measured in years. 300 months translates to 25 years, again not so surprising. How about a negative value, say -4 in the age column? Not too surprising if you're looking at a birthing center's data for babies that are yet to be born, and the negative value makes sense suddenly. The key idea is that specific aspects of the domain reflect peculiarities in the data. The wise data scientist must understand these peculiarities and account for them to create a valuable machine learning / AI solution.

Influence of the task at hand

The considerations for an unsupervised machine learning problem are usually very different from those for a supervised one. The data processing needed is, therefore, also very different. For example, a clustering activity may require you to standardize the features to give them equal importance and the output can vary greatly with and without standardizing. Standardization isn't necessary for several supervised machine learning techniques. It can help with faster convergence for some machine learning algorithms but usually doesn't result in wildly different outputs.

The case study

Azra Inc. is a leading private financial institution with various financial products and wealth management services. The bank wishes to run a telemarketing campaign for its new product which is a deposit scheme with great returns. The bank had run a similar campaign for a comparable product a few months back and wishes to use that data to identify customers that are most likely to convert, that is, buy the product and commit to a deposit. The assumption is that the type of customers who responded positively to the previous campaign are likely to do so for this campaign as well. The data science objective is to build a highly performant predictive model. As you appreciate by now, the natural first step is gathering and pre-processing the data.

The data is in the file **`Azra_Bank_Marketing_v1.zip`** is a compressed CSV. The first few records are shown in *Figure 3.2*:

age	job	marital	education	balance	housing	loan	contact	month	duration	poutcome	deposit
59	admin.	married	secondary	2343	yes	no	unknown	may	1042	unknown	yes
56	admin.	married	secondary	45	no	no	unknown	may	1467	unknown	yes
41	technician	married	secondary	1270	yes	no	unknown	may	1389	unknown	yes
55	services	married	secondary	2476	yes	no	unknown	may	579	unknown	yes
54	admin.	married	tertiary	184	no	no	unknown	may	673	unknown	yes
42	management	single	tertiary	0	yes	yes	unknown	may	562	unknown	yes
56	management	married	tertiary	830	yes	yes	unknown	may	1201	unknown	yes
60	retired	divorced	secondary	545	yes	no	unknown	may	1030	unknown	yes
37	technician	married	secondary	1	yes	no	unknown	may	608	unknown	yes
28	services	single	secondary	5090	yes	no	unknown	may	1297	unknown	yes
38	admin.	single	secondary	100	yes	no	unknown	may	786	unknown	yes
30	blue-collar	married	secondary	309	yes	no	unknown	may	1574	unknown	yes
29	management	married	tertiary	199	yes	yes	unknown	may	1689	unknown	yes
46	blue-collar	single	tertiary	460	yes	no	unknown	may	1102	unknown	yes

Figure 3.2: A glimpse of the dataset

Brief descriptions of the key fields in the dataset are as follows:

- **age**: The age of the customer at the time of the marketing campaign
- **job**: The customer's occupation
- **education**: Highest education level of the customer (primary to tertiary)
- **balance**: Bank balance at the time of the campaign
- **housing**: Whether the customer had a housing loan (yes/no)
- **loan**: Whether the customer had a personal loan (yes/no)
- **contact**: Preferred contact channel of the customer (telephone/cellular)
- **month**: Month on contact in the campaign
- **duration**: The duration (seconds) of the phone call in the campaign
- **poutcome**: Outcome of the campaign before this campaign
- **deposit**: Whether the customer bought the product (yes/no) – the outcome

There is quite a lot of information about the customer, their financial state (balance, loan or not and so on), and some information about the campaign itself (contact month, duration). Using these columns, the goal is to make a model that predicts the 'deposit' field (the outcome).

So, the model would be as follows:

$$\textbf{deposit} = f\,(\textbf{age, job, ..., poutcome})$$

That is, we are modeling deposit as a function of the features.

Note: All the columns we see might not eventually be a part of the model. We will likely discard some of the columns we see as not valuable for our task. *Feature selection* is the process of choosing the required set of features. Additionally, we might create some new features derived from the existing features. This is part of *feature engineering* that we will perform shortly.

We will use this data and case study throughout the chapter. We will perform all the data pre-processing steps to make all the ideas concrete. But what are those steps? Is there a standard 'pipeline' of steps that applies to all modeling tasks? Or is each case special? Let us discuss this in the next section.

The pre-processing process

Pre-processing refers to all the steps from data gathering to the point where you are ready to fit the model. This includes basic checks and fixes like formatting fixes and complex operations like imputation of missing values. Generally, these steps can be considered part of a process or a *pipeline*. One such pipeline is shown in *Figure 3.3*. You can see that there are varied tasks included in this process. We will study each step in detail in this chapter and apply the learnings to the marketing case study. Refer to *Figure 3.3* for the steps in the pipeline:

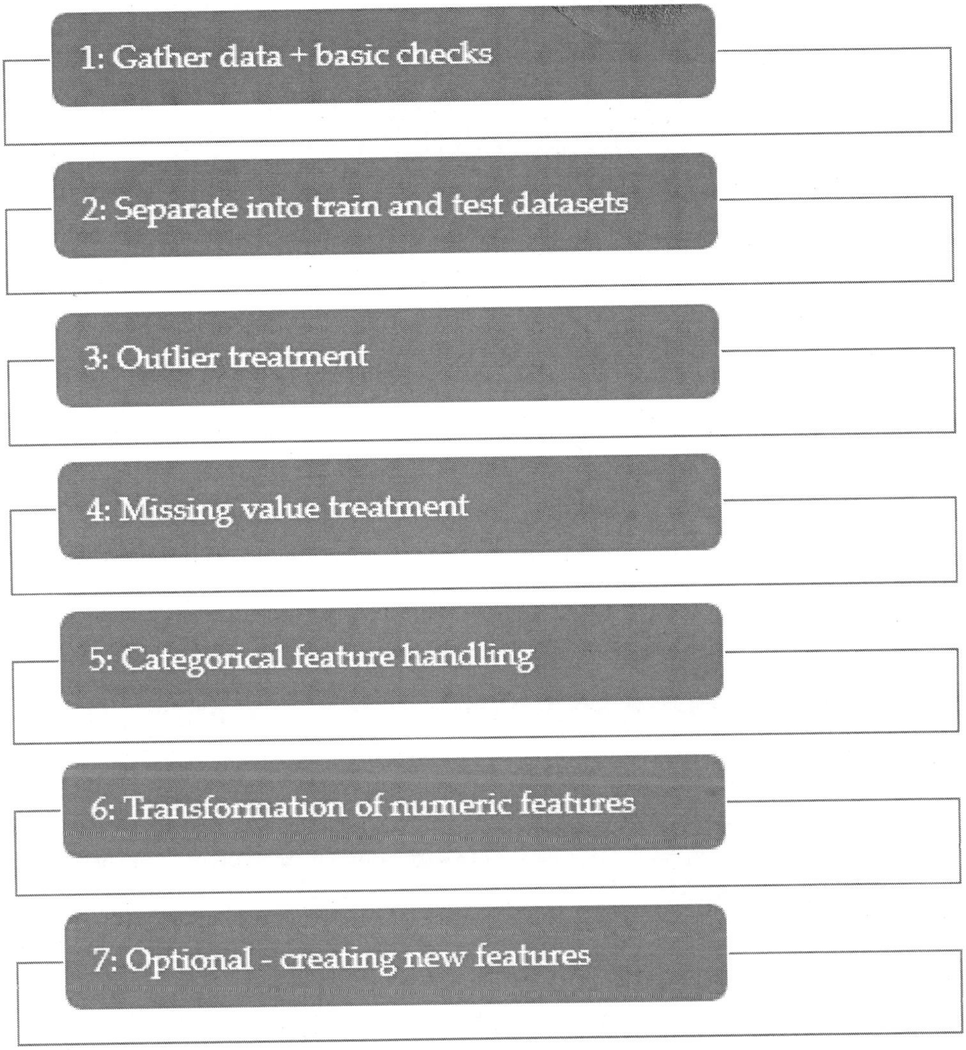

Figure 3.3: *Some general pre-processing steps*

It is important to understand that there is no standard pipeline. There is no standard process for *any* of these steps. As we discuss throughout the chapter, a lot of data and domain specifics must be accounted for, along with the task's requirements. This makes standardization extremely difficult. You can potentially automate some parts of individual steps and maybe even have a guiding template of steps. However, a wise data scientist should not leave this critical step to automated processes and must always perform the final checks.

Step 1: Gather data + basic checks

The first step in the processing pipeline is obtaining the data. This could mean loading CSV files into Python or working with tables from databases/data lakes. This could mean reading in a single table or joining multiple tables using distributed storage. This could be done using a single script or employing multiple scripts and interacting back and forth with a database to painstakingly create a dataset from multiple sources. This could also be using APIs to fetch JSONs of data. As mentioned in the previous section about the *Data Collection Process*, as a data scientist you must understand this process and the artefacts this can create in the data.

You then need to check whether the data loading was performed correctly and fix any issues. For instance, if you realize that the loading process induced incorrect formats or did not read certain special characters correctly, you must alter the loading process to fix these issues. Often, there are issues with date formats not being read correctly because of which you must fix them manually. Think of this as a "basic clean-up of the data".

Note: We will perform cleanup on the data again later. Which will include outlier treatment, missing value treatment and so on. You can think of that as the *deep clean* compared to the clean-up mentioned in this section.

For our case study on bank marketing for Azra Inc., we will obtain the data by reading a CSV file into Python and performing some of these checks.

Let us head towards the exercise:

Exercise 3.1: Loading and exploring bank marketing dataset

In this exercise, we will gather the data for the bank marketing case study for Azra Inc. and perform some basic exploration to understand the data, followed by identifying issues (and fixing relevant ones):

- Import the libraries **`pandas`**, **`numpy`**, and **`pyplot`** from **`matplotlib`** and **`seaborn`** using the following code:

  ```
  import numpy as np, pandas as pd
  import matplotlib.pyplot as plt, seaborn as sns
  %matplotlib inline
  ```

- Using the **`read_csv`** function from Pandas, read the CSV file named Azra_**`Bank_Marketing_v1.zip`**. Since you are reading a compressed file, specify compression = **`'zip'`** in the command:

  ```
  bank0 = pd.read_csv('Azra_Bank_Marketing_v1.zip', compression='zip')
  ```

  The file has been successfully loaded into Python.

- Using the **`head`** method of the pandas DataFrame, get a glimpse of the first 5 rows of the dataset:

  ```
  bank0.head()
  ```

  Figure 3.4 shows the output:

age	job	marital	education	balance	housing	loan	contact	month	duration	poutcome	deposit
59.0	admin.	married	secondary	2343	yes	no	unknown	may	1042	unknown	yes
56.0	admin.	married	secondary	45	no	no	unknown	may	1467	unknown	yes
41.0	technician	married	secondary	1270	yes	no	unknown	may	1389	unknown	yes
55.0	services	married	secondary	2476	yes	no	unknown	may	579	unknown	yes
54.0	admin.	married	tertiary	184	no	no	unknown	may	673	unknown	yes

***Figure 3.4:** First 5 records of the dataset*

You can see the columns of the dataset and some of the values. We will understand these values better in the next section. For now, we can see that most of these columns have text values and there seem to be 3 numeric columns age, duration, and balance:

- Using the **info** method of the pandas **DataFrame**, get a simple data profile.

  ```
  bank0.info()
  ```

  Refer to the following figure for the output:

```
<class 'pandas.core.frame.DataFrame'>
RangeIndex: 11162 entries, 0 to 11161
Data columns (total 12 columns):
 #   Column     Non-Null Count  Dtype
---  ------     --------------  -----
 0   age        11152 non-null  float64
 1   job        11162 non-null  object
 2   marital    11162 non-null  object
 3   education  11162 non-null  object
 4   balance    11162 non-null  int64
 5   housing    11162 non-null  object
 6   loan       11162 non-null  object
 7   contact    11162 non-null  object
 8   month      11162 non-null  object
 9   duration   11162 non-null  int64
 10  poutcome   11139 non-null  object
 11  deposit    11153 non-null  object
dtypes: float64(1), int64(2), object(9)
```

***Figure 3.5:** Basic profile of the dataset*

The basic profile from the `info` method shows the number of records and columns, the data types of the columns, and the number of non-null values. The `deposit` column is of particular interest (the outcome of our case study), let us understand its distribution next.

- List the values in this column and their counts using the **value_counts** method of the Pandas series using the following code:

  ```
  bank0.deposit.value_counts()
  ```

The output should be:

```
no      5869
yes     5284
Name: deposit, dtype: int64
```

- To get normalized counts (adding to 100%), use **value_counts** with normalize specified as **True** as in the following command:

  ```
  bank0.deposit.value_counts(normalize=True)
  ```

  The output should be:

  ```
  no      0.526226
  yes     0.473774
  Name: deposit, dtype: float64
  ```

  About 47% of records have a **yes** in the **deposit** column.

With these simple commands, you have gathered the data, performed some basic profiling, checked out some sample records, and investigated the unique values, and counts of a particular column of interest. Using these outputs, let us understand the dataset and the case study better.

A basic profiling of the dataset shows that it has 12 columns in total and 11,162 records. The profiling also shows that the number of non-null values does not match the number of records for all the columns that is some columns have missing values. Doing a basic distribution check on the target column, that is **deposit**. we see that about 52% of the customers did not make a deposit, while the campaign was successful for about 47% of customers. Next, we should perform more checks on the data and make some basic corrections.

At this stage, we should check for imperfections in the data and fix those we can already. Data format issues during loading are common as Python may not be able to correctly detect all of them (for example, common for date fields,). We must identify such issues and fix them. Some formats may have been correctly loaded, but not optimal for us. For example, in the dataset, we see that **deposit** is a categorical field with values "yes" and "no". We would require this to be a numerical value (0/1) for modeling. This is yet another quick fix we can perform at this stage itself.

Another extremely important check is to identify missing information. Note that this is not as straightforward as identifying the number of null values. Data logging/creation processes often enter a placeholder value when the true value is unavailable, and these commonly appear as *unknown* or *N/A*. In other cases, there are domain-specific codes for such missing information. Therefore, understanding the domain is also essential to correctly identify missing values.

Note: At this stage, we only identify the missing values and do not handle them. Handling will be performed at a later stage as an explicit step. The only exception is missing values in the outcome/ target variable, and such records can be dropped. For all others, we need to perform careful handling.

Exercise 3.2: Fixing formats and identifying missing values

In this exercise, we will explore the dataset a little more to identify format issues and detect missing values. First, we will convert the target variable ('deposit') to numeric. Next, we will identify obvious 'null' and 'hidden' missing values. We will also drop the unnecessary columns that we're sure we will not use for modeling. Let us get started:

- First, copy the dataset before modifications to avoid losing the original.

```
bank1 = bank0.copy()
```

- Next, modify the target variable to have 0 and 1 values corresponding to **no** and **yes**. Check the distribution of the values to ensure the change was done correctly.

```
bank1.deposit = bank1.deposit.map({'yes':1, 'no':0})
bank1.deposit.value_counts(normalize=True)
```

The following is the output:

```
0.0    0.526226
1.0    0.473774
Name: deposit, dtype: float64
```

- Get the counts of the (obvious) missing values, i.e., the number of null values and print the non-zero values:

```
nulls - bank1.isnull().sum()
nulls[nulls>0]
```

The result is:

age 10

poutcome 23

deposit 9

- Print the distribution of the values for the fields **poutcome**, **contact**, **education:**

```
bank1.poutcome.value_counts()
unknown     8309
failure     1226
success     1069
other        535
Name: poutcome, dtype: int64

bank1.contact.value_counts()
The result is -
```

```
cellular     8042
unknown      2346
telephone    774
```

```
bank1.education.value_counts()
The output should be -
secondary    5476
tertiary     3689
primary      1500
unknown      497
```

- Drop the records where the field **deposit** is missing:

```
bank1 = bank1.dropna(subset=['deposit'])
```

- Drop the **duration** column:

```
bank1.drop('duration',axis=1, inplace=True)
```

Caution: Leakage during pre-processing

These activities before the train test split can lead to leakage – detailed univariate analysis, correlation and other multivariate analyses, scaling/standardizing features, and outlier handling. Unfortunately, these are sometimes done before the train test split. This is not a good practice and leads to leakage, that is, you end up learning information from the test set and use it for pre-processing.

Caution: Category encoding before train-test split

It is common to handle categorical data (for example, one hot encoding) before the train test split. This could be problematic in real-world situations where the test set contains a new value that was not encountered in the train set. As a best practice, such handling should be performed after the train-test split.

Step 2: Separate into train and test datasets

The primary purpose of most predictive models is to not do well on the existing data for which we have the ground truth. Indeed, the true value of the predictive model is that it can make useful predictions on new data that the model has never encountered before. We can only trust that the model generalizes well and can be employed.

Such an assessment of model performance is only possible if a dataset is reserved solely for this purpose. This is accomplished by splitting the available dataset into two parts train and test. This is the most common validation scheme, that is, a method to assess the model's general performance. The act of deriving these two sets from the data is called a **"train test split"**. Let us now understand how to best use the train and test datasets:

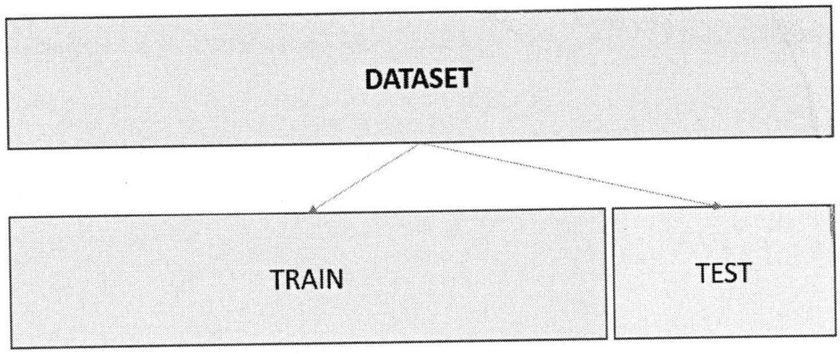

Figure 3.6: Train test split

Using the train set

For the entire learning and training process, understanding the distributions of the fields, logic for defining and treating outliers, and information that informs any of the eight steps in the pre-processing pipelines. The train set is used for eventually fitting the model, deciding on the model's hyper-parameters (*Chapter 6, Hyperparameter Tuning*) and debugging the same (*Chapter 4, Model Evaluation and Debugging*).

Using the test set

The test set is used only for validation of model performance, no information from this dataset is derived until then. You must not learn any patterns or make any decisions pertaining to training using the test set, and this dataset is to be kept aside until the very end.

We reiterate that the test set must not be used to influence the training process in any way. Not adhering to this, leads to "**data leakage**" where you effectively used the test set to train the model. The risk is that you overestimate model performance (on a good day). On a bad day and if done incorrectly, this could lead to drastic differences between performance on the seen versus unseen data, potentially rendering the model useless.

Note: If the dataset was created painstakingly using multiple sources, you might have already performed many integrity and sense checks, and maybe even outlier checks and performed descriptive summaries. In such cases, you can't unlearn what you learned about the data already. But it is important to recognize that what you learned might not apply to a completely fresh test dataset and you should closely monitor the model performance after deployment.

Let us perform a train-test split for our bank marketing for Azra Inc. in the next exercise.

Exercise 3.3: Splitting the data into train and test sets

In this exercise, we will divide the marketing dataset for Azra Inc. into train and test sets. To verify that the split happened properly, and the test data is representative, we will check some numerical summaries of the test and train sets:

- From sklearn, import the **train_test_split** method from the **model_selection** module:

```
from sklearn.model_selection import train_test_split
```

- Perform an 80-20 train-test split, specifying **42** as the random state and stratifying by the outcome, that is, the deposit column using the following code. Print the dimensions of the train and test datasets after division:

```
df_train, df_test = train_test_split(bank1, \
                                     test_size=0.2, \
                                     random_state=42, \
                                     stratify=bank1.deposit)
df_train.shape, df_test.shape
```

The shapes get printed as:

((8922, 11), (2231, 11)

We can see that the test contains about 20% of the overall records, as expected.

Note: A stratified split was not needed here but is generally a good practice. This ensures that both test and train sets have the same distribution of the outcome labels. This can be very useful in situations with a low number of records and especially useful when dealing with imbalanced classes (that is, uneven distribution of the labels).

- Print the **mean**, standard deviation, and **median** values of the numeric fields in the train dataset using the following code:

```
df_train.apply([np.mean, np.median, np.std])
```

The output is:

	age	balance	deposit
mean	41.191160	1504.879848	0.473773
median	39.000000	542.500000	0.000000
std	11.891117	3119.918931	0.499340

Figure 3.7: Summary of the numeric fields

- To check whether the train and test splits are similar, we print the same metrics for the test set as well:

```
df_test.apply([np.mean, np.median, np.std])
```

Which should give the following output:

	age	balance	deposit
mean	41.401974	1620.630659	0.473779
median	39.000000	580.000000	0.000000
std	12.001119	3614.739282	0.499424

Figure 3.8: *Summaries of the test data*

We can see from the preceding output that the train-test split was performed correctly with an 80-20 split. The numerical summaries show that mean, median and standard deviation are very similar between the test and the train datasets. This tells us that the split was done properly, and we are ready to move to the next step: outlier detection and treatment.

Step 3: Outlier treatment

There are many ways to define (univariate) outliers, and the appropriate choice depends on the nature of the feature and the observed values. Therefore, the first question should be *What is an outlier to me in this feature?*

A few clarifying questions; Are both high and low values outliers? Are outliers only values that are *sufficiently high* (For example, an age value of 25 for high schoolers)? Or are sufficiently low values also outliers (For example, age 5 for high schoolers)? Are negative values outliers (For example, item delivery time)?

Let us look at a couple of definitions of the term outlier:

- **The usual/classic definition**: Unusual values that differ from the others in the data. This definition defines outliers as usually much higher/lower than regular values, and simply numerical approaches are sufficient to identify such outliers.
- **A more holistic definition**: In this definition, some values could be rare, but make sense from a domain perspective and not surprising. These could point to genuine extremes that we observe (For example, a 25-year-old high schooler), albeit rarely. Another example is negative bank balances it is rare, but not surprising and makes perfect sense from a domain perspective.

It is important to note that we must think about the definition of outlier for each feature separately.

Note: Remember that defining outliers, rules to identify them, and handling strategy must ALL be based on the training data alone. Otherwise, this would be a classic case of data leakage. Once decided, only the outlier detection logic and handling can be applied to the test set.

Once you have defined what is surprising for each feature, you can proceed to use one of the methods from the following (non-exhaustive) list:

- Percentile threshold/ cut-off (e.g., p99, p995)
- Z score approach
- Box plots / Tukey criterion

Let us understand each of them briefly.

Percentile threshold approach

This approach is used when we believe a sufficiently high/sufficiently low value is an outlier. Consider item delivery times for an e-retail giant. E-retail companies typically keep track of delivery times by way of percentiles p95 (95th percentile), or p99 (99th percentile) are common measures and these companies have a notion of healthy levels for these metrics. For example, a p99 value of 5 days might be acceptable/expected, but the p99 value rising to 10 days could point to a major problem. Quite simply, 1% of orders being delivered after 10 days could be alarming.

Such percentile values, therefore, capture what surprising values should be and are a good approach for outlier detection. Likewise, order value on an e-commerce platform also sees extremely high values. Values of 0 are not very surprising (no order was placed), but a p99 value of $100,000 could be surprising for a B2C clothing platform.

Pause and ponder: Consider the 'balance' feature in our bank marketing case study that captures the customer's bank balance. What kind of values do you expect in it? Which values would be surprising to you? Sufficiently high values?

Translating this idea to a simple rule that can be implemented in Python is as simple as saying any value above a certain percentile is considered an outlier. For example, the highest 0.5 percentile values are outliers (above the 99.5th percentile):

```
cutoff = quantile(feature, p)
```

where `p` could be high percentiles like 95, 99, 99.5, and so on, or very low percentiles like 0.05, 1, and so on. Let us now take a look at the Z Score approach for outlier detection.

Z score approach

The Z score approach is suitable when we believe the feature loosely follows a Gaussian distribution, meaning that we expect most values to belong to a certain central range. Values significantly away from this central range are considered outliers. In this approach, both extremes high and low are considered surprising.

For each observation, the Z score is calculated as:

```
Z-Score = (X - mean) / std
```

where `mean` is the simple average of the feature value and `std` is its standard deviation. In a Gaussian distribution, values with a sufficiently high or low Z score are considered less probable and more surprising. It is therefore usual to assign some thresholds based on the Z score to define outliers.

Pause and ponder: Considering that this approach uses mean and standard deviation in the criteria. Is this approach robust to outliers? If your answer is "no", can you think of ways to mitigate this?

A common threshold is 3, that is, values with Z scores greater than 3 or lower than -3 are considered outliers. In a normal distribution, values beyond these scores are expected to occur only 0.3% of the time. Another popular cut-off is 2.5 which, as expected, is slightly more relaxed. Choose these or any other cut-off that you deem suitable for the data at hand. Let us now look at the third approach the Tukey criterion.

Box plots/Tukey criterion

Another extremely popular approach is the Tukey criterion. Like the Z score approach, the Tukey criterion is a simple numerical approach suitable when you expect the data to behave somewhat normally and both high and low extremes are considered surprising. The Tukey criterion overcomes the biggest drawback of the Z score approach and is more robust to extreme values.

Mathematically, values outside the following interval are considered outliers:

$[Q1 - k \times IQR, Q3 + k \times IQR]$;

where IQR = Inter Quartile Range is defined as Q3 (75th percentile) – Q1 (25th percentile)

From this criterion, the lower threshold for regular value is $Q1 - k\,(Q3 - Q1)$ and the higher threshold is $Q3 + k(Q3 - Q1)$.

A very common value of k is 1.5. This value is employed in the standard implementation of box plots (including matplotlib and seaborn packages in Python). This is also known as the Tukey criterion. For k = 1.5, the interval for regular values is:

$[Q1 - 1.5 \times IQR, Q3 + 1.5 \times IQR]$

Note: Many distributions in the real world follow exponential distributions, where you have a very large number of observations at the lower end and a few extremely high values. Think of wealth – a very small percentage typically commands a very high proportion of the total wealth. Another example could be the number of orders a customer places in a visit on an e-retail platform where most customers have 0 orders placed.

Pause and ponder: Consider an exponential distribution like that of bank balance. Do you think the Tukey criterion/Box plot approach is suitable for this?

With this, we have learnt 3 approaches to detecting outliers. As a wise data scientist, you must understand these approaches, the considerations in using each and their strengths, and drawbacks. Now, let us try these approaches in our bank marketing case study.

Exercise 3.4: Outlier detection and treatment

In this exercise, we will apply the outlier detection techniques we learned to the marketing case study for Azra Inc. We will evaluate the 2 numeric fields for outliers, viz. age and balance. We will employ suitable outlier handling approaches for each case if outliers are detected. Let us begin.

1. Create a box plot for the age feature from the **df_train** dataset using the pandas series plot method, using the following code:

```
df_train.age.plot.box(figsize=[3,5])
plt.show()
```

You should get the following output:

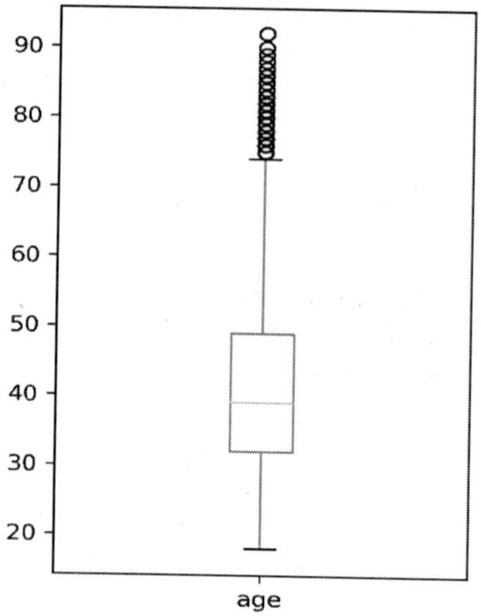

Figure 3.9: *Box plot of age*

The box plot shows that there are some high values above 75. Using the Tukey criterion, these can be considered potential outliers (i.e., the cut-off would be 75). Let us check out the true cut-offs as per the Tukey criterion.

2. Calculate **Q1**, **Q3**, IQR (Q3 – Q1) and subsequently the lower and upper thresholds based on the Tukey criterion. Display the obtained thresholds. Use the following code:

```
Q3 = df_train.age.quantile(0.75)
Q1 = df_train.age.quantile(0.25)
```

```
IQR = Q3 - Q1
print("Lower cutoff:", Q1 - 1.5*IQR, \
      "; Upper cutoff:", Q3 + 1.5*IQR)
```

The cut-offs should be printed as:

```
Lower cutoff: 6.5; Upper cutoff: 74.5
```

Note that the **upper cutoff** matches with the box plot.

Based on our domain understanding, values preceding 75 are not problematic, and we do not consider these as genuine outliers and therefore do not handle them.

Note: The age column has a continuous range with a few high values. These are not far off and seem connected to the main values. These seem to be genuine high values and not truly outliers. One approach would be to NOT perform any outlier treatment for this column. Instead, we could transform this column to follow any preferred distribution (in a later section).

3. Create a box plot for the **balance** feature using the following code:

```
df_train.balance.plot.box(figsize=[4,5])
plt.show()
```

This should result in the following output:

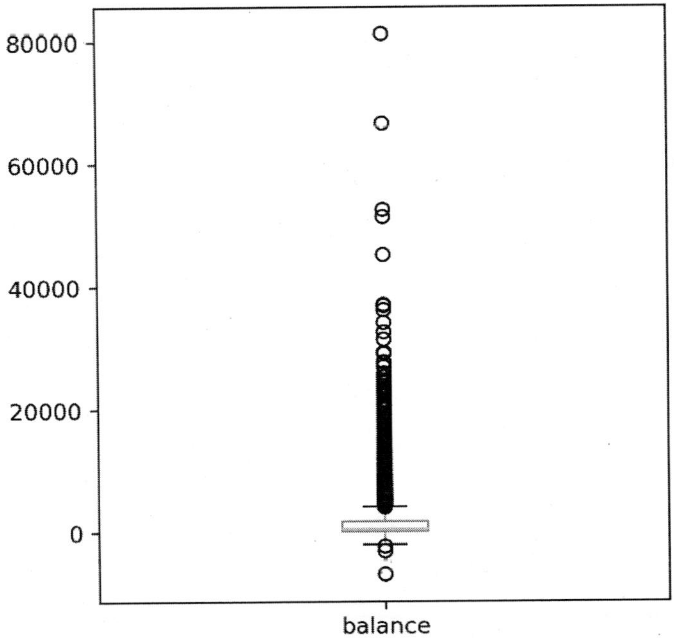

Figure 3.10: Box plot of balance

We seem to have some values far from the usual, and values like 60,000 are way higher than the median, which seems much closer to 0. Let us find out the thresholds based on the Tukey criterion.

4. Calculate and display the thresholds for **balance** based on the Tukey criterion. Use the following code:

   ```
   Q3 = df_train.balance.quantile(0.75)
   Q1 = df_train.balance.quantile(0.25)
   IQR = Q3 - Q1
   print("Lower cutoff:", Q1 - 1.5*IQR, \
         "; Upper cutoff:", Q3 + 1.5*IQR)
   ```

   The thresholds get printed as:

   ```
   Lower cutoff: -2245.5; Upper cutoff: 4062.5
   ```

   The **upper cutoff** seems to be **4,062.5**, which is way lower than the observed highs around 80,000. Recall that we expect the **balance** feature to not follow a Gaussian, but an exponential/power distribution. Let us see the top percentiles for it:

5. Calculate percentiles p95, p99, p995 for the balance variable:

   ```
   df_train.balance.quantile([0.95, 0.99, 0.995])
   ```

   You should get the following output:

   ```
   0.950     5915.900
   0.990    13341.160
   0.995    20061.165
   Name: balance, dtype: float64
   ```

The 95th percentile is around 5.9K (note that this is higher than the Tukey criterion value). Also, note that around 5.9K, we have a fair number of observations. A higher cut-off is therefore more suitable, and a cut-off of around 20K seems more suitable.

6. Using 20K as the **cutoff**, drop all records with a higher balance value. Print the shape of the dataframe to see the updated number of records:

   ```
   cutoff_balance = 20000
   df_train = df_train[df_train.balance <= cutoff_balance].copy()
   df_train.shape
   ```

   The dimensions get printed as:

   (8876, 11)

7. Now, apply the same cut-off to remove outliers in balance from the test data. Print out the updated dimensions of the test dataset.

```
df_test = df_test[df_test.balance <= cutoff_balance].copy()
df_test.shape
```

The updated dimensions are:

(2220, 11)

In this exercise, we applied different outlier detection methods to the numeric fields in our dataset. We observed that while 'age' has higher values, we do not consider them genuine outliers and therefore did not perform any outlier treatment. The feature **`balance`** has some extremely high values that are quite different. Using the percentile cut-off approach, we dropped the outliers from the train and test set. Note that the cut-off was obtained solely from the train set and only the cut-off was applied on the test set. With this, we are ready to learn to tackle another common problem with real-world data – missing values.

Step 4: Missing value treatment

Missing values are a reality of data science projects that plague practically every machine learning project. Every machine learning practitioner meets them virtually in their first machine learning project. This problem is particularly challenging because dealing with missing values is not simple. Doing it right involves several steps and a great deal of understanding of the data, the domain, and the task at hand. Let us discuss a few considerations.

Note: About the impact of the task at hand. For time series forecasting, the approach to handling missing values completely differs from usual predictive models where the observations are independent. A new observation in time series data inherently depends on the previous. The strategies for dealing with missing values must be different. Handling missing values in time series is out of the scope of this book. This Arxiv paper (https://arxiv.org/abs/2011.11347) discusses some approaches.

First, not all missing values are obvious. In *Exercise 3.2*, we saw some null values in the Pandas dataframe with obvious misses that are easy to identify. We also saw that three columns had values indicating that the information was somehow missing –p_outcome, contact, and education had an unknown value. This indicates that the information is missing, but because these are not null values in the dataframe, it was not easy to detect them. This is a good example of **hidden missing values**.

Once the missing values are identified, the practitioner must meditate on the cause of these missing values. This understanding (to the best of your capacity) is critical for a good outcome. Sometimes, the missing value could be due to random factors that have nothing to do with the customers or their information (For example, random drops when logging streaming data with a high event rate). Such missing values are known to be **Missing**

completely at random (**MCAR**). These are the least harmless missing values as they are truly non-informative and do not cause systematic issues with the data.

The other, insidious, extreme is the **Missing not at random** (**MNAR**) situation. In such a case, there is an underlying logic because of which certain observations or features are missing more than the others. Revisiting the survey data example, surveys containing potentially sensitive questions may be skipped by some respondents more than others. In such a case, these missing values are not uninformative the fact that they are missing itself is information. Extreme care must be taken in handling these missing values.

The approach to handling missing values changes with the type of missing value and the mechanism from which the values stemmed. Consider the case of e-commerce customer data with the number of orders they placed in the past month as a field. The field could be missing for a lot of customers. But this could simply be because of the way the data was joined which resulted in null values for customers who did not place any order. In this case, **a missing value had a meaning**. Handling this case could be as simple as replacing the null values with 0.

In general, there are a few approaches to handling missing values:

- Replace by true meaning (if known).
- Replace (impute) with a simple central tendency (mean and median).
- Estimate (impute) the probable value using multivariate analysis.
- Drop the records.
- Use techniques that work with missing values.

We have already seen an example of option 1 – the e-commerce data where null values could be replaced by their true meaning, that is, a 0. Options 2 and 3 are related in that both replace the missing value with some expected value, with the second approach being more complex. Option 5 is also safe, even though it restricts the options for machine learning techniques you can use. Option 4 is a special case and a tricky one at that.

Losing records drops potential information in the dataset that could be useful in improving your predictive model's performance. This could be a viable option if the missing values are few and are missing completely at random. But if you believe these are not missing at random, that is systematic misses, then dropping these would drop information and potentially some important records. The dataset may not represent the general data and the true performance of the model will suffer. Therefore, we must be careful and drop only when we do not suspect systematic misses.

There are various approaches to handling such situations, and Option 5 is one. Additionally, in case the field must be dropped, the fact that the field was missing for certain records could be informative and can be provided to the model using an indicator variable containing 1 when the original field was missing a value, 0 otherwise. If there is a pattern in missingness, the model can potentially detect it with the help of this field.

Note: All the techniques we discussed here are for dealing with the features/ independent variables. In a predictive modeling exercise, records with values missing for the outcome must be dropped, as we did for the 'deposit' field in *Exercise* 3.2.

Note: Handling missing values is a very complex topic. Over the past decades, various techniques have been developed for handling them. While the techniques could be complicated, the principles aren't different from what we discussed.

It is important to remember that handling the missing values in the data should be done separately for train and test datasets. Even if you take the simple approach of mean imputation the mean must be calculated using the train data alone and using the entire dataset would lead to data leakage.

Let us see these techniques in action and handle the missing values in our data in the next exercise.

Step 5: Categorical feature handling

In general, the dataset will have variables of mixed types numerical and categorical. All implementations of predictive modeling techniques in Python are built to handle numerical features, and most predictive modeling technique implementations in Python do not handle categorical values. Therefore, the categorical values must be encoded into numerical values. But before we start encoding, there are some smart approaches you can employ. These are often ignored but can help greatly simplify this part of the pre-processing and help avoid losing potential information from the data. A more holistic approach would have the following steps:

1. **Reduce levels (club similar ones) in a feature**:

   We look at the unique values in the feature and how they relate to the outcome/ target. Levels that contain similar information and have a similar relation to the target (For example, similar average outcome value) can be clubbed/condensed into a single level. This step alone can help you reduce the levels significantly.

2. **Combine features with similar/complementary information**:

   Often, we have features that contain similar or even complementary information. A classic example from the health domain is weight and height contain complementary information for heart disease prediction. These can be combined into **Body Mass Index** (**BMI**) which is a simple ratio between weight and height. Similarly, in our case study, both features around a personal loan or a housing loan capture similar information that the customer has taken a loan and can potentially be clubbed. We will see these details later in the section on feature engineering.

3. **Encoding (dummy, target, effect, and so on)**:

   After making these simplifications, we can proceed to convert the categorical values to numbers by using one of the many encoding strategies. Schemes like One Hot Encoding/Dummy Encoding, Label Encoding, Target Encoding, Effect Encoding, and Deviation Coding are a few examples. At the end of this process, the original categorical column is replaced by one or more numerical features.

Note: Steps 1 and 2 are non-standard and again require an understanding of the data and the domain and are task dependent. A thorough analysis of the train data must be performed to perform these steps efficiently.

Solving our case study

In our case study for marketing for Azra Inc., we have a few categorical features:

- **job**: The customer's occupation
- **education**: Highest education level of the customer (primary to tertiary)
- **housing**: Whether the customer had a housing loan (yes/no)
- **loan**: Whether the customer had a personal loan (yes/no)
- **contact**: Preferred contact channel of the customer (telephone/cellular)
- **month**: Month on contact in the campaign
- **poutcome**: Outcome of the campaign before this campaign

Pause and ponder: For our case study, which strategies can you already think of? Which features can be potentially clubbed? For which columns would you like to evaluate condensing levels?

First, we will explore the different values in the column and how they relate to the target/outcome. This will help us identify some candidate levels that we can potentially club. The simplest way to do this will be to calculate the average value of the target for each of the levels in the categorical feature and plot them. Let us begin by doing so for the job column. Use the following code to plot the average target value for each job category:

```
bank1.groupby('job')['deposit'].mean().sort_values().plot.barh()
plt.title()
plt.show()
```

The output should be as follows:

***Figure 3.11:** Job categories and corresponding success rates*

We notice that there are 12 unique job categories in the field, and we can see that the success rate varies significantly by category. We also observe that some categories, though logically very different, seem to have very similar values for the outcome. This understanding will help immensely while handling this feature. Let us create similar views for all the categorical features in one go. Use the following code:

```
cat_cols = df_train.select_dtypes("object").columns
plt.figure(figsize=[15,12])
for ind, col in enumerate(cat_cols):
    plt.subplot(3,3,ind+1)
    bank1.groupby(col)['deposit'].mean().sort_values().plot.barh()
    plt.title(col)
plt.show()
```

The output should be as follows:

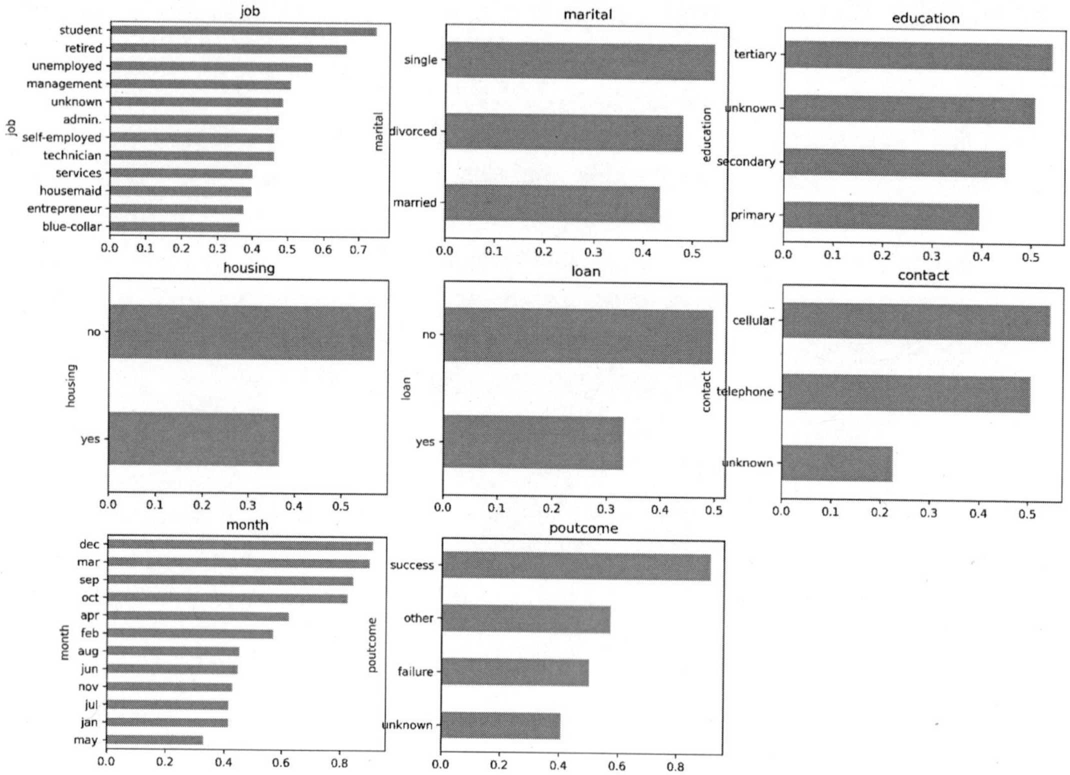

Figure 3.12: Levels and success rates for all categorical features at once

Figure 3.12 is extremely informative. An analysis of each of the sub-plots is necessary to understand each feature and gain first ideas on handling them. Let us start with the handling strategy for the feature job.

We saw that the feature job has 12 unique levels. Using an encoding scheme like Dummy Encoding or One Hot Encoding directly on this would create 11 or 12 new features from a single feature. This is not a great idea as it increases model complexity, and you can potentially lose information when dropping some of these new features later. A better idea would be to perform target encoding. Let us understand it better.

The job categories services, housemaid, entrepreneur, and blue-collar have similar success rates. These jobs themselves are very different, but for our modeling activity, they are expected to have a similar effect on the outcome. In our encoding, therefore, we can assign similar numerical values to these. The value is simply the average value of the target. If we replace the category with the average target value, then we have a different value for each level in a single column and the difference between the levels is also retained.

Note: Another option here was clubbing the categories. However because the job categories are logically very different, we do not club them using our domain understanding. Additionally, there could be some other information in the dataset related to the job category that we do not want to lose out on.

Let us implement target encoding for the job feature. For this, we could either create our own simple mappings or use the **category_encoders** library in Python. We recommend using the library as it has a host of other approaches that you can employ with ease using sklearn-styled syntax. You can install the package using the pip command:

```
pip install category_encoders
```

More details about the package can be found at **https://pypi.org/project/category-encoders/.**

Let us begin by importing and instantiating a target encoder from the **category_encoders** package using the following code:

```
from category_encoders.target_encoder import TargetEncoder
enc_target = TargetEncoder()
```

To fit the **encoder**, that is, calculate the average outcome levels, and to extract these values, we will use the **fit_transform** method of the **encoder**. We will extract these values into a new column (**job_encoded**) that we will create on the **df_train** dataset. The method needs two inputs the categorical column to encode, and the target values. Use the following code:

```
df_train['job_encoded'] = enc_target.fit_transform(df_train.job,
df_train.deposit)
```

This simple command should do the job. To verify if this was done correctly, we can use the following **groupby** command and see the value assigned to each level. Use the following code:

```
df_train.groupby(['job','job_encoded']).size()
```

The output should be:

```
job            job_encoded
admin.         0.467317       1025
blue-collar    0.359274       1542
entrepreneur   0.380435        276
housemaid      0.384956        226
management     0.511133       2066
retired        0.659539        608
self-employed  0.463190        326
services       0.404601        739
student        0.749104        279
technician     0.464187       1452
unemployed     0.577061        279
unknown        0.482759         58
dtype: int64
```

***Figure 3.13:** Result from the target encoding*

We can see that for each job category, the **job_encoded** field has a single value. It is easy to verify that these are the same values that we saw in the exploratory plot earlier. Target encoding was as simple as that. Now, we need to apply this encoding to the test data. Note that we are fitting on the train, but only transforming on the test data. Use the following code:

```
df_test['job_encoded'] = enc_target.transform(df_test.job)
```

Caution: Because Target encoding directly uses the target values for creating a feature, there is a risk of overfitting and therefore a lack of generalization to new data. It is therefore advised that some *smoothing* or *regularization* be applied when using target encoding. This can be done via some variations of the target encoding like 'Leave One Fold Out' or with noise addition. Or, can be done via explicit regularization while modeling (more on this in future chapters).

With that, the target encoding is complete for the job field. The original column job can be dropped from both train and test datasets. Using other encoders is just as simple with similar syntax.

Let us now handle the outcome categorical field. We saw earlier in *Figure 3.12* that this field has 4 levels. Revisiting the figure, we observe that the success rates for the categories vary, but one category that stands out from the rest is success. Customers who had previously responded positively to a campaign were much more likely to respond positively to a new campaign. This makes logical sense from a domain perspective. The other categories have values like each other. For our task, we can see that one category is special.

A natural strategy could be to **condense the levels** from 4 to 2. The two levels would be a *success* and *all others*. Realize that if we are reducing to two levels, we need not create 2 new categories. Instead, we could create an **indicator feature**. The feature would hold a value of 1 to indicate success and 0 otherwise. We can achieve this by a simple mapping, as we did for the deposit column in *Exercise 3.2*.

Let us now approach the field **marital**. We see that there are 3 levels, and all have different success rates. No category stands out. One hot encoding / dummy encoding is a good choice for such cases. Essentially, we create indicator variables for each of the columns. Therefore, there would be three indicator variables one for each of married, single, and divorced. Let us use the **OneHotEncoder** method from **category_encoders** for this purpose. Begin by importing and instantiating the **onehotencoder,** using the following code:

```
from category_encoders.one_hot import OneHotEncoder
enc_onehot =  OneHotEncoder(return_df=True, use_cat_names=True)
```

Specifying **use_cat_names** ensures that the indicator variable names are descriptive and contain the level name as a prefix. Specifying **return_df** ensures that a dataframe is returned for easy joining with the main dataset. Now, let us fit and transform the **df_train** dataset using the marital feature using the following code and print out the first 5 records of the result:

```
dumms = enc_onehot.fit_transform(df_train.marital)
dumms.head()
```

The output should be as follows:

	marital_single	marital_married	marital_divorced
3785	1	0	0
1748	0	1	0
5314	0	1	0
10907	1	0	0
6796	0	0	1

Figure 3.14: Columns from one hot encoding

We can see that, as expected, 3 columns were created by the encoder, one for each level. It is important to note there is redundancy in these 3 new columns, all 3 columns are not needed to infer the marital status. For instance, if indicators for both married and divorced are 0, then the original value must be single. We can therefore drop one of these. Let us go ahead and drop the column for divorced, and append it to the original dataframe. Let us also drop the original column marital from **df_train** to remove all redundancy. Use the following code:

```
df_train = df_train.join(dumms.drop('marital_divorced', axis = 1))
df_train.drop('marital', axis=1, inplace=True)
df_train.head()
```

You should get the following result:

	age	job	education	balance	housing	loan	contact	month	poutcome	deposit	job_encoded	marital_single	marital_married
3785	40.0	services	secondary	1038	no	no	unknown	jun	unknown	0.0	0.404601	1	0
1748	55.0	technician	tertiary	-466	yes	no	cellular	may	unknown	1.0	0.464187	0	1
5314	37.0	blue-collar	secondary	454	yes	no	unknown	may	unknown	0.0	0.359274	0	1
10907	30.0	blue-collar	secondary	228	no	no	cellular	feb	failure	0.0	0.359274	1	0
6796	57.0	retired	secondary	316	no	no	cellular	jan	unknown	0.0	0.659539	0	0

Figure 3.15: After dummy encoding for marital

To complete the handling of this field, we need to apply this encoding to the test data as well. To do so use the following code:

```
dumms_test = enc_onehot.transform(df_test.marital)
df_test = df_test.join(dumms_test.drop('marital_divorced',axis = 1))
df_test.drop('marital',axis=1,inplace=True)
```

With that, we have completed the encoding for the field **marital** as well. So far, we have discussed/handled 3 fields already. The remaining categorical fields can be approached similarly. The field month could be target encoded. Field education can be dummy encoded. An indicator feature could be helpful for the field poutcome. In the next exercise, we will handle most of the remaining features in our case study.

Exercise 3.5: Handling remaining categorical features

In this exercise, we will first create an indicator variable for the **poutcome** field. Similarly, we will create an indicator feature for **contact** indicating if the value is unknown. Then, we will perform target encoding for the column **month**. For **education** as well, we will create an indicator variable. Let us begin.

1. Create the indicator variable to replace the original **poutcome** feature that indicates **success** using the following code. Do so for the test set as well:

```
df_train['poutcome'] = np.where(df_train.poutcome ==
"success", 1, 0)

df_test['poutcome'] = np.where(df_test.poutcome == "success", 1, 0)
```

2. Create an indicator variable to replace the original **contact** feature that indicates if the value was **unknown**. Do so for the test dataset as well:

```
df_train['contact'] = np.where(df_train.contact == "unknown", 1, 0)

df_test['contact'] = np.where(df_test.contact == "unknown", 1, 0)
```

3. Perform target encoding for the **month** feature. Transform the test dataset as well:

```
enc_target = TargetEncoder()

df_train['month_enc] = enc_target.fit_transform(df_train.month,
df_train.deposit)

df_test['month_enc] = enc_target.transform(df_test.month)
```

4. Create an indicator feature for **education** that is 1 when the value is either **primary** or **secondary**. These are the low success rate categories. Do the same for the test data as well. Verify that it worked on the train set by printing out the value against the original values:

```
ind_vals = ['primary', 'secondary']

df_train['edu_enc'] = np.where(df_train.education.isin(ind_vals), 1, 0)

df_test['edu_enc'] = np.where(df_test.education.isin(ind_vals), 1, 0)

df_train.groupby(['education', 'edu_enc']).size()
```

The output should be as follows:

```
education  edu_enc
primary    1         1187
secondary  1         4324
tertiary   0         2963
unknown    0          402
dtype: int64
```

Figure 3.16: Result of encoding education

5. Clean up the datasets by dropping the original columns **education**, **month**, **job**. Print out the first five records of the train data:

```
df_train.drop(['job','education','month'],
              axis=1, inplace=True)
df_test.drop(['job','education','month'],
              axis=1, inplace=True)
df_train.head()
```

The output should be as follows:

age	balance	housing	loan	contact	poutcome	deposit	job_encoded	marital_single	marital_married	edu_enc	month_enc
40.0	1038	no	no	1	0	0.0	0.404601	1	0	1	0.457819
55.0	-466	yes	no	0	0	1.0	0.464187	0	1	0	0.332447
37.0	454	yes	no	1	0	0.0	0.359274	0	1	1	0.332447
30.0	228	no	no	0	0	0.0	0.359274	1	0	1	0.568106
57.0	316	no	no	0	0	0.0	0.659539	0	0	1	0.403571

Figure 3.17: First 5 records of the train data

In the exercise, we implemented the categorical data handling techniques that we learned. We have completed the handling of all the categorical features except **housing** and **loan**. We reserved this for the end as to handle them, we will take a slightly different approach. This is a non-standard step but important to be aware of as it helps combine the value of two or more columns into one. Let us learn about it.

Let us view again how the values in the fields of housing and loans relate to the outcome. *Figure 3.18* shows the relationship. We see that for both cases when the customer has a loan, the success rate is much lower. This makes sense a customer who has already taken a loan does not usually have the necessary liquidity to make a term deposit. Because both features capture similar information (the customer has taken a loan) and they have very similar values for the levels, these would be good candidates to combine into a single feature. We could have one feature called **loan_any** that holds a value of **1** when either **housing** or **loan** is "yes", and **0** otherwise:

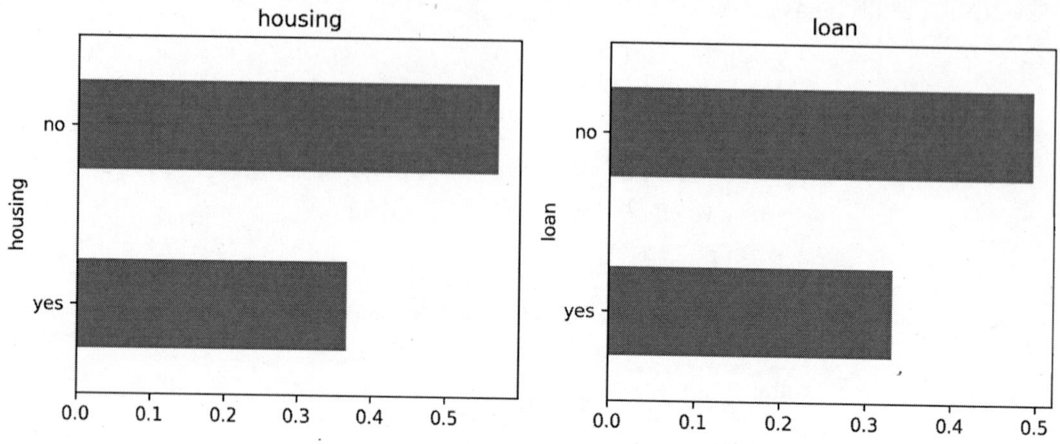

Figure 3.18: housing and loan vs. the outcome

Let us now create this new column, **loan_any** first on the train dataset. We will concatenate the values for housing and loan into a new column which will have values like "yesyes", "yesno", and so on. The value **nono** would indicate the customer has neither type of loan nor we can create an indicator for this value. Use the following code:

```
df_train['loan_any'] = df_train.housing + df_train.loan
df_train.loan_any = np.where(df_train.loan_any=='nono',1,0)
```

This should create the indicator variable. Let us print out 5 records with just these 3 columns to check whether this worked:

```
df_train[['housing','loan','loan_any']].head()
```

	housing	loan	loan_any
3785	no	no	1
1748	yes	no	0
5314	yes	no	0
10907	no	no	1
6796	no	no	1

Figure 3.19: Indicator for any loan

Create a similar feature for the test dataset and drop the original features housing and loan using the following code:

```
df_test['loan_any'] = df_test.housing + df_test.loan
df_test.loan_any = np.where(df_test.loan_any=='nono',1,0)
df_train.drop(['housing','loan'], axis=1, inplace=True)
df_test.drop(['housing','loan'], axis=1, inplace=True)
```

With these commands executed, we have now completed the handling for all the categorical features. A quick print of the first 5 rows of the train dataset can confirm this. *Figure 3.20* shows what the dataset looks like after all the pre-processing so far:

age	balance	contact	poutcome	deposit	job_encoded	marital_single	marital_married	edu_enc	month_enc	loan_any
40.0	1038	1	0	0.0	0.404601	1	0	1	0.457819	1
55.0	-466	0	0	1.0	0.464187	0	1	0	0.332447	0
37.0	454	1	0	0.0	0.359274	0	1	1	0.332447	0
30.0	228	0	0	0.0	0.359274	1	0	1	0.568106	1
57.0	316	0	0	0.0	0.659539	0	0	1	0.403571	1

Figure 3.20: *Train data after pre-processing so far*

We are one step closer to completing the pre-processing of the data and have completed the core and essential steps. This leaves us with one more, somewhat standard step in pre-processing of numerical features, that is, scaling.

Step 6: Transformation of numeric features

Another very common pre-processing step for numerical features is transformation. The most common forms of transformations are scaling, standardization, or normalization (non-standard usage). All of them usually attempt to bring the different numerical features to a similar value range. Depending on the task at hand, this could be an essential step or just an optional one.

For most supervised machine learning techniques, scaling the features does not drastically influence the model accuracy. This is especially true for smaller datasets where the background calculations in fitting the model can be done quickly regardless of the different value ranges. This is not the case for situations involving large datasets and modeling techniques like deep neural networks. The optimisation algorithms employed by these techniques are sensitive to scale in the sense that reaching an optimum is much faster if features are on a similar scale. Such situations prefer that the features are 0-centered (have a mean close to 0) and values close by on either side. When all features are 0-centered and have a similar range of values, the optimisation algorithms are expected to work fastest. Therefore, for efficiency, it is a good idea to scale the features.

Another benefit of scaling for supervised machine learning is the ease of interpretation. For a linear or logistic regression model, for example, it is much easier to interpret and compare the impact of each feature if the scales are the same. In the absence of scaling, practitioners resort to calculating standardized coefficients to compare them. This step is not needed if you scale the features before fitting the model.

Some popularly applied transformations are:

- **Standard scaling**: Makes the field 0 mean, unit standard deviation (Z scores).
- **Min-Max scaling**: Limits to a value between 0 and 1.
- **Other Transformations**: Converts the distribution to approximate Gaussian (or even uniform) using Quantile/Power/Log transforms.

Note: For a larger list of transformations implemented in sklearn, you can refer to the official sklearn documentation: https://scikit-learn.org/stable/modules/classes.html#module-sklearn.preprocessing

For most situations, it is sufficient to constrain the different features to similar values. Standard scaling replaces values effectively with Z scores, making it 0 mean and unit standard deviation. This would also mean that most data points would be in the range [-3,3] as values outside them have low probabilities. Such a transformation benefits deep neural networks particularly owing to the nature of optimization algorithms employed.

For our marketing model for Azra Inc., let us perform transformation for the two numerical features age and balance in the next exercise.

Exercise 3.6: Transforming numerical variables:

In this exercise, we will perform transformations on the two numerical features in the dataset for marketing for Azra Inc., age, and balance. Note that we do not wish to change the way the values are distributed (that is, no power/log/quantile transforms) but merely change the range of the values. We will use the standard scaling approach for this purpose. Let us begin the transformations.

1. First, plot the two variables on box plots to understand their distribution better:

   ```
   vars_num = ['age', 'balance']
   df_train[vars_num].plot.box(subplots=True, figsize=[10,5])
   plt.show()
   ```

   The output is as follows:

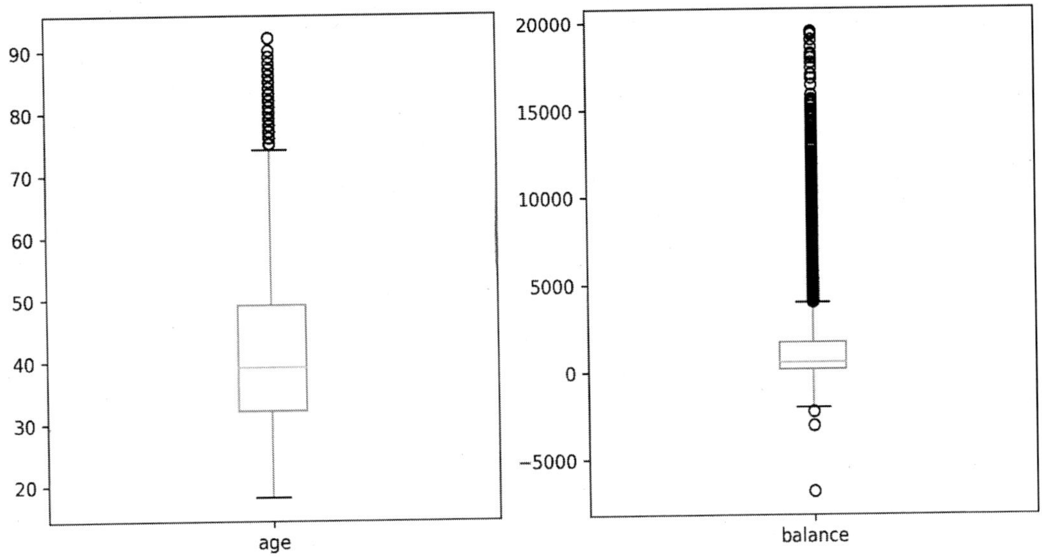

Figure 3.21: Box plots of the numeric features

2. Check the current mean and standard deviation of the columns:

```
df_train[vars_num].apply([np.mean, np.std])
```

The results are printed as follows:

	age	balance
Mean	41.148850	1360.832470
Std	11.861231	2233.509819

Table 3.1: Current mean and standard deviation

3. For both features, we will perform standard scaling. Import and instantiate standard scaler from **sklearn**:

```
from sklearn.preprocessing import StandardScaler
scaler_std = StandardScaler()
```

4. Now, using the **fit_transform** method, transform the features on the train set. Check the new mean and standard deviation for these columns to ensure they worked:

```
df_train[vars_num] = scaler_std.fit_transform(df_train[vars_num])
df_train[vars_num].apply([np.mean, np.std])
```

You should get the following output:

	age	balance
Mean	6.162063e-17	4.140822e-17
Std	1.000056e+00	1.000056e+00

Table 3.2: *Updated mean and standard deviation*

The mean values are practically 0 and the standard deviation is 1, as we expected.

5. Using the transform method, apply the scaling to the columns in the test data as well. Check the mean and standard deviation of the columns in the test data:

```
df_test[vars_num] = scaler_std.transform(df_test[vars_num])
df_test[vars_num].apply([np.mean, np.std])
```

	age	balance
Mean	0.020065	0.040063
Std	1.009910	1.053442

Table 3.3: *Mean and std of the test data*

Note: On applying the scaler to the test dataset, the values might not be exactly as expected. If standard scaling was used, the mean of the columns in the test data might not be exactly 0 and the standard deviation might not be exactly 1. This is because the mean and standard deviation of the train data could be slightly different from the test data (it usually is). This is perfectly fine and doesn't cause any significant drop in model performance.

6. Print the first 5 records of the train dataset to have a look at it after all the pre-processing:

```
df_train.head()
```

The records get printed as follows:

age	balance	contact	poutcome	deposit	job_encoded	marital_single	marital_married	month_enc	edu_enc	loan_any
-0.096742	-0.144549	1	0	0.0	0.404601	1	0	0.457819	1	1
1.168505	-0.817966	0	0	1.0	0.464187	0	1	0.332447	0	0
-0.349791	-0.406035	1	0	0.0	0.359274	0	1	0.332447	1	0
-0.940240	-0.507227	0	0	0.0	0.359274	1	0	0.568106	1	1
1.337205	-0.467825	0	0	0.0	0.659539	0	0	0.403571	1	1

Figure 3.22: *Data after the pre-processing*

This exercise concludes the eighth and final step in our data pre-processing pipeline. The data is now ready to be supplied to a model and the entire model fitting process can now begin.

Case study steps review

For the Azra Inc. marketing case study, we performed several steps. Let us take a complete look at all the steps we performed in *Table 3.4*:

Step 1: Load data + basic checks + corrections Loaded data Fixed `deposit` format Identified obvious and hidden missing values
Step 2: Separate into train and test datasets Performed a stratified 80-20 split
Step 3: Outlier treatment Identified outliers for each numeric feature Dropped outliers for relevant fields
Step 4: Missing value treatment Handled obvious and hidden missing values Median imputation, clubbing with 'unknown'
Step 5: Categorical feature handling Target encoding Indicator features One hot / dummy encoding
Step 6: Creating new features 'loan_any' combined `housing` and `loan` features
Step 7: Transform numerical features Standard scaling for 'age' and 'balance' features

***Table 3.4**: Pre-processing steps employed*

You may have noted that this is not the same as the process we described in the section "The pre-processing process". Specifically, steps 6 and 7 have swapped positions. This should not be surprising, as we now understand that there is no standard process that applies to all machine learning solutions.

Pause and ponder: Is there any other order of steps that would have worked for our case study? Could any steps have changed the order? Could we have created the new features before transforming the numerical features?

Conclusion

In this chapter, we focused on data pre-processing, a core step in building a machine learning solution, that comes in between *Business Understanding* and *Model building* in the CRISP-DM framework. There are several steps involved in data pre-processing. This process is rarely standardized and can/should not be automated. The primary reason is that there are numerous domain, data, and task specifics that must be accounted for in the process.

Azra Inc. bank needed a machine learning solution for their marketing campaign. Through our numerous pre-processing steps, we helped them go from somewhat raw data to a much more refined and tuned dataset that will help build a high-performing predictive model. To begin, we fixed formats, identified issues and fixed the simple ones right away. A train-test split is essential before proceeding further with detailed analysis and data processing. We do not want data leakage and analyzing the train dataset alone is a good way to ensure this. Outlier treatment, numerical transformations, categorical feature handling and other feature engineering decisions were all made using the train data. The decisions were then only applied to the test set.

With redundancies removed, additional features generated (all informed by data analysis), along with the incorporation of our domain knowledge, we are far better off than where we began. We have optimized the dataset that goes into the model. This completes one major step towards a more optimized machine learning/ AI model.

In the next chapter, we will learn how to assess the performance of the predictive model that we build on this pre-processed data. We will learn the best way to assess the generalized performance of our model. If things are not right, debug the model and figure out improvement areas.

CHAPTER 4
Model Evaluation and Debugging

Introduction

As a data scientist in a large, multinational fast fashion giant, Azra Inc., you have been working on a model to show users the most helpful product reviews. Products can gather several reviews on the platform, and popular items have thousands of them. The goal is to identify reviews the user finds most helpful and display them at the top when the product page loads. You choose a classification-based approach - predicting whether the user will find the review helpful. The review with the highest predicted probability of being helpful gets ranked at the top. What do you suppose is a good model for this situation? Additionally, you may have identified the right technique and aimed to improve the model. How do you diagnose poor model performance and identify corrective actions? Model debugging is also important for a practitioner.

How would you evaluate the various competing models? Is the low latency (faster predictions) model with decent accuracy better than a high accuracy model with higher latency? Is an interpretable model more important than a black box model? Numerous considerations go into defining and choosing the best model and pure accuracy is seldom the sole criterion. In this chapter, we will understand these considerations in detail. We will also learn a principled way to diagnose and debug models to identify the cause of poor performance and improve our models. We will go through real-world examples to practice and solidify these learnings.

Structure

This chapter will cover the following topics:

- Ad click prediction case study
- Model evaluation considerations
- Model evaluation metrics
    - o Metrics for classification
    - o Metrics for regression
- Model evaluation schemes
- Model debugging
    - o Overfitting and underfitting
    - o Handling overfitting

Objectives

In this chapter, we will learn about model evaluation in the context of solving business problems. We will understand the various considerations that make one model better than another. We will learn about metrics for model evaluation, classification, and regression problems. Not all errors are equally problematic, and we will understand several metrics that are beyond simple accuracy. We will also learn a principled way to diagnose and debug models to identify the cause of poor performance. Thereafter, we will discuss several ways to handle underfitting and overfitting. At the end of the chapter, we will go through real-world examples to practice and solidify these learnings.

Ad click prediction case study

Azra Inc. is a multi-national fast fashion giant with millions of daily active users visiting the mobile app. The home page of the app is prime digital real estate and brands are keen on advertising their brand/selection to gain maximum visibility. On-platform advertisement on e-commerce platforms is extremely popular and a great revenue stream for the platforms. Azra Inc., though, needs to make sure the ads are relevant to the customer. Irrelevant ads dilute customer experience and impact customer retention. Azra Inc. therefore needs to identify the ads relevant to the customer.

A popular approach is to display only those ads that have a higher chance of being clicked by the customer. An ad being clicked is a reasonable indicator of relevance; customers are less likely to click on irrelevant ads. Like most major platforms, Azra Inc. wishes to deploy a **click prediction model that will predict whether a user will click on a given ad**. Such a model can be used to rank ads and the company can surface only those that have a high chance of being clicked. The input to such models usually consists of (but not limited to) demographic information of the customer, information about the context (device type, OS, and so on), and information about the ad itself (item category, brand, and so on).

Azra Inc. has collected historical data containing some demographic information about the customer, their estimated salary, and whether they clicked on the ad that was displayed. Your task as a data scientist is to create the ad click prediction model using this data. That is, given user demographic data, predict if they will click on the ad. Let us understand the data that we have at hand.

Exercise 4.1: Load and prepare the data

Let us begin by understanding the data for our case study that will be used throughout the chapter.

Perform the following steps:

1. Import the necessary libraries (**numpy**, **pandas**, **seaborn**) using the following command:

```
import pandas as pd, numpy as np, seaborn as sns
import matplotlib.pyplot as plt
%matplotlib inline
```

2. Using the **read_csv** method, read the file into a pandas dataframe, and display the first 5 rows:

```
inp0 = pd.read_csv("Social_Network_Ads.csv")
inp0.head()
```

You should get the following output:

	User ID	Gender	Age	EstimatedSalary	Clicked
0	15624510	Male	19	19000	0
1	15810944	Male	35	20000	0
2	15668575	Female	26	43000	0
3	15603246	Female	27	57000	0
4	15804002	Male	19	76000	0

Figure 4.1: *The first 5 records of the social network ads dataset*

3. Drop the column User ID as we will not be using it, using the following command:

```
inp0.drop("User ID", axis=1, inplace=True)
```

4. Convert the gender column into a numeric field by mapping male to 0 and female to 1. Display the counts of the values in the gender column after modification, as in the following command:

```
inp0['Gender'] = inp0.Gender.map({'Female':1, 'Male':0})
inp0.Gender.value_counts()
```

You should get the following output:

```
1    204
0    196
Name: Gender, dtype: int64
```

5. Print the first 5 records of the modified dataset using the head method of the dataframe:

```
inp0.head()
```

You will get the following output:

	Gender	Age	EstimatedSalary	Clicked
0	0	19	19000	0
1	0	35	20000	0
2	1	26	43000	0
3	1	27	57000	0
4	0	19	76000	0

Figure 4.2: *First 5 records of the modified dataset*

Model evaluation considerations

Revisit the review ranking situation (as mentioned in the *Introduction* section) for the data scientist at Azra Inc. How would you define a good model? The models must generalize well to the unseen data which is a basic requirement in all situations, and therefore something other than what we need to focus on. Let us discuss the other considerations.

We know the ranking is user-specific and a thousand reviews (as mentioned in the *Introduction* section) may need to be ranked. The reviews need to be ranked as soon as the page is loaded. The scoring and ranking need to be extremely quick. This means that speed (low latency) is an extremely important criterion - a model that takes several seconds to rank these thousand reviews is simply unacceptable. The good model must be quick.

Another consideration is that user preferences and behaviors keep changing frequently, and what interests the user today might not be relevant on the next visit. This means that frequent retraining of the model is a requirement and you may need to retrain the model daily. Therefore, a good model must be easy and quick to retrain. Model interpretability is another consideration - in this case, the model is an internal model employed for a (relatively) less risky task (compared to disease diagnosis or loan approvals). For such a situation, a highly interpretable model that allows auditing for fairness is optional. Therefore, while interpretability would be nice, it is optional for a good model in this situation.

Coming to accuracy - does the situation have very steep accuracy requirements? That is, does the most helpful review always need to be ranked first? We display several reviews at once. It is okay if the most helpful review is ranked second or third. The user will potentially read multiple reviews, so the top review does not have to be the winner. We have a low accuracy requirement, and a good model can have acceptable accuracy.

Putting it all together, we now have an idea of a good model for our situation: a low-latency model with acceptable accuracy that is easy and quick to retrain.

In the example, accuracy was discussed at the end. Indeed, accuracy is only one of the criteria for evaluating a model. In general, there are several considerations in evaluating a model. Refer to the following figure:

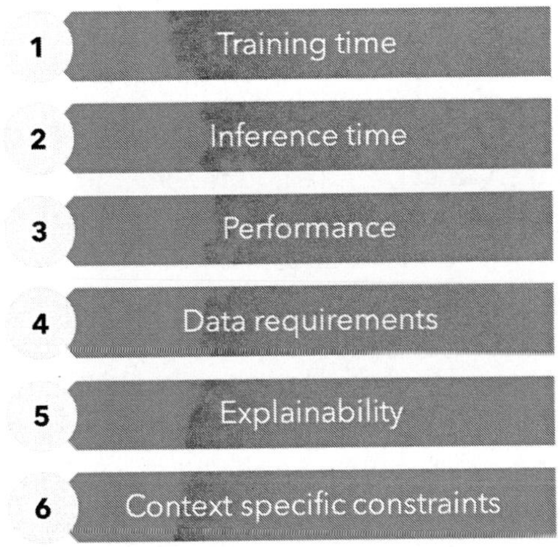

***Figure 4.3**: General considerations in model evaluation*

The following list is the main considerations:

- **Training time**: Higher training time often equates to higher costs and might make frequent retraining prohibitively time-consuming and expensive. For example, models needing to be retrained once a month can afford significantly higher training times than those needing daily retraining.
- **Inference time**: This is when the model predicts a record (referred to as the latency of the model). In online, near real-time systems, inference times have hard constraints that must be respected to be useful (for example inference time of at most five milliseconds). A higher latency can be acceptable in offline scoring systems with fewer predictions.

Pause and ponder: In a real-time situation, where inference time needs to be extremely short, which modeling technique might be more appropriate - a K Nearest Neighbor model, or a decision tree model? Which of these approaches is expected to have faster inference times?

- **Performance**: We refer to how well the model predicts the outcome. For classification problems, this could be plain accuracy, precision, recall, or one of the many available measures (discussed in the next section). This could be R2, MAE, MAPE, and so on for regression problems.

Note: Choosing from the various model performance metrics itself has several considerations. Certain situations have very specific requirements on model performance that dictate the choice of the metric, and we will learn these in the next section.

- **Explainability**: Situations where model bias can have serious consequences necessitate that the model be interpretable and can be audited for fairness, this is a necessity for several regulatory environments. Additionally, it is critical for explanatory models (the purpose is to explain behavior). However, there are several situations where explainability is not a concern.
- **Data requirements**: A linear regression model and a deep neural network surely have different data requirements. The former can do with a hundred records, but the latter usually needs thousands at the least. Low data size is typical in several domains necessitating fewer data-hungry models. On the other hand, platforms with millions of customers typically have millions of data points in Terabytes of data that the most complex models can work with.
- **Context-specific constraints**: Constraints can also emerge from the specific context and models that do not respect these constraints can be useless. For example, if a situation needs predictions to have confidence intervals, then only a few models can even be considered.

To summarize, there are multiple considerations in model evaluation and accuracy is merely one of them. We must respect the constraints of the system in which the model is to be employed. The model is useless otherwise. A good model depends on the situation, and it is up to the data scientist, to use the domain understanding and judgment to choose the best model. In the next section, we will learn model evaluation metrics in detail to help us concretely evaluate model performance. Before we get there, to make things more concrete, let us prepare a baseline model to predict ad clicks.

Exercise 4.2: Building the competing models

We will make 3 models - a decision tree model, a random forest model, and a support vector classifier. Later sections of the chapter will evaluate and compare these models' performance. Perform the following steps:

1. Divide the data into train and test sets using the **train_test_split** method from **sklearn**, as shown in the following code. Print out the shapes of the train and test datasets:

```
from sklearn.model_selection import train_test_split
df_train, df_test = train_test_split(inp0, train_size=0.7, random_
state=42)
df_train.shape, df_test.shape
```

   The shapes get printed as follows:

```
((280, 4), (120, 4))
```

2. Separate the features and the target (**X_train, y_train, X_test, y_test**) using the following code. Print the first 5 records of the **X_train** dataset:

```
X_train = df_train.drop("Clicked", axis=1)
y_train = df_train[['Clicked']]
X_test = df_test.drop("Clicked", axis=1)
y_test = df_test[['Clicked']]
X_train.head(5)
```

   You should get the following output:

	Gender	Age	EstimatedSalary
157	0	29	75000
109	1	38	80000
17	0	45	26000
347	1	54	108000
24	0	46	23000

Figure 4.4: *First 5 records of X_train*

3. Import decision tree from **sklearn**, instantiate with **random_state** assigned to 42 (for repeatability of results) and **max_depth** to 5, fit on the train data. Use the following code:

```
from sklearn.tree import DecisionTreeClassifier
dt = DecisionTreeClassifier(max_depth=7, random_state=42)
dt.fit(X_train, y_train)
```

4. Import **RandomForest** from **sklearn.ensemble**, instantiate with **random_state** assigned to 42 and **max_depth** to 5 and 50 estimators, fit on the train data. Use the following code:

```
from sklearn.ensemble import RandomForestClassifier
rf = RandomForestClassifier(max_depth=7, \
                                    random_state=42, \
                                    n_estimators=50)
rf.fit(X_train, y_train)
```

5. Import SVC from **sklearn.SVM**, instantiate with **random_state** assigned to 42, fit on the train data. Use the following code:

```
from sklearn.svm import SVC
svc = SVC(random_state=42)
svc.fit(X_train, y_train)
```

With these few lines of code, you have trained 3 predictive models already. In the next few sections, we will see how to perform an in-depth evaluation of these models, diagnosing for poor performance and fixing them. Let us begin with metrics for evaluation in the next section.

Model evaluation metrics

Model performance evaluation to assess how well the model predicts the outcome - is a core criterion for evaluating the goodness of a model. While this is not the only criterion in general, as we saw in the previous section, this becomes the deciding factor in several situations. It is therefore imperative for a data science practitioner to be proficient in model performance evaluation by skillfully identifying:

- The right metrics for assessment
- The evaluation scheme to reliably estimate the generalized performance of the model

The various evaluation schemes will be discussed in a bit. This section will focus on the right metrics for assessment, which has various considerations, as you will learn. Let us begin by appreciating the machine learning problem; there are numerous metrics to evaluate model performance. We will list and define some metrics for classification and regression problems and calculate them for the click prediction case study. Let us begin with metrics for classification.

Metrics for classification problems

In classification problems, the task is correctly predicting the outcome/ label/ category that the item belongs to. The outcome can have two or more categories. For binary classification problems, the outcome has two possible values. The outcome of our click prediction case study can be clicked or not clicked. Likewise, the outcome for a spam detection model would be either spam or not spam. Indeed, binary classification problems are everywhere- predicting customer churn, device failure, ad clicks, loan default, lead conversion, and so on.

Multi-class classification problems have more than two classes to predict.

Accuracy

We have already seen and employed accuracy in *Chapter 3, Data Collection and Pre-processing*. Accuracy measures the proportion of cases that were correctly classified that is the model predicted their true category/label. If 90 of the 100 records were correctly predicted, we say the model has 90% accuracy. This is extremely useful and one of the most commonly used metrics.

It is important to note that accuracy does not care about the labels. It does not treat positives as different from negatives and getting a positive example right is considered as good as getting a negative example right. As a corollary, it considers getting a positive example wrong as problematic as getting a negative one wrong. We therefore need to think beyond accuracy and consider metrics that closely match our business requirements and make our model more suitable for the problem at hand. Let us look at some options.

Pause and ponder: Think about a model to detect HIV. Is not detecting HIV as problematic as a false positive that is a non-HIV case identified as an HIV case? If there is a difference, which type of error do you think is more important to avoid?

Confusion matrix

We saw that plain old accuracy does not care about class and looks at the overall correctness of the model. Often, we care about one outcome and getting it right more than the other. Coming back to the question around HIV detection - we asked if identifying one outcome is more important than the other. You may have identified that this question needs to be more concrete. Let us formulate this better by understanding the types of errors that can occur in this situation.

For binary classification problems, there are two real outcomes and two predicted outcomes. This means that four possible situations can occur for each prediction/record which a confusion matrix can conveniently express. *Table 4.1* shows a general-purpose confusion matrix. We have actual outcomes in the rows, while the columns contain the predictions. *Table 4.1* uses positive/negative labels for the outcomes, but the confusion matrix works the same if the outcomes are 1/0, True/False and so on.

Confusion Matrix	Prediction	
Ground truth	**Positive**	**Negative**
Positive	True Positives (A)	False Negatives (B)
Negative	False Positives (C)	True Negatives (D)

***Table 4.1**: Confusion Matrix showing the possible cases*

The four cases are through A and D and are easy to understand. A and D are cases that the model got right:

- **True positives (A):** The positive outcome was correctly predicted as positive.
- **True negatives (D):** The negative outcome was correctly predicted as negative.

While cases B and C are errors made by the model:

- **False negatives (B):** The positive outcome was incorrectly predicted as negative.
- **False positives (C):** The negative outcome was incorrectly predicted as positive.

To make things more concrete, look at the conceptual confusion matrix for our ad click prediction case study in *Table 4.2*. The rows represent the truth, actual click or no click, while the columns contain the model predictions. The four cases contextualized to the case study, mean:

- True positives: Clicks correctly predicted by the model
- True negatives: Non-clicks correctly predicted by the model
- False positives: Non-clicks incorrectly predicted as clicks
- False negatives: Clicks incorrectly predicted as non-clicks

Click Prediction Confusion Matrix	Prediction	
Ground truth	**Click**	**No Click**
Click	True Positives (A)	False Negatives (B)
No Click	False Positives (C)	True Negatives (D)

***Table 4.2**: Confusion Matrix for the Click Prediction Case Study*

Revisiting the question from earlier: Are all error types equally problematic in all situations? Taking the case of HIV detection think about the consequences of each error type. A False positive, a healthy patient incorrectly identified as HIV positive, is typically followed by another confirmatory test to rule out the error. While it may cause emotional trauma to the patient for a while, the error is usually identified. Now, consider a false negative an HIV positive case not detected. This patient would go out unaware of their true condition, risking their lives and potentially of others around them. The consequences of a false negative can be dire. A model for HIV detection must therefore focus on detecting all true cases, even if it means getting a few more false positives. A confusion matrix is a perfect tool to check this breakdown and identify these cases. Let us now create the confusion matrix for the ad click prediction case study and evaluate the performance of the various models.

Exercise 4.3: Confusion matrix for click prediction models

In this exercise, we will create the confusion models for the 3 models we trained for the ad click prediction case study. We will evaluate the different models' false positives and negatives on the training data. Continue in the same Jupyter notebook that we have been using so far. Perform the following steps:

1. Import the **ConfusionMatrixDisplay** and **confusion_matrix** modules from **sklearn** using the following command:

   ```
   from sklearn.metrics import confusion_matrix
   from sklearn.metrics import ConfusionMatrixDisplay as CM
   ```

2. Print out the simple confusion matrix (without formatting) for the Decision Tree Classifier on the train data:

   ```
   confusion_matrix(y_train, dt.predict(X_train))
   ```

   The matrix gets printed as follows:

   ```
   array([[180,   4],
          [  5,  91]])
   ```

   While this has the information, the formatting could be better. Let us plot a better-formatted confusion matrix.

3. Using the **CofusionMatrixDisplay** module to plot the confusion matrix for the decision tree:

   ```
   CM.from_estimator(dt, X_train, \
                     y_train, cmap="Blues", colorbar=None)
   plt.show()
   ```

You should get the following output:

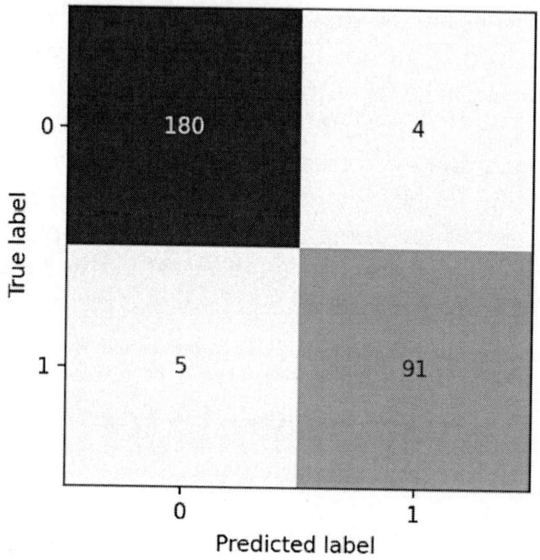

Figure 4.5: *CM for Decision Tree*

4. Plot the confusion matrix for the **RandomForest** model using the same method:

```
CM.from_estimator(rf, X_train, \
                  y_train, cmap="Blues", colorbar=None)
plt.show()
```

You should get the following output:

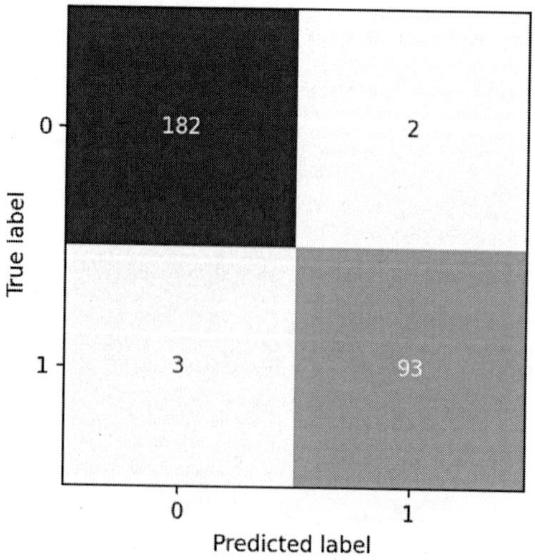

Figure 4.6: *CM for RF*

5. Similarly, plot the confusion matrix for the SVC model:

```
CM.from_estimator(svc, X_train, \
                  y_train, cmap="Blues", colorbar=None)
plt.show()
```

You should get the following output:

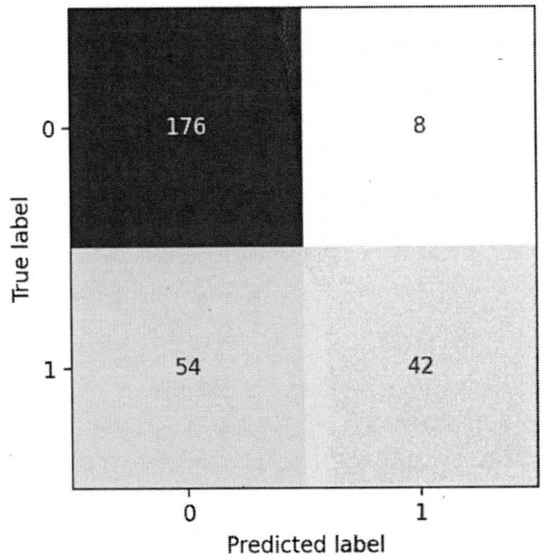

Figure 4.7: CM for SVC

We created confusion matrices for the three models to get a detailed breakdown of model performance (on the train dataset). From the confusion matrices, we could also see which class is getting misclassified more than the other. It is easy to derive the extent of true positives, false negatives, and so on. from the confusion matrix, making it a useful tool for assessing model performance. We will now take a look at some more metrics which can be used for specific ways of evaluation and can programmatically be calculated easily and used for model comparison.

Precision, Recall, and F1 Score

As discussed earlier, in many situations, we care about one class more than the other. This is particularly true when the objective is to detect an event. For a loan default prediction exercise, for example, most loans are not defaulted, and detecting a default is more interesting than identifying non-defaults. Likewise, the actual fraud cases are more interesting in a fraud detection situation than the regular, non-fraud cases. Note that this is also true for the ad prediction case study where we are more interested in identifying true clicks. This is true of many practical situations. We, therefore, need metrics that focus on model performance in one of the classes. For the ad click prediction case, we would be interested in metrics that help us understand the performance around true clicks better. While these metrics can be applied to the positive and negative classes, they are employed for the positive classes in most situations. We define the metrics in *Table 4.3*. Let us understand these metrics better with some concrete examples.

Metric	Calculation	Intuition
Precision	$\frac{\text{True Positives}}{\text{All Predicted Positives}}$	% of predicted positives that are correct
Recall	$\frac{\text{True Positives}}{\text{All Actual Positives}}$	% of actual positives detected
F1 Score	$\frac{\text{2x Precision x Recall}}{\text{Precision + Recall}}$	Combined measure balancing precision & recall

Table 4.3: Precision, Recall, and F1 score

Precision score answers the question, what proportion of the predicted positives are positive? For a fraud detection situation, this would indicate what proportion of the fraudulent cases we identified as fraud. Naturally, we would want this to be as high as possible; we would not want the model to identify genuine transactions as fraudulent. For the ad click prediction situation, a low precision would mean that many cases we predicted as clicks were not clicks.

Recall score answers the question, what proportion of the positives did we detect? This is particularly relevant when dealing with fraud, where the recall score tells us the proportion of fraud cases the model detects. In event detection situations (for example disease detection tests), we would like the recall to be as high as possible. A high recall score would mean we could detect the most clicks for the ad click prediction case.

F1 score tries to balance the precision and recall scores. But why is this balance needed? Because there is a trade-off between precision and recall. Increasing the recall of the model often comes at the cost of precision that is when we attempt to increase the proportion of positives we detect, we often also increase the number of false positives that is cases that are not positives but predicted as so. Likewise, increasing precision leads to a reduction in recall. The F1 score therefore is a needed metric that measures the balance between precision and recall. Unlike the arithmetic mean, the harmonic mean is more inclined towards the lower of the two values. This means we will obtain a low score even if one value is extremely high and the other is low. To get a high F1 score, both precision and recall need to be high. The F1 score effectively captures the tradeoff between precision and recall and is a great metric when both precision and recall are important.

As you may have figured, these metrics can all be derived from the confusion matrix with a little calculation. However, this is optional as all these metrics are very conveniently derived with a single module **`classification_report`** in sklearn. We can use the **`classification_report`** method as shown in the following code for the ad click prediction example for the SVC model:

```
print(classification_report(y_train, svc.predict(X_train)))
```

The preceding single line command provides the very detailed output in *Figure 4.10*. The command calculates precision, recall, and F1 score for both classes. As discussed, we are interested in these metrics for the positive class. The second row of the output corresponds to the positive class and contains the precision, recall, and F1 score. For our example, recall (0.44) is much lower than the precision. Accordingly, the F1 score is at 0.58, more towards the lower value (Recall) as expected. The overall accuracy is available in the third row in the output as 0.78. Refer to *Figure 4.8*:

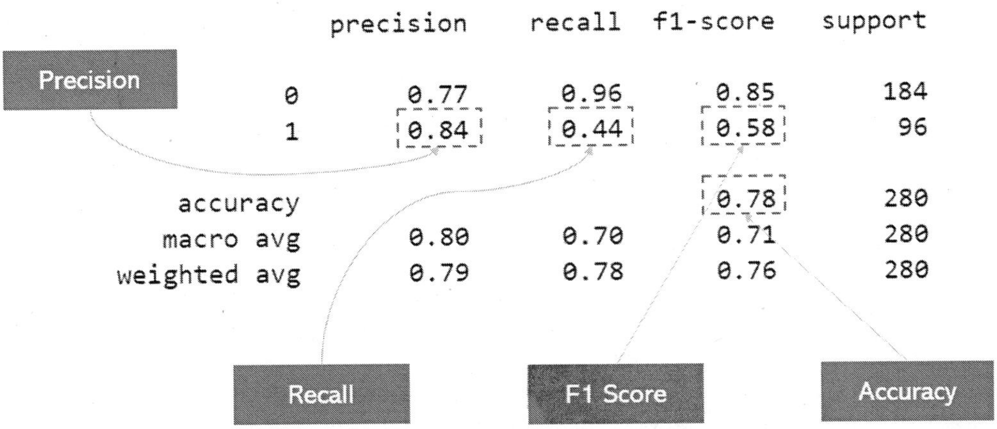

***Figure 4.8:** Metrics from the classification_report*

Note: While the classification report provides a lot of detailed metrics, you can only employ this method if you are interested in any specific metric. To get only precision, recall or f1 score for the model, you can use the `precision_score`, `recall_score`, `f1_score` methods from sklearn.metrics.

To calculate only precision, recall or F1 score, you could use the associated methods in **`sklearn.metrics`**. Let us calculate accuracy and recall values for the three models on the train dataset. Start with importing the functions from **`sklearn`** using the following code:

```
from sklearn.metrics import accuracy_score, recall_score
```

Next, generate and store predictions from the decision tree model on the train dataset into a **`numpy`** array and use the **`accuracy_score`** and **`recall_score`** methods as shown in the following code:

```
y_train_pred = dt.predict(X_train)

print("DT Accuracy:", accuracy_score(y_train, y_train_pred))

print("DT Recall:", recall_score(y_train, y_train_pred))
```

You should get the following output:

```
DT Accuracy: 0.9678571428571429

DT Recall: 0.9479166666666666
```

Similarly, calculate the training accuracy and recall for the **RandomForest** model using the following code:

```
y_train_pred = rf.predict(X_train)

print("RF Accuracy:", accuracy_score(y_train, y_train_pred))

print("RF Recall:", recall_score(y_train, y_train_pred))
```

You should get the following output:

```
RF Accuracy: 0.9821428571428571

RF Recall: 0.96875
```

Finally, print the training accuracy and recall for the SVC model:

```
y_train_pred = svc.predict(X_train)

print("SVC Accuracy:", accuracy_score(y_train, y_train_pred))

print("SVC Recall:", recall_score(y_train, y_train_pred))
```

The output should be as follows:

```
SVC Accuracy: 0.7785714285714286

SVC Recall: 0.4375
```

We observe that the accuracy and recall are the highest for the RandomForest model, followed closely by the decision tree model, with the SVC model lagging.

Precision, recall, and F1 score are extremely useful metrics for the positive class. These are essential for a data scientist to understand and be proficient in situations where one class is more interesting and extremely common. But there are also several situations where the model should balance performance in both classes and show high skill in differentiating between the classes. The ROC curve and the area under it are must-learn metrics for such situations. Let us learn and implement them.

Area Under ROC curve (AUC)

Area under the **Receiver Operator Characteristic** (**ROC**) curve is another extremely useful and popular metric. The name is a mouthful, but the intuition is straightforward. The area under the ROC curve measures how well the model balances false positives and negatives. *Figure 4.9* illustrates the idea of the ROC curve and how it can be used:

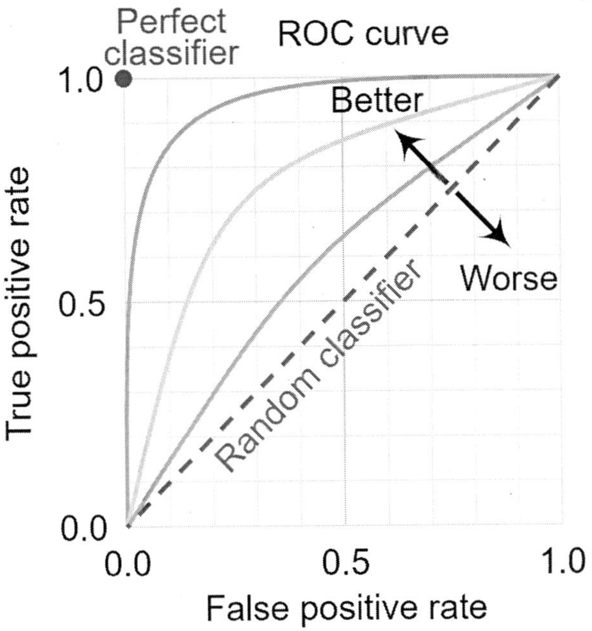

Figure 4.9: *ROC Curve* [1]

The **False Positive Rate (FPR)** makes the X axis, while the Y axis represents the **True Positive Rate (TPR)**. The false positive rate (False positives/ Total actual negatives) measures the proportion of negatives the model got wrong. True positive rate (True positives/Total actual positives) measures the proportion of positives correctly predicted. TPR therefore focuses on the positives and FPR on the negatives. The curve is generated using different thresholds from 0 to 1 and plotting the point on the graph for the TPR and FPR obtained. The ROC curve therefore shows how skilled the model is that is how well the model differentiates the classes.

A perfect model would not have any False Positives (FPR of 0) and would have a 100% True positive rate. As shown in *Figure 4.9*, the perfect classifier would be represented by the dot at the upper left corner as it would have 0 FPR and 100% TPR. A model with no skill, that is, a model which is as good as randomly assigning the classes (say using a coin flip) would have equal TPR and FPR at all thresholds. The diagonal dotted line represents this in *Figure 4.9*. A way to summarize model performance is therefore the area under this curve.

The no skill, random classifier will have a 50% area under the curve as it represents the diagonal line. A perfect classifier will have 100% area under the curve as it has 100% TPR and 0% FPR and immediately reaches the top left corner. Most models will be between the no skill and the perfect classifier that is the area under the ROC curve for most models will be between 0.5 and 1. This is visually represented in *Figure 4.9*. As the curve gets more

[1] *source: roc curve (wikimedia.org)*

towards the upper left corner, the model's skill is higher and therefore the area under the ROC curve.

Note: For a more detailed explanation of the ROC curve, its interpretation and how it relates mathematically to other concepts, you can refer to the Wikipedia page - Receiver operating characteristic - Wikipedia

Let us plot the ROC curve and calculate the AUC (area under the ROC curve) for our ad click prediction case study for the SVC model. Use the following code to import the plotting module from **`sklearn`** and plot the ROC curve on the training data. The **`from_estimator`** method of **`RocCurveDisplay`** needs the trained classifier, the features and the true labels using which the ROC curve can be generated. Refer to the following code:

```
from sklearn.metrics import RocCurveDisplay as roc

roc.from_estimator(svc, X_train, y_train)

plt.show()
```

You should get the following output:

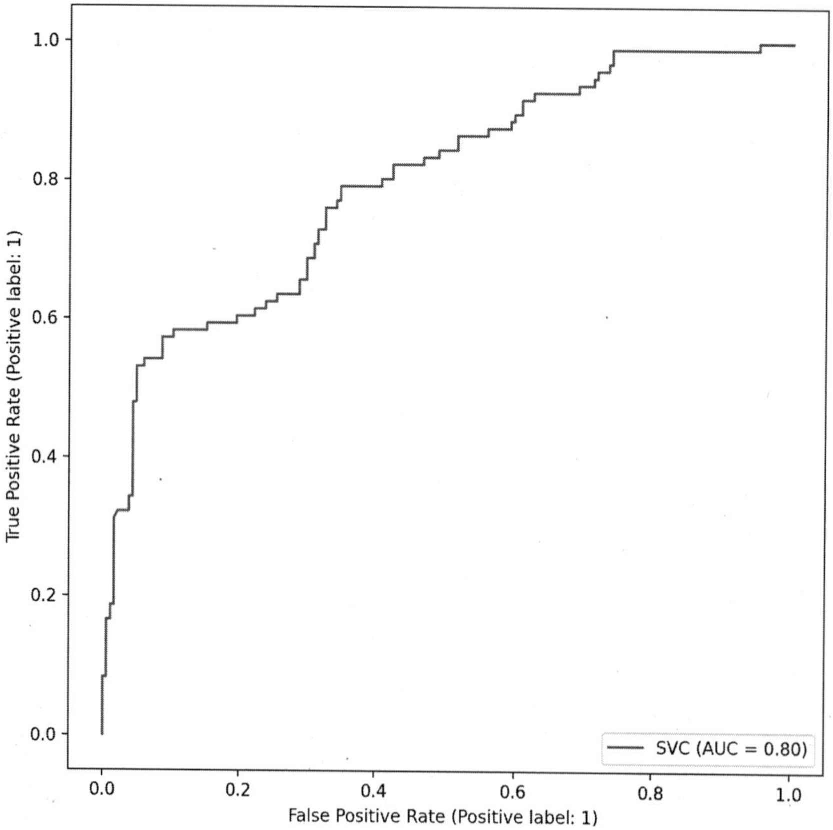

***Figure 4.10**: ROC Curve for SVC model*

The ROC Curve for our SVC model (on the training data) is doing a decent job. As the graph indicates, the AUC is 0.8, significantly better than a no-skill classifier (0.5). Note that you can only plot the entire curve if interested in the AUC. The AUC can be calculated using the **`roa_auc_score`** method in **`sklearn.metrics`**. The **`roc_auc_score`** method needs the class probabilities to calculate the TPR and FPR at different thresholds. We extract the probabilities from the SVCs' '**`predict_proba`**' method. Let us use it in the following code:

```
from sklearn.metrics import roc_auc_score

y_pred_train_probs = svc.predict_proba(X_train)[:,1]

roc_auc_score(y_train, y_pred_train_probs)
```

The AUC printed is 0.7967 which matches the value displayed on the ROC curve (rounded to two decimals). The **`roc_auc_score`** can be used to compare multiple models for performance directly.

To summarize, the ROC curve and the AUC are extremely informative and useful methods when both classes are important to balance performance on. The AUC summary metric can help compare the performance of multiple models and help select the best one. To complete our discussion on classification performance metrics, we will now take a look at the area under the PR curve, a great choice when balancing precision and recall is required.

Area under PR curve

Area under PR curve (**AUPRC**) is similar to the ROC curve (which balances TPR and FPR) and the **precision-recall curve** (**PR curve**) can be used to see how a model balances precision and recall. As discussed earlier, there is a tradeoff between precision and recall, and an improvement in recall often comes at the cost of reduced precision and vice versa. The PR curve therefore shows how well a model makes this tradeoff.

As shown in *Figure 4.11*, the X axis of the PR curve represents the recall, while the Y axis represents the precision of the model. To generate the plot, the values of precision and recall are noted and plotted for different probability thresholds. The perfect classifier would have 100% precision and 100% recall, represented by a point at the upper-right corner. A random classifier would have precision like the event rate (% positives) and a recall that would decrease linearly with the threshold, representing the dotted line in *Figure 4.11*:

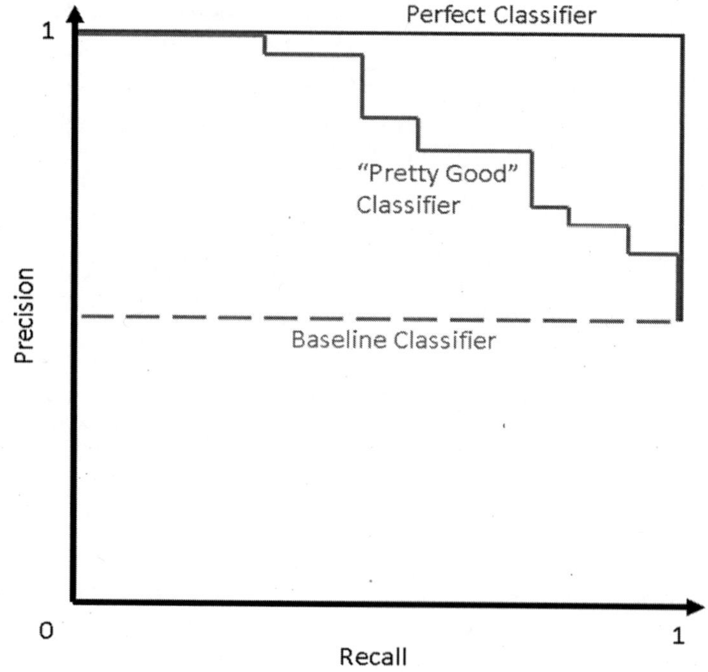

Figure 4.11: Precision Recall Curve 2

The area under the PR curve varies between 0 and 1 and summarizes the trade-off between precision and recall made by the model. Let us plot the PR curve and check the area under it for our ad click prediction case study for the SVC model on the training data. We will use the **PrecisionRecallDisplay** module from **sklearn**, as shown in the following code:

```
from sklearn.metrics import PrecisionRecallDisplay as prc

prc.from_estimator(svc, X_train, y_train)

plt.show()
```

Note: Similar to the roc_auc_score method, you can extract only the area under the PR curve using the pr_auc_score.

This results in the PR curve as shown in *Figure 4.12*. The area under the PR curve is 0.72 as displayed in the plot. This is significantly higher than a no skill classifier (which will have a 0 area), and we perform well on the train data. Since this is on the training data, the model's true performance is unknown and can be assessed only on unseen data:

[2] *Source: Precision-Recall curve and AUC-PR - Hasty.ai*

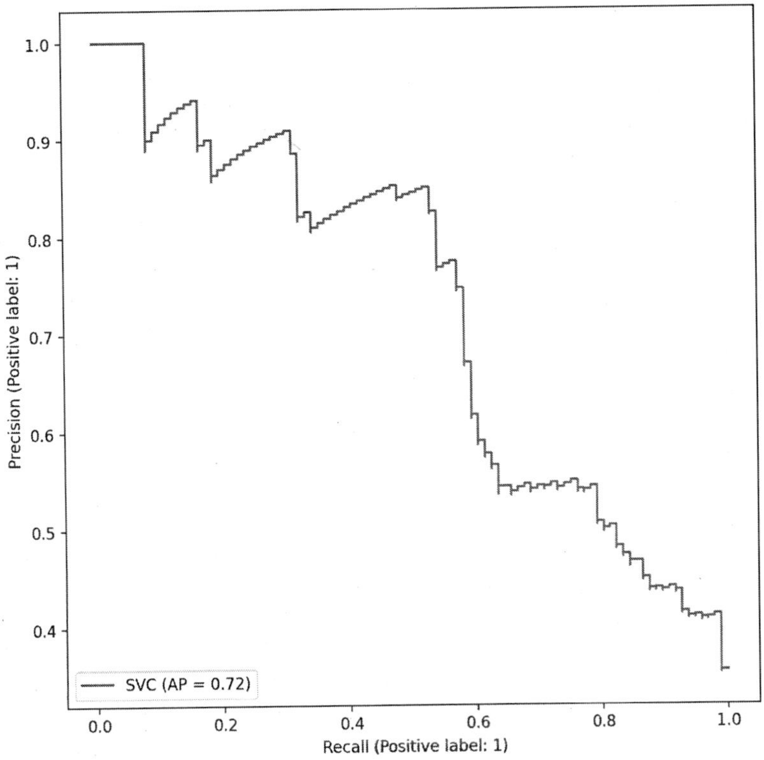

***Figure 4.12**: PR Curve for Ad Click SVC model (train data)*

To summarize, the PR curve is another extremely useful model evaluation measure that captures the tradeoff between precision and recall. This is useful when one class is in focus, which is extremely common to note that in situations with heavy class imbalance (For example, fraud detection, where the event rate is typically very low) the PR curve is a more reliable indicator of performance than the ROC curve. We will discuss this in more detail in *Chapter 6, Imbalanced Machine Learning*.

We discussed classification metrics in a great amount of detail. Let us now turn our attention to regression problems. We will look at the most common and useful metrics for evaluating model performance for regression tasks.

Metrics for regression

In regression problems, the target/outcome is a number (as opposed to a category for classification problems). A classic example of a regression task is predicting the sales of a product on an e-commerce platform. Likewise, tasks like stock price prediction, product rating prediction, delivery time prediction, ride arrival time prediction, and temperature prediction are all regression tasks.

Therefore, the notion of error in regression tasks is how far the predicted value is from the true value. For instance, how far the predicted sales were from the actual sales of the product. If **`y_true`** is the actual value and **`y_pred`** is the prediction for a record, then in the simplest form the error for this record could be defined as:

$$error = y_{true} - y_{pred}$$

This term is also called residual. The error aggregated over all the records gives us the overall model error or goodness of fit. There are various ways in which this error term can be aggregated over all the records, and normalized in multiple ways, resulting in several metrics for evaluating regression models. Let us look at a few of them, beginning with the popular R squared.

The **R squared** for a regression model is defined as:

$$R^2 = 1 - \frac{SS_{res}}{SS_{tot}}$$

Where SS_{res} is the sum of squares of the residuals that is sum of squares of the errors and SS_{tot} is the total variance of the outcome. The R squared metric therefore represents the proportion of variance in outcome that the model explains. A perfect model would have 0 error and predict the outcome perfectly (SS_{res} would be 0) and R squared would be 1. A poor model that does not explain the variance in the outcome has a value closer to 0. The R squared is a normalized metric and does not depend on the number of records and is therefore a widely used metric for regression. R squared' s drawback is that it uses squared error terms, and a single large error value can significantly impact its value. We therefore also must look at metrics that are more robust to outliers in error values.

Median absolute percentage error is a very robust alternative. The MAPE is defined as:

$$MAPE = median\left(\left|\frac{y_{true} - y_{pred}}{y_{true}}\right|\right)$$

The MAPE uses the absolute value of the error and normalizes it by the true value of the instance. This ensures that the value for each instance is between 0 and 1. Next, because the median of this value is taken, it is not influenced by extremely high or extremely low values. Another benefit of the MAPE metric is that it is highly interpretable as how bad the typical error is relative to the data and provides an intuitive understanding of the model's goodness.

Model evaluation schemes

In most real-world situations, a model is trained on historical data to use it on newer data. For instance, a loan default prediction model trained on historical data is useful only if it can be used to help identify future default cases. Indeed, the true assessment of the goodness of a model is its performance on data that has not been seen before. This is the reason for the train test split scheme. A part of the data is reserved as the test is set for final validation, as illustrated in *Figure 4.13*. The 80-20 split in the figure is only an example and a completely different split can rightfully be chosen by the data scientist if they see fit for the situation.

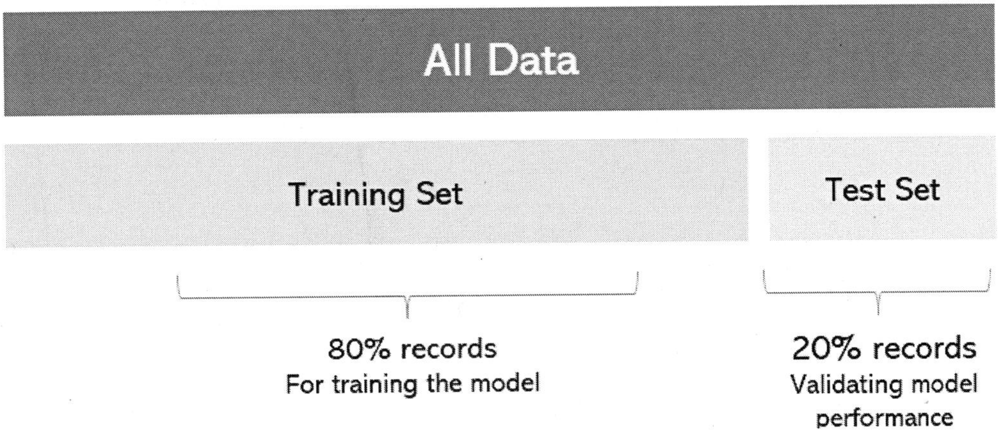

***Figure 4.13:** Using holdout set for validation*

The single holdout validation set approach has its merits, but also a few drawbacks. First, the test set needs to be used only at the end of the development process. This makes it difficult to estimate generalized performance at any intermediate step. Second, the assessment on the test set is based on a single sample and the estimate is therefore less reliable. In smaller datasets, this estimate could be based on very few records making the estimate unreliable, as you might expect.

A better approach would be a cross-validation approach; a popular example of which is the k-fold cross-validation technique. *Figure 4.14* illustrates the working of a k-fold cross-validation scheme, taking the example of 5 folds. The data is divided into 5 folds. Each time, one-fold acts as the validation fold while the rest of the folks form the training data for the model. For the first row, the last 20% records of the data become the validation set. The model is trained on the remaining 4 folds of 80% of data. Next, block 4 becomes the validation set and the remaining 4 folds constitute the training data. In this manner, a fold is held out each time as a validation set while the other blocks are used for training. At the end of this process, each fold has once become a validation set. Each time the validation set was unseen by the model. The average of performance on the 5 folds is the final estimate of the generalized performance of the model. An average of over 5 folds is reasonably expected to be a more robust estimation. Refer to *Figure 4.14*:

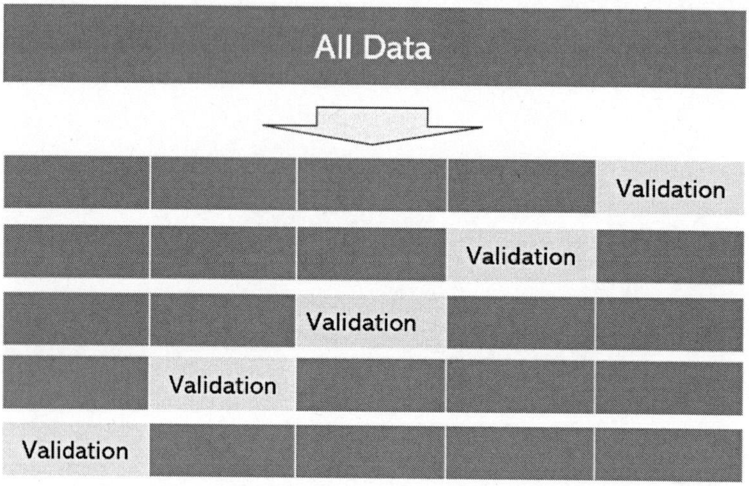

Figure 4.14: Example of a 5-fold cross-validation scheme

Note: For hyper-parameter tuning, we will use a slightly modified K-fold scheme. We will see this in detail in *Chapter 6, Hyperparameter Tuning.*

Note: The number of folds to use is different and depends on the amount of data you have at hand, the time you can spend on this assessment and the number you as an individual need to trust the numbers. 3-5 folds are used commonly.

Let us now see model evaluation using cross-validation in action on the ad click prediction models we prepared.

Exercise 4.4: Model evaluation using cross-validation

This exercise will evaluate the three ad click models using a 3-fold cross-validation. We will choose the metrics of precision, recall, and accuracy. We will calculate the average of these metrics for each model to get a sense of generalized accuracy. Continue in the same Jupyter notebook that we have been using so far. Perform the following steps:

1. Import the **cross_validate** method from **sklearn.metrics** and create a list containing the metrics to use, as shown in the following code:

```
from sklearn.model_selection import cross_validate
scoring = ['accuracy','precision','recall']
```

2. Evaluate the decision tree model by using a 3-fold cross-validation by specifying cv =3 using the following code. Print the metrics for each fold as a pandas dataframe:

```
cv_scores = cross_validate(estimator=dt,\
                           X = X_train,\
```

```
                    y = y_train,\
                    cv = 3,\
                    scoring = scoring)
pd.DataFrame(cv_scores)
```

You should get the following output:

	fit_time	score_time	test_accuracy	test_precision	test_recall
0	0.009386	0.008029	0.882979	0.862069	0.78125
1	0.006439	0.006635	0.849462	0.821429	0.71875
2	0.007134	0.006898	0.860215	0.756757	0.87500

Figure 4.15: Decision tree performance on each fold

Note that the method also provides details on the fit and scoring time. This can be extremely valuable when scoring and training times are decision criteria for model selection.

Note: The output uses the term test_accuracy to refer to the accuracy on the validation fold. This is separate from the accuracy on the test (final hold out data) set that we will finally evaluate.

3. We are interested in the average. Print out the average of the fit and score times and the performance on the metrics:

```
pd.DataFrame(cv_scores).mean()
```

The following will be the output:

```
fit_time            0.007653
score_time          0.007187
test_accuracy       0.864219
test_precision      0.813418
test_recall         0.791667
```

The generalized accuracy is expected to be around 87%, precision and recall at 81%.

4. Evaluate the RandomForest model and print out the mean scores:

```
cv_scores = cross_validate(estimator=rf,
                    X = X_train,
                    y = y_train,
                    cv = 3,
                    scoring = scoring)
pd.DataFrame(cv_scores).mean()
```

The following will be the output:

```
fit_time           0.178056
score_time          0.029179
test_accuracy       0.885648
test_precision      0.816784
test_recall         0.864583
```

We observe that accuracy and recall are much higher for the **RandomForest** model than for the decision tree.

5. Evaluate the SVC model and print out the mean scores:

```
cv_scores = cross_validate(estimator=svc,
                          X = X_train,
                          y = y_train,
                          cv = 3,
                          scoring = scoring)
pd.DataFrame(cv_scores).mean()
```

The following will be the output:

```
fit_time           0.014643
score_time          0.005495
test_accuracy       0.771334
test_precision      0.833007
test_recall         0.416667
```

We observe that accuracy and recall are much higher for the RandomForest model than the decision tree, as are the training and scoring times. Remember that while accuracy is an important consideration, training times are also important in many situations and your evaluation of the model must consider all relevant criteria.

Model debugging

The astute reader would have noticed a big difference between the training and the models' cross-validated performance. This is particularly true for the decision tree and random forest models. *Table 4.4* lists the training and cross-validated recall for the three models:

Model	Training Recall	Cross Val Recall	Difference
Decision Tree	94.8%	79.2%	-15.6%
Random Forest	96.9%	86.4%	-10.5%
SVC	43.8%	41.7%	-2.1%

***Table 4.4**: Difference between training and cross-validated recall*

Focusing on the decision tree model to understand the behavior, we see that the performance is high on seen data (what it trained on) and much lower on unseen data. We realize the decision tree model's performance on the train data does not generalize well to unseen data, and this is a classic case of overfitting. In the next section, we understand this behavior better and learn how to handle this.

Overfitting and underfitting

In the previous section, we studied the training vs. cross-validated performance of the three models used in the ad click prediction case study. *Table 4.4* showed a big difference in the performance of the decision tree model: a high recall score on seen data, and a much lower score on unseen data. On the other hand, the SVC model has a much lower recall on both seen and unseen data.

These are very good examples of overfitting and underfitting respectively. In both cases, the model behavior could be better. We want a model that does well on seen and unseen data. Overfitting and underfitting are therefore two extremes, but sides of the same coin a model that does not learn patterns in the data well. Let us understand these concepts, what causes them and how to handle them.

Overfitting

Revisiting the performance of the decision tree model, the numbers from *Table 4.2* tell us the following:

- Does the tree perform well on the training data? **Yes**
- Does the tree perform well on unseen data? **No**

This is classic overfitting behavior, as we mentioned earlier when the machine learning model performs too well on the training data but does not generalize well. Why does this happen? Recall that the objective and utility of training a model is usually to make predictions on unseen data.

Using the training data, we wish for the model to learn the patterns and relationships hidden in the data that help us make predictions. Noise in the (training) data is a reality of the world and we have artefacts in the data, some deviations from the true patterns. Consider a very flexible and complex model that is so flexible that it learns even the noise. That is a model that learns noise as a pattern. Such a model is expected to perform extremely well on the training data. Indeed, complex tree-based models (like boosted trees in XGBoost, GBMs, and so on) and neural networks can learn each point in the dataset, giving you even close to 100% accuracy scores. *Figure 4.16* illustrates how an overfitting model might work:

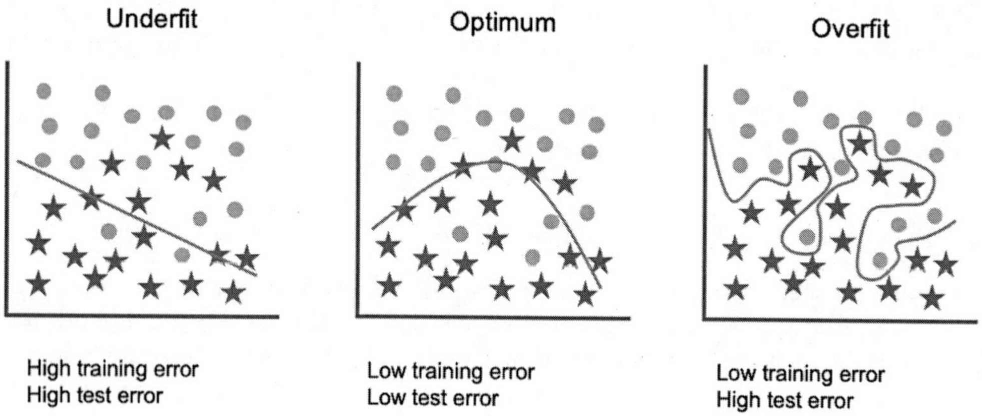

Figure 4.16: *Underfitting, Overfitting, a good fit* [3]

However, is an overfitting model expected to do well on unseen data? Do we expect the same noise in the unseen data? Of course not. The models are expected to perform poorly on new data. This is exactly what happened with the decision tree model in the ad click prediction case study: ~95% recall on the training data but around 79% recall on the test data. The model could have been better because it understood the training data too well (including its noise) and needed a better understanding of the overall patterns.

With an understanding of overfitting, let us now turn towards the other case of a poor fit - underfitting:

Underfitting

Now consider the performance of the SVC model on the ad click prediction case study. Revisiting *Table 4.4*:

- Does the SVC perform well on the training data? **No**
- Does the SVC perform well on unseen data? **No**

A natural inference from this information could be that the SVC model is not flexible enough to capture the patterns in the data. The model is likely behaving like the leftmost plot in *Figure 4.17*. The underfit case is where the boundary is not flexible enough to separate the two classes. Underfitting can be due to a few reasons:

- The modeling technique is not flexible enough (think linear regression vs. XGBoost).
- The set parameters of the technique do not allow for flexibility (For example, k in KNN methods, or shallow vs. deep decision tree, more on this in *Chapter 6, Hyper-parameter Tuning*).
- Input features are not informative enough.

[3] *Source: What is Overfitting? | IBM*

- Too much noise in the data that is not enough patterns or signals (related to point 2; about flexibility).
- The model has not been trained long enough (this is particularly true for techniques like neural networks that are often trained incrementally in batches).

Handling underfitting therefore can be done by addressing each of the points appropriately. This is often done by using a complex model, adding more informative features, or sometimes simply training the model for a longer duration. Before we start fixing these issues in our models, we need to be able to detect overfitting or underfitting. Training/learning curves are an excellent tool for this purpose. Let us understand them better and learn how to use them in our ad click prediction case study.

Validation curves and goodness of fit

We learnt that model complexity/flexibility is a key factor for performance and has a big bearing on the model's fit. A high complexity model is often the main reason for overfitting and low complexity is often the reason for underfitting.

Complexity in the model can come from:

- Highly flexible modelling technique (think linear regression vs. neural network)
- Model parameter choices (shallow vs. deep decision trees)
- High number of features
- Overtrained models (relevant for techniques that learn in batches, for example, neural networks or boosted trees)

A simple yet extremely powerful way to identify the overfitting/underfitting of the model is through validation curves (variations are also called learning curves). This common variation is shown in *Figure 4.17*. The X-axis represents model complexity, and the Y-axis represents model accuracy (any metric like recall, accuracy, and so on). Two curves are plotted on these axes: the training and validation errors. This simple view tells us a lot about the learning situation.

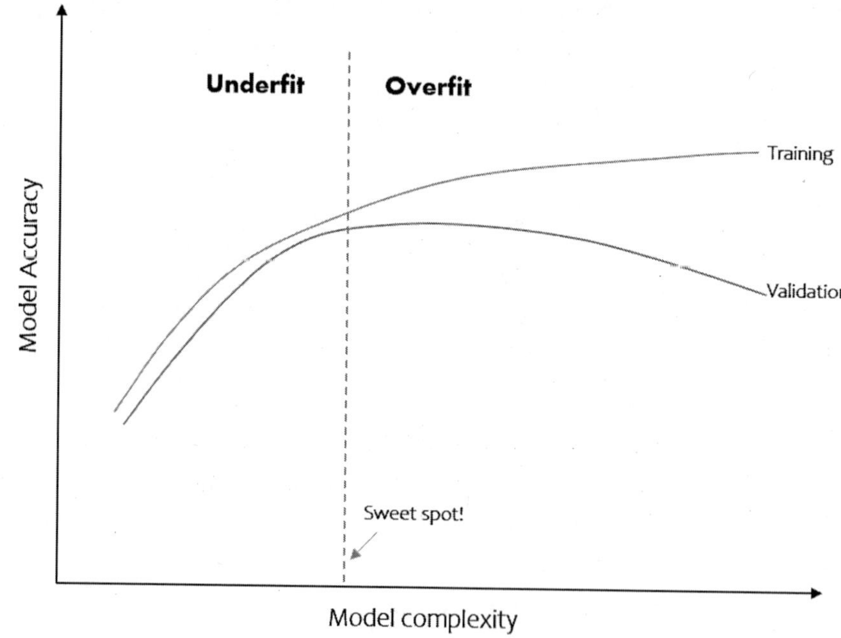

Figure 4.17: *Model complexity vs. performance*

Note: Model complexity on the X-axis can be represented in many ways. It could be the number of training batches (For example, neural networks), or parameters that define flexibility (depth of the tree for tree-based methods). It could also be the number of features.

As the complexity of the model increases, the model gets more flexible and after a point begins to learn the noise components. This situation can be detected by looking at the validation accuracy, representing the generalized performance on unseen data. As long as the model learns genuine patterns, its training and validation accuracy improve. This is because these genuine patterns also work well on the validation data. When the model begins to learn the data too well, including the noise, we see that the training and validation curves start diverging. Further training only increases the gap between these curves. Therefore, a sweet spot is a level of complexity where the performance is good on both training and validation data. Finding this optimizes the fit of the model.

A similar understanding can be derived from another variation of the validation curves. Instead of plotting accuracy, we could plot the loss of the model on the training and the validation data. Note that the key difference is that the error or the definition of loss can also be linked to the underlying optimization that the model does (often utilizing loss functions). In principle and practice, this curve gives us similar results to the previous version (accuracy on the Y axis). In an overfitting situation, the model keeps reducing errors in the training data. Still, the validation error is stable or keeps increasing as the noise influences the model and fails to generalize. Refer to *Figure 4.18*:

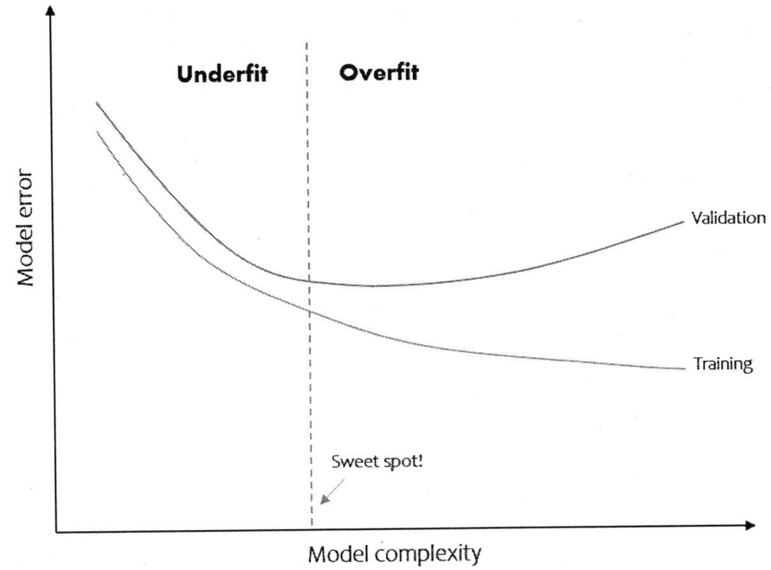

Figure 4.18: Model complexity vs. error rates

To make this understanding more concrete and test these ideas for ourselves, let us create such validation curves for the ad click prediction models we prepared for Azra Inc. and evaluate when we started to overfit the data.

Exercise 4.5: Validation curves for Ad click prediction

In this exercise, we will continue working on the ad click prediction case study for Azra Inc. We will plot the validation curves for the decision tree model. We will use the handy **validation_curve** method in **sklearn** for this purpose and then evaluate when we started overfitting the decision Tree. Our proxy for the complexity of the decision tree will be the parameter **max_depth**. Higher depth leads to more flexible and complex trees. We employed a depth of 7 earlier, and through the curves, we will see how deep we are in the overfitting zone. Perform the following steps:

1. Import the **validation_curve** method from **sklearn–model_selection** module:

   ```
   from sklearn.model_selection import validation_curve
   ```

2. We need to specify the list of **max_depth** values that we will use to build the plot. Specify values from 1 through 10 using the following code:

   ```
   param_values = np.arange(1,10,1)
   ```

3. Use the **validation_curve** method to get the train and validation accuracies using a 3-fold CV scheme. Supply **max_depth** as the parameter and **param_values** list as the values to try for this parameter:

```
param_values = np.arange(1,10,1)
res = validation_curve(dt, X_train, y_train, \
                       param_name='max_depth',
                       param_range=param_values,
                       scoring="accuracy",
                       n_jobs=-1,
                       cv=3)
```

4. The details are available in the **res** variable. Extract the train and test scores using the following code and calculate the means over the folds for each parameter value.

```
train_scores, test_scores = res[0], res[1]
train_scores_mean = np.mean(train_scores, axis=1)
test_scores_mean = np.mean(test_scores, axis=1)
```

5. Plot these scores with the parameter values on the X-axis using the following code:

```
plt.plot(param_values, train_scores_mean,label="Train Recall")
plt.plot(param_values, test_scores_mean,label="Test Recall")
plt.ylim(0,1.1)
plt.legend()
plt.title("Training & Validation scores - DT Max Depth")
plt.show()
```

You should get the following output:

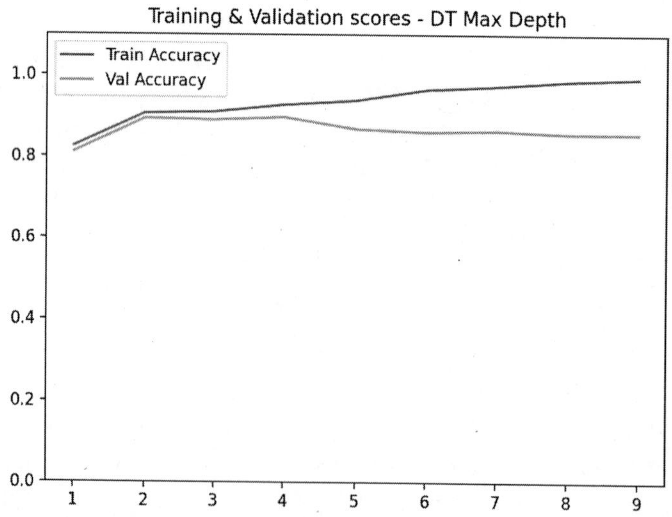

Figure 4.19: *Decision Tree validation curves for varying max_depth*

Recall that our decision tree model had a depth of 7 and we observed that it was overfitting. Does the validation curve agree that 7 is in the overfitting zone?

The validation curve shows us that as expected, when we initially increased the complexity of the tree, we got performance benefits as both training and validation accuracy kept increasing. Around max_depth of 4, however, the curves started to diverge, indicating that we entered the overfitting zone. Beyond that, the curves diverged further as the complexity increased. Our value of 7 for max_depth is well in the overfitting zone, as seen in this curve.

Note: Max depth is an important setting that controls the tree's flexibility and is called a "hyper-parameter". This is merely one hyper-parameter; we generally need to tune multiple such hyper-parameters to optimize the model. We will explore this topic in detail in *Chapter 6, Hyperparameter Tuning*.

Now that we understand how to identify overfitting, the next natural question is – how do we handle overfitting? Let us now look at a few ways to do so.

Handling overfitting

In a previous section, we saw some of the reasons for overfitting. While the reasons could be aplenty, the result is always an overly complex and flexible model. Handling overfitting, logically, is about simplifying the model. There are multiple ways to achieve this.

Feature selection

One of the simplest ways models become complex is by adding way more features than needed. This could happen even for classically less flexible models like linear regression. The impact is much more pronounced for more flexible models like boosted trees or neural networks. By nature, a linear regression with 3 features is much simpler than one with 200 features.

Data scientists often collect more features than they finally use in the model. Having more features and eliminating them is better than having very few and creating them individually in a tedious and stretched project. But how many features and which of these should be included in the model? First, dumping all the possible features is seldom a good idea. This is particularly true of models that need to be maintained. Maintaining a pipeline for 200 features is much more complex than a pipeline for 10. How do we go about choosing then?

The most practical and intuitive approaches are around recursive/iterative/stepwise feature selection. In principle, three approaches are used:

- **Stepwise feature addition (forward)**: Start with one feature and add only those features that provide a meaningful performance improvement. This is continued until there is no benefit of adding any more features.

- **Stepwise feature elimination (backward)**: Start with all the features in the model and keep eliminating features one by one, each time dropping the feature that added the least information to the model. This continues until dropping any further feature leads to a significant drop in performance.
- **Recursive feature elimination (mixed)**: A combined approach that adds and drops features. At each step, the approach evaluates if a feature can be dropped without losing significant performance. Then. the model checks whether adding any leftover features provides any performance boost. This continues until we arrive at an optimal feature set.

  Note that all these approaches can be combined, and indeed are better, with cross-validation to determine if we are impacting performance.

Note: A useful implementation of Recursive Feature Elimination is available in sklearn as RFE under the feature selection module (sklearn.feature_selection). More details and some examples can be found in the official documentation.

Hyper-parameter control

We have already seen that certain model settings control its complexity / flexibility. We saw how the setting max_depth is a hyper-parameter for a decision tree and that changing this can significantly improve how well the model generalizes. It was a good example of the extent of impact hyper-parameters can have. Let us first see the impact of changing max depth of the decision tree and see if we can achieve more generalizable results.

Let us begin by instantiating a **`DecisionTreeClassifier`** from **`sklearn`** with a **`max_depth`** value of 4. Use the following code:

```
from sklearn.tree import DecisionTreeClassifier
dt_4 = DecisionTreeClassifier(max_depth=4, random_state=42)
```

Now, let us calculate this model's (3 fold) cross-validated accuracy score using the following code:

```
cv_scores = cross_validate(estimator=dt_4,
                           X = X_train, y = y_train,
                           cv = 3, scoring = "accuracy")
pd.DataFrame(cv_scores).mean()
```

The validation accuracy would be close to 90% as shown in the following output:

```
fit_time      0.008755
score_time    0.005416
test_score    0.896324
```

Now, let us create another decision tree with a **max_depth** of 10 and calculate its cross-validated accuracy using the following code:

```
dt_10 = DecisionTreeClassifier(max_depth=10, random_state=42)
cv_scores = cross_validate(estimator=dt_10,
        X = X_train, y = y_train,
        cv = 3, scoring = "accuracy")
pd.DataFrame(cv_scores).mean()
```

The generalized accuracy of the tree with **max_depth** 10 gets printed as about 86% as you can see in the following output:

```
fit_time      0.004431
score_time    0.001893
test_score    0.860673
```

Comparing the 90% validation accuracy at depth 4 with 86% accuracy at depth 10, it is clear that controlling hyper-parameters can significantly help with overfitting and improve the generalized performance of the model.

Most modeling techniques have their own set of hyper-parameters. The humble decision tree itself has several hyper-parameters defining the maximum depth of the tree, features to evaluate at each split, minimum samples allowed in a leaf after the split, minimum leaves before a split, the information criterion and many more. When the decision tree is employed in an XGBoost, the hyper-parameters increase. There are a reasonable number of hyper-parameters for deep learning models, which we will see in the later chapters. Therefore, evaluating these settings ensures we have an optimal model.

Note: Hyper-parameter tuning is a core topic in model optimization and we will study this in detail in this book. ***Chapter 6, Hyper-parameter Tuning*** **focuses on choosing hyper-parameters for classical machine learning models.** ***Chapter 8, Optimizing Deep Learning Models*** **teaches getting the most out of the deep learning models.**

Regularization

Regularization is a general machine learning concept that applies well to classical and deep learning techniques. The term regularization has more popularity due to its usage in deep learning models. The term shrinkage has been around in classical machine learning techniques for decades. The model is regularized by shrinking the parameters/coefficients of the predictors in the model.

For example, a linear regression model could be complex with many predictors. Regularization would mean reducing the coefficients in magnitude for the predictors. Note that this does not necessarily drop predictors, but rather subdue the impact of the predictors. The effect is reduced flexibility in the model which effectively helps reduce overfitting. *Figure 4.20* illustrates this impact. Regularizing the coefficients makes the highly fluctuating and flexible curve much less flexible. The result is a less overfitting model.

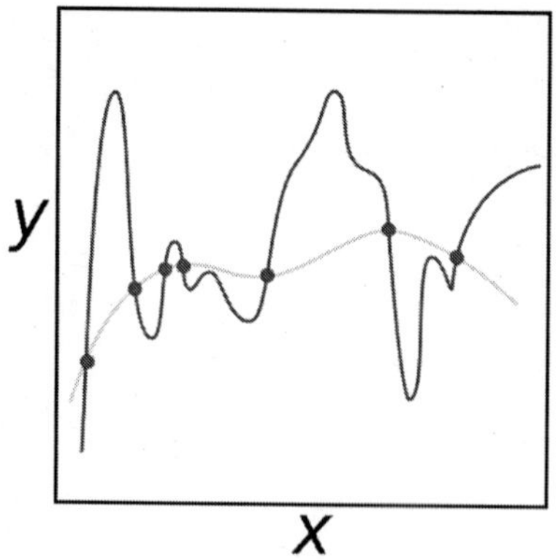

***Figure 4.20**: Regularization of coefficients; source: Wikipedia*

Regularization of linear regression models gives us techniques like ridge regression and lasso both of which regularize in slightly different ways. While ridge regression suppresses the values of all coefficients, lasso can reduce some coefficients to 0. Lasso, therefore, also helps with feature selection. If you want a compromise between the approaches, you could also use the ElasticNet approach which is simply a weighted combination between ridge and lasso.

Note: Ridge and Lasso regression are less popular but are well supported in sklearn. The methods work well with other sklearn utilities making them easy to use. More details on the ideas of regularization are available at Regularization (mathematics) - Wikipedia,

In the context of deep learning models, there are several regularization methods. The most straightforward way is to add a penalty for higher weights. A model with a lot of high weights will be less preferred, resulting in the weights being subdued exactly the way linear regression coefficients are subdued. Additionally, some penalties allow regularization to work exactly like ridge and lasso work for regression. In *Chapter 8, Optimizing Deep Learning Models*, we will study regularization in greater detail.

Data augmentation

Data augmentation techniques are primarily used in deep learning for images and textual data. However, they can also be employed with classical Machine Learning approaches for tabular data. Data augmentation can be considered another form of regularization for highly complex models. Highly complex models' overfit small datasets very easily and increasing the data size should help mitigate the problem.

However, getting more data is impractical sometimes. A smart workaround is to generate data variations to provide more examples for the model to learn from. Consider an image classification model developed to detect dogs in pictures. To create more training examples, you must make minor alterations to the image. For instance, you could rotate the image by a few degrees, zoom into the image a bit, and flip it horizontally and vertically. In all cases, you are not changing the image's subject and the fact that it contains a dog. Effectively, you can generate several samples from one for the same label. In this way, data augmentation helps you get more from your data by:

- Creating more variety in the data for the model to learn from; in many cases, it provides that much-needed variation
- Regularizing and making the model generalize better

Data augmentation is a useful tool in your arsenal as a data scientist. We will study this in detail in later chapters.

Optimal training (early stopping)

For modeling techniques that either learn in batches or from data sequentially, stopping at the right time can prevent overfitting. For neural networks, this would mean the right number of epochs. For other techniques, this could mean setting the right number of learning iterations. Taking the example of neural networks, an epoch is said to be passed when the entire data has gone through the network once for training. Neural networks are typically trained over several epochs in dozens, hundreds, or even thousands. This increases the training time and significantly maximizes the tendency to overfit.

A practical and effective strategy to prevent overfitting and choosing the optimal number of epochs is to use early stopping. The idea is simple while training the neural network, keep monitoring the validation loss/accuracy. If the validation loss does not decrease (or the accuracy does not increase) for a few epochs, the model will stop training further. The rationale should be obvious now. If the training score is increasing, but the validation score is not, we are overfitting. This approach is very effective and is employed commonly in practice with great success.

Note: A detailed exploration of techniques for overfitting neural networks and how to use early stopping is covered in *Chapter 8, Optimizing Deep Learning Models.*

Conclusion

In this chapter, we saw a principled way of comparing models. We began with the idea that accuracy is among many considerations in choosing models. We saw metrics like precision, recall, ROC curves, PR curves, F1 scores, and more in action. We learned that they can help ensure the model performance is aligned with the business objectives in different situations.

We then saw that because models need to be employed on unseen data, we need that they generalize well. We saw the pitfalls of assessing the training data saw different evaluation schemes to estimate generalized performance and implemented the K-fold cross-validation scheme for different models.

In the process, we realized that overfitting is a common problem that plagues most machine learning projects. We learnt about overfitting and underfitting and ways to diagnose them using learning/validation curves where we saw the models' performance vs. complexity. We discussed multiple ways and implemented some ways in the Ad click prediction case study. This completes the very important chapter on model evaluation.

In the next chapter, we will discuss and overcome another extremely common challenge in several real-world machine learning problems – imbalanced classes.

CHAPTER 5
Imbalanced Machine Learning

Introduction

In the chapters so far, when dealing with binary classification, the classes we saw had a somewhat equal distribution (close to 1:1) which was convenient. However, there are several real-world situations in which you will find many more records belonging to one class than the other. Fraud detection, that is, identifying fraudulent transactions is a classic example of such a situation where you typically have less than 0.1% (or fewer) that are fraudulent. This is an example of highly **imbalanced classes** with a ratio between the non-fraud and fraud classes around 999:1 (for 0.1% of fraud cases). It is important to note that such situations are not rare. Some common tasks where the imbalance is usual are:

- Fraud detection (<0.1% to <1%, banking, e-commerce)
- Spam detection (<1%)
- Disease (for example, cancer) prediction (<1% usually)
- Device failure prediction (varies, but <1% usually)
- Customer conversion prediction (<5% on top e-commerce sites)
- Email campaign click prediction (<1% open the email)
- Anomaly detection (usually <1%)
- Outlier detection (usually <1%)

If you have noticed, most of these are about predicting or detecting an event of interest (for example, the presence of a disease). The event occurs rather rarely and thus has a low event rate (records where the event occurred/total records). In all the tasks mentioned above, detecting one outcome is more important. How does this play out in the whole data science process? Well, there are two main key challenges from such low event rates (imbalanced classes):

- Model evaluation is tricky
- Getting the model to handle imbalance is tricky

In this chapter, we will understand and see these two problems playing out for ourselves. Beginning with model evaluation, we will see how standard metrics like accuracy are not sufficient and a more involved evaluation is needed to make the model useful. We will explore key alternative metrics and examine the difference between them on the same task. After we understand a better way of evaluation, we will tackle the next challenge which is handling the imbalance. We will learn and implement techniques of varying complexities, right from the simplest sampling approaches to more sophisticated approaches that use complex algorithms for careful data selection. We will implement all these hands-on using Credit Card Fraud Detection as our problem statement.

Let us begin by understanding the most important aspect first: the difficulty in model evaluation. But before that, let us understand the business problem that we are solving and familiarize ourselves with the data at hand.

Structure

In this chapter, we will discuss the following topics:

- Understanding the business problem
- Difficulty in model evaluation
- Evaluation metrics for imbalanced classes
  - o F1 score
  - o Precision-Recall curve
  - o Summary of model evaluation
- Handling imbalance
  - o Adjusting the cost function
  - o Data Balancing
- Undersampling
  - o Model evaluation with rebalancing
  - o Using Pipelines for evaluating re-balanced data
  - o Tomek Links
  - o Undersampling methods: edited nearest neighbour

- Oversampling
  - o SMOTE
  - o ADASYN
- Combination of undersampling and oversampling
- Comparing the approaches

Objectives

After reading this chapter, you will be able to tackle one of the most common and challenging problems in machine learning/artificial intelligence. You will understand how imbalance impacts our evaluation of the model and be able to diagnose issues due to imbalance. You will identify better metrics for evaluation. You will also be able to use multiple approaches to tackle imbalance. You will also be adept at using under/over sampling techniques to balance the dataset better for a more optimized machine learning solution.

Understanding the business problem

Aiza, Inc. is a leading insurance company offering products in the life, health, property, and liability insurance categories. The company wants to expand to vehicle insurance for 4-wheelers. Its existing policyholders are a natural target segment, given that they already own insurance policies, it is reasonable to assume they are more likely to buy the new offering. Additionally, the company has enough details about the customers to target them effectively.

Aiza, Inc. recently ran a large marketing campaign, reaching out to about 37 thousand of its existing policyholders. The data from the campaign coupled with some demographic information about the customers (**Gender**, **Age**), and some knowledge of their vehicles can potentially provide good insights into which customers are more likely to convert. Training a Machine Learning model that predicts whether a customer will convert or not can be extremely useful in optimizing future campaigns by limiting the target to those having a higher chance of converting.

Campaign data responses are typically imbalanced, and our data is no exception. In this chapter, we will use this as our case study and help build a high-performance model for identifying better leads and learning how to handle imbalanced classes along the way. First, let us load, understand, and prepare the data.

Exercise 5.1: Understanding and staging the data

In this exercise, we will use various simple analyses to understand the data and the business problem better. Let us begin.

1. First, let us import the necessary libraries using the following commands:

```
import numpy as np, pandas as pd
import matplotlib.pyplot as plt, seaborn as sns
%matplotlib inline
```

2. Next, we will import the data from the file Aiza Insurance **`Data.csv`** into a Pandas dataframe and print out the top 5 records. Use the following code:

```
ins0 = pd.read_csv('Aiza Insurance Data.csv')
ins0.head()
```

This should produce the following output as shown in *Figure 5.1*:

	Gender	Age	Previously_Insured	Vehicle_Age	Vehicle_Damage	Annual_Premium	Response
0	Male	28	1	< 1 Year	No	28885.0	0
1	Female	24	1	< 1 Year	No	25093.0	0
2	Male	47	0	1-2 Year	Yes	2630.0	0
3	Male	29	0	< 1 Year	Yes	46835.0	0
4	Male	68	1	1-2 Year	No	26908.0	0

***Figure 5.1:** First 5 records of the dataset*

We have some basic demographics like the gender and age of the customer. Additionally, we have their insurance history from Hina, Inc. and relevant details about their current vehicle. The target variable is Response which captures whether the customer converted during the campaign.

3. Let us now examine the data types and the number of records using the info method of the data frame as shown in the following output:

```
ins0.info()
```

You will see the details of the data as shown in *Figure 5.2*:

```
ins0.info()
```

```
<class 'pandas.core.frame.DataFrame'>
RangeIndex: 37258 entries, 0 to 37257
Data columns (total 7 columns):
 #   Column              Non-Null Count  Dtype
---  ------              --------------  -----
 0   Gender              37258 non-null  object
 1   Age                 37258 non-null  int64
 2   Previously_Insured  37258 non-null  int64
 3   Vehicle_Age         37258 non-null  object
 4   Vehicle_Damage      37258 non-null  object
 5   Annual_Premium      37258 non-null  float64
 6   Response            37258 non-null  int64
dtypes: float64(1), int64(3), object(3)
memory usage: 2.0+ MB
```

Figure 5.2: basic profile of the dataset

We see that there are 37,258 records in the dataset. We do not have any missing values in the data, which is convenient. Let us now examine the target field Response.

4. Using the value counts method of the Pandas series, we print out the number of responses for each class in Response and also print out the percentage records in each:

```
ins0.Response.value_counts()
```

We see the counts as shown in *Figure 5.3*:

```
0    31189
1     6069
Name: Response, dtype: int64
```

Figure 5.3: Distribution of the dependent variable

```
ins0.Response.value_counts(normalize=True)
```

We see the percentages as shown in *Figure 5.4*:

```
0    0.837109
1    0.162891
Name: Response, dtype: float64
```

Figure 5.4: Normalized distribution of the dependent variable

There seems to be a significant imbalance in the classes, with only about 16.3% of records belonging to the minority class. This can cause problems, as we will see shortly in the next section. Let us continue and prepare the data for modeling.

The features 'Gender', 'Vehicle_Age', and 'Vehicle_Damage' are categorical.

5. Let us perform dummy encoding on these features to get numeric representations, using the `get_dummies` method of Pandas as shown in the following code:

```
ins1 = pd.get_dummies(data=ins0,
                      columns=['Gender', 'Vehicle_Age', 'Vehicle_
                      Damage'],
                      drop_first=True)
ins1.head()
```

	Age	Previously_Insured	Annual_Premium	Response	Gender_Male	Vehicle_Age_< 1 Year	Vehicle_Age_> 2 Years	Vehicle_Damage_Yes
0	28	1	28885.0	0	1	1	0	0
1	24	1	25093.0	0	0	1	0	0
2	47	0	2630.0	0	1	0	0	1
3	29	0	46835.0	0	1	1	0	1
4	68	1	26908.0	0	1	0	0	0

Figure 5.5: First 5 records of the dataset

Note: In this case, we knew exactly the values that would be present in the categorical features and therefore performing dummy encoding before the train-test split did not do any harm. On the off chance that you anticipate newer values in the categorical fields when the model is in production, you should handle unknown categories explicitly. The encoders in sklearn. preprocessing modules are worth exploring and have options for handling unseen categories.

With this, we performed the basic pre-processing of the data. We acknowledge that the classes are significantly imbalanced. Let us now understand how the imbalance is problematic.

Difficulty in model evaluation

In *Chapter 4, Model Evaluation and Debugging,* we discussed that one of the most unexpected ways in which a model breaks or a modeling process breaks is when the evaluation is not done as per the objective and the characteristics of the data. This is particularly problematic with imbalanced datasets or situations where one class is much more prevalent than the other. Working with imbalanced datasets requires a lot of careful consideration and a good understanding of the business objectives and the application of the model to arrive at a good evaluation approach. Regular metrics like classification accuracy are rarely enough. As a quick recap, consider a case where you are creating a model for fraud detection. Let us say only about 0.1% of the transactions in the data are fraudulent transactions. Now, let us say you have a model which predicts everything as not fraud. What would be the accuracy of this model? The model would still have a 99.9% accuracy.

Pause and ponder: Let us say you are evaluating a model to detect a serious disease like HIV. Which of the following errors is more serious? A false positive (a person not having HIV, getting diagnosed with HIV), or a false negative (a person having HIV and not getting detected).

Hint: Think of the consequences of each error. An unaware HIV-infected patient or a healthy person who gets scared by the result and can go for a re-test?

While this performance sounds great on paper, the model is completely useless for the purpose. This is because, in our situation, we are not very concerned about getting the non-fraud cases right. Rather, we are interested in detecting cases of fraud. We are more interested in the minority class. The metrics, therefore, need to be chosen accordingly. Accuracy as a metric is unreliable because it does not distinguish between the minority and majority classes.

By now you must have realized that the solution is simple, at least conceptually. We need asymmetric metrics to allow us to weigh one class more than the other. Let us first see for ourselves if accuracy is suitable for our insurance case study in the next exercise.

Exercise 5.2: Accuracy for imbalanced classes

We will now build and evaluate a Machine Learning model using accuracy as our metric. First, we will perform the train-test split on the dataset, followed by scaling the numeric features. After preprocessing is complete, we will train a Logistic Regression model on the data. Alongside seeing the accuracy of the model, we will perform an involved evaluation by analyzing the performance of the individual classes.Please bear in mind that our classes are imbalanced and we, therefore, need to perform a **stratified split** to ensure that the proportions of the classes are maintained in the derived datasets. Perform the following steps.

1. Let us begin by performing a 70:30 train-test split on the data using the following code:

   ```
   From sklearn.model_selection import train_test_split
   df_train, df_test = train_test_split(ins1, test_size=0.3, random_
   state=42,
                                        stratify=ins1.Response)
   df_train.shape, df_test.shape
   ```

   The shapes of the new datasets are printed as shown in *Figure 5.6*:

   ```
   ((26080, 8), (11178, 8))
   ```

   Figure 5.6: *Shapes of the train and test datasets*

2. To confirm that the class proportions are maintained in the new datasets, print them for both datasets using the value counts method:

```
df_train.Response.value_counts(normalize=True)
```

```
df_test.Response.value_counts(normalize=True)
```

We see the output as shown in *Figure 5.7*:

```
df_train.Response.value_counts(normalize=True)

0     0.837117
1     0.162883
Name: Response, dtype: float64
```

```
df_test.Response.value_counts(normalize=True)

0     0.837091
1     0.162909
Name: Response, dtype: float64
```

Figure 5.7: *Distribution of response in the train and test datasets*

The proportions of the classes have been retained from the original dataset, just as we expected.

3. Scale the numeric features ('Age', 'Annual_Premium') using the StandardScaler utility from sklearn, as shown in the following code.

   Remember to use 'fit_transform' on the train set and use 'transform' on the test set:

```
df_train[cols_to_scale] = scaler.fit_transform(df_train[cols_to_
scale])
```

```
df_test[cols_to_scale] = scaler.transform(df_test[cols_to_scale])
```

4. Print out the average values for these columns to confirm that the scaling worked:

```
df_train[cols_to_scale].mean()
```

```
df_test[cols_to_scale].mean()
```

We see the output as shown in *Figure 5.8*:

```
df_train[cols_to_scale].mean()

Age               6.796710e-17
Annual_Premium    3.897700e-16
dtype: float64
```

```
df_test[cols_to_scale].mean()

Age               0.021344
Annual_Premium    0.005766
dtype: float64
```

Figure 5.8: Mean values after scaling

The mean values for the train set are practically 0. The values for the test set are also close to 0, as we expected these aren't exactly zero as the mean can slightly change between the datasets.

5. Separate the data into X and Y variables for both train and test sets using the following code:

```
X_train = df_train.drop('Response', axis=1)
y_train = df_train['Response']
X_test = df_test.drop('Response', axis=1)
y_test = df_test['Response']
```

6. Fit a Logistic Regression model on the train set using sklearn and specify 42 as the random seed for the reproducibility of the results:

```
from sklearn.linear_model import LogisticRegression
logreg = LogisticRegression(random_state=42)
logreg.fit(X_train, y_train)
```

The model has been trained. Let us evaluate the model performance on the train set.

7. Import the necessary utilities and calculate and print the accuracy score:

```
from sklearn.metrics import accuracy_score, confusion_matrix, classification_report
y_train_pred = logreg.predict(X_train)
accuracy_score(y_train, y_train_pred).round(3)
```

You should get the following accuracy:

0.837

This accuracy in the first attempt seems impressive, but is it any good? Remember that we care more about the customers who converted. How did our model perform for them? Let us print out the confusion matrix that presents a better picture of the classes.

8. Print the confusion matrix using the following code:

```
confusion_matrix(y_train, y_train_pred)
```

The matrix gets printed as shown in *Figure 5.9*:

```
array([[21339,   493],
       [ 3768,   480]], dtype=int64)
```

***Figure 5.9**: The output confusion matrix*

The second row belongs to the customers who converted, the second column represents the customers who were predicted to convert. Let us first talk about the 'detection rate' of conversions. Of the 4,248 customers who converted, the model predicted only 480 correctly. This means that the model could detect only about 11% of the conversions. Additionally, out of the 973 customers the model predicted would convert, only 480 or 49% were actual conversions. Therefore, the precision of the model is 49% and the recall is 11%.

Note: Please revisit the definitions in *Chapter 4, Evaluation and Debugging*, if you need a refresher.

9. Let us see the precision and recall calculated by the **`classification_report`** utility:

```
print(classification_report(y_train, y_train_pred))
```

```
              precision    recall  f1-score   support

           0       0.85      0.98      0.91     21832
           1       0.49      0.11      0.18      4248

    accuracy                           0.84     26080
   macro avg       0.67      0.55      0.55     26080
weighted avg       0.79      0.84      0.79     26080
```

***Figure 5.10**: Classification report for the model*

The classification report provides us with a detailed report for each class. This view confirms that the precision is around 49% and recall is around 11% for the conversions.

The model isn't performing well even on the train set. This model's performance is not sufficient. It should be clear that accuracy is not a good metric when evaluating performance in imbalanced classes. We always need to perform a more detailed analysis and choose our success metric according to our situation. Let us discuss some potential metrics for such imbalanced situations.

Evaluation metrics for imbalanced classes

We did a detailed discussion of accuracy, precision, and recall in *Chapter 4, Model Evaluation and Debugging*. The previous hands-on activity made it clear that we need better metrics than accuracy. Precision and Recall are much better alternatives for such cases. There is a tradeoff between precision and recall and may need to prioritize one over the other for our business problem. While these are good alternatives, they are not our only options. Let us evaluate some more key metrics.

Pause and ponder: Going back to the example of evaluating a model to detect HIV. Which metric is more important? Precision or recall?

Hint: You would want to detect all possible true HIV cases, even if at the expense of some false positives.

F1 score

We know that there is a tradeoff between precision and recall, higher precision leads to lower recall and vice versa. While in some situations we have a clear prioritization between them, choosing is not always possible. In such situations, we need a metric that captures the model's performance on both precision and recall. An effective metric is the F1 score. The F1 score is the harmonic mean between precision and recall, as shown in *Figure 5.11*:

$$F1 = \frac{2 \cdot \text{Precision} \cdot \text{Recall}}{\text{Precision} + \text{Recall}}$$

Figure 5.11: *F1 score is the harmonic mean of precision and recall*

As depicted in *Figure 5.12*, the harmonic mean between two variables is the highest when both are high. Even if one of the variables has a low value, the harmonic mean drops significantly, even if the other variable is close to 1. Consequently, a high F1 score is achieved when both precision and recall are high, indicating a well-balanced trade-off between these two metrics.

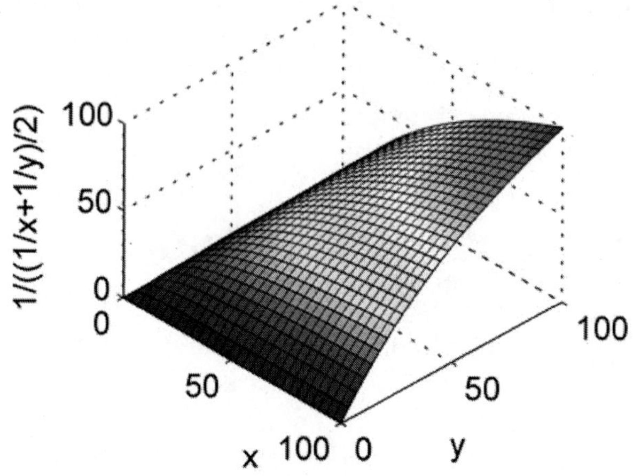

Figure 5.12: Harmonic mean visualized

It is important to note the implicit assumptions and therefore the situations where the F1 score is suitable to use are as follows:

- The F1 score assumes that a false positive is equally bad as a false negative.
- True negatives are uninteresting because we look at precision and recall, both of which are focused on the positive class.

In practice, the F1 score is a very popular metric for imbalanced classes. The F1 score metric is conveniently available in sklearn among many other metrics. As a consequence, the metric can be easily used in other sklearn modules for cross-validation and other extremely useful utilities that we will encounter later will help us optimize the model performance to obtain better F1 scores.

Warning: Do not use Area under ROC curves!

One of the most common mistakes while working with imbalanced data sets is using the ROC curve. This mistake is so prevalent that even many experienced data science professionals commit this. We know people who have more than a decade of experience in building statistical models make this mistake. Therefore, this can be considered one of those data science sins that one should be extremely careful around.

Let us plot the ROC curve for our case study to see for ourselves how misleading it could be. We'll use the plot ROC curve utility from sklearn using the following code:

```
from sklearn.metrics import plot_roc_curve

plot_roc_curve(logreg, X_train, y_train)

plt.show()
```

The ROC curve is plotted as shown in *Figure 5.13*:

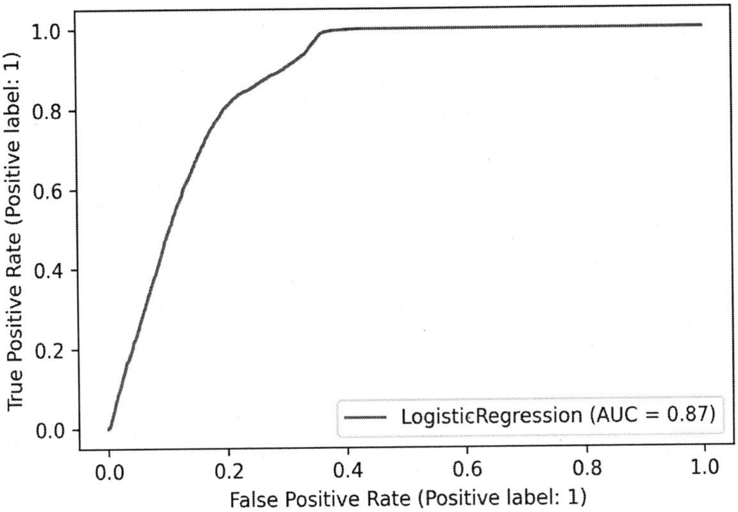

***Figure 5.13**: ROC curve for the classifier*

The area under the ROC curve is **0.87**, which is impressive. But we already have seen that the model is not useful for our purpose. The area under the ROC curve is therefore misleading. But why is that? Let us understand.

The ROC curve, as seen in *Chapter 4, Evaluation and Debugging*, attempts to measure how well the model can distinguish between the two classes. A model with high skill will be able to distinguish between the classes very well, whereas a model with low skill can easily be confused. A common mistake is to use ROC curves for highly imbalanced situations. The idea seems to have merit prima facie, if a model differentiates between two classes well, the imbalance should not be a problem. But to understand why this is problematic, we need to understand the metrics that the ROC curve works on True Positive Rate and False Positive Rate. A true Positive Rate is the same as Recall, so the Recall part is somehow captured. But the other metric is concerned more about the proportion of total negatives that were identified as positive (False Positive/Total Negatives). When you have a severe imbalance, the False Positive Rate will inevitably be very low as the denominator (Total Negatives) is typically high. A better alternative would be to use the area under the Precision-Recall curve an extremely useful metric that we will learn next.

Precision-Recall Curve

The PR curve is generated like the ROC curve but using precision and recall metrics. This is the trade-off that is often most relevant to us. Given that the recall metric is precisely about detecting the true positive cases and the precision metric is about not creating a lot of false positives, the area under this curve would be far more useful for evaluating imbalanced situations.

Plotting the PR curve is also simple using the 'plot_precision_recall_curve' utility from sklearn. Let us plot the curve for our model for vehicle insurance campaigns using the following code:

```
plot_precision_recall_curve(logreg, X_train, y_train)

plt.show()
```

The curve is plotted as shown in *Figure 5.14*:

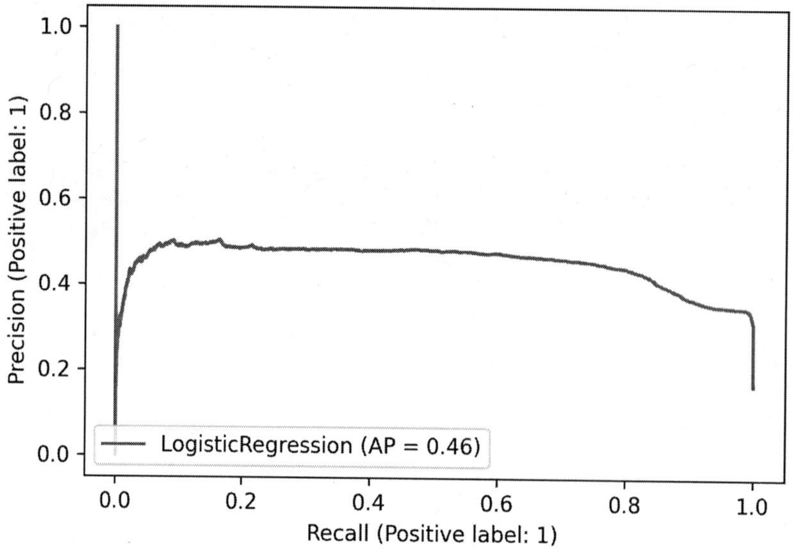

***Figure 5.14**: PR curve of the classifier*

As seen in *Figure 5.14*, the area under the PR curve is just about 0.46. This is far lower than the area under the ROC curve (0.87). The PR curve gives us a much more reliable picture of the model performance. The reason is that both metrics precision and recall that are used to generate this curve are of importance for situations like ours.

Summary of model evaluation

There are many metrics available for evaluating models, even for imbalanced situations. The key point is to understand which one is most relevant to the problem statement. In some cases, a single metric like the F1 score may suffice. In other cases, a combination of metrics may be used with one as the primary metric and the other as a guardrail. This is especially true when the model can have a serious business impact or for critical applications. If you are in doubt, make sure to take inputs from the business teams and align the criteria for a good model.

With the first challenge of model evaluation addressed, let us turn our attention to the second biggest challenge in machine learning for imbalanced classes, making the model handle the imbalance and thereby improving the model performance. Let us discuss the main approaches to doing so.

Handling imbalance

With a better understanding of a proper way of evaluating the model, we are now ready to evaluate a single model as well as compare multiple models. This also now allows us to improvise on a model, or at least know how one model is better than the other. But the key question remains how do we improve the model? How do we make the model pay more attention to a certain class while training? How do we make the model learn the patterns that we want it to learn? Now, there are several approaches to this. We will look at the 3 main approaches.

Adjusting the cost function

The first approach is influencing the way the machine learning model 'learns' that is influencing the model training itself. Recall from *Chapter 1, Optimizing a Machine Learning/ Artificial Intelligence Solution* that "model training" is, simply put, making the model learn the patterns in the data while providing an objective or a cost function that the model needs to minimize. While training, if we can tell the model to pay more attention to a certain class and that getting the minority class right is more important than getting the majority class right, then we would be close to a better solution.

For example, if you could tell the model that classifying a fraud case correctly is 10 times more important than getting a not-fraud case right, the model would detect more fraud cases. Model training is an optimization problem after all. All optimization problems have a cost or objective function. If you can modify the objective function to give more weight to a certain class, then the model learning can be influenced very easily. This is indeed a simple, straightforward, yet powerful first approach to handling imbalance.

The logistic regression loss function is shown in *Figure 5.15*:

$$log\ loss = \frac{1}{N}\sum_{i=1}^{N}[-(y_i * log(\widehat{y_i}) + (1-y_i) * log(1-\widehat{y_i}))$$

***Figure 5.15**: Regular log loss for classification*

Class weights to weigh one class more than the other is shown in *Figure 5.16*:

$$log\ loss = \frac{1}{N}\sum_{i=1}^{N}[-(w_0(y_i * log(\widehat{y_i})) + w_1((1-y_i) * log(1-\widehat{y_i})))]$$

***Figure 5.16**: Log loss with class weights*

The simplest way is to modify the class weight setting that several classification models in sklearn have. Let us relook at the arguments to the LogisticRegression module in sklearn using the line of the following code:

```
?LogisticRegression
```

You will see the arguments for the model in *Figure 5.17*:

```
Init signature:
LogisticRegression(
    penalty='l2',
    *,
    dual=False,
    tol=0.0001,
    C=1.0,
    fit_intercept=True,
    intercept_scaling=1,
    class_weight=None,
    random_state=None,
    solver='lbfgs',
    max_iter=100,
    multi_class='auto',
```

Figure 5.17: *The class_weight parameter in LogisticRegression*

Notice the class weight parameter. By default, it is set to 'None', which means that the cost function weighs both classes equally. To learn more about the parameter and how to use it, scroll down further in the help pop-up to look at the 'Parameters' section of the docstring of LogisticRegression. You will see the description of this parameter as shown in *Figure 5.18:*

```
class_weight : dict or 'balanced', default=None
    Weights associated with classes in the form ``{class_label: weight}``.
    If not given, all classes are supposed to have weight one.

    The "balanced" mode uses the values of y to automatically adjust
    weights inversely proportional to class frequencies in the input data
    as ``n_samples / (n_classes * np.bincount(y))``.
```

Figure 5.18: *Description of the class_weight parameter*

We can specify the weight for each class using a dictionary. This weight will be used in the adjusted cost function for LogisticRegression. If you wish to weight the positive class, 10 times more than the negative, you can specify class weight as {0:1, 1:10} as an example (the weights don't need to add up to 1, it is the ratio that matters). If you want to weigh the classes in inverse proportion to their proportions in the data, use 'balanced'. If the ratio between the minority and majority classes is 1:5, using a 'balanced' scheme would assign class weights with a 5:1 ratio. This simple approach is usually effective and a good starting point.

Note: While we saw the class_weight parameter in the context of LogisticRegression, most classification methods in sklearn have the class_weight parameter implemented. For all those classification methods, adjusting the cost function is as simple as modifying the class_weight parameter.

Exercise 5.3: Adjusting class_weight

In this exercise we will assess the impact of adjusting class weights for the logistic regression model. We will use a stratified k-fold validation scheme to get a generalized performance score. Perform the following steps.

1. Create an instance of LogisticRegression with **`class_weight`** specified as `balanced`L:

   ```
   logreg_wt = LogisticRegression(class_weight='balanced', random_
   state=42)
   ```

2. To assess model performance, use the 3-fold scoring scheme and print out the cross-validation scores as a dataframe. Use the code in the following commands:

   ```
   from sklearn.model_selection import StratifiedKFold
   from sklearn.model_selection import cross_validate
   folds = StratifiedKFold(random_state=42, n_splits=3, shuffle=True)
   cv_scores = cross_validate(logreg_wt,
                              X_train,
                              y_train,
                              cv=folds,
                              scoring=['precision','recall','f1'])


   pd.DataFrame(cv_scores)
   ```

   The CV scores are printed as shown in *Figure 5.19*:

	fit_time	score_time	test_precision	test_recall	test_f1
0	0.057687	0.006759	0.353906	0.959746	0.517123
1	0.056166	0.003168	0.348629	0.960452	0.511567
2	0.051804	0.003353	0.349011	0.959040	0.511777

   ***Figure 5.19**: Cross-validation scores*

Data balancing

Here is an insight that is extremely simple and fundamental: models learn patterns from the data presented to them. If you want the model to pick up the patterns relevant for detecting the minority class better, it simply needs more representation. We often come across situations where the imbalance in the data is so severe that merely modifying the cost function does not suffice. In such cases, we need to explore the option of data balancing. Data balancing means that we reduce the imbalance of the classes in the data, which means that we see more records, as a percentage, from the minority class. This will help the model see a little more of the minority class records and the patterns the model learns are less dominated by the majority class. We need not always completely balance the classes 50:50, even 5:1 is a significant improvement over 999:1.

How do we do this? Well, we have only two options, undersampling and oversampling, sometimes you may use a combination of the two. Undersampling refers to taking a subset of the records for the majority class. As an example, in a dataset with 1 million records, we may have 999,000 records in the majority class and only 1,000 records in the minority class, a ratio of 999:1. But while preparing the training data, instead of choosing all 999,000 records, we could choose just 5000. The 5000 records can be chosen using Random undersampling that is choosing the records at random, or some other sophisticated strategy (for example, Near Miss). This would create the ratio or modify the ratio to 5:1. As discussed earlier, 5:1 is still somewhat imbalanced, but is a huge improvement over 999:1. The two approaches are illustrated in *Figure 5.20*:

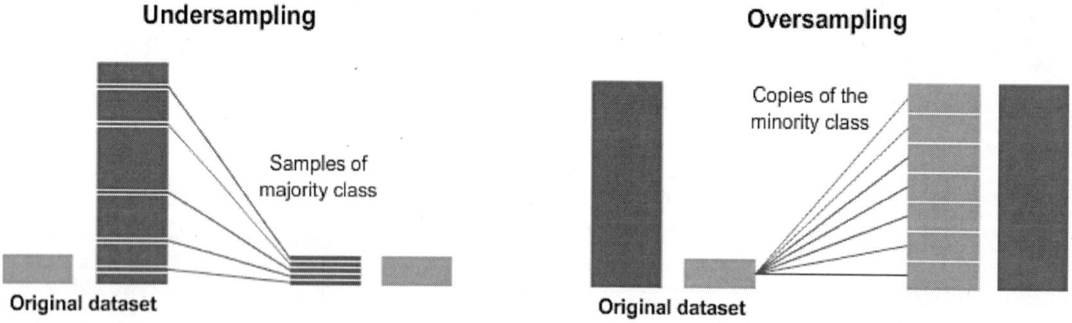

***Figure 5.20**: Undersampling vs. oversampling*

The idea of oversampling is on similar lines, while preparing the data set, we include more records from the minority class. The simplest way of achieving this is to merely duplicate or create copies of the records from the minority class, either replicating all records or choosing a random portion (Random Oversampling) of the records to duplicate. The most sophisticated approaches don't just replicate points but generate new data points that are similar to existing data points. Techniques like SMOTE, and ADASYN fall into this category. We will understand and implement these in later sections of this chapter.

The result of both undersampling and oversampling is the same; a more favorable ratio for the minority class. But the practical difference between the two approaches can be significant, while doing an under-sampling of the majority class you may end up losing some important information or patterns in the data. The loss of information can lead to extremely poor performance, especially when there is a severe imbalance in the labels. Therefore, exercise caution, while performing under-sampling. As a common-sense guiding principle, always prefer retaining information to losing information.

Pause and ponder: Is simple oversampling of the minority class fundamentally significantly different from assigning a higher-class weight to the minority class? In both cases, we do not provide any new information and are effectively providing a higher weight to the minority class.

Undersampling

We saw that the idea behind under-sampling is extremely simple, balance the classes in favour of the minority class by reducing the records from the majority class. The simplest and most naive method is simply dropping some or many records from the majority class while preparing the training dataset. By performing Random under-sampling, we can choose the proportion of records to drop or retain from the majority class.

Exercise 5.4: Random undersampling of insurance data

To understand how it works, let us see Random Undersampling in action. We will use the imblearn library for Random Undersampling and all the subsequently discussed approaches. If you don't have the library installed, install it using the following command:

```
!pip install imblearn
```

We will use the handy **fit_resample** method from imblearn to balance the data. As you might expect, the **fit_resample** method identifies the number of records in the minority class. Next, it randomly selects a matching number of records from the majority class, resulting in a perfectly balanced set. Let us perform the undersampling and subsequent analysis.

1. Import **RandomUnderSampler** from the **under_sampling** module in imblearn and create an instance of the undersampler. Use the following code:

   ```
   from imblearn.under_sampling import RandomUnderSampler
   u_sampler = RandomUnderSampler(random_state=42)
   ```

2. Resample the dataset and verify the new class distributions using the following code. Note that we are using new variables to store the balanced datasets.

   ```
   X_train_under, y_train_under = u_sampler.fit_resample(X_train, y_train)
   y_train_under.value_counts()
   ```

The new class frequencies get printed as shown in *Figure 5.21*:

```
y_train_under.value_counts()
```

```
0    4248
1    4248
Name: Response, dtype: int64
```

***Figure 5.21:** Distribution after under-sampling*

Note: Class balancing must always be done AFTER performing the train-test split. Any manipulations or rebalancing must be done on the train dataset alone. Performing balancing before train-test split will make the test data non-representative of the true data and can render the final model useless.

3. Create an instance of **LogisticRegression** (specify only the random state) and assess its performance on the balanced dataset using the cross-validation scheme we have been using so far. Use the following code:

```
logreg = LogisticRegression(random_state=42)
cv_scores = cross_validate(logreg,
                           X_train_under,
                           y_train_under,
                           cv=folds,
                           scoring=['precision','recall','f1'])
pd.DataFrame(cv_scores)
```

The model performance gets printed as shown in *Figure 5.22*:

	fit_time	score_time	test_precision	test_recall	test_f1
0	0.032670	0.008817	0.741740	0.951271	0.833540
1	0.025311	0.005804	0.730937	0.947740	0.825338
2	0.019999	0.004668	0.733224	0.949153	0.827331

***Figure 5.22:** Performance after Random Undersampling*

This seems like a huge improvement over the previous models. It seems like we have struck gold with just a simple change, a recall of about 94% and F1 scores > 82%. Is this the generalized performance we can expect on new and unseen data? Have we created a great model with just this change? No, we have not. This a very insidious 'gotcha' that you should be extremely careful about while working with imbalanced datasets. Let us understand this pitfall better.

Model evaluation with re-balancing

After re-balancing the training data, we are ready to build a model and evaluate its performance. We usually look at the cross-validation score for this purpose. K-fold cross-validation creates folds from the training data and measures the performance on the held-out fold. The idea is that the average score over these validation folds gives us an estimate of the generalized performance of the model, which we hope is similar to the test set. However, after you have re-balanced the training data, the cross-validation score does not serve its purpose.

This is because when you create the cross-validation folds after rebalancing, even the 'test' folds have the same, balanced class distribution. Therefore, the performance seen in the cross-validation results is based on balanced classes. In the actual data and the unseen data that the model will encounter in the future, the class distribution is heavily skewed. The balanced test set is therefore **not representative of true data**, and the performance of the model is not indicative of generalized performance.

The following steps indicate the process we followed:

1. Rebalance the training data
2. Split into k folds
3. Model evaluation on balanced test folds

Instead, this is what we need to do:

1. Split into k fold
2. Rebalance the training folds
3. Evaluation of untouched test folds

The difference between the two approaches is highlighted in *Figures 5.23* and *5.24*:

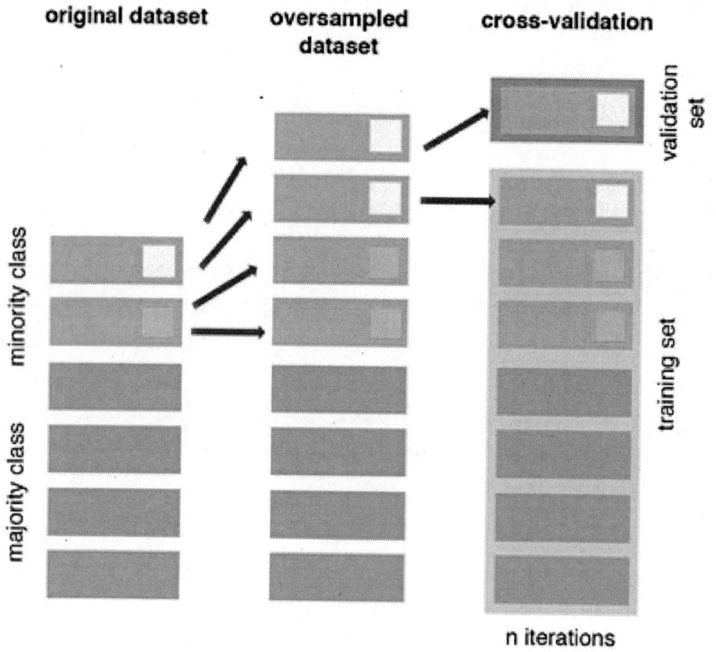

Figure 5.23: *Rebalancing before creating validation splits*

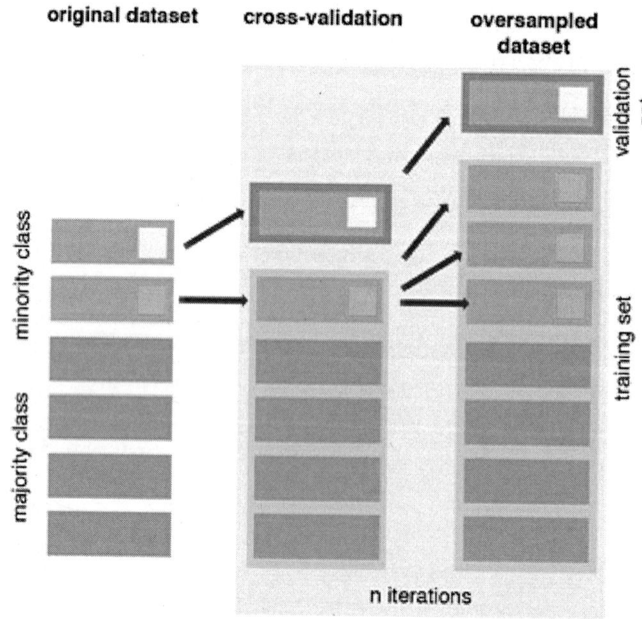

Figure 5.24: *Splitting before rebalancing*

Using Pipelines for evaluating re-balanced data

We now understand that the right order in model evaluation with class re-balancing is as follows:

split into k folds | rebalance the training folds | evaluation on untouched test folds

This can be coded manually using a loop. Manual coding would give you full control over each step in the process. Note that the steps listed above are a general outline - you might have task-specific steps in the process. In general, the loop would split the data into the folds, then perform all the necessary steps to rebalance (more than one sometimes) and fit the model on the training folds. Finally, the evaluation on the validation fold is performed and the score is stored. As mentioned earlier, this can be coded manually, but is less convenient compared to the handy Pipeline utility in the imblearn library. The Pipeline module allows us to chain multiple steps into a single pipeline that includes the re-balancing steps and can also include the model. The pipeline module conveniently handles the looping and fold division part. It allows you to specify the rebalancing step(s) conveniently. It also allows you to add the predictive model as a pipeline component. The fold creation, rebalancing, model fitting, and scoring are all handled very easily by the pipeline module. Let us see how it works in the following steps:

1. First, we import the Pipeline utility from imblearn using the following code:

   ```
   from imblearn.pipeline import Pipeline
   ```

2. Next, we instantiate the rebalancer that is the random undersampler and the **LogisticRegression** instance. The following code does this:

   ```
   u_sampler = RandomUnderSampler(random_state=42)
   logreg = LogisticRegression(random_state=42)
   ```

3. Next, both these steps are combined in a pipeline. The steps in the pipeline can be specified as named steps, as shown in the following code:

   ```
   p_steps = [('under', u_sampler),
              ('model', logreg)]
   pipeline = Pipeline(steps = p_steps)
   ```

4. The pipeline is now ready and works just like a sklearn model would. You can assess the cross-validation performance of this pipeline by using it just like you would use the **cross_validate** method on the sklearn model:

   ```
   cv_scores = cross_validate(pipeline,
                              X_train,
                              y_train,
                              cv=folds,
                              scoring=['precision','recall','f1'])
   pd.DataFrame(cv_scores)
   ```

The output is shown in *Figure 5.25*:

	fit_time	score_time	test_precision	test_recall	test_f1
0	0.162583	0.059897	0.353577	0.970339	0.518295
1	0.154315	0.050736	0.349638	0.954096	0.511742
2	0.167563	0.056456	0.348819	0.959746	0.511672

***Figure 5.25:** Realistic results on using Pipeline*

This performance is much more believable and closer to the performance we have seen so far. The generalized recall is high, but the precision is poor, leading to F1 scores similar to what we saw when using the **`class_weight`** parameter.

The performance is much more reliable and realistic because the pipeline does exactly what needs to be done. The under sampler is applied only to the training folds created after the K-fold splits. The test fold is not re-balanced. While predicting, the under-sampler step doesn't do anything (it just passes the values through). Thanks to the Pipeline module in imblearn, we now have a much better model evaluation scheme that works with re-balancing approaches. Let us now turn our attention towards more re-balancing approaches.

Undersampling methods: Tomek Links

The approach of Random undersampling is extremely simple. When dropping records from the majority class, it treats all points equally. This isn't such a good idea. Points belonging to the majority and minority classes need not be well separated in space. Near the decision boundary, we may have points from both classes close together. This could be confusing for the model, which may not be able to identify a clear decision boundary because of the 'unclean' space. Therefore, points of the majority class that are very close to the minority class points and vice versa are 'nuisance' points that confuse the model.

A smarter undersampling approach would identify that dropping such nuisance points is more beneficial than dropping points in the majority class that are far away from the minority class points. Points from the opposite classes that are nearest neighbours of each other form a Tomek Link. The Tomek Link is illustrated in *Figure 5.26*. Points in Tomek Links can be considered to be 'nuisance' points that confuse the model.

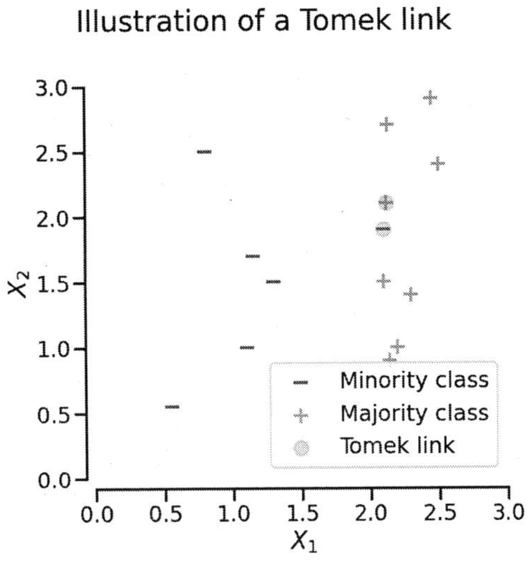

Figure 5.26: *Tomek Links visualized.*

Under-sampling approaches using Tomek Links would drop these nuisance points. *Figure 5.27* shows the undersampling using Tomek Links in action. The initial space has many cases where points of opposite classes are very close to each other (forming a Tomek Link). The under-sampler identifies these links and drops points from the majority class belonging to these links. The result is a much cleaner space with the opposite classes better separated. Refer to *Figure 5.27* for the detailed working of the technique:

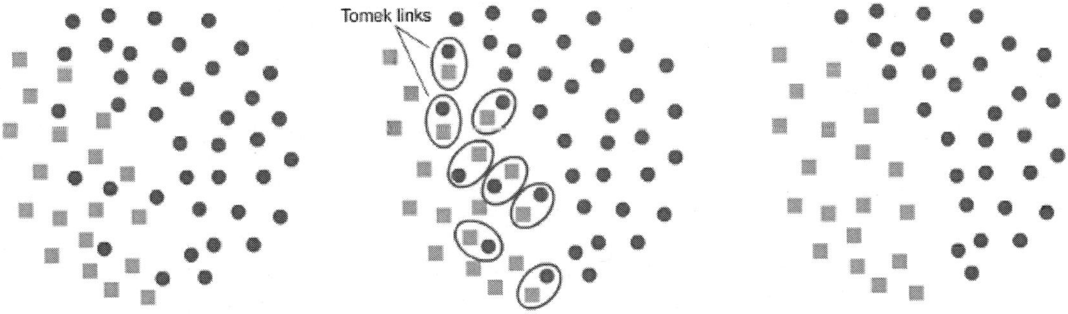

Figure 5.27: *Clean-up using Tomek Links*

It is important to note that this approach is not truly a rebalancing approach. The approach does not guarantee, and indeed in most cases does not lead to well-balanced classes. This is because it removes only the records from the Tomek links. Points that do not belong to Tomek Links are not omitted. Therefore, Tomek Links based under sampler can be thought of as a **cleaning method**, but not a strong under sampler. We will now see the Tomek Links under sampler in action on the insurance case study.

Exercise 5.5: Tomek Links applied to insurance data

In this hands-on exercise, we will perform Tomek Links based on a sampling of the insurance case study and evaluate model performance. Let us get started:

1. First, import the `TomekLinks` utility from the `under_sampling` module in imblearn using the following code:

   ```
   from imblearn.under_sampling import TomekLinks
   ```

2. Next, instantiate the TomekLinks under sampler and using the fit_resample method, rebalance the training data as in the code:

   ```
   u_sampler =  TomekLinks()
   X_train_under, y_train_under = u_sampler.fit_resample(X_train, y_train)
   ```

3. To verify the extent of re-balancing on applying the over sampler, display the class frequencies before and after rebalancing. Use the following code:

   ```
   y_train.value_counts()
   y_train_under.value_counts()
   ```

   The output is shown in *Figure 5.28*:

   ```
   y_train.value_counts()

   0    21832
   1     4248
   Name: Response, dtype: int64

   y_train_under.value_counts()

   0    20523
   1     4248
   Name: Response, dtype: int64
   ```

   Figure 5.28: *Distribution before and after under-sampling*

   Notice from the output that very few points (1,309) have been dropped from the majority class. We still have a lot of imbalances in the classes. Let us see if the model performance is good. To assess the performance of this under sampling scheme, we will use the imblearn pipeline approach as we did for random under sampling.

4. Create a pipeline with TomekLinks under Sampler and Logistic Regression as the steps:

   ```
   u_sampler =  TomekLinks(n_jobs=-1)
   ```

```
logreg = LogisticRegression(random_state=42)

p_steps = [('under', u_sampler),
           ('model', logreg)]
pipeline = Pipeline(steps = p_steps)
```

5. Evaluate the model using the cross-validation scheme we have been using so far and display the results as a Pandas dataframe using the following code:

```
cv_scores = cross_validate(pipeline,
                           X_train,
                           y_train,
                           cv=folds,
                           scoring=['precision','recall','f1'])
pd.DataFrame(cv_scores)
```

The model performance gets printed as shown in *Figure 5.29*:

	fit_time	score_time	test_precision	test_recall	test_f1
0	3.417831	0.025506	0.464316	0.381356	0.418767
1	0.270339	0.003847	0.487424	0.396893	0.437524
2	0.252036	0.007791	0.501832	0.387006	0.437002

Figure 5.29: *Cross-validation scores*

The performance is very poor compared to the random over-sampler we saw previously. Note that the performance is still an improvement over the completely imbalanced data. This should not be surprising considering that we understand that Tomek Links is not rebalancing to a significant extent. Regardless, undersampling using Tomek Links is an extremely important conceptual approach and we will explore its full potential in a subsequent section in this chapter. For now, we evaluate another powerful undersampling approach, Edited Nearest Neighbour-based under-sampling.

Undersampling methods: edited nearest neighbour

We saw the Tomek Links under the sampling approach is a cleaning approach that drops points that form a Tomek Link when a point from the majority class is the closest neighbour to one from the minority class. We saw that this drops very few points and in our case study, it did not affect the imbalance in a significant manner. The Edited nearest neighbour approach is a variation of this approach. For each point, the approach forms a neighbourhood of the K nearest neighbours (default value of 3 in sklearn implementation) and attempts to clean this neighbourhood by dropping the disagreeing point. For example, if a neighbourhood contains mostly the minority class, then the majority point class from this neighbourhood will be dropped. Such an approach can potentially drop more points and clean the space better, leading to potentially better balance in the data. Again, this too is a cleaning approach, and we cannot be sure of the extent of rebalancing of the data. Let us see how well it works for our insurance case study.

Exercise 5.6: Edited nearest neighbour undersampling

In this hands-on exercise, we will perform Edited Nearest Neighbours based on sampling on the insurance dataset. We will use the EditedNearestNeighbours utility from the under_sampling module in imblearn, similar to the way we used TomekLinks and evaluated model performance.Perform the following steps.

1. Import the EditedNearestNeighbours utility, instantiate, and apply it to the train data. Display the class frequencies before and after the under sampling:

   ```
   from imblearn.under_sampling import EditedNearestNeighbours
   u_sampler = EditedNearestNeighbours(n_jobs=-1)
   X_train_under, y_train_under = u_sampler.fit_resample(X_train, y_train)

   y_train.value_counts()
   y_train_under.value_counts()
   ```

   The frequencies get output as shown in *Figure 5.30*:

   ```
   y_train.value_counts()

   0    21832
   1     4248
   Name: Response, dtype: int64

   y_train_under.value_counts()

   0    16967
   1     4248
   Name: Response, dtype: int64
   ```

   Figure 5.30: *Class distribution before and after under-sampling*

   Note that this time we have a higher number of points dropped (4,865). This is an improvement from TomekLinks and the balance is slightly better, but we still have an imbalance and this is somewhat expected as Edited Nearest Neighbour is a cleaning method. Let us see how this approach fares on the data.

2. Create a pipeline with Edited Nearest Neighbour and Logistic Regression and evaluate its performance using the following code:

```
p_steps = [('under', u_sampler),
           ('model', logreg)]
pipeline = Pipeline(steps = p_steps)

cv_scores = cross_validate(pipeline,
                           X_train,
                           y_train,
                           cv=folds,
                           scoring=['precision','recall','f1'])
pd.DataFrame(cv_scores)
```

The performance output is shown in *Figure 5.31*:

	fit_time	score_time	test_precision	test_recall	test_f1
0	0.228495	0.004845	0.431321	0.807203	0.562223
1	0.235231	0.005180	0.438258	0.817090	0.570513
2	0.279949	0.004522	0.431843	0.825565	0.567063

***Figure 5.31**: Cross-validation scores*

The recall is now more than 80% and the F1 score is above 56%. This is an improvement in terms of precision and the best result we achieved so far on the F1 score. The Edited Nearest Neighbour approach cleaned up the data better than Tomek Links and improved model performance.

We have seen a few variations of the under-sampling approach by now. Random undersampling was the simplest approach that dropped a significant chunk of the majority class points and can balance the classes perfectly. It treats all majority points equally and was thus a naïve approach. Data clean-up approaches like Tomek Links and Edited Nearest Neighbour clean up the space instead. The approaches attempt to clean up spaces where points from the majority and minority classes are close to each other and drop the points to make the region less mixed. These approaches do not guarantee class balance. Indeed, on our data, the Tomek Links approach dropped very few majority class points and the model performance was poor. The Edited Nearest Neighbour method dropped more points and gave us better model performance. Note that in all the under-sampling approaches, we are losing data points and therefore information contained in the data. With this summary, let us now look at the other major approach to balancing the classes of oversampling.

Oversampling

Under-sampling attempted to balance the classes better by omitting points from the majority class. Oversampling also has the same objective, but the approach is to increase the records of the minority class. There are various ways to achieve this. The simplest and most naive approach is to merely duplicate or create copies of the records from the minority class. You can do this as much as you want to achieve better balance. One such approach is **Random Oversampling** where you randomly choose a certain proportion of the records to duplicate. The benefit of over-sampling is that unlike under sampling, we do not lose any information from the data. We will soon see better ways of over-sampling. But let us first implement Random Oversampling and assess the performance of the model ourselves.

An important decision that we need to make when performing oversampling is the extent of the balance that we want to achieve. We can look at the ratio of the minority to the majority class to measure the imbalance. In our problem statement, the ratio is 4,248/21,832 which is 0.195. We surely want to increase this ratio to achieve a greater balance. In situations where we have extreme ratios, to begin with, say 1:1,000, rebalancing to a 1:1 ratio would mean replicating the minority class 1,000 times. As your intuition might tell you, this isn't a great idea. As mentioned earlier, a ratio of 1:10 is a good deal better than 1:1,000. The necessary extent of rebalance varies by case and the data scientist should aim to get the best performance without replicating the data too much. For our case study, we will rebalance to a ratio of 0.75 that is records of the minority class/records of the majority class would be 0.75 (3:4). The oversampling algorithms in the imblearn package can be supplied via the 'sampling_strategy' parameter. If unspecified, the default value is 1 which is a complete rebalance of the classes. Let's see all of this in action in the following points:

1. We first import the `RandomOverSampler` utility from the `imblearn.over_sampling` module using the following code:

   ```
   from imblearn.over_sampling import RandomOverSampler
   ```

2. Next, create an instance 'o_sampler' of the RandomOverSampler specifying 0.75 as `sampling_strategy' and 42 as `random_state`:

   ```
   o_sampler = RandomOverSampler(random_state=42, sampling_strategy=0.75)
   ```

3. Now, use the `fit_resample` method of the sampler, supplying X_train and y_train to it. The method returns resampled versions of X_train and y_train - collect them in X_train_over and y_train_over variables using the following code:

   ```
   X_train_over, y_train_over = o_sampler.fit_resample(X_train, y_train)
   ```

4. Check the counts for each class in Y_train using the value_count method using the following command:

```
y_train_over.value_counts()
```

You will see the frequencies in *Figure 5.32*:

```
0    21832
1    16374
Name: Response, dtype: int64
```

***Figure 5.32:** Updated distribution of response*

The number of records with class 0 does not change, but it has significantly increased for class 1 (it was 4,284 earlier). The ratio between the classes is now 16,374/21,832, exactly 0.75, just as we specified using the 'sampling_strategy' parameter.

5. Now, create an instance of LogisticRegression with 42 as `random_state` and create a pipeline with the oversampler followed by Logistic Regression:

```
logreg = LogisticRegression(random_state=42)
p_steps = [('over', o_sampler),
           ('model', logreg)]
pipeline = Pipeline(steps = p_steps)
```

With the pipeline specified, now we will evaluate the performance of the approach by using the 3-fold cross-validation scheme we have been using so far. Print the cross-validation performance in terms of precision, recall, and F1 score:

```
cv_scores = cross_validate(pipeline,
                           X_train,
                           y_train,
                           cv=folds,
                           scoring=['precision','recall','f1'])
pd.DataFrame(cv_scores)
```

	fit_time	score_time	test_precision	test_recall	test_f1
0	0.166409	0.021935	0.375790	0.881356	0.526916
1	0.189867	0.029945	0.366282	0.897599	0.520262
2	0.114642	0.004199	0.383494	0.872881	0.532873

***Figure 5.33:** Cross-validation scores*

We observe that the precision of the pipeline is not the best, but recall is decent overall. The overall F1 score also seems to be acceptable. The oversampling strategy seems to fare decently overall. But is this the best oversampling approach we have?

Note: Reiterating that we do not need a perfect 1:1 balance between classes. Especially for cases with extreme imbalance (class ratio of, say, 1:1,000 ratio), a perfect rebalancing would mean oversampling the minority class 1,000 times. Regardless of the technique you employ, it is likely that you are not adding significant useful information.

Pause and ponder: If you increase the `sampling_strategy` value to 1, how do you expect the recall to change? Would you expect it to increase or decrease? And why?

It is important to note that when performing Random Oversampling, you are not adding any new information to the dataset. You could argue that this approach is not different from simply adjusting the class weights in the model. The additional observations we created were simply dumb copies of existing records. A smarter approach would be to use the patterns in the data to generate new records. Data generation approaches like SMOTE and ADASYN do just that. Let us now understand these approaches and see for ourselves if they help us with the model performance.

Synthetic Minority Oversampling Technique

Synthetic Minority Oversampling Technique (**SMOTE**). The idea behind the SMOTE technique is elegant and powerful. *Figure 5.34* illustrates the workings of the technique. Instead of creating duplicates of all records or randomly selected records from the minority Class, the technique generates synthetic observations representing the minority class by interpolating the points. More concretely, there are 3 steps in the SMOTE algorithm:

1. Identify a point from the minority class
2. Find its nearest neighbours from the *minority* class
3. Create a synthetic observation along the line between the point and the nearest neighbours

For each point in the minority class, the SMOTE algorithm looks at a few of its nearest neighbours (defaults to 5 in the imblearn implementation). A link is created between the point and its neighbours and the new synthetic points lie on these links. By design, SMOTE aims to create synthetic records of the minority class that are 'in-between' other points of the minority class. The number of points created depends on the extent of the rebalancing specified. See *Figure 5.34* which illustrates the working of SMOTE:

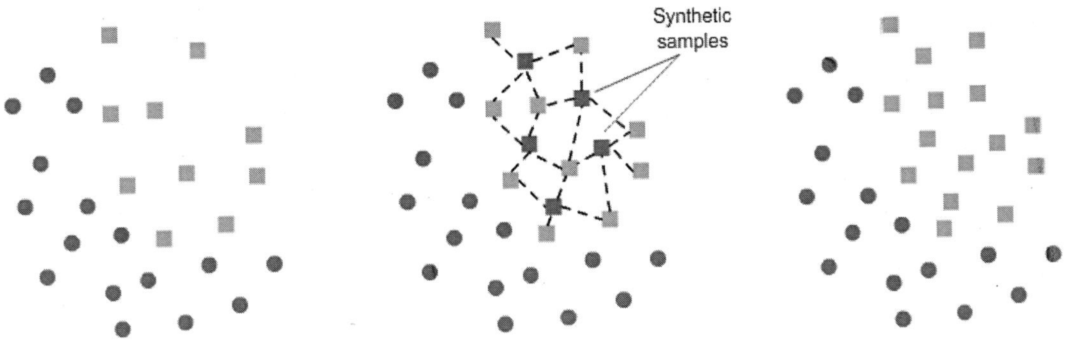

Figure 5.34: The SMOTE technique in action

As you can imagine, the separation between the classes isn't always as clean as in the illustration. We may (and usually do) have points belonging to the minority class right between the majority class points. This can lead to situations where you have newly generated minority class points, even though such a point didn't exist in the original data. This leads to 'noise' in the data, as we are now seeing data that are not helpful towards our objective. For larger datasets, however, this could be a benefit. The additional points effectively make the decision boundary larger, effectively leading to regularization. When using larger datasets and high-variance classifiers, SMOTE can therefore provide a performance boost. A data scientist working with SMOTE should always be cognizant of the consequences of the nature of the algorithm.

Note: The SMOTE technique interpolates a significant number of points between marginal outliers and inliers, leading to noisy samples. This issue can be solved by cleaning the space resulting from over-sampling, which we will explore in an upcoming section on combining over and under-sampling approaches.

Exercise 5.7: Synthetic Data Generation with SMOTE

In this hands-on exercise, we will use SMOTE to generate synthetic samples using the minority class points to balance the data. We will use the SMOTE utility from the over-sampling module in imblearn. Perform the following steps.

1. Import the SMOTE utility and create an instance of the over-sampler specifying 0.75 as sampling_strategy. Use the following code:

```
from imblearn.over_sampling import SMOTE
o_sampler = SMOTE(random_state=42, sampling_strategy=0.75)
```

2. Create a pipeline with SMOTE and Logistic Regression and evaluate the model performance using the 3-fold cross-validation scheme we have been using so far:

```
logreg = LogisticRegression(random_state=42)
p_steps = [('over', o_sampler),
           ('model', logreg)]
pipeline = Pipeline(steps = p_steps)

cv_scores = cross_validate(pipeline,
                           X_train,
                           y_train,
                           cv=folds,
                           scoring=['precision','recall','f1'])
pd.DataFrame(cv_scores)
```

The performance gets printed as shown in *Figure 5.35*:

	fit_time	score_time	test_precision	test_recall	test_f1
0	0.177532	0.021886	0.376136	0.877119	0.526494
1	0.170648	0.023446	0.380574	0.879944	0.531343
2	0.182826	0.040372	0.375113	0.881356	0.526249

***Figure 5.35**: Cross-validation scores*

We notice that the performance is very similar to the performance of the random oversampling approach. A detailed diagnosis is not prudent at this stage, but we do suspect that because of its nature, the SMOTE technique could be creating noisy points that are not helping the model in any way. Let us now discuss another approach that overcomes the drawbacks of SMOTE.

ADASYN - Adaptive Synthesis

Recall that the issue with SMOTE is that for the minority class points very close to majority class points, it creates a lot of noise points that can make classification more difficult for the model. ADASYN solves this by effectively de-prioritizing such points. ADASYN creates more synthetic points for minority class points that have fewer majority class points around them. The points generated will be the least for minority class points that lie in between majority class points thus the 'adaptive' in the name.

Theoretically, ADASYN should perform better than SMOTE. Let us see for ourselves if that is practically true for our vehicle insurance case study.

Exercise 5.8: Synthetic Data Generation with ADASYN

In this hands-on exercise, we will use ADASYN to generate synthetic samples. We will use the ADASYN utility from the over_sampling module in imblearn. Let us start by importing ADASYN and creating an instance of the over sampler (sampling strategy at 0.75) using the following code:

```
from imblearn.over_sampling import ADASYN

o_sampler = ADASYN(random_state=42, sampling_strategy=0.75)
```

Now, create a pipeline with ADASYN followed by Logistic Regression and evaluate the model performance using the 3-fold evaluation scheme we have been using so far:

```
logreg = LogisticRegression(random_state=42)

p_steps = [('over', o_sampler),

          ('model', logreg)]

pipeline = Pipeline(steps = p_steps)

cv_scores = cross_validate(pipeline,

                           X_train,

                           y_train,

                           cv=folds,

                           scoring=['precision','recall','f1'])

pd.DataFrame(cv_scores)
```

The result gets printed as shown in *Figure 5.36*:

	fit_time	score_time	test_precision	test_recall	test_f1
0	0.186126	0.004014	0.358352	0.927260	0.516929
1	0.236511	0.024699	0.350956	0.932910	0.510039
2	0.190876	0.004452	0.355033	0.916667	0.511830

Figure 5.36: *Cross-validation scores*

As seen in *Figure 5.36*, there was no improvement in the F1 score. However, there was an improvement in the recall score. Note that the higher recall comes at the cost of reduced precision. This score is an improvement in terms of recall.

Let us now discuss another aspect of handling imbalance: the extent of rebalancing. Let us look at the considerations and explore smarter ways of rebalancing.

Extent of rebalancing

Do you always need to rebalance the classes 1:1? Most real-world situations do not have a perfect balance between the classes, so do we always need to rebalance them? The answer to this depends on the data as well as the machine learning algorithm. If the observations are easily separable using the available features, techniques like Logistic Regression and SVC with linear kernels may work fine without extreme rebalancing. In other cases, algorithms like Boosting and RandomForest (with sufficient depth) can also work well without the classes being equally distributed. Of course, it is not practical to know Apriori which approach will work better. We, therefore, need to evaluate what works best for our situation. We used 0.75 as the ratio of minority to majority class in the examples above and it seemed to be working well for our situation. It is always a good idea to try different extents of rebalancing.

Note: The ratio of minority to majority class observations is a user choice that affects the performance of the model. It is therefore a hyper-parameter. We will learn how to tune hyper-parameters in *Chapter 7, Hyper-parameter Tuning.*

Combination of under and oversampling

Under-sampling of the majority class may drop a significant number of records and therefore information from the data. On the other hand, oversampling of the minority class in certain cases may not add significant value and might lead to mere replication of the data already contained. Additionally, we discussed that oversampling methods like SMOTE and ADASYN are effective, but there is a potential problem of 'noise', where the techniques generate some noisy samples when they interpolate. One way to fix this is by "cleaning the space".

Under-sampling methods like Tomek Links (or Edited Nearest Neighbours) can help us clean the space by dropping these noisy records. The idea is fundamentally simple, add a cleaning step to the pipeline after the SMOTE step. SMOTE would generate synthetic samples from the minority class (albeit with some noise) and the Tomek Links method reduces this noise. We could manually build pipelines composed of these components. For example, we could chain a SMOTE and ENN to create a combo pipeline ourselves. However, very conveniently for us, the pipelines have been implemented in the imblearn package. This means that a combination sampler like SMOTE Tomek or SMOTEENN can be used just like any other sampler. Let us see it in action in the following exercise.

Exercise 5.9: Using a combination of over and undersampling

In this exercise, you will evaluate the combination of over and under-sampling for rebalancing the data. First, you will use **SMOTE + Tomek Links (SMOTETomek)**, create a pipeline, and evaluate the cross-validation performance of the model. Then, you use **SMOTE + Edited Nearest Neighbours (SMOTEENN)** for rebalancing and compare the performance of the two approaches. Perform the following steps:

1. Import the SMOTEENN and SMOTETomek utilities from **`imblearn.combine`** module:

```
from imblearn.combine import SMOTEENN, SMOTETomek
```

2. Create an instance of Logistic regression, specify 42 as `random_state`:

```
logreg = LogisticRegression(random_state=42)
```

3. Create an instance of SMOTETomek specifying 0.75 as `sampling_strategy`:

```
combo_sampler = SMOTETomek(random_state=42, sampling_strategy=0.75)
```

4. Create a pipeline of SMOTETomek and Logistic Regression, calculate and print the cross-validation scores (Precision, Recall and F1 score as metrics) as a dataframe:

```
p_steps = [('combo', combo_sampler),
           ('model', logreg)]
pipeline = Pipeline(steps = p_steps)

cv_scores = cross_validate(pipeline,
                           X_train,
                           y_train,
                           cv=folds,
                           scoring=['precision','recall','f1'])
pd.DataFrame(cv_scores)
```

	fit_time	score_time	test_precision	test_recall	test_f1
0	0.547454	0.004731	0.376014	0.883475	0.527514
1	0.420873	0.004719	0.378133	0.884181	0.529723
2	0.522618	0.004694	0.373659	0.885593	0.525566

***Figure 5.37:** Cross-validation scores*

5. Create an instance of SMOTEENN specifying 0.75 as `sampling_strategy`:

```
combo_sampler = SMOTEENN(random_state=42, sampling_strategy=0.75)
```

6. Create a pipeline of SMOTEENN and Logistic Regression, calculate, and print the cross-validation scores (Precision, Recall, and F1 score as metrics) as a dataframe:

```
p_steps = [('combo', combo_sampler),
           ('model', logreg)]
pipeline = Pipeline(steps = p_steps)cv_scores = cross_validate(pipeline,
                              X_train,
                              y_train,
                              cv=folds,
                              scoring=['precision','recall','f1'])
pd.DataFrame(cv_scores)
```

You should get results as shown in *Figure 5.38*:

	fit_time	score_time	test_precision	test_recall	test_f1
0	0.497906	0.004154	0.375298	0.888418	0.527685
1	0.490681	0.004365	0.376161	0.887006	0.528286
2	0.546317	0.003815	0.373731	0.884181	0.525388

Figure 5.38: *Cross-validation scores*

What do you observe? Which works better?

We see that the results from both approaches are very similar and practically equal. We do not have a clear winner. Also, note that the overall performance of the combination approach is decent and gives us among the best recall and F1 scores so far.

Comparing the approaches

We saw a variety of approaches for handling imbalance, from the simplest approach of adjusting the cost function to using a sequence of oversampling and clean-up techniques. We saw that some of these approaches worked better than the others in our vehicle insurance case study. But so far, we have been looking at the cross-validation scores. Let us now see which approaches work best on the unseen test data, the true test of the approaches.

We begin by creating a list containing the different techniques we want to evaluate. Based on the cross-validation results, we saw that the following approaches gave among the best results:

- Random Over Sampling (over sampling)
- Edited Nearest Neighbours (under sampling)
- ADASYN (over sampling)
- SMOTEENN (over sampling + under sampling)

We create a `sampler_list` containing instances of these 4 samplers. We will specify 0.75 as the sampling_strategy for RandomOverSampler, ADASYN, and SMOTEENN. Use the following code:

```
sampler_list = [EditedNearestNeighbours(n_jobs=-1),
                RandomOverSampler(random_state=42, sampling_strategy=0.75),
                ADASYN(random_state=42, sampling_strategy=0.75),
                SMOTEENN(random_state=42, sampling_strategy=0.75)]
```

Instantiate a Logistic Regression classifier. Also import the utilities precision_score, recall_Score, and f1_score from sklearn.metrics. We will calculate these metrics for each sampler:

```
logreg = LogisticRegression(random_state=42)
from sklearn.metrics import precision_score, recall_score, f1_score
```

For each sampler, we will create a pipeline (sampler + logistic regression) and train on the train set. We will then predict the test classes and calculate and print the precision, recall and F1 score on the test set for each sampler. Use the following code:

```
for sampler in sampler_list:
    p_steps = [('sampler', sampler),
               ('model', logreg)]
    pipeline = Pipeline(steps = p_steps)
    pipeline.fit(X_train, y_train)
    print(sampler)
    y_pred = pipeline.predict(X_test)
    print('Precision:', precision_score(y_test, y_pred).round(2),
          'Recall:', recall_score(y_test, y_pred).round(2),
          'F1 Score:', f1_score(y_test, y_pred).round(2),
          '\n')
```

The performance of the sampling approaches is printed as shown in *Figure 5.39*:

```
EditedNearestNeighbours(n_jobs=-1)
Precision: 0.43 Recall: 0.83 F1 Score: 0.57

RandomOverSampler(random_state=42, sampling_strategy=0.75)
Precision: 0.38 Recall: 0.9 F1 Score: 0.53

ADASYN(random_state=42, sampling_strategy=0.75)
Precision: 0.36 Recall: 0.93 F1 Score: 0.52

SMOTEENN(random_state=42, sampling_strategy=0.75)
Precision: 0.39 Recall: 0.9 F1 Score: 0.54
```

***Figure 5.39**: test performance of the methods*

From the results, we observe that if F1 were our only criterion, the Edited Nearest Neighbour approach would be the clear winner. However, we need to get good recall as well. Note that the results are close, and most approaches achieve a similar recall. The SMOTEENN approach has an F1 score of 0.54, a good recall of 0.9, and a precision is 0.39. This result seems to be the most balanced. For our vehicle insurance case study, we will therefore go ahead with SMOTEENN.

Conclusion

Imbalanced classes in Machine Learning are a common situation, many real-world situations have a skewed balance of the classes. This is particularly common when the object is to 'detect' an event, a purchase on an eCommerce platform, or a disease. We first discussed the difficulty in the model evaluation due to imbalance. We saw that we needn't limit ourselves to simple accuracy and have a variety of metrics available. A well-thought-out choice of metric goes a long way in setting us up for success.

Handling class imbalance by making a high-performance machine learning model that handles the imbalance is not straightforward. There are several approaches which broadly fall into two categories, sampling of the majority class and over-sampling of the minority class. While both aim to achieve a more balanced class representation, the approaches can be wildly different. Under-sampling approaches can either randomly drop points from the data (Random Under Sampling) or perform involved clean-up (Tomek Links, Edited Nearest Neighbour) of the data to make the classification easier for the modeling technique. Under-sampling drops points and therefore potentially loses some information contained in the dataset.

In contrast, over-sampling does not lose any data. It derives newer data points from the existing minority class points. This derivation could be simple replication, as in the case of Random Over Sampling. Or, as in the case of SMOTE and ADASYN, we could generate newer points similar to the minority class points. We noted that these methods tend to generate noisy data. The combination approach – using oversampling followed by cleanup of the data is also a promising option. We saw all these approaches in action in our vehicle insurance case study.

Imbalanced classes are frequent in real-world problems. Imbalanced Machine Learning is therefore an essential skill for a data scientist to excel in today's world. Apart from a good understanding of the problem statement and the domain, solving imbalanced problems also requires a good understanding of machine learning techniques. With this chapter, you have learned the essential skills and implemented them. Well done!

In the next chapter, we will learn about a very direct way of optimizing the model: modifying the hyper-parameters of the model. Hyper-parameter tuning is one of the most powerful methods of getting the most optimized ML/AI skill that any data scientist must master.

CHAPTER 6
Hyper-parameter Tuning

Introduction

You are a data scientist in the marketing team at a bank. The bank is gearing up for its next major marketing campaign. The product to be promoted is not new, and there have been marketing campaigns in the past. Surely, the past campaign's data can be used to improve the upcoming campaign. A good assumption is that the kind of customers who responded positively to the previous campaign will respond positively again. Therefore, you could analyze the data to identify the customer segments that are likely to respond positively. The constraints are that the output/model should be interpretable by non-technical marketers. The number of segments for the marketing team to act on should be limited. High accuracy is not an important requirement.

Pause and ponder: Which modeling technique(s) do you think works best in such a situation? Make a list of techniques suitable for the task and rank them in order of your preference.

Hint: Go through the constraints again. Interpretability disqualifies many high-performance models.

After much discussion with your team, you chose to use Decision Trees. But how do you influence the Decision Tree model to make it respect your constraints? Controlling the depth seems like a good option! But how do we decide the best depth? Very low depth may lead to a model too simple and low in performance to be useful. How do you strike a balance?

In another situation, the only requirement could be to get the maximum possible accuracy, without having to worry about interpretability. The only constraint could be the speed of making predictions. Let us say that you're planning to use tree-based models (Decision Trees, Random Forests, Boosting, etc.). You need to make choices again - what should be the maximum depth of the tree? What depth gives you the best result without overfitting the data?

Yet another situation could be where the model doesn't need to be interpretable, but there is an upper limit on the time it needs to make predictions. In such a situation, you would look for a model that gives you the highest accuracy and does not exceed the allowed prediction time.

In all the aforementioned situations, the task is similar - you wish to find the value of a 'setting' that gives you the best/optimal result while respecting the constraints. This process of searching for the best setting is called 'hyper-parameter tuning'. Let us understand 'hyper-parameters' and what it means to 'tune' them.

Structure

In this chapter, we will cover the following topics:

- Parameters and hyper-parameters
- Importance of hyper-parameters
- Hyper-parameter tuning and approaches
- Manual looping
- GridSearchCV - Grid Search with Cross-Validation
- Limitations of exhaustive methods
- RandomizedSearchCV
- Grid Search versus Randomized Search
- Choosing a hyper-parameter tuning approach
- Choosing the 'best' model
- Training on the entire data and making predictions
- The complete process

Objectives

After reading this chapter, you will be able to optimize the model to get the best generalized performance by way of finding the best set of "settings" for the model, i.e., hyper-parameters. You will be able to assess the impact of hyper-parameters on model performance and be able to choose the "best" model. You will also learn some considerations in defining "best". You will learn multiple automated approaches to searching for the best hyper-parameters – from exhaustive methods like grid search to approaches like Randomized search that work better for larger datasets and hyper-parameter combinations. You will then be able to use these hyper-parameters to train on the entire dataset, get the best generalized performance and start making predictions on unseen data.

Parameters and hyper-parameters

Hyper-parameters are parameters that are 'external' to the model and control the behavior and learning of the model. By 'external' we mean that the model does not learn these parameters. Instead, these need to be provided to the modeling algorithm by the user. They are not to be confused with 'model parameters.'

Let us understand 'model parameters' first. Let us take the example of a linear regression model. The output of a linear regression model are the coefficients corresponding to the predictors. The coefficients are what define the model and learning these coefficients is what training is all about. These coefficients are internal to the model and are learned by the model during the training process. Hyper-parameters, by definition, are not learned by the model.

To make the idea more concrete, let us take the example of a decision tree. A very important characteristic of a decision tree is its depth, that is, the number of levels in the tree, or the maximum number of decisions/questions allowed to get to a prediction. A tree with a depth of just 1 will ask just one question to make a prediction - a single question to decide whether, say, an individual will default on a loan or not. This decision stump is the simplest of models. Another extreme could be a decision tree with a depth of 15 - meaning that it could ask 15 questions to get to a prediction and is therefore far more complex. Modeling packages have a standard 'setting' for Decision Trees which is 'maximum depth' - the maximum depth that the tree is allowed to grow to. The decision tree does not learn this and is to be provided by the user. Depending on the specified 'maximum depth', the resulting tree and therefore the model can be very different. The maximum depth of the tree is, therefore, a ***hyper-parameter***.

Pause and ponder: We are basing the definition on one key feature - hyper-parameters need to be specified by the user. But what if this can be automated? What if I have a code that automatically finds the best depth for a Decision Tree? Does it then become a parameter?

Hint: Hyper-parameters are external to the model and influence the model training.

Each algorithm has its own set of different hyper-parameters. For a KNN classifier, the number of neighbours is an important hyper-parameter that the user must specify. Similarly, for a K-means clustering, the number of clusters needs to be specified by the user. For Deep Neural Networks, the activation functions are among the many hyper-parameters. For SVM, the type of Kernel needs to be specified. These, along with some other key hyper-parameters, control how the algorithm learns and influences the resulting model.

For most standard packages, you can easily find the list of hyper-parameters that can be specified by the user for that algorithm. For example, for a Decision Tree Classifier in SciKit Learn, you can find the available hyper-parameters by using the following code:

```
from sklearn.tree import DecisionTreeClassifier

?DecisionTreeClassifier
```

You will see the signature of the class (*Figure 6.1*), which includes the parameters the user can provide:

```
Init signature:
DecisionTreeClassifier(
    *,
    criterion='gini',
    splitter='best',
    max_depth=None,
    min_samples_split=2,
    min_samples_leaf=1,
    min_weight_fraction_leaf=0.0,
    max_features=None,
    random_state=None,
    max_leaf_nodes=None,
    min_impurity_decrease=0.0,
    min_impurity_split=None,
    class_weight=None,
    ccp_alpha=0.0,
)
```

Figure 6.1: *Hyper-parameters in a decision tree*

All the above are hyper-parameters that you can specify. We see that for an algorithm as simple as a Decision Tree, you can have several hyper-parameters that control how the tree model grows. Moving to tree-based ensemble methods only increases the hyper-parameters.

Task 1: Go ahead and check out the hyper-parameters for any other algorithm that you are curious about. If you can't think of any algorithm, go ahead with LogisticRegression. Which hyper-parameters do you think are most important? Which of these have you already adjusted in the previous chapters?

Importance of hyper-parameters

We mentioned that hyper-parameters impact how the model learns and the resulting model can be very different for different choices of hyper-parameters. Let us continue with the example of the Decision Tree as it is extremely suitable and makes for a great example of the importance of hyper-parameters. Instead of discussing theoretically, we will demonstrate this significance.

Let us first make a decision tree with the maximum depth specified as 2. The parameter to specify while creating an instance of the DecisionTreeClassifier is 'max_depth'. We won't specify any other hyper-parameter. Use the following code:

```
from sklearn.tree import DecisionTreeClassifier

dt = DecisionTreeClassifier(max_depth=2)

dt.fit(X_train, y_train)
```

With that, the first decision tree with a maximum depth of 2 has been trained. To understand the tree and see what it looks like, we can use the plot_tree method in sklearn. You can do so using the following code:

```
from sklearn.tree import plot_tree

plt.figure(figsize=[10,6])

plot_tree(dt, feature_names=X_train.columns, filled=True, rounded=True)

plt.show()
```

You should get a tree as shown in *Figure 6.2*:

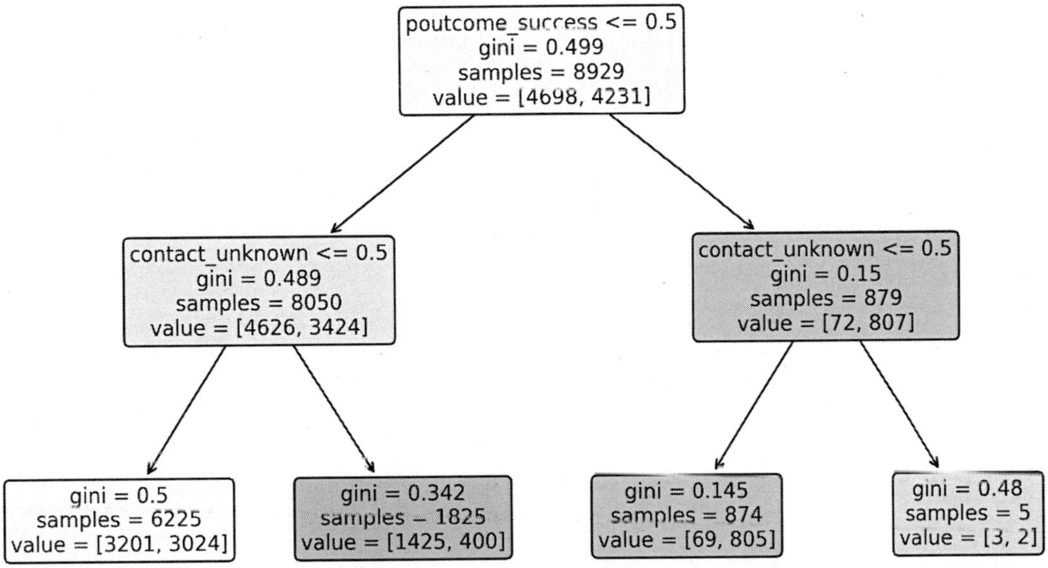

Figure 6.2: *Decision Tree for Depth 2*

The Decision tree in *Figure 6.2* has two levels, i.e., it asks at most two questions to get to a leaf (that contains the prediction). This tree is simple to read and it's easy to see how a decision is being made. If you have difficulty understanding the tree in *Figure 6.2*, make sure to read the following optional explanation. Note that understanding the tree itself is not required for this chapter and that you can proceed even if the interpretation of the tree isn't crystal clear to you.

Optional: Interpreting a decision tree

The decision tree can be read and interpreted like a flow chart, a rather simple one. The arrows indicate the direction you need to move. The arrows are from top to bottom, which means that you begin at the top (root node) and traverse to the bottom (leaf nodes). A question is asked at each node. If the answer to the question is yes, then you move to the left in the next level. A 'No' means you move to the right.

Consider the path leading to the orange box (second from left in the last row) in *Figure 6.2*. The first question that is asked at the top (the root node) is if the previous outcome success is <= 0.5 (that is, 0, meaning a failure). Let us say the answer is 'Yes', that is, the previous outcome was a failure. You, therefore, move to the left in the next level. The next question asked is if contact_unknown <= 0.5 (that is, 0, is the contact known?). If the answer to this question is no (i.e., contact is not known), then you move to the right to the next level. This leads to the leaf node where no further question is asked. In this node, you can see that most of the records belong to the first class, i.e., class 0, the customers with whom the campaign did not work. These are customers who meet both the conditions:

1. The previous campaign was a failure.
2. Contact is unknown.

It makes sense that these customers have a very low chance of success.

The way you read the tree above is the standard way in which you can read any decision tree. As you can see, for small trees, it is extremely easy to look at each path and understand exactly how the model works.

If you need more explanation and examples, head over to the following link:

https://www.ibm.com/topics/decision-trees

Now, let us train another Decision Tree; this time with no depth control. It would be an interesting experiment to 'see' this tree with much higher depth. Do not specify any max_depth value, which will allow the tree to grow to its fullest. Train the model and plot the tree like we did for the previous tree. Note that if the tree has high depth, it may take a while to display the plot:

```
dt = DecisionTreeClassifier(random_state=42)
dt.fit(X_train, y_train)
plt.figure(figsize=[15,10])
```

```
plot_tree(dt, feature_names=X_train.columns, filled=True, rounded=True)
plt.show()
```

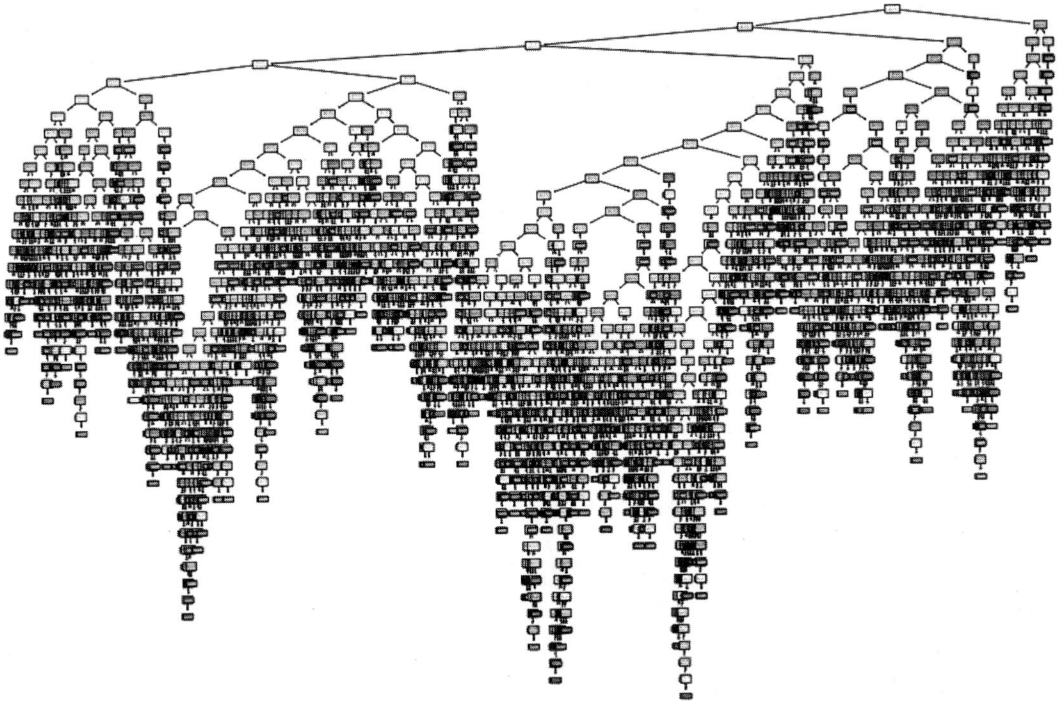

Figure 6.3: Decision Tree with no depth control

Clearly, the second tree is far more complex than the first. In this plot, the tree isn't even readable. You'll be excused if you do not want to put the effort into understanding this tree - neither did we.

Let us now compare the performances of the models on the train and test sets. For the first model, let us calculate the accuracy score on the train and test sets using the following code and make note of the scores:

```
y_train_pred = dt_2.predict(X_train)
print("Train accuracy:", accuracy_score(y_train, y_train_pred))
y_test_pred = dt_2.predict(X_test)
print("Test accuracy:", accuracy_score(y_test, y_test_pred))
```

The train and test accuracy should be around 0.609 and 0.593, respectively. The simple model has similar performance on both train and test sets. Let us now see how the complex model with no depth control fares:

```
y_train_pred = dt.predict(X_train)
print("Train accuracy:", accuracy_score(y_train, y_train_pred))
y_test_pred = dt.predict(X_test)
print("Test accuracy:", accuracy_score(y_test, y_test_pred))
```

The train accuracy should be around 0.999 - nearly perfect predictions. The test performance, however, is drastically lower at around 0.63. Clearly, this model is overfitting!

Depth	Assessment
2	+ Simple and interpretable - Underfitting
Max	- Very complex - Overfitting

Table 6.1: Comparing the two decision trees

Not only do the models look very different, but their performances are also strikingly different. A simple comparison between the two trees is shown in *Table 6.1*. The key takeaway ***is that the choice of hyper-parameters can result in very different models.*** We employed only one hyper-parameter - this was the only difference between the two training attempts. In other situations, you may need to set multiple hyper-parameters leading to potentially greater differences in the resulting models. Hyper-parameters are therefore extremely important and can have a significant impact on the resulting model. It is, therefore, essential that we understand the approaches to finding the right set of hyper-parameters, a process commonly referred to as 'hyper-parameter tuning'. The trees are visualized in *Figure 6.4*:

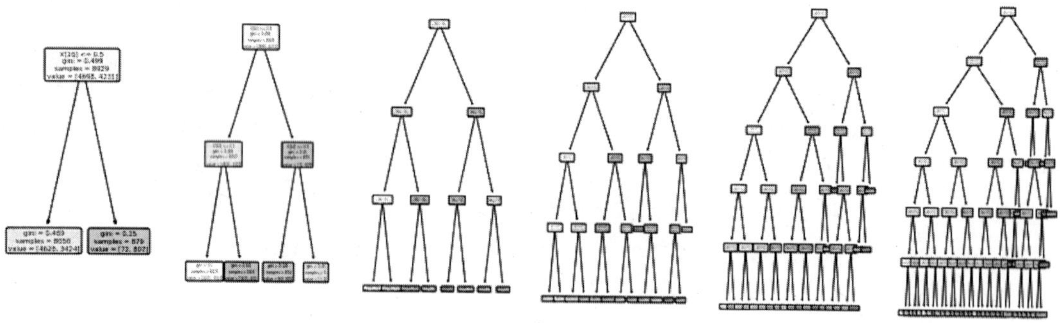

***Figure 6.4**: Decision trees on our dataset for different values of max_depth.*

Hyper-parameter tuning

By now we have seen that hyper-parameters greatly impact the resulting model. A poor choice of hyper-parameters is often the reason for the underwhelming performance of a model. Even if you have good data and if you are employing an extremely powerful algorithm, a bad set of hyper-parameters can lead to a poor model that just does not utilize the information in the data or the potential of the algorithm. The other way to look at this is -

Choosing the right set of hyper-parameters gets you the maximum out of the data and the modeling algorithm.

Determining the right set of hyper-parameters can be considered a search problem. Going back to the Decision Tree example - a very low depth (2) gave a very simple model that was too simple, whereas a high depth (no depth control) model was unnecessarily complex and overfitting. Somewhere between these two extremes is the optimal model - that has good generalized performance. Hyper-parameter tuning in this example would be finding the optimal value of maximum depth for the decision tree model.

In general, we work with multiple hyper-parameters. Hyper-parameter tuning can therefore be thought of as finding the right combination of hyper-parameters to get optimal model performance. As with search problems in general, there are multiple approaches to hyper-parameter tuning. These approaches could be manual or automated, could be exhaustive searches or smarter ones that quickly zone into the optimal values. However, the essence of these approaches is the same and can be simplified to a few key steps. For a given dataset, estimator (modeling algorithm), success metric is as follows:

1. Perform a k-fold split on the training data.
2. For a candidate set of hyper-parameters (i.e., a particular combination), obtain the cross-val score using the scoring metric specified.
3. Store the candidate hyper-parameter combination, its cross-validation scores, training scores, and timing details.
4. Choose the 'best estimator' as one that provides the 'best' performance.

Note: It is important to recall at this juncture that the definition of 'best' depends on the situation and there are several considerations in declaring an estimator the best. We touched upon this idea in *Chapter 4, Model Evaluation and Debugging*. We will discuss this further in this chapter in the section Choosing the 'best' model.

The scoring metric is also specified by the user. Recall from the discussion in Chapter 4, *Model Evaluation and Debugging*, that this is an important choice that defines the utility of your model and must be aligned with the overall objective of the project.

Note: Notice that we use cross-validation scores for model evaluation, and not training scores or the test scores. We have discussed model evaluation extensively in *Chapter 4, Model Evaluation and Debugging,* and saw that cross-validation score is a great way to estimate the generalized performance of the model on unseen data. For this reason, most hyper-parameter tuning algorithms use the cross val score for evaluating a candidate hyper-parameter set.

The preceding steps are general steps in any hyper-parameter tuning approach. Extensive research has gone into solving this search problem as quickly as possible, using minimal resources, by way of smartly identifying the high-potential candidate combinations. This has spun multiple hyper-parameter tuning algorithms. We will discuss some prominent approaches. But first, we will perform this search ourselves manually in the simplest possible manner - manual looping.

Manual looping over hyper-parameters

This first approach is simple enough for us to code ourselves with ease. We will manually loop through the candidate hyper-parameter combinations, calculate, and store the cross-validation scores. We can then pick the best based on the performance. Let us begin!

The general approach for manual looping is very simple and can be described as a sequence of 4 simple steps:

1. Store the candidate values of the hyper-parameter in a list.
2. Loop over the list and for each candidate value, fit the model.
3. Calculate and store the cross-validation score.
4. Choose the 'best estimator' as one that provides the 'best' performance.

Perform your own manual hyper-parameter tuning

We will continue using the same dataset and use the Decision Tree modeling algorithm. We will pick one hyper-parameter - max_depth - for our implementation. We will loop through the values 1 through 15, in increments of 1 (stored in a list) and store the cross-validation score using a 4-fold cross-validation scheme.

Note: We need to be mindful of the number of models fits we are planning to execute. In the preceding example, we will be trying 15 values of the hyper-parameter, performing a 4-fold cross-validation each time. This would mean 15 times 4, i.e., 60 model fits. This is a small number for this example but can get out of hand very easily with a higher number of hyper-parameters.

Begin with defining a list 'depth_val' that contains the range of values from 1 through 15 using the range function. Also, define an empty list (`candidate_score`) that will contain the mean cross-validation score for each candidate, as shown here:

```
depth_vals = range(1,16)
candidate_score = []
```

Next, we will loop through the values of depth. For each depth value, we will instantiate a **DecisionTreeClassifier** with that depth. Then, calculate the mean cross val score with a 4-fold CV scheme, and append it to the **candidate_score** list. We do this using the following code:

```
for depth in depth_vals:
    dt = DecisionTreeClassifier(max_depth=depth, random_state=42)
    cv_scores = cross_val_score(estimator=dt, X=X_train, y=y_train, cv=4,
    scoring='accuracy')
    candidate_score.append(cv_scores.mean())
```

The **candidate_score** list will now contain the score for each depth value. To analyze the results visually, we'll plot the score against each depth value using the following code:

```
plt.figure(figsize=[10,6])
plt.plot(depth_vals, candidate_score)
plt.xlabel("Max Depth")
plt.ylabel("Cross Validation Accuracy")
plt.show()
```

We get the graph shown in *Figure 6.5*:

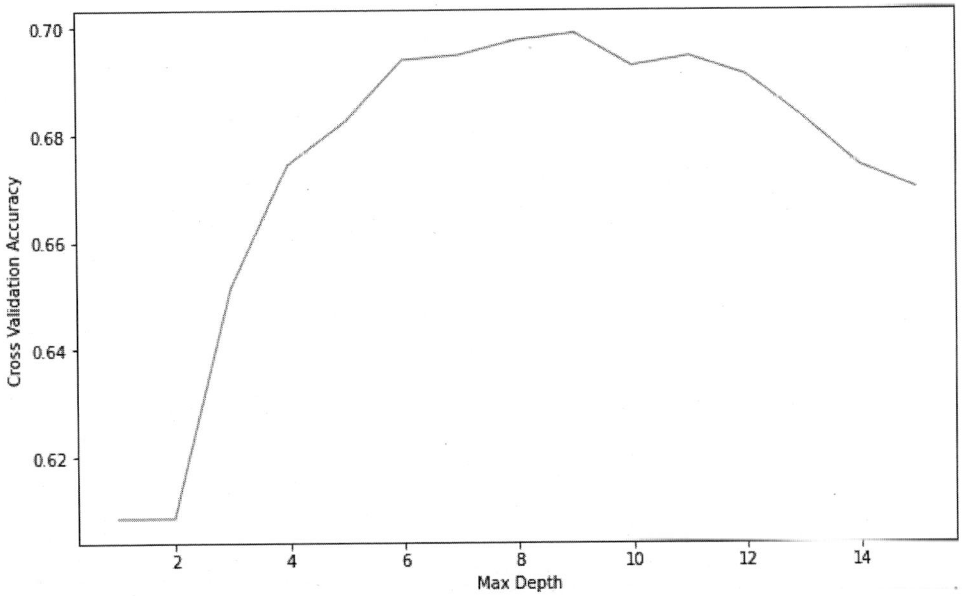

***Figure 6.5**: Accuracy vs. Max depth*

The graph of accuracy vs. max depth in *Figure 6.5* shows that the accuracy is maximized at slightly less than 70% for depth 9. This is where the model gets us the best-generalized performance and is the optimal value of the hyper-parameter.

The manual approach we used is very useful because it gives us a lot of control. We needn't restrict ourselves to storing just the mean accuracy - we could add more metrics and custom metrics too. We could also add more details - about the training time, perhaps, or the median accuracy from the different folds, or even the training accuracy. You get the drift. We have total control over the code we write and can customize it heavily if needed. This approach is very useful and we encourage you to try out variations of the same that include more details on the performance.

While very promising, the manual looping approach has a couple of limitations:

- Adding more details and extending it to multiple hyper-parameters combinations could be cumbersome to code manually.
- The method employs brute force and is dumb in the sense that it must go through all the combinations.

Despite its drawbacks, in some cases where you need a very high level of customization, this approach may be your only option. But in general, we now have standard libraries which cover most of the typical use cases. In that sense, you do not need to re-invent anything and can employ the methods available in popular packages like Scikit Learn. These are very simple to use, very convenient, and store a lot of details that you would ordinarily require. Let us begin understanding the first of these automated approaches available in Scikit Learn - GridSearchCV.

GridSearchCV - Grid Search with Cross-Validation

What GridSearchCV search does is not very different from the manual looping approach. But it does so in an automated fashion that greatly reduces our coding efforts and helps save significant time. If you need to tune multiple hyper-parameters, GridSearchCV makes the code much simpler. Note that this is still an exhaustive, simple approach that tries every possible combination of the specific hyper-parameters.

Let us now use the convenient GridSearchCV method for hyper-parameter tuning for the same Bank Marketing example. We'll assess the same candidates for using GridSearch and discover for ourselves its benefits and drawbacks.

First, let us understand the parameters needed for GridSearchCV. Begin with importing it from sklearn using the following command:

```
from sklearn.model_selection import GridSearchCV
```

Use the following command to invoke a good description of the method and usage examples:

```
?GridSearchCV
```

The parameters should be printed as shown in *Figure 6.6*:

```
Init signature:
GridSearchCV(
    estimator,
    param_grid,
    *,
    scoring=None,
    n_jobs=None,
    refit=True,
    cv=None,
    verbose=0,
    pre_dispatch='2*n_jobs',
    error_score=nan,
    return_train_score=False,
)
```

***Figure 6.6**: Parameters for GridSearchCV*

Not all parameters are equally important to us. You need the following key parameters:

- `estimator`: The predictor you want to use.
- `param_grid`: The hyper-parameters and their values you want to try, passed as a dictionary.
- `cv` : To specify the cross-validation scheme you want to use; you can supply an integer which will be considered the number of folds in the k-fold scheme. E.g. use 4 for 4-fold cross-validation.

Additionally, you can use the following parameters to further customize the process:

- `scoring`: The metric to assess performance on. You can choose accuracy, precision, recall, or any of the standard metrics available in sklearn. If scoring isn't specified, the default measure of the estimator is used, which is 'accuracy' for most classifiers.
- `n_jobs`: To utilize multi-core setup for parallel processing, if available. If -1 is supplied, all available cores can be utilized for maximum execution speed.
- `verbose`: The level of detail in the progress updates. If 0, no progress is displayed. The higher the number, the greater the detail of the progress printed out to you. A value of 2 gives enough information for most situations.
- `return_train_score`: True would return the performance on the training folds as well. By default, it is False and only the validation set performance is returned.

Using GridSearchCV for hyper-parameter tuning

Let us now use GridSearchCV to replicate the example we did with manual looping. Let us begin with instantiating the estimator:

```
dt = DecisionTreeClassifier(random_state=42)
```

Note that we did not specify any parameter to the classifier except for **random_state**. This will ensure that the **random_state** is fixed to what we want. In case there is another parameter you want to fix, you can do so by specifying it in the instantiation command. For example, if you used **DecisionTreeClassifier(random_state=42, max_features=4)**, then both **random_state** and **max_features** would be fixed at 42 and 4, respectively. The remaining parameters will be their default values or be tuned through GridSearchCV.

The hyper-parameters to be tuned and their values to try are specified using a 'parameter grid' - a dictionary. For our case, we want to try values 1 to 15 for the 'max_depth' hyper-parameter. The 'parameter grid' dictionary will be as follows:

```
hyper_params = {max_depth: range(1, 16)}
```

We will also use a 4-fold cross-validation scheme, so 'cv' would be 4. We will set verbose to 2 to get some basic progress status. To return the train score, we will set 'return_train_score' to True and set n_jobs to -1 to utilize all cores. We will use 'accuracy' to score:

```
model_cv = GridSearchCV(estimator=dt,
            param_grid=hyper_params,
            scoring='accuracy',
            cv=4,
            n_jobs=-1,
            verbose=2,
            return_train_score=True)
```

The preceding command specifies the settings we want to and returns a 'GridSearchCV' object into 'model_cv'. To try out the different hyper-parameters on the training data, we need to 'fit' this on the data. The syntax is the same as fitting any sklearn model on training data:

```
model_cv.fit(X_train, y_train)
```

This will 'fit' on the data and try out the different combinations of hyper-parameters and store performance information for each combination. Because we used verbose = 2, the progress will be displayed on the screen, as shown in *Figure 6.7*:

```
model_cv.fit(X_train, y_train)
```

```
Fitting 4 folds for each of 15 candidates, totalling 60 fits
GridSearchCV(cv=4, estimator=DecisionTreeClassifier(random_state=42), n_jobs=-1,
             param_grid={'max_depth': range(1, 16)}, return_train_score=True,
             verbose=2)
```

Figure 6.7: Output from fit command

There are 15 candidate hyper-parameter combinations. Since we're using a 4-fold CV scheme, 4 fits were done for each candidate, totaling 60 fits. This is very useful as sometimes when you're trying multiple hyper-parameters, the number of combinations gets out of hand quickly and this serves as a good reminder.

With the hyper-parameters tried, let us see which value of **max_depth** gave us the best cross-validation accuracy. We can use the 'best_estimator_' and the 'best_score_' attributes of **model_cv** to find the best estimator and its cross-validation performance:

```
print(model_cv.best_estimator_)
print(model_cv.best_score_)
```

The output should be as shown in *Figure 6.8*:

```
print(model_cv.best_estimator_)
print(model_cv.best_score_)
```

```
DecisionTreeClassifier(max_depth=9, random_state=42)
0.6987342236925107
```

Figure 6.8: Best estimator and score

The best value of **max_depth** seems to be 9 which is exactly the result we got from manual looping. The cross-validation accuracy is also very close to what we got from manual looping. This shows that GridSearchCV does whatever we do using manual looping, just in a cleaner, modular manner.

So far, we just looked at the best estimator and its cross-validation score. GridSearchCV stores far more information than that in the 'cv_results_' attribute. It contains rich information about the performance on each validation fold, the scoring time, the fit time and more, to give you a very detailed understanding of the performance beyond just the overall score. Let us extract this information into a Pandas dataframe and explore it a bit, using the following code:

```
cv_df = pd.DataFrame(model_cv.cv_results_)
print(cv_df.shape)
cv_df.head()
```

You'll see the output as shown in *Figure 6.9*:

```
(15, 19)
```

	mean_fit_time	std_fit_time	mean_score_time	std_score_time	param_max_depth	params	split0_test_score	split1_test_score	split2_test_score	split3_test_score
0	0.022916	0.002014	0.007120	0.003108	1	{'max_depth': 1}	0.605464	0.616487	0.605287	0.606631
1	0.034954	0.003914	0.007783	0.001203	2	{'max_depth': 2}	0.605464	0.616487	0.605735	0.606183
2	0.040063	0.006354	0.008105	0.000896	3	{'max_depth': 3}	0.649798	0.652330	0.648746	0.655018
3	0.043027	0.003465	0.007007	0.007217	4	{'max_depth': 4}	0.672638	0.680556	0.669803	0.674283
4	0.047670	0.004696	0.008099	0.003841	5	{'max_depth': 5}	0.682938	0.689068	0.676523	0.680556

Figure 6.9: *Shape and first 5 records of the dataset*

There are 15 rows in the dataset - one for each parameter value/combination tried. There are 19 columns giving you rich detail about each fit. Go ahead and explore the dataset and see for yourself the details available. You will see that it does a lot of work for us while requiring minimal coding skills for us. We will use this detailed information shortly to see the utility of having all this in addition to the highest accuracy.

GridSearchCV with multiple hyper-parameters

The true utility of GridSearchCV is apparent when tuning multiple hyper-parameters at once. The hyper-parameters and their values to be tried are supplied as a dictionary to 'param_grid' - this is all the change you need to do in code to work with several hyper-parameters.

Let us continue with the Decision Tree example and tune several hyper-parameters at once. We will tune - **`max_depth`**, **`max_features`**, and **`min_samples_leaf`**. Use the following code to set up the parameter grid:

```
hyper_params = {'max_depth': [3, 5, 7, 9, 11, 13, 15],
                'max_features': [3, 4, 5, 6, 7],
                'min_samples_leaf': [5, 10, 15, 20, 35, 50]
               }
```

It should be easy to understand the combinations we are trying here. We are trying multiple depth values - 3 to 15 in increments of 2. We are trying **`max_features`** from 3 to 7. We are also trying to find the best value for **`min_samples_leaf`** among [5, 10, 15, 20, 35, 50]. GridSearchCV will try all combinations of these hyper-parameters. How many combinations would there be? As many as the product of the number of unique values being tried for each hyper-parameter - 7 x 5 x 6, i.e., 210 combinations.

Let us now use GridSearchCV to find the best combination of these 3 hyper-parameters - by supplying the hyper-parameter grid and fitting on the train data using the following code:

```
model_cv = GridSearchCV(estimator=dt,
                param_grid=hyper_params,
                verbose=1,
                cv=4,
                n_jobs=-1,
                return_train_score=True)

model_cv.fit(X_train, y_train)
```

You should get the following output:

```
Fitting 4 folds for each of 210 candidates, totalling 840 fits
GridSearchCV(cv=4, estimator=DecisionTreeClassifier(random_state=42), n_jobs=-1,
             param_grid={'max_depth': [3, 5, 7, 9, 11, 13, 15],
                         'max_features': [3, 4, 5, 6, 7],
                         'min_samples_leaf': [5, 10, 15, 20, 35, 50]},
             return_train_score=True, verbose=1)
```

Figure 6.10: GridSearchCV fit output

We see that there are 210 candidates, just as we expected, and that there are a total of 840 fits (since we are using a 4-fold CV scheme). Note that this number can significantly increase with just one more parameter as the candidates would increase in a multiplicative manner.

Now that the search is complete, what is the best hyper-parameter combination? And what is its performance? Use the following code to find out:

```
print(model_cv.best_estimator_)
print(model_cv.best_score_)
```

```
print(model_cv.best_estimator_)
print(model_cv.best_score_)

DecisionTreeClassifier(max_depth=13, max_features=7, min_samples_leaf=15,
                       random_state=42)
0.6983983025070345
```

Figure 6.11: Best DT hyperparameters and score

The best estimator is one with the following hyper-parameters:

```
max_depth: 13
max_features: 7
min_samples_leaf: 15
```

This is the hyper-parameter combination that would give us the best generalized accuracy.

The effect of each hyper-parameter

We saw earlier that the cv_results_ attribute of the trained GridSearchCV contains detailed performance information for each combination. Since all combinations of the hyper-parameters have been tried, this data is useful to us. It can tell us how, on average, the performance of the estimator changes with the value of the hyper-parameter. This can easily be plotted to give us a great visual summary of the effect of the hyper-parameter on the performance.

First, we load the results into a Pandas dataframe, inspect it, and understand what details we have to work with:

```
cv_df = pd.DataFrame(model_cv.cv_results_)
print(cv_df.shape)
cv_df.columns
```

You'll see in the following output that there are 210 rows in the dataframe, corresponding to the 210 candidates/combinations:

```
(210, 21)
Index(['mean_fit_time', 'std_fit_time', 'mean_score_time', 'std_score_time',
       'param_max_depth', 'param_max_features', 'param_min_samples_leaf',
       'params', 'split0_test_score', 'split1_test_score', 'split2_test_score',
       'split3_test_score', 'mean_test_score', 'std_test_score',
       'rank_test_score', 'split0_train_score', 'split1_train_score',
       'split2_train_score', 'split3_train_score', 'mean_train_score',
       'std_train_score'],
      dtype='object')
```

Figure 6.12: *Columns available in the CV results*

Let us take a look at the top 3 records to understand the values contained in the columns beginning with 'param':

```
cv_df.head(3)
```

	mean_fit_time	std_fit_time	mean_score_time	std_score_time	param_max_depth	param_max_features	param_min_samples_leaf	params
0	0.018949	0.000706	0.006982	0.000705	3	3	5	{'max_depth': 3, 'max_features': 3, 'min_sampl...
1	0.023457	0.004085	0.006483	0.000498	3	3	10	{'max_depth': 3, 'max_features': 3, 'min_sampl...
2	0.019199	0.000432	0.007230	0.000432	3	3	15	{'max_depth': 3, 'max_features': 3, 'min_sampl...

Figure 6.13: First 3 records from the CV results

There are many columns in the dataframe. We are interested in the parameter values, **mean_train_score** (training accuracy), and **mean_test_score** (cross-validation accuracy) column. The hyper-parameter values for the candidate tried are conveniently available in the columns beginning with 'param'. We can use this to see the average train and cross-validation accuracy at a certain value of the hyper-parameter and observe how the accuracy changes with the values tried. You can do so using the following code:

```
res = cv_df.groupby('param_max_depth')['mean_train_score', 'mean_test_
score'].mean()
res.plot(figsize=[8,5])
plt.show()
```

You should get the following output:

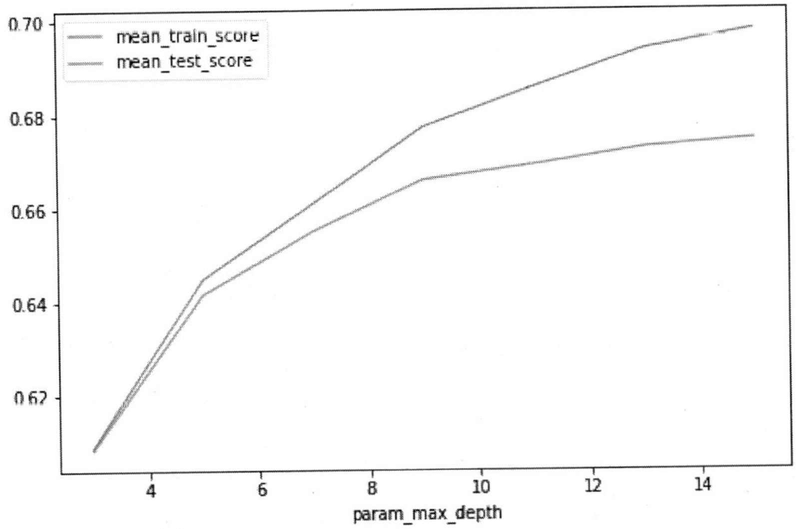

Figure 6.14: Avg cross val score for max_depth candidates

Take a moment to understand this plot. You have the training accuracy and cross-validation accuracy for each value of the hyper-parameter. What do you infer from the plot?

As the **max_depth** increases, the training accuracy as well as the cross-validation accuracy increase. The cross-validation accuracy increases significantly at first but almost flattens at around 0.67. The train score increases at a much faster rate and continues to do so.

Pause and ponder: Look at the plot in *Figure 6.14*. Is the model overfitting? If yes, at what depth does it start to overfit?

Hint: Be mindful of the scale of the Y axis before concluding.

Let us see the impact of **min_samples_leaf**. This is also an important parameter that affects the tree growth and ensures the leaf nodes aren't smaller than the specified value. Use the following code:

```
res = cv_df.groupby('param_min_samples_leaf')['mean_train_score', 'mean_
test_score'].mean()
res.plot(figsize=[8,5])
plt.show()
```

You should get the following output:

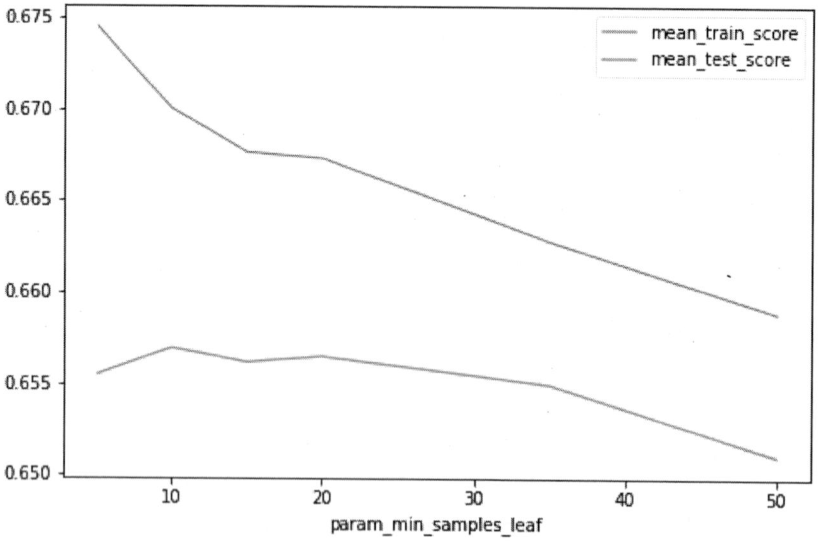

***Figure 6.15:** Effect of min_samples_leaf hyper-parameter*

The effect of the **min_samples_leaf** hyper-parameter is rather interesting. As the value increases, the training accuracy seems to be dropping significantly. The test score however is stable between 0.65 and 0.655 - all values are performing the same on the test set. So, it looks like lowering the value is only leading to overfitting and is not helping with the generalized model performance.

Task 2: Perform a similar analysis for the hyper-parameter 'max_features'. What pattern do you observe and how do you explain it? What do you infer from the analysis?

Thus, with some simple commands, you can understand the impact of each hyper-parameter on the model performance. This was possible because of the detailed information that GridSearchCV stores for each run, requiring minimal code from us. Very useful indeed! This seems like a great method and indeed it is. But it is not perfect. We must study its drawbacks as well, as we will do in the next section.

Limitations of exhaustive methods (looping, GridSearchCV)

The manual looping method is great if you need to customize metrics and want perfect control over the processing. The GridSearchCV method is also great because it simplifies the code tremendously and gives you rich performance information by default. Both these methods are of the 'exhaustive' type, i.e., they need to go through every candidate in a dumb fashion to identify the best. These approaches work fine for quick-to-train algorithms like Decision Trees, Logistic Regression, etc. and small-sized datasets where you could perform hundreds of fits in a few minutes. But when you have large datasets and are employing computationally heavy algorithms, you need to look further. Let us understand the limitations of these exhaustive methods first.

We will continue with the Bank marketing example. The dataset is rather small (about 8K observations) and we expect quick run times. For this small dataset, we will employ the RandomForest algorithm. We will tune the same parameters we did earlier while keeping the number of estimators fixed at 100. Note that the number of estimators is an important hyper-parameter and should be tuned, but we'll omit it for simplicity. For this simple setup, we will note the execution time (%%time cell magic in Jupyter). First, let us import **RandomForestClassifier** and instantiate:

```
from sklearn.ensemble import RandomForestClassifier
rf = RandomForestClassifier(n_estimators=100, random_state=42, n_jobs=-1)
```

We specified the number of estimators (**n_estimators**), fixed **random_state** for reproducible results, and specified **n_jobs** as -1 to use all possible cores for quicker execution. We will use the same **param_grid** we used for our Decision Tree model. Tune the hyper-parameters and observe the timing using the following code:

```
hyper_params = {'max_depth': [3, 5, 7, 9, 11, 13, 15],
                'max_features': [3, 4, 5, 6, 7],
                'min_samples_leaf': [5, 10, 15, 20, 35, 50]
               }

rf_grids = GridSearchCV(estimator=rf,
```

```
                param_grid=hyper_params,
                verbose=1,
                cv=4,
                n_jobs=-1,
                return_train_score=True)
```

```
%%time
rf_grids.fit(X_train, y_train)
```

You should get the following output:

```
%%time
rf_grids.fit(X_train, y_train)

Fitting 4 folds for each of 210 candidates, totalling 840 fits
Wall time: 2min 5s

GridSearchCV(cv=4, estimator=RandomForestClassifier(n_jobs=-1, random_state=42),
             n_jobs=-1,
             param_grid={'max_depth': [3, 5, 7, 9, 11, 13, 15],
                         'max_features': [3, 4, 5, 6, 7],
                         'min_samples_leaf': [5, 10, 15, 20, 35, 50]},
             return_train_score=True, verbose=1)
```

Figure 6.16: Output of the fit command

Note: The run time here is indicative and of course, varies with the system you are using. Nevertheless, the relative duration of tasks should be similar. So, if you're comparing the timings of different approaches, the inference should be the same.

The number of fits remains the same as earlier, as we didn't change the parameter grid or the cross-validation scheme. The *%%time* cell magic tells us that the cell took more than 2 minutes* to run. Now that the search is complete, let us see the best hyper-parameter combination it found and the cross-validation accuracy of the best estimator:

```
print(rf_grids.best_estimator_)
print(rf_grids.best_score_)
```

You will get the following output:

```
print(rf_grids.best_estimator_)
print(rf_grids.best_score_)
```

```
RandomForestClassifier(max_depth=15, max_features=5, min_samples_leaf=5,
                       n_jobs=-1, random_state=42)
0.7199025251722693
```

Figure 6.17: *Best RF estimator and score*

The hyper-parameter combination is different from what we got earlier. This is not surprising because the model is now very different. The accuracy of the best estimator is significantly higher at about 72%.

Pause and ponder: The best hyper-parameter set for Random Forest is somewhat different from the Decision Tree. Which difference in hyper-parameter seems most significant to you? Also, the accuracy is significantly higher now. Is this expected?

Let us discuss the timing a bit. 2 minutes does seem like a lot. But consider this - we used a rather small dataset (~8K records) and limited hyper-parameters. What if we used the same setup (same hyper-parameters) on a dataset with 200K records? Surely, the timing would be several times higher. We didn't even try a different number of estimators - it is not uncommon to try several hundred estimators. What if we also try more values of n_estimators and other hyper-parameters on a dataset having, say, 500K records? The run time estimate would be in hours, or even days.

A training time of days is not very practical for many industry scenarios. This is a limitation of the exhaustive approach (even after parallelizing and using all processing cores).

Key takeaway: Exhaustive methods are great for small datasets as they are thorough. However, they require a lot of time and computation which could make them impractical in situations with large datasets and many hyper-parameters.

Exhaustive methods are great because you can be as thorough as you want and can be confident that all possible specified values have been tried. With manual looping, you have far more control over the processing and the information you store. GridSearchCV is another solution that gives you richer information using minimal code. But both these approaches struggle with large datasets. While useful, both these approaches were dumb in the sense that they tried every possible combination. These work very hard but we need approaches that work Smarter as well. We need approaches that, instead of going through all the possible candidates, allow us to identify high-potential candidates and zone in into them quickly. One such approach is RandomizedSearchCV. Let us understand and explore this approach.

RandomizedSearchCV

The approach used by RandomizedSearchCV is different. Instead of going over all hyper-parameter values, sampling is done to try out a fixed number of times. Consider a situation in which you are tuning multiple hyper-parameters and the number of candidates (unique combinations) is 2,000. GridSearchCV would try all 2,000 candidates. But if you use RandomizedSearchCV and specify that you want to try at most 50 combinations, RandomizedSearchCV honours it. This is the first major difference and you can see that this can reduce the run time significantly. But how does RandomizedSearchCV select those 50 from the 2,000 candidates?

Here is where the 'Randomized' in the name comes from. RandomizedSearchCV randomly selects the 50 (or any specified number) combinations. There's another difference in the way the values are tried. Grid Search tries only the values that are available in the grid. For continuous hyper-parameters (for example, learning rate of Boosting), this isn't ideal because you need to provide discrete steps or very limited values. Whereas with RandomizedSearchCV, you can specify that the hyper-parameter is continuous and can even use a distribution to pick the values. This makes the search much better for continuous hyper-parameters. The difference in the approaches is illustrated in *Figure 6.18*:

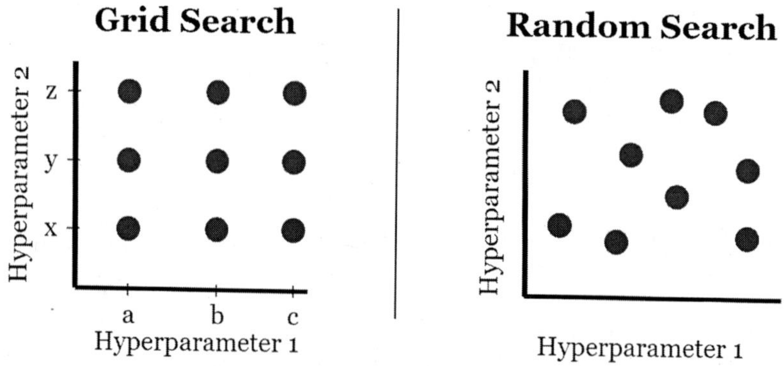

Figure 6.18: *Grid Search vs. Randomized Search*

Figure 6.18 shows a situation with two hyper-parameters. GridSearchCV searches only values from the grid. Whereas RandomizedSearchCV can choose randomly from the search space and potentially values 'off the grid'.

Pause and ponder: Do you think there are benefits of Randomized Search (other than speed)? Do you expect Randomized Search to work as well as Grid Search? If yes, under what conditions?

Hint: Randomized Search is faster but at the cost of thoroughness. But it can explore values different from Grid Search.

Let us see RandomizedSearchCV in action on our data and see for ourselves what kind of results we get. To begin, import **RandomizedSearchCV** from **sklearn.model_selection** and instantiate the **RandomForestClassifier** estimator as in the following code. Use the same hyper-parameter grid that we used for GridSearchCV:

```
from sklearn.model_selection import RandomizedSearchCV


rf = RandomForestClassifier(n_estimators=100, random_state=42, n_jobs=-1)


hyper_params = {'max_depth': [3, 5, 7, 9, 11, 13, 15],
                'max_features': [3, 4, 5, 6, 7],
                'min_samples_leaf': [5, 10, 15, 20, 35, 50]
               }
```

Next, instantiate **RandomSearchCV** and supply to it the estimator, the hyper-parameter grid, a 4-fold cross-validation scheme using the code below. The syntax for RandomizedSearchCV is very close to that of GridSearchCV:

```
rf_randoms = RandomizedSearchCV(estimator=rf,
             param_distributions=hyper_params,
             cv=4,
             n_iter=10,
             verbose=1,
             n_jobs=-1)
```

Note: In the preceding example, we specified values by manually creating lists. It is also possible to provide ranges and even distributions. For example, you could provide a uniform distribution using scipy.stats (or any other distribution). For continuous hyper-parameters, using distributions allows you to search for more possible values.

Notice that we have **param_distributions** for RandomizedSearchCV where we had **param_grid**. For GridSearchCV. As mentioned, this is because you can also supply distributions instead of a list of values. Also note the value of `n_iter`. This tells RandomizedSearchCV to try not more than 10 combinations. Of course, this is something you can change. But to begin, let us use this small value and see what outcome we get. Let us tune these hyper-parameters, the same way we did earlier, using the 'fit' method. Use %%time cell magic to record the execution time.

```
%%time
rf_randoms.fit(X_train, y_train)
```

The output should be as below:

```
%%time
rf_randoms.fit(X_train, y_train)
```

```
Fitting 4 folds for each of 10 candidates, totalling 40 fits
Wall time: 4.05 s

RandomizedSearchCV(cv=4,
                   estimator=RandomForestClassifier(n_jobs=-1, random_state=42),
                   n_jobs=-1,
                   param_distributions={'max_depth': [3, 5, 7, 9, 11, 13, 15],
                                        'max_features': [3, 4, 5, 6, 7],
                                        'min_samples_leaf': [5, 10, 15, 20, 35,
                                                             50]},
                   verbose=1)
```

***Figure 6.19**: Output of RandomizedSearch*

You can see that we are trying 10 candidates - as expected because we specified **`n_iter`** as 10. But look at the time it took - just 4 seconds! GridSearchCV took about 140 seconds. The difference in execution time should not be very surprising because we're trying very few combinations in comparison to GridSearch (210). We got the speed we wanted. But is the result any good and is the best hyper-parameter set close? Let us find out by extracting the best estimator and its accuracy:

```
print(rf_grids.best_estimator_)
print(rf_grids.best_score_)
```

The output you get is as shown in *Figure 6.20*:

```
print(rf_randoms.best_estimator_)
print(rf_randoms.best_score_)
```

```
RandomForestClassifier(max_depth=15, max_features=5, min_samples_leaf=5,
                       n_jobs=-1, random_state=42)
0.7199025251722693
```

***Figure 6.20**: Best estimator and score*

Compare this with the best estimator and accuracy from Grid Search. You will see that it is the same result. We got the same result in a fraction of the time! Did we simply get lucky? Perhaps. But this raises an important question - which of the two approaches performs better, or how do we choose between them? We will answer this in the next section.

Grid Search versus Randomized Search

Grid Search and Randomized Search are very different approaches and comparing them boils down to comparing the merits of one approach over the other - exhaustive search versus randomized search.

We reiterate that each method has its advantages, but you also need to know about and benefit from the extensive research that has been done on this topic.

In 2012, *Bergstra* and *Bengio* (**https://www.jmlr.org/papers/v13/bergstra12a.html**) extensively studied the performance of both methods on various datasets. They also employed various algorithms ranging from extremely simple to complex algorithms like Deep Belief Nets. They showed that Random Search performs as well as Grid Search in most cases, even beating it in some cases. This may seem counterintuitive at first, because we have good reasons to be pragmatic, such as:

- Grid Search is thorough, while Random Search is not.
- Random Search is much faster, we expect to lose some performance to achieve this speed.

It turns out, there are a few reasons for the good performance on Random Search.

The first is that in real-world situations, especially with a high number of predictors and a fair volume of data - there exist multiple local minima. Meaning that there isn't necessarily a unique, golden solution that outperforms all the rest. Rather, many good solutions are close to each other in performance. With the random sampling that Random Search does, with enough number of iterations, there is a good chance that you encounter one of these 'good' solutions.

The second reason is that not all hyper-parameters are equally important to tune. Grid Search was very exhaustive in evaluating all the combinations. Many of these combinations were simply wasteful because they were variations on unimportant hyper-parameters. So, even if Random Search searches fewer combinations, it doesn't necessarily lose many valuable combinations.

The third major reason is that Random Search can explore more and do a finer search. This is especially true when you provide distributions for continuous hyper-parameters. Grid Search searches 'on the grid' and is therefore limited in what it can try. If as a user you made the search intervals too granular, Grid Search would not perform well. Consider *Figure 6.21*, which is an example from the 2012 paper by Bergstra and Bengio. The example beautifully illustrates this. In the data, the performance is extremely sensitive to the important hyper-parameter in a small interval where the true maximum lies. The Grid Search intervals could be broad and miss this. Randomized Search, on the other hand, is more exploratory and has a higher chance of discovering the true maxima because it is not forced to follow the wide, rigid intervals. This is illustrated in *Figure 6.21*:

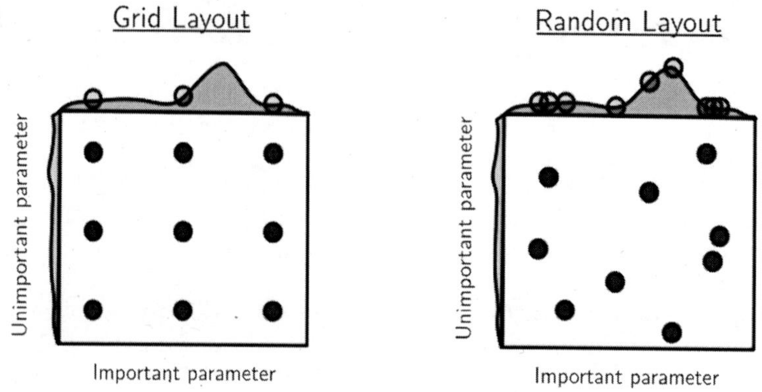

Figure 6.21: *Grid Search vs. Random Search*

Choosing a hyper-parameter search approach

We have seen different approaches and it is natural to ask - how do we choose? Is there a 'best method'? Here are some tips and considerations to help you choose the best approach for your situation.

If the dataset is small and the number of hyper-parameters is small, then you can use either Grid Search or Randomized Search. If the hyper-parameters to search have all integer values, then the Grid Search option is the most thorough. But if you have many continuous hyper-parameters, a Random Search with a higher number of iterations will make the search more exhaustive.

If you are using a computation-heavy algorithm on a large dataset, then Random Search is a more attractive option. Especially if the number of hyper-parameters is large. In such a case, Random Search may be the only feasible option. Even if the algorithm is quick but there are many hyper-parameters, Grid Search may not be feasible as it may need to try several combinations for a large dataset.

If you want highly customized metrics and want to record information that is not captured by Random Search or Grid Search, you may want to manually loop over the hyper-parameters. This option gives you the most control and may be the only feasible one in specific situations.

Note: Another approach gaining popularity is performing Bayesian optimization over hyper-parameters. The approach does not perform an exhaustive search. A fixed number of parameter combinations is sampled from the specified distributions. The key difference from random search is that the search is directed using Bayes Theorem. A handy implementation is available in scikit-optimize as BayesSearchCV. Read more about it here: https://scikit-optimize.github.io/stable/modules/generated/skopt.BayesSearchCV.html

Having stated the above, please bear in mind that these are merely guidelines and may not address all situations. In such a case, understand the constraints and requirements of your project and choose. In case you have the time, it is wise to explore both Grid Search and Random Search approaches and maybe even use them in succession. Indeed, another good idea could be to use both - maybe use Random Search for coarse tuning, followed by Grid Search for fine-tuning. There are no set rules and you can be creative in finding out what works best for you.

Pause and ponder: Hyper-parameter tuning is essentially a search activity and there are various search/optimization algorithms to quickly find the maximum/minimum. Can you think of any search approach that can be used for hyper-parameter tuning?

Choosing the 'best' model

In this section, we will discuss the notion of 'best'. We have already discussed in *Chapter 4, Model Evaluation and Debugging*, that the notion of 'best' depends on the context and objective. At the beginning of this chapter, we presented 3 different situations where the objective and constraints were different. To understand the ideas and the considerations better, let us revisit the example where we did manual looping and re-examine the results:

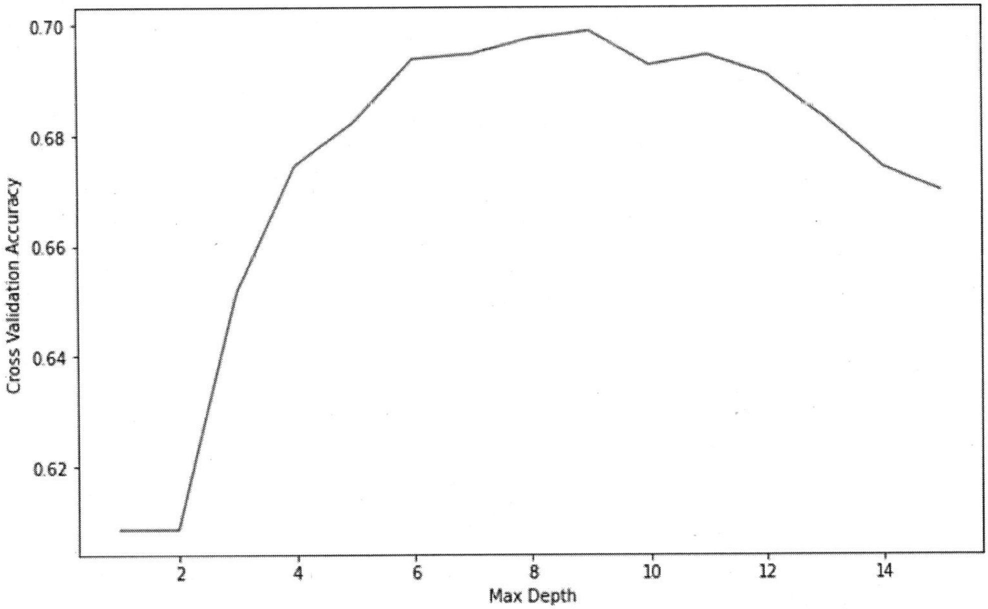

Figure 6.22: Manual looping for Bank marketing example

Note that while maximum accuracy was achieved when 'max_depth' was 9, the other values were quite close. At depth 6 too, the accuracy was above 69% (it is 69.4%, to be precise). At this stage, you should think if the slight gain in accuracy is worth the 3 extra levels of decisions and the added complexity. Furthermore, if the highest accuracy is not paramount and interpretation is important, then you should seriously consider choosing a depth 4 where you have around 68% accuracy and much higher interpretation (compared to depth 9). In the situation that we started the chapter off with - where interpretation is important and accuracy needs to be reasonable, depth 4 would be the preferred choice.

Note: It is also possible to use multiple metrics and derive a notion of *best*. The *scoring* argument of the search method accepts a customer scoring function. A simple example can be found at: https://scikit-learn.org/stable/modules/model_evaluation.html#multimetric-scoring.

Let us also revisit the Grid Search results for the Decision Tree that we had stored in a **`dataframe (cv_df )`**. Instead of looking at all the columns, we will limit ourselves to the hyper-parameters that we tuned and the 'mean_test_score'. We will look at the top 20 hyper-parameter combinations by sorting on the **`mean_test_score`** column. Use the following code:

```
sel_cols = ['param_max_depth',
            'param_max_features',
            'param_min_samples_leaf',
            'mean_test_score']

cv_df.sort_values(by='mean_test_score', ascending=False)[sel_cols]\
        .head(20)\
        .reset_index(drop=True)
```

The best 10 performers get printed as in *Figure 6.23*. We can see that all the top 20 models are very close in performance. Let us say that we define 'best' as the model which gives us good performance while being the simplest. Which of the following hyper-parameter combinations is 'best'?

	param_max_depth	param_max_features	param_min_samples_leaf	mean_test_score
0	13	7	15	0.698398
1	13	7	10	0.694814
2	13	7	20	0.694255
3	15	7	20	0.693583
4	15	7	10	0.693023
5	15	7	15	0.692575
6	11	7	10	0.691567
7	11	5	10	0.691456
8	11	7	15	0.691454
9	11	5	5	0.690447
10	15	7	5	0.690447
11	15	7	35	0.689327
12	9	5	10	0.689216
13	13	7	35	0.688992
14	11	7	20	0.688878
15	9	5	5	0.687424
16	13	5	20	0.687311
17	13	7	5	0.686191
18	11	5	20	0.685967
19	15	7	50	0.685631

***Figure 6.23:** The top 20 models from Grid Search*

The answer changes. When we looked purely at performance, the first set (index 0) was the best. But with the new definition of 'best' that includes simplicity as a criterion, the 13th combination (index 12) is far more appealing.

Training on the entire data and making predictions

So far, we used a cross-validation scheme to evaluate the hyper-parameter candidates. Because of this, we never trained a model on the full training data. Even 'best_estimator_' from Grid Search or Random Search was based on the cross-validation score. For a 4-fold cross-validation scheme, we use at most 75% of the training data, using the remaining 25% as validation. Therefore, our estimates of generalized performance are derived from models that did not see the entire training data. Why not use the entire training data?

At the end of the hyper-parameter tuning activity, we know the best hyper-parameter combination. The next step is to use these hyper-parameters and train the model on the entire training set. This way, the best hyper-parameter combination gets the most data to train the best model.

Let us do this for our example. For simplicity, we will define best as 'highest accuracy'. We begin by extracting the best estimator from Grid Search by using the 'best_estimator_' attribute. We then train it on the entire training dataset. Use the following code:

```
dt_best = model_cv.best_estimator_
dt_best.fit(X_train, y_train)
```

You should see the following output which confirms that the model has been trained:

```
dt_best.fit(X_train, y_train)

DecisionTreeClassifier(max_depth=13, max_features=7, min_samples_leaf=15,
                       random_state=42)
```

***Figure 6.24**: Decision Tree has been fit*

Next, we come to the true test of the model - its performance on an unseen dataset, that is, the test dataset that we had set apart in the beginning. We will make predictions using the 'predict' method of the Decision Tree classifier and calculate the accuracy score. Use the following code:

```
y_test_pred = dt_best.predict(X_test)
print(accuracy_score(y_test, y_test_pred))
```

The output accuracy is about 68%. This is good and not significantly different from the estimates from the cross-validation score. The performance of the chosen hyper-parameters is indeed generalizable on unseen datasets.

The complete process

This completes the process of hyper-parameter tuning and using the best resulting model. A high-level summary of the steps involved is as below. For a dataset and a modeling algorithm:

1. Define the hyper-parameter combinations you want to evaluate.
2. Use any hyper-parameter search approach and evaluate the candidates.
3. Use cross-validation scores with metrics of choice to measure performance.
4. Choose the 'best' candidates as per your requirements.
5. Train on the entire training data with the best hyper-parameters.
6. Evaluate true model performance using the test set.

It is important to remember that there are many choices that you, the Data Scientist, need to make. These could be choices on the search approach to use or the candidates for a given search approach. Also important is the definition of 'best' for the resulting models.

Conclusion

In getting the best out of the data and modeling algorithm, choosing the right hyper-parameters is an important step. Hyper-parameters are parameters that are external to the model - these are not learnt by the algorithm, but can significantly impact how it learns and influences the resulting model. We saw three approaches to hyper-parameter tuning, beginning with the simplest approach that gives you the most control and flexibility - manually looping over the hyper-parameter candidates. The Grid Search approach is an improvement over manual looping in the sense that it provides far more information with minimal code.

Both these approaches are exhaustive, evaluating every candidate, and are therefore 'dumb'. Random Search randomly selects a pre-specified number of candidates for evaluation and can handle continuous hyper-parameters better. We implemented and contrasted all of these approaches in a banking case study and also learned from research on the topic. We are now conversant with hyper-parameter tuning, which is an extremely important step in optimizing our machine-learning models,

Now that we understand how to optimize how a modelling algorithm learns, let us turn our attention to a common challenge in supervised machine learning – imbalanced classes. *Chapter 5, Imbalanced Machine Learning,* will teach you the issues with imbalanced classes and how to handle them to optimize the machine learning model and derive maximum impact from the solution.

CHAPTER 7

Parameter Optimization Algorithms

Introduction

Mathematical optimization is at the core of machine learning. All machine learning algorithms, whether supervised, unsupervised, or reinforcement learning, use optimization. Machine learning is essentially learning patterns from data. For instance, supervised machine learning approaches attempt to capture the relationships in the data and best predict the dependent variable. A good model's predictions are sufficiently close to the true values, that is, it minimizes the difference between the true and the predicted value. This is a form of optimization, as you may have recognized.

Likewise, other machine learning styles also perform optimization in one way or the other and the practitioner benefits from understanding this. Understanding the fundamentals of mathematical optimization helps practitioners understand the workings of the models and helps them make important choices (for example, we will learn loss function and optimization algorithm in this chapter) to maximize the performance of the model.

Structure

In this chapter, we will discuss the following topics:

- Optimization in machine learning
- Fundamentals of numerical optimization

- Objective/loss function
- Local and global optima
- Convex vs. non-convex loss functions

- Numerical optimization for machine learning
  - Regression
  - Classification
  - Regularization
- A general solving approach
  - Stopping criterion
  - Gradient descent
- Faster gradient descent variants
  - Momentum
  - AdaGrad optimizer
  - RMSProp optimizer
  - Adam optimizer
  - Choosing the optimization approach

Objectives

In this chapter, we will first obtain a general understanding of the essential components of mathematical optimization. We will then see how it is contextualized for machine learning and discuss some aspects that make optimization for machine learning unique. Further, we will learn a general, principled approach to solving optimization problems. The variations developed for machine learning, especially deep neural networks, will then be discussed. We will implement these methods using a hands-on case study. By the end of this chapter, you will be able to learn the optimization algorithms for modern machine learning and make all the right choices to develop a truly optimized machine learning solution.

Optimization in machine learning

Machine learning, regardless of the style (supervised vs. unsupervised), learns patterns from data. To learn these patterns, the machine learning algorithm must optimize some outcomes. For example, in supervised machine learning, we try to capture the relationship between the independent and the dependent variables. Naturally, we want the model to describe the relationship accurately and our errors to be as low as possible. Fitting the model is learning these patterns.

We have fit many models in this book so far. The process of fitting the model is essentially optimization - finding the model parameters that best describe the data. For example, in linear regression, fitting the model amounts to finding the right coefficients that best capture the relationships in the data (and therefore minimize errors). When we use the **`fit`** method in **`sklearn`**, it starts an optimization process in the background and fitting/training is complete when the optimization is finished.

In unsupervised learning, we look for structures/groups in the data. For example, clustering tries to find natural groups in the data and groups similar points. To evaluate any particular grouping of points and to iterate, there are numerical quantities that are minimized (for example, within the sum of squares for the k-means algorithm). An unsupervised approach like clustering also has optimization at its core. As another example, **Principal Component Analysis (PCA)** tries to find new features (principal components) that capture the information in the data. It is important to note how this loss in information is assessed. In simple terms, a reconstruction error is typically used - the difference between the original data and the reconstructed data (using the new principal components). This holds true for other dimensionality reduction methods as well.

As mentioned in the introduction, understanding the fundamentals of mathematical optimization helps practitioners understand the workings of the models and helps them make important choices in the model-building process. We will learn various aspects of optimization, contextualize them to machine learning, and discuss principled approaches to solving such optimization problems. Let us start by understanding key ideas and salient features of mathematical optimization.

Fundamentals of mathematical optimization

An optimization problem consists of the following three components.

- An objective function, f(x), that needs to be minimized or maximized
- Decision variables, x, that can be chosen
- Constraints that need to be respected

Let us begin by understanding the most important and consequential component first, the objective function, also known as the loss function.

Objective/loss functions

The objective/loss function measures the quality of optimization for any given set of parameters. Finding the choice of parameters for which the loss function has the optimal (minimum) value is the objective of the optimization process. The objective function must therefore be expressed as a function of the parameters to tweak. A general articulation of the loss function in terms of parameters is as follows:

$$\textit{Loss function: } f(w) = f(w_1, w_2, \ldots, w_n)$$

Where w_1 through w_2 are the n parameters to tweak.

The function *f* can be a simple, linear combination of the parameters, or a complex function involving multiple transformations on the parameters. This relationship between the parameters and the loss function is a choice to be made by the modeler. In the machine learning context, different techniques have different objective/loss functions defined.

The loss function needs to be carefully chosen, it captures your intent behind optimization and naturally has a big impact on the result. As mentioned earlier, most/all machine learning algorithms optimize. Supervised machine learning methods have a loss function that must be minimized. The loss function usually captures the difference (in some form) between the actual values and the predicted values.

Note: The design of the loss function can lead to an entirely different algorithm. A good example is the regularization of the loss function for multiple linear regression. The form of the coefficients in the loss function leads to a Ridge (square of the coefficient) or a Lasso (absolute value of coefficient) regularization.

The shape of the loss function plays an extremely important role in whether there can be a good solution to the optimization problem. It is possible that the solution we find is not the best overall solution, but just one of the many **local minima**. Let us understand these concepts better.

Local and global optima

Mathematical optimization works by finding stationary points in the data. These are the points where the slope of the curve becomes 0. Mathematically, these are points where the derivative is 0. *Figure 7.1* illustrates the different types of stationary points. While the diagram is for one parameter, the principles apply to multiple parameters as well. Take a look at *Figure 7.1*:

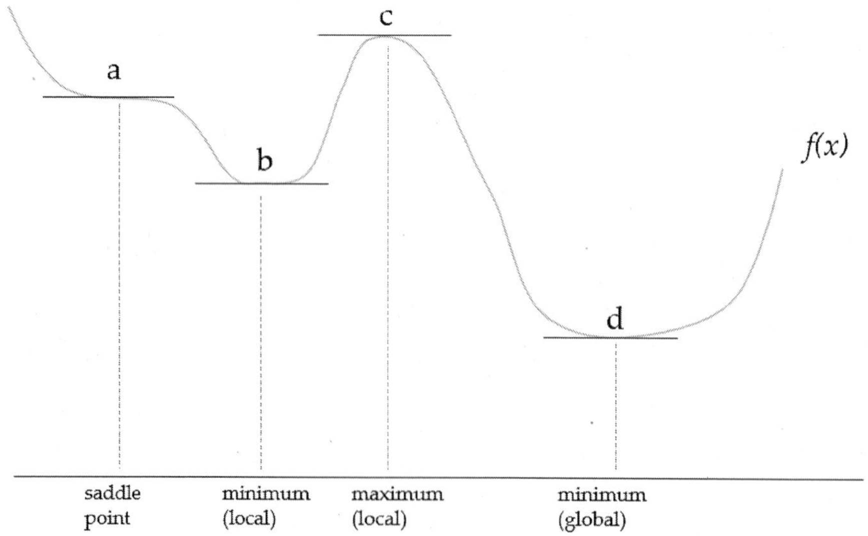

Figure 7.1: *Types of stationary points for a loss function*

It is important to note that there could be more than one minimum to the loss function. In *Figure 7.1,* both points b and d are minima. However, point d is the global minimum while point b is just a local minimum. Point c is a local maxima, as the function has higher values for very low values of x. You may have surmised that finding the global minimum is challenging for functions with multiple stationary points and minima. This property of a function, that defines if it has multiple optima, is called **convexity**. Let us understand this important concept.

Convex vs. non-convex loss functions

The convexity of a curve is simplest to understand visually with the help of a 1D function. In simple terms, the convex function is shaped like a cup. This leads to some properties that are very convenient for optimization. Most importantly, convex functions have strictly one minimum. For such a function, the local minimum and the global minimum are the same. These properties hold true even in very high-dimensional spaces. Additionally, optimization is easy because it does not matter where you start the optimization process from, you will end up at the global minimum. This is illustrated in *Figure 7.2:*

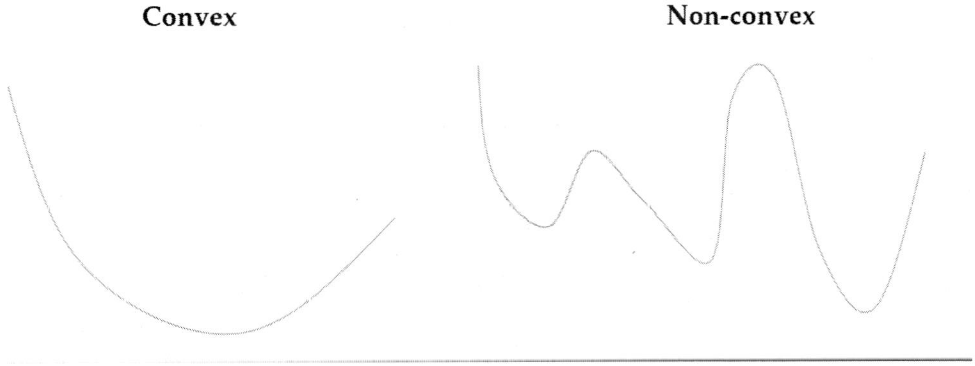

Figure 7.2: *Convex vs. non-convex loss functions*

In contrast, the non-convex function is more complex. It can have irregular shapes and multiple minima. One might end up at a local minimum while falsely believing they found the global one. Additionally, as we will discuss later in the chapter, the starting point for optimization makes a difference in the solution we end up with. This makes optimization more challenging for non-convex functions.

Numerical optimization for machine learning

In the previous section, we built a general understanding of numerical optimization. Let us now contextualize this understanding of machine learning and discover some nuances that make optimization for machine learning special. Let us first discuss the idea of loss functions for machine learning and look at some loss functions for popular machine learning algorithms.

Regression

For supervised regression problems, the machine learning model predicts a numeric value. Naturally, a good model's predictions are close to the true values. The loss function measures how far these values are. There are numerous ways to quantify this difference between the true and predicted values and therefore numerous choices for a loss function.

The most used plain vanilla linear regression algorithm is **Ordinary Least Squares (OLS)** regression. The method is named after the loss function: ordinary least squares. Specifically, the method minimizes the sum of the squares of the error, hence the name least squares. The loss function is also called **Residual Sum Squares (RSS)**:

$$RSS = \sum_{i=1}^{N} (y_i - \hat{y}_i)^2$$

The RSS loss function is convex, differentiable, and therefore easy to optimize. This is the default loss function for most implementations of linear regression. `Sklearn` also uses this loss function as its default. Other notable loss functions are the **Mean Absolute Error (MAE)** and the Huber loss. The Huber loss is a balance between RSS and MAE. Let us now look at some loss functions for classification.

Classification

In classification problems, the task is to identify the right label for a record. The output is usually a numerical value that captures the probability of the item belonging to a particular class. The probability is compared with the true label to assess the quality of the prediction. The cross-entropy loss or log loss captures this difference well. The loss function is defined as follows:

$$Log\ Loss = -\frac{1}{N}\sum_{i=1}^{N} y_i .\ log(\hat{y}_i) + (1 - y_i).log(1 - \hat{y}_i)$$

Note that in this equation $\hat{y}_i$ represents the probability score of the sample belonging to the class.

Note: In the equation for log loss, if the true label is 1 and the predicted probability is 0, the first term of the equation becomes which is negative infinity. In practice, a large negative constant is used instead to make the calculation feasible.

This loss function is convex and differentiable and therefore easy to optimize for. For this reason, log loss is by far the most common loss function applied for classification problems and is the default loss for most packages/algorithms.

There are several other options for loss for classification problems, each having its merits and demerits. Some of these loss functions have been visualized in *Figure 7.3*. These functions are available in **`sklearn`**.

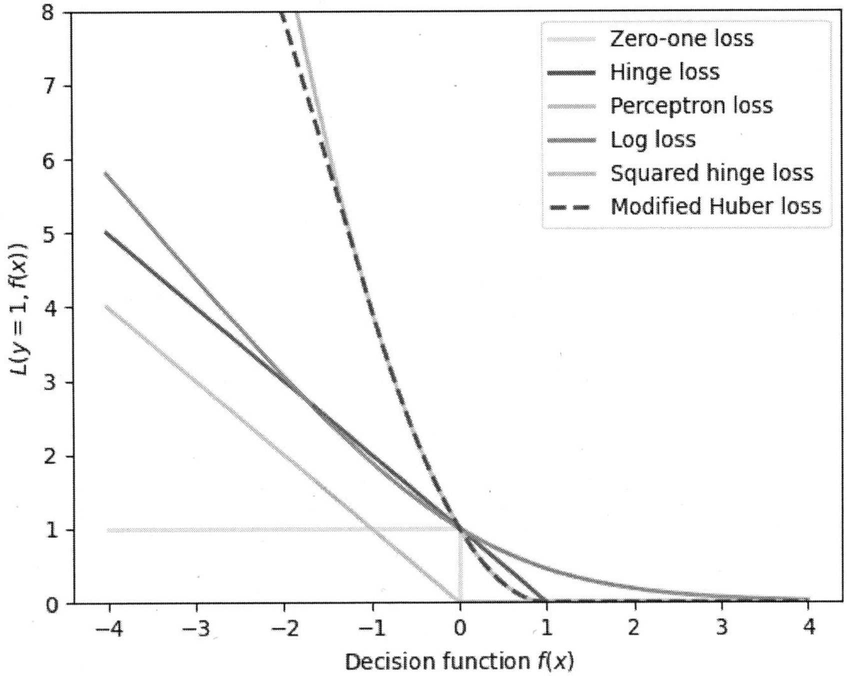

***Figure 7.3:** sklearn classification loss functions*

We have seen the general loss functions for classification as well as regression problems. Optimization of these functions with respect to the parameters amounts to training the model on the data. These loss functions are sufficient for simple use cases. In practice, you also need to be able to prevent overfitting by using regularization while model building. Modifying the loss function is a direct way to implement regularization. Let us look at regularization in depth in the next section.

Regularization

One of the approaches to regularization is to apply a penalty term in the loss function. The penalty term usually is on the parameter coefficient. Larger coefficients lead to larger penalties. This approach keeps the coefficients under control and in effect controls the flexibility and variance of the model. Such modification of the loss function is the most popular approach for regularization. For example, the loss function for Ridge regression (L2 penalty) is as follows:

$$Ridge\ Loss = RSS + \lambda \sum_{j=1}^{p} \beta_j^2$$

Where, the $RSS = \sum_{i=1}^{N} (y_i - \hat{y}_i)^2$

$\lambda \Sigma_j \beta_j^2$ is the penalty term added to the loss function for regular regression. The term is small when the values of β are close to 0. The penalty term therefore ensures lower values of the coefficients. The parameter λ is the tuning parameter which controls the impact of the regularization term. If λ is high, the coefficients get diminished more. Likewise, Lasso regression (L1 penalty) also has a penalty term proportional to the magnitude of the coefficient. Note that by contrast Ridge regression (L2 penalty) has a penalty term proportional to the square of the coefficients.

Most algorithms provide a regularization term. **`Scikit-learn`** in Python provides a **`penalty`** parameter that allows you to choose the penalty type you want to apply. Fitting the model at this point would optimize the modified loss function. This is a simple and direct way to modify the loss function to your benefit.

Now that we understand how loss functions are defined for typical machine learning problems, we also understand how minimizing this loss is formulated as a mathematical optimization problem. We are ready to learn how to solve these optimization problems. Let us learn a fundamental approach to doing so.

A general solving approach

Numerical optimization schemes for the minimization of a general function f work as follows:

- Start the minimization process from some initial point $w0$.
- Take iterative steps denoted by $w1$, $w2$, ..., going downhill towards a stationary point of f.
- Repeat step 2 until the sequence of points converges to a stationary point of f (or until a stopping criterion is met).
- The process starts at $w0$, which could be arbitrarily chosen. After the first downhill step we reach $w1$. After a few more steps we reach wk, which is the minimum for the function. This is illustrated in *Figure 7.4:*

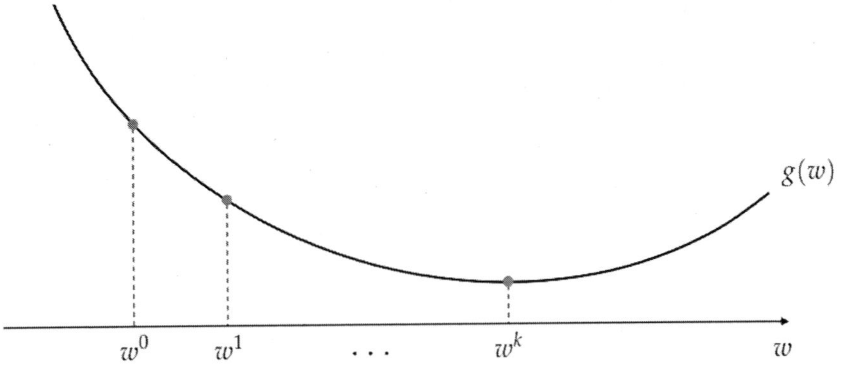

Figure 7.4: Descent method for optimization

The idea is simple conceptually. The important part is deciding mathematically the direction and size of the step. The most common approach (used extensively in machine learning) is **Gradient Descent**. Let us understand this method.

Gradient descent

The gradient descent method works by calculating the gradient (partial derivative) of the cost function with respect to the parameters. Recall that the derivative/gradient captures the slope of the function at that point. Therefore, the larger the gradient, the larger the increase in the cost function. The direction opposite to this is the direction of the **steepest descent**. Taking repeated steps, each time in the direction of the steepest descent (direction opposite to the gradient) will lead to a minimum. This is shown in *Figure 7.5*:

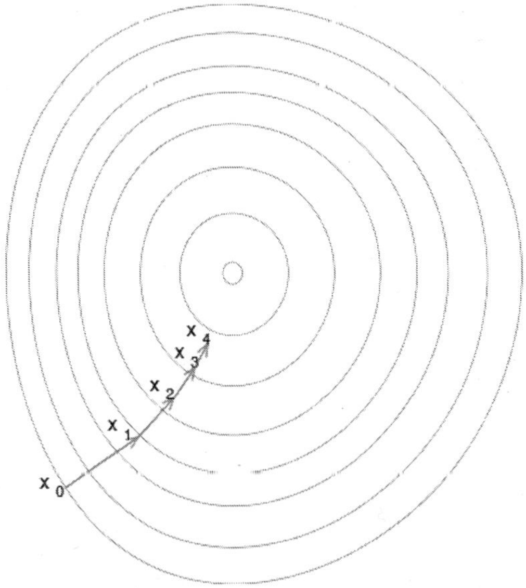

Figure 7.5: Gradient descent in a 2D parameter space

It is important to note that for convex cost functions, the local and global minima being the same, the gradient descent method would lead to the global minimum. For non-convex and complex cost functions, applying the method once will lead to a local minimum. This is illustrated in *Figure 7.6:*

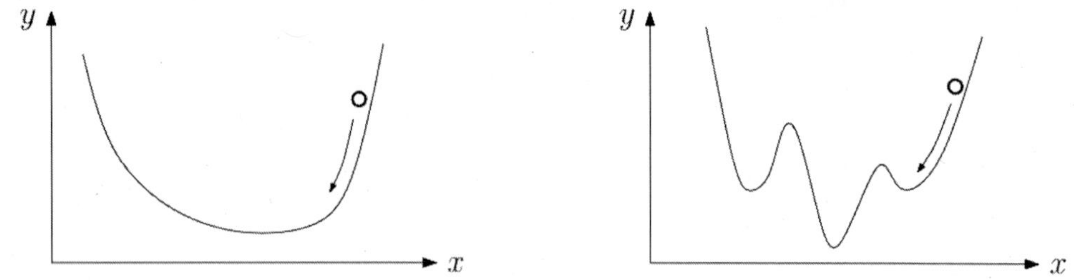

***Figure 7.6:** Gradient descent can lead to a local minima*

The stationary point of a non-convex function found via numerical optimization is dependent on the choice of initial point w_0. In the left panel in *Figure 7.7*, our initialization leads us to find the global minimum. In the right panel, the initialization can lead to the local minimum or the global minimum. Therefore, trying out different starting points and a high number of iterations is a common feature of modern optimization algorithms. We will discuss the ways to overcome this throughout the chapter.

The negative of the gradient provides the direction of the step. We must also define another hyper-parameter, the **size of the step** to take. This parameter is called the **learning rate** **(η)** of the optimizer. When the step size is too large, it can cause the optimization process to overshoot the minima. On the other hand, choosing a very small step size would mean that convergence (arriving at the solution) can take an extremely large number of steps, slowing the optimization process significantly.

Note: We will learn about optimizing the learning rate for deep neural networks in *Chapter 8, Optimizing Deep Learning Models.*

The gradient descent approach is a practical solution that has found great success in deep neural networks. It provides us with a mathematical way to find the direction of movement that can be operationalized. We also saw that the step size is another hyper-parameter that we must carefully choose, otherwise, the convergence might never happen or might happen extremely slowly. This brings us to another important aspect of optimization algorithms, the stopping condition. That is, knowing when to stop. Let us understand this further.

Stopping condition

In the plain vanilla gradient descent implementation, the gradient is exactly 0 when we reach a minimum. This means that no further steps need to be taken and the algorithm would **converge** in the ideal way. It is important to note that landing on exactly a stationary point is not straightforward. As discussed, a poor step size/learning rate can lead you to overshoot the minima or take painfully long to get there. We therefore need a principled way to decide when to stop.

One approach could be to limit the number of iterations, that is, halt the process after a predetermined number. This is a very naive approach but is useful in terminating the process in the absence of other criteria. Another approach could be to stop when additional steps do not provide a sufficient decrease in the loss function. This is also a common approach that is applied in conjunction with the cap on the iterations.

Note: We will see these strategies in action in *Chapter 8, Optimizing Deep Learning Models.*

The two components, searching logic and stopping criterion form the core approach, and can work wonders for most use cases. Over the years, there have been multiple additions to this approach to make it work faster and increase the chances of finding a global minimum. Deep neural networks have especially complex loss functions, and the optimization process is extremely time consuming. Deep neural networks, therefore, benefit tremendously from these updates. We will learn about the most important variations now.

Faster gradient descent variants

The simple gradient descent approach we discussed in the previous section is theoretically sufficient to solve the optimization problems we encounter in machine learning in building deep neural networks. In practice, this plain version is inefficient. We have already discussed that one problem is high sensitivity to the step size, leading to the optimization converging extremely slowly, or not converging at all. Another significant and practical problem is the lack of **momentum**. Let us understand this important idea.

Momentum

The analogy provided by *Geoffrey Hinton* is effective in understanding the idea of momentum. A ball rolling down a slope moves slowly initially but keeps gaining momentum as it progresses. The ball builds up speed in directions with gentle but consistent gradients. On gaining significant momentum, the ball does not easily change direction on minor changes in the terrain. This makes the ball more stable as well. Such a ball would reach the bottom faster, despite some minor changes in the terrain on the way.

Momentum-based optimization works the same way. The optimizer will take larger steps in the direction of consistent gradients and be more stable in its descent. Simple gradient descent will simply take small regular steps and might take much longer to reach the minimum. The key difference in implementation is that simple gradient descent does not care about the previous gradient (or direction; making it irregular and unstable), while the momentum approach considers the previous direction/gradient. It uses statistics from the previous iterations to make the convergence process more robust and faster.

A key hyper-parameter in momentum-based methods is momentum (denoted by β). It controls the level of momentum that builds up and effectively the sensitivity to changes in the gradients. The momentum term typically has a value between 0 and 1. A higher value of the momentum parameter would lead to less sensitivity to changes and therefore smoother movement towards the minimum. Sounds good in principle. Let us discuss the benefits and drawbacks of momentum-based optimization.

Benefits:

- Faster convergence
- Better overcomes local minima

Drawbacks:

- Adds another hyper-parameter (β) to tune

Momentum is a simple but powerful idea that provides significant gains in practice. The simple gradient descent optimizer is seldom used for deep neural networks and has been replaced by momentum-based variants. There are several such variants developed in the past decades. Some prominent ones available as optimizers in **Keras** are listed in *Figure 7.7:*

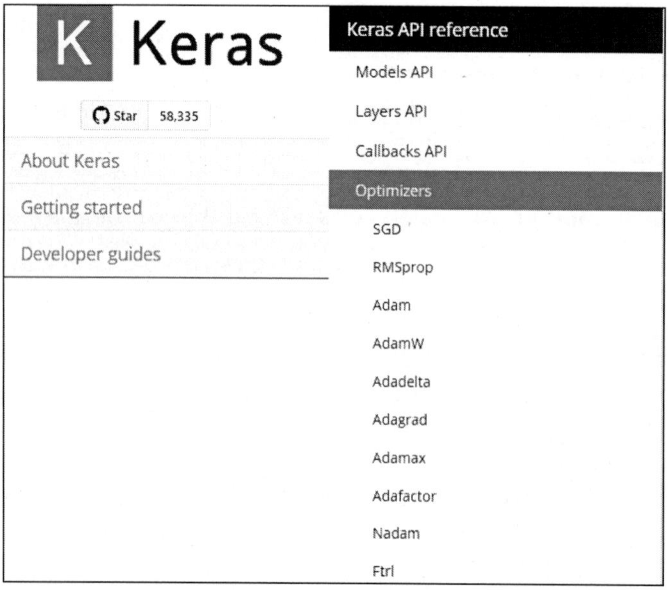

Figure 7.7: *Optimizers available in Keras*

Note: For an overview of the main approaches to optimization, refer to this paper by *Bottou et al.*, 2018. 1606.04838.pdf (arxiv.org).

Note that the simple gradient descent optimizer that implements momentum is the **Stochastic Gradient Descent Optimizer (SGD)** in *Figure 7.7*. We have discussed its working already in this section. Some of the optimizers listed in *Figure 7.7* are minor variations over a base approach. For example, **`Adam, AdamW, and Nadam`** are modifications to the **`Adam`** optimization algorithm. We will now understand the most prominent base approaches, beginning with the **`AdaGrad`** optimizer.

AdaGrad optimizer

A feature of the standard stochastic gradient descent approach (with or without momentum) is that it uses a single value of learning rate (η) to update all the parameters. This approach is too simple in the way that it does not consider the data at hand and the true geometry of the loss function. Additionally, the learning rate is not adaptive, that is, does not change based on the progress in optimization. The **`AdaGrad`** optimizer improves over the standard approach by introducing two key ideas:

- Parameter-specific learning rate
- Adaptive learning rate

The first key idea is that each weight has a different learning rate. This simple modification makes a great difference in practice. In real-world data, not all features and their parameters are equally important or populated. Some features are extremely sparse (for example, most values for a bag of words features for text are usually 0 while some others are extremely dense. A common learning rate is not optimal in such situations. In **`AdaGrad`**, the features occurring frequently are given lower learning rates relative to low-frequency features. Therefore, this approach can also help pay necessary attention to features that are predictive but rare. This simple modification of using different weights gives the **`AdaGrad`** optimizer a performance edge over simple stochastic gradient descent.

Elaborating on the second idea, **`AdaGrad`** adapts the learning rate (for each parameter) depending on the progress of optimization. The algorithm decays the learning rate over time. This decay is low for dimensions with gentler slopes and faster for dimensions with steep slopes. Note that this modification also reduces the impact of the predetermined learning rate. That is, we do not need to very carefully tune the hyper-parameter η. With the workings understood, let us look at some benefits and drawbacks of **`AdaGrad`**.

Benefits:

- Faster convergence (for simpler problems)
- Attention to rare but predictive features

Drawbacks:

- Stops too early for complex deep neural networks

The **AdaGrad** optimizer's drawback could be a deal breaker for large neural networks. In practice, it is seldom used. The idea and the updates it brought are quite significant, though, and will help us understand the next major variant, the **RMSProp** optimizer.

RMSProp optimizer

The **RMSProp** approach is fundamentally similar to that of **AdaGrad** and carries over its benefits. The problem with **AdaGrad** is that it slows down too fast and might not converge for large neural networks. The **RMSProp** overcomes this drawback. The **AdaGrad** optimizer effectively considers all the past gradients while making an update. In contrast, the **RMSProp** applies an exponential decay and therefore effectively considers only the most recent iterations.

The name **RMSProp** comes from the fact that the algorithm maintains a moving average of the **square of the gradients**. The average is of course discounted for earlier iterations effectively using the exponential decay. The gradient is then divided by the square root of this moving average, thus justifying its name. The key differentiating steps in **RMSProp** are:

- Maintain a moving (exponentially decayed) average of the square of gradients
- Divide the gradient by the square root of this average

Note that the rate of decay is another hyperparameter. But unlike other parameters, you do not need to carefully tune the decay rate. The default rate of 0.9 works well generally. For most situations, you do not need to tune this parameter at all. Let us now look at the benefits and drawbacks of the algorithm:

Benefits:

- Faster convergence (as compared to **AdaGrad**)
- Works well for deep neural networks

Drawbacks:

- Superseded by newer optimizers (for example, Adam)

Adam optimizer

The **Adam** optimizer is an extremely handy, high-performing optimizer that works well without much fine tuning. The Adam algorithm combines ideas from simple momentum and **RMSProp** approaches and elegantly overcomes their limitations. The result is a computationally efficient algorithm that has little memory requirement and is suitable for problems like large deep neural networks.

Adaptive Moment Estimation (Adam) estimates the first and second-order moments of the gradient. This is a technical detail you can learn more about here: ***https://arxiv.org/abs/1412.6980***. The intuition is that Adam uses the discounted average of past gradients as the simple momentum approach does. The optimizer also uses the squared gradients (decayed, averaged) as the **`RMSProp`** algorithm does. These two ideas work together to minimize oscillation when the optimizer reaches the global minimum. At the same time, the optimizer also takes big enough steps so that it does not get stuck at a local minimum.

The 2018 paper titled *An improvement of the convergence proof of the ADAM-Optimizer by Bock et al.* demonstrated that Adam outperforms other optimizers significantly. The comparison is shown in *Figure 7.8*, which compares the loss/ cost function after multiple iterations on the same dataset:

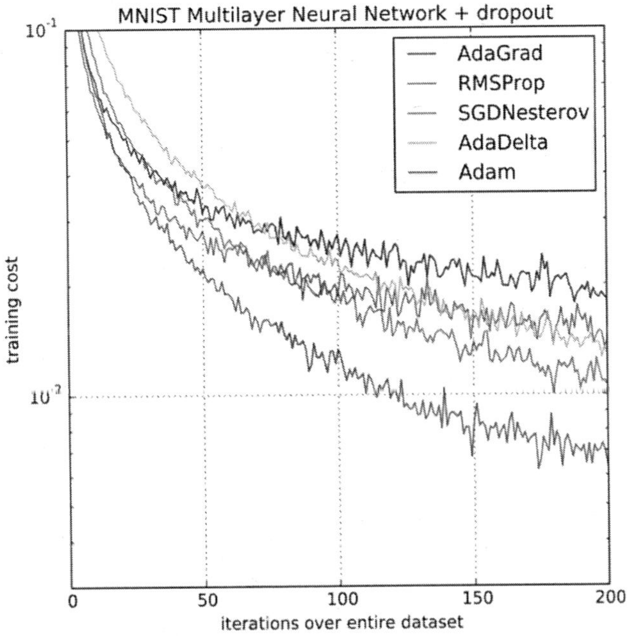

***Figure 7.8:** Adam compared with other optimizers*

The paper makes a strong argument for using Adam as a default. However, it is important to note that this result might not generalize to all situations. Let us learn some ways to choose between the optimizers.

Choosing the optimization approach

After understanding some major approaches to optimization and studying three prominent optimizers in depth, we need to be able to choose the right one for the situation. Theoretically, all the approaches should converge to the same solution (albeit with different speeds). However, an empirical analysis is needed on real-world data to understand the tradeoffs better.

The 2015 paper by *Kingma et al.*, titled *Adam: a Method for Stochastic Optimization* showed that the **`Adam`** optimizer outperforms **`RMSProp`** and **`SGD`**. However, the gains were marginal and may not generalize to other solutions. Therefore, if pure performance is the criterion, we may not have a clear winner.

However, the Adam optimizer does have the benefit of being extremely easy to use. The optimizer is adaptive in many ways. As a user, you need not carefully choose the initial hyperparameters around decays and the default values work. Therefore, **`Adam`** works well out of the box in many situations.

However, if pure model performance (lowest error) is paramount, then we suggest trying out **`RMSProp`** as well with some hyper-parameter tuning. Recent research also shows that **`SGD`** with careful hyper-parameter tuning is also a good candidate. Please refer to the 2019 paper **https://arxiv.org/abs/1910.05446** which compares different optimizers and highlights the role of the hyper-parameter tuning approach.

Conclusion

In this chapter, we first understood some core ideas of optimization. The objective function, the parameters and the constraints define the optimization problem at hand. The most important aspect, especially for machine learning/artificial intelligence, is the objective function/loss function. Once defined well, the learning/model fitting part of machine learning reduces to solving an optimization problem. We saw how loss functions are formulated in machine learning tasks and saw loss functions for regression and classification tasks. We also saw how regularization can be easily implemented by modifying the loss function.

To solve these problems, we discussed the fundamental approach of gradient descent. It is the most employed technique, but simple gradient descent falls short for deep learning problems. Deep neural networks have complex loss functions, and the choice of the optimization algorithm can make a significant difference in the outcome. Momentum-based approaches are the present norm. Some prominent momentum-based approaches are **`SGD, AdaGrad`**, **`RMSProp`** and **`Adam`**. All three provide significant performance gains over simple gradient descent approaches. When it comes to choosing one of them, Adam is a good general-purpose first candidate. But for high accuracy, we recommend trying out the **`RMSProp`** and **`SGD`** algorithms with hyperparameter tuning.

This brings us to the focus of the next chapter, hyper-parameter tuning for deep learning models. Deep learning problems are special cases for hyper-parameter tuning and in the next chapter, we will learn principled approaches for achieving a finely optimized, high-performance deep learning/artificial intelligence model.

CHAPTER 8
Optimizing Deep Learning Models

Introduction

You are a Data Scientist at a leading online fashion company which is facing a problem. When new items are listed on the platform, the sellers need to provide which category the item belongs to - whether it is a dress, a coat, a sneaker, or any of the many other categories. The team has discovered growing cases of mids-categorization by the sellers, and this leads to items being sold in the wrong category. This also means the item is not available for customers looking for it in the desired category. This is clearly a problem.

As a Data Scientist, you assert that this problem can be solved using Deep Learning. At this point, you need to make several decisions. What neural network architecture should be used? Would a deep network without convolutions be sufficient for the task, or are convolutions essential? How deep should the model be i.e., how many layers should it contain? Should the model have high depth and be narrow or should it have low depth shallow and be wide? Should you use ResNet-like architectures or simpler designs like LeNet? You also heard that transformer architectures perform well for image tasks as well - should you explore them? So many questions - and you haven't even begun thinking about hyper-parameters like activation functions and learning rate!

Pause and ponder: Without a systematic approach, what do you think are your best options for finding good settings, or even a reasonable starting point? Try to think of a couple of approaches other than trial and error.

Clearly, extremely high flexibility in the architectures of neural networks necessitates that the data scientist makes more decisions. Classical machine learning algorithms largely have hyper-parameters related to the training of the model while the structure is already pretty much defined. Neural networks, on the other hand, additionally have decisions/ hyper-parameters about structure. Any practitioner looking to get the best result from deep neural networks must know how to tune the structure in addition to the training-related hyper-parameters (which are plenty too).

Another aspect of deep learning models is that they typically contain a high number of parameters (often millions). The problem becomes 'overparameterized' when the number of parameters exceeds the number of data points. A big issue with deep learning models is that they are complex enough to completely overfit the data. Of course, with great predictive power comes great responsibility to not overfit. This implies that preventing overfitting to make the model useful is a constant consideration when training deep learning models.

As practitioners, we need to solve both aspects of working with neural networks. As you may expect, training neural networks is much more involved and complex. But a principled and systematic approach always helps. Let us discuss, in this chapter, some ways to efficiently optimize our deep learning models to get the maximum out of them.

Structure

In this chapter, we will cover the following topics:

- The image processing case study
    - o The overall modeling approach
- Building a baseline model
- Hyper-parameters in neural networks
    - o Activation function
    - o Learning rate
    - o Network structure
    - o Optimizer
    - o Other hyper-parameters
- Coarse plus fine tuning
- Practical tips for tuning neural networks

- Beyond hyper-parameters: other approaches to boost performance
  - o Regularization
  - o More data
  - o Data augmentation
  - o Ensembles
  - o Inject domain knowledge through features

Objectives

In this chapter, we will learn about optimizing neural networks to get the best out of the data and the modeling technique. There are several aspects to the optimization of neural networks. One major aspect is hyper-parameter tuning, of course. Recall from *Chapter 6, Hyper-parameter Tuning* that hyper-parameter tuning is the process of setting the right parameters that are external to the modeling algorithm but define the way the model learns from the data. Like we did for classical Machine Learning algorithms, we will perform automated hyper-parameter tuning for deep neural networks too. Note that we will focus on a simple deep learning architecture in this chapter – the fully connected network. This is to keep the focus on hyper-parameter tuning. In Chapter 9, *Optimizing Image Models* and Chapter 10, *Optimizing NLP Models*, we will learn about special architectures for image and text processing, respectively and how to optimize them.

Then, we will address many other ways of improving model performance other than hyper-parameter tuning. We will discuss how adding data helps the neural network extract more patterns from the data and how to observe such models to do better with more data. We will discuss how techniques like data augmentation can help achieve better performance by deriving more samples from existing data. We will also discuss how making an ensemble from multiple models can almost always help you get better performance. Finally, we will discuss perhaps the most undervalued approach – injecting your domain and data understanding by manually adding features.

The image processing case study

The Fashion-MNIST dataset was introduced in 2018 by the research team at Zalando SE, Europe's leading online fashion store. It consists of about 70,000 images of products along with their labels. The images are resized 28x28 grayscale images. There are 10 unique product categories in the data that need to be predicted using the images. Some sample images from the dataset are shown in *Figure 8.1*:

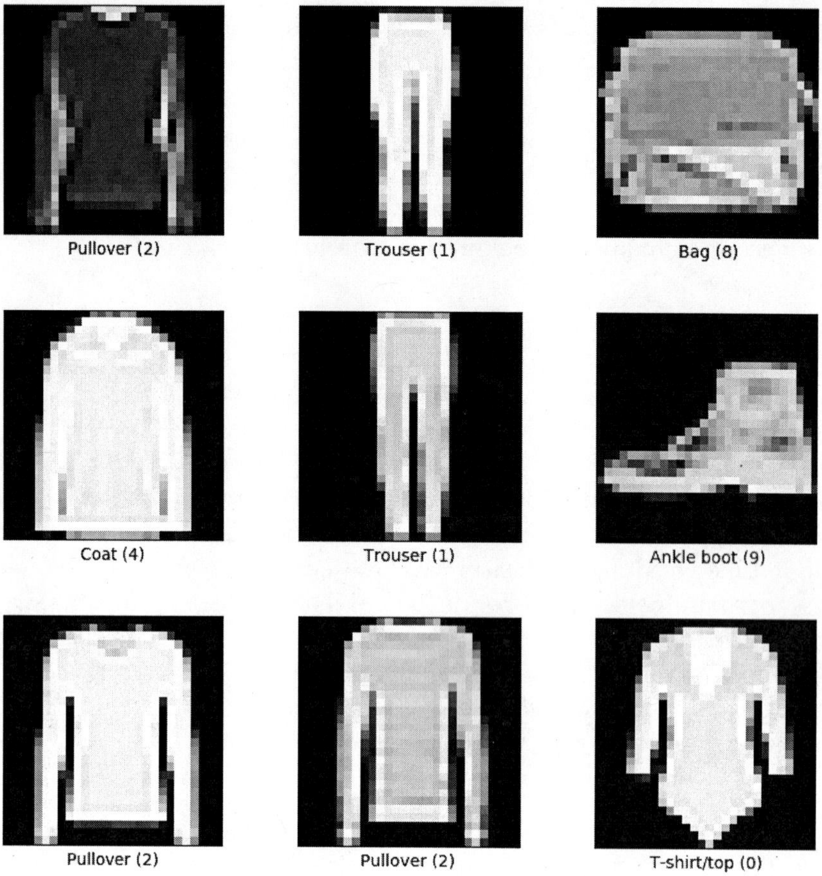

Figure 8.1: *Sample images and categories from the Fashion-MNIST dataset*

Note: More details on the dataset are available on the TensorFlow documentation at: tensorflow.org/datasets/catalog/fashion_mnist.
There is also a very interactive visualization of the dataset available at the following link: knowyourdata-tfds.withgoogle.com/#tab=STATS&dataset=fashion_mnist

The 10 unique product categories and their labels in the dataset are mentioned in *Table 8.1*:

Label	Description
0	T-shirt/top
1	Trouser
2	Pullover
3	Dress
4	Coat
5	Sandal

Label	Description
6	Shirt
7	Sneaker
8	Bag
9	Ankle boot

Table 8.1: *Product categories and their labels in the Fashion-MNIST dataset*

The dataset is available as an inbuilt dataset in Tensorflow, within the `datasets` module of Keras (part of Tensorflow 2). This makes it very convenient for us to load the dataset and divide it into train and test sets. Let us explore and understand the data that we will be working with. An understanding of the data is the first step towards building a good model. We begin by loading Tensorflow and the usual libraries using the following code:

```
import matplotlib.pyplot as plt

import numpy as np

import tensorflow as tf

np.random.seed(42)

tf.random.set_seed(42)
```

Note that by setting the random seed for Numpy and Tensorflow, we make sure that the results are reproducible and that you get results that are similar, if not the same, to ours. Now that we have Tensorflow imported, we can load import the Fashion-MNIST dataset using the `fashion_mnist` module. The load_data function conveniently divides the data into train and test images and labels. Use the following code to import the data:

```
fashion_mnist = tf.keras.datasets.fashion_mnist

(train_images,train_labels), (test_images,test_labels) = fashion_mnist.
load_data()
```

The dataset is loaded into the 4 variables. Let us examine the shapes of the train and test image variables:

```
train_images.shape, test_images.shape
```

The shapes are output as follows:

((60000, 28, 28), (10000, 28, 28))

As we expected, there are 60,000 training examples and 10,000 test examples. Each example is a 28x28 matrix corresponding to the 28x28 grayscale image. Let us confirm the number of unique categories in the data using the following command:

```
np.unique(train_labels, return_counts=True)
```

The values of the categories and their counts are printed as follows:

```
(array([0, 1, 2, 3, 4, 5, 6, 7, 8, 9], dtype=uint8),
 array([6000, 6000, 6000, 6000, 6000, 6000, 6000, 6000, 6000, 6000],
       dtype=int64))
```

We see that indeed there are 10 unique categories in the data; each having exactly 6,000 records. The dataset is balanced among the categories. The description of each label can be found in Table 1. Let us also see the values in the matrix corresponding to the train images. Because it is a grayscale image, we expect the value to be an integer between 0 and 255. Let us confirm by printing the maximum and minimum values in the matrix for one of the images. Use the following code:

```
np.min(train_images[0]), np.max(train_images[0])
```

The maximum and minimum get printed as follows:

```
(0, 255)
```

This confirms that the values are between 0 and 255. As a good practice in dealing with image data, we will normalize the matrix values to limit them between 0 and 1. We will do this for both the training and test datasets. This is a basic, common pre-processing step that helps train the neural networks faster. The following code will help us do so:

```
train_images = train_images.astype('float32') / 255.0

test_images = test_images.astype('float32') / 255.0
```

That completes our exploration and understanding of the Fashion-MNIST dataset. We have also done a basic pre-processing step and we are now ready to start building some neural networks for predicting a product's category from just its image. But before we do so, we need to briefly discuss our overall approach towards the entire model-building process. We also need to fully understand and appreciate the notion of hyper-parameters and what it means to tune them. Let us begin by creating a plan of action.

Note: The complete code can be found at the GitHub link mentioned at the beginning of the book.

The overall modeling approach

Now that we have the dataset ready for predictive modeling, it is imperative that we think over our approach and make a plan of action before jumping in. First, we need to define a success metric for evaluating the models. This is a multi-class classification problem and the 10 labels we have in the target are all balanced. In such a situation, a straightforward overall accuracy metric works just fine. We will therefore use 'accuracy' as our model evaluation metric.

With the success metric defined, we need to decide on the model-building process. A reasonable plan is as follows:

1. Build a baseline model without tuning.
2. Start with tuning one key hyper-parameter.
3. Tune more hyper-parameters using the best hyper-parameters learned so far.
4. Tune multiple hyper-parameters in an automated manner.

Let us begin by building a baseline model. This will also help us recap some relevant Tensorflow and the code relevant to training deep neural networks in Python.

Building a baseline model

Before we start systematically tuning the model, we need to have a baseline model. The baseline model is our first guess at what a reasonable neural network design could be. Its performance provides us with a number to anchor our expectations around and provides us with the first benchmark to beat. A naïve approach is to start with some arbitrary design. A better baseline model would be informed or inspired by existing results on a similar dataset and task. We will revisit this subject later in the chapter.

In this industry, we often deal with unique datasets, and it is difficult to identify architectures that are known to work well. Therefore, we will start with a simple and rather arbitrary architecture.

First, we will import Keras and all the necessary modules from it. This includes the specific layers we wish to use and utilities for performance monitoring and training control. Use the following code:

```
from tensorflow.keras.models import Sequential

from tensorflow.keras.layers import Flatten, Dense, Dropout

from tensorflow.keras.callbacks import EarlyStopping, ModelCheckpoint
```

Our simple model will use the Dense layer for our hidden layers with the basic sigmoid activation function. To transform the 28 x 28 image matrix into a flat 'record'/row for the model to process, we will use the Flatten layer. Additionally, we will use the Dropout layer to regularize, that is, lower the chances of overfitting the model.

The layers in the model would therefore be as follows:

- Flatten layer (28 x 28 corresponding to the image size)
- Dense layer with 64 units and sigmoid activation
- Dropout layer with 20% dropout
- Output Dense layer with 10 units and softmax activation

Initiate a simple Sequential model and add layers to it one at a time. Add the layers as described above using the following code:

```
model1 = Sequential()

model1.add(Flatten(input_shape=(28,28)))

model1.add(Dense(64, activation='sigmoid'))

model1.add(Dropout(0.2))

model1.add(Dense(10, activation='softmax'))
```

Note: In the preceding model definition, you must have noticed that we have set a lot of hyper-parameters. How did we choose these? These are completely arbitrary for now. Learning to tune them is precisely the objective of this chapter and something we will start very shortly.

Now that the architecture has been defined, we need to specify the optimizer and the loss function for the training. While there are plenty of choices for optimization algorithms (many of which we discussed in *Chapter 7, Parameter Optimization Algorithms*) in Keras, Adam optimizer (Adaptive Momentum) is always a good starting point. Later in the chapter, we will see how to pick the best optimizer systematically. In Adam, the loss function will be Sparse Categorical Cross Entropy, which is the natural choice for a multi-class classification problem. Specify these using the following code:

```
model1.compile(

  optimizer='adam',

  loss='sparse_categorical_crossentropy',

  metrics=['accuracy']

)
```

View the model summary using the summary method of the model object:

```
model1.summary()
```

You should see an output similar to that in *Figure 8.2:*

```
Model: "sequential"
_________________________________________________________________
Layer (type)                 Output Shape              Param #
=================================================================
flatten (Flatten)            (None, 784)               0
_________________________________________________________________
dense (Dense)                (None, 64)                50240
_________________________________________________________________
dropout (Dropout)            (None, 64)                0
_________________________________________________________________
dense_1 (Dense)              (None, 10)                650
=================================================================
Total params: 50,890
Trainable params: 50,890
Non-trainable params: 0
_________________________________________________________________
```

***Figure 8.2:** Summary of the baseline model*

Note: For a recap of these terms and utilities and some more examples of using these Keras utilities, the following links are a good reference.

Different layers in Keras: **`keras.io/api/layers/core_layers/`**

Using callbacks and checkpoints: **`keras.io/api/callbacks/model_checkpoint/`**

Keras built-in methods for training: **`keras.io/guides/training_with_built_in_methods/`**

For a refresher on any of these terms, visit the ML glossary page by Google:

https://developers.google.com/machine-learning/glossary

We will also use EarlyStopping which helps us stop training if we don't see an improvement after training for a specific number (5) of epochs. This helps avoid unnecessary epochs and saves time. The restore best weights option is also very handy as it retains the best weights the process encountered and thus makes it convenient for us to work with the best model weights. The following code will help us accomplish this:

```
callbacks = EarlyStopping(monitor='val_accuracy', patience=5, restore_best_
weights=True)
```

With the callbacks setup, we will now fit the model on the train data. Some additional settings that we will implement are given below. We will learn later how to tune some of them.

- Validation split of 20%, i.e., use 20% data for validation
- Limit training to 50 epochs
- Use batch_size of 256

Use the following code for training the model and storing the model performance after each training epoch in the 'history' variable:

```
history = model1.fit(train_images, train_labels,
                     validation_split=0.2, shuffle=True,
                     epochs=50, batch_size=256,
                     callbacks=[callbacks])
```

During the training, the progress is printed out after each epoch and the accuracy of the training and validation set is printed. This performance is also supplied to the 'history' variable:

```
Epoch 1/50
188/188 [==============================] - 1s 3ms/step - loss: 1.0
832 - accuracy: 0.6545 - val_loss: 0.6751 - val_accuracy: 0.7848
Epoch 2/50
188/188 [==============================] - 0s 2ms/step - loss: 0.6
406 - accuracy: 0.7855 - val_loss: 0.5377 - val_accuracy: 0.8182
Epoch 3/50
188/188 [==============================] - 0s 2ms/step - loss: 0.5
440 - accuracy: 0.8127 - val_loss: 0.4899 - val_accuracy: 0.8272
Epoch 4/50
188/188 [==============================] - 0s 2ms/step - loss: 0.4
994 - accuracy: 0.8276 - val_loss: 0.4562 - val_accuracy: 0.8388
Epoch 5/50
188/188 [==============================] - 0s 2ms/step - loss: 0.4
723 - accuracy: 0.8345 - val_loss: 0.4315 - val_accuracy: 0.8460
Epoch 6/50
```

Figure 8.3: *Model training progress printed*

In this case, the training occurs over 50 epochs, i.e., there was no early stopping. We will plot the learning curve for the model to see how the training and validation accuracy developed with each epoch in the training. Use the following code to plot the learning curves:

```
plt.plot(history.history['accuracy'], label='Train Accuracy')
plt.plot(history.history['val_accuracy'], label='Validation Accuracy')
plt.xlabel("Epochs")
plt.ylabel('Accuracy')
plt.legend()
plt.show()
```

The learning curves appear as shown in *Figure 8.4*:

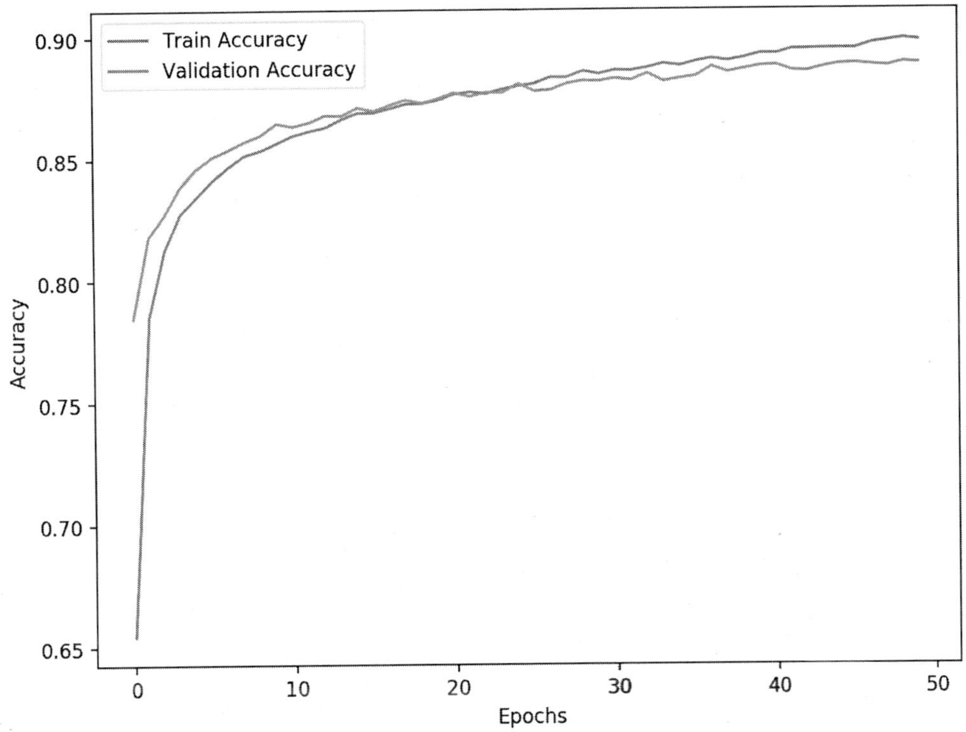

***Figure 8.4**: Training curves for the baseline model*

From the learning curves, we see that the training accuracy overtook the validation accuracy around 20 epochs. The validation accuracy flatlined around 40 epochs, while the training accuracy kept increasing. While usually this is a sign of overfitting, the curves are not too far away for us to suspect serious overfitting. The true test of the model, however, is on the test set. To assess how good our baseline model does on the test data, we will use the 'evaluate' method of the model object using the following code:

```
model1.evaluate(test_images, test_labels)[1]
```

The model accuracy gets printed as follows:

```
0.8808000087738037
```

We get an accuracy of about 88%. This is good for an arbitrary baseline model. Now, we must optimize the model and improve it. Before beginning to 'optimize the model' by 'adjusting the hyper-parameters', it is imperative that we understand what hyper-parameters are, and what tuning them means, and discuss a principled and systematic approach to tuning them to get the best model.

Hyper-parameters in neural networks

There is no dearth of hyper-parameters in neural networks. We have core hyper-parameters that define how the neurons fire and use the output from other neurons, i.e., the activation functions. Then, some hyper-parameters control how the network learns - learning rate, batch size, etc. We also have hyper-parameters specific to the optimization algorithms (e.g. learning rate decay, momentum). Using dropout is another choice, as is the extent of it. Then, there is the choice of the loss function, which directly affects how your model learns from the mistakes in predictions.

The structure of the neural network too is flexible and therefore needs to be optimized. Hyper-parameters like the number of layers, and the number of neurons in each layer define the structure of the neural network. All of these play a role in the behavior and therefore the performance of the neural network.

Rather than addressing each possible hyper-parameter, we will focus on some key hyper-parameters that have a stronger bearing on the performance of the neural network. Tuning these hyper-parameters will help you get the most out of your model quicker.

Activation function

A very simple way to look at activation functions is that they define how a neuron gets activated based on the inputs. As we know, the inputs to the neuron can be the outputs of the preceding layers' neurons. The activation function, thus, plays a key role in how these neurons come together and cooperate. Activation functions also bring in the powerful non-linearity that allows neural networks to solve complex real-world problems with amazing accuracy.

Over the past decades, several activation functions have been developed - beginning with the simple and humble sigmoid function, to the staple ReLu and now popular ELu (then, there are Swish, Mish and more). For brevity, we will omit a detailed list of available activation functions. Some key activation functions are illustrated in *Figure 8.5*:

Note: For the curious, Wikipedia has a great list you can read.
en.wikipedia.org/wiki/Activation_function
For the list of activation functions currently supported in Keras, check out the Keras documentation at the following link: keras.io/api/layers/activations/

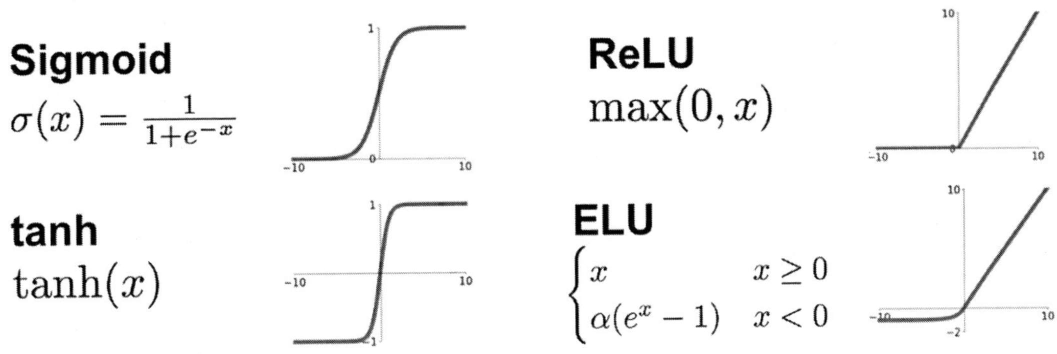

Figure 8.5: Some popular activation functions

Theoretical explanations are insufficient for understanding the impact of the activation function on the performance of the neural network. We will therefore see the impact through a demonstration. TensorFlow Playground is a very useful resource for this purpose. You can refer to `https://playground.tensorflow.org` in your web browser. This is a great way to visually try out neural networks. You can modify a neural network design with a few clicks, change some settings, and see how it performs on the toy datasets for illustration. When you land on the page, you should see the setup as shown in *Figure 8.6*:

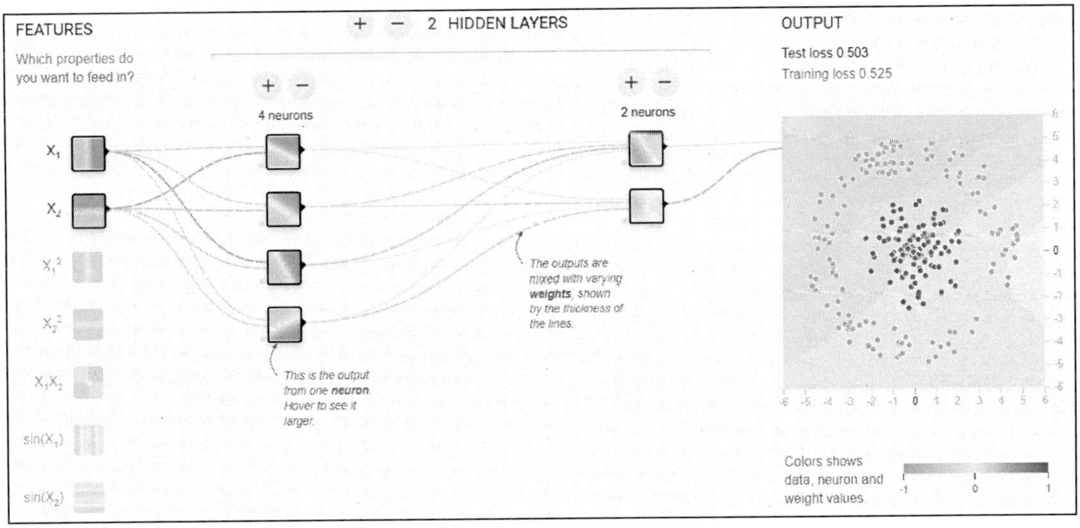

Figure 8.6: Tensorflow playground

In this demo, we will not modify the pre-defined model architecture and task. The task is to design a neural network that correctly classifies or separates the two classes (blue and orange). The configuration that does so faster is better for our purpose. The neural network architecture we have is as follows:

- 4 neurons in the first hidden layer
- 2 neurons in the second hidden layer

We are interested in seeing the impact of the activation function. To do so, we will run the model twice – once with the Sigmoid activation function and then with TanH. Let us begin with the Sigmoid activation function. Select 'Sigmoid' from the drop-down for the activation function, as shown in *Figure 8.7*. Leave the other options untouched:

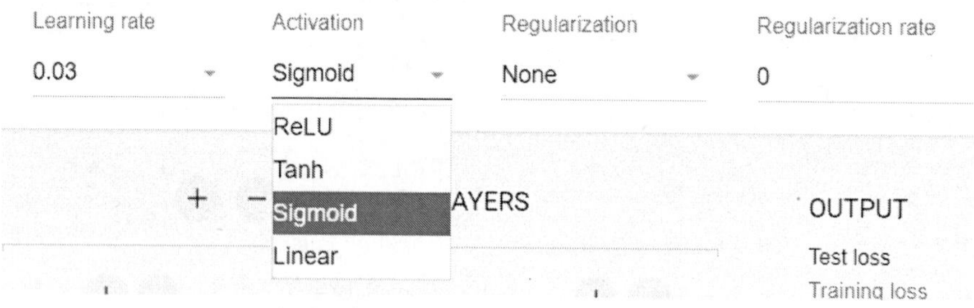

***Figure 8.7:** Choose the Sigmoid activation function*

Now, you have a Neural Network configured with 2 hidden layers and Sigmoid as the activation function. Let us proceed and see for ourselves how this model performs.

Hit the 'Run/Pause' button and monitor the Output section as you wait for the model to classify the points correctly. After about 600* epochs (see *Figure 8.8*), the model does very well in separating the two classes.

Let us now see how a different activation function performs on the same task:

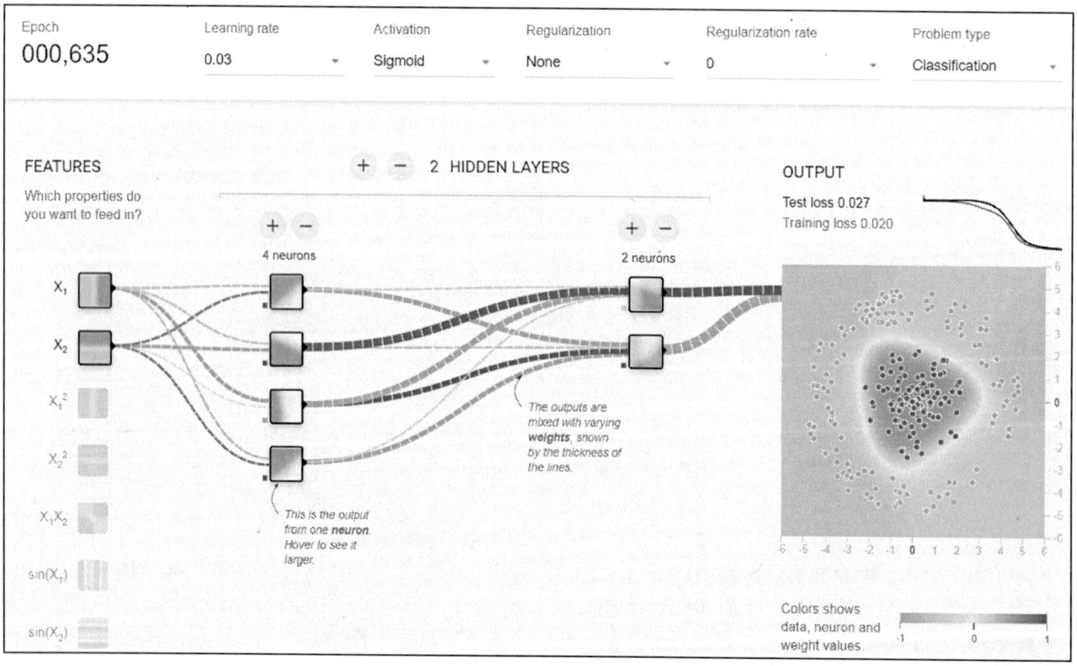

***Figure 8.8:** Sigmoid model after about 600 epochs*

Note: Due to the nature of Neural Networks and training, the number of epochs needed to get a good output may vary. But in most cases, this number is beyond 500.

We will now choose the TanH activation function from the drop-down. This is the only change that we will make so that our comparison is fair. We now have the same architecture and only the activation function has changed. Hit the **Run/Pause** button and monitor the output section. How long does it take to get a well-performing model? *Figure 8.9* shows the output:

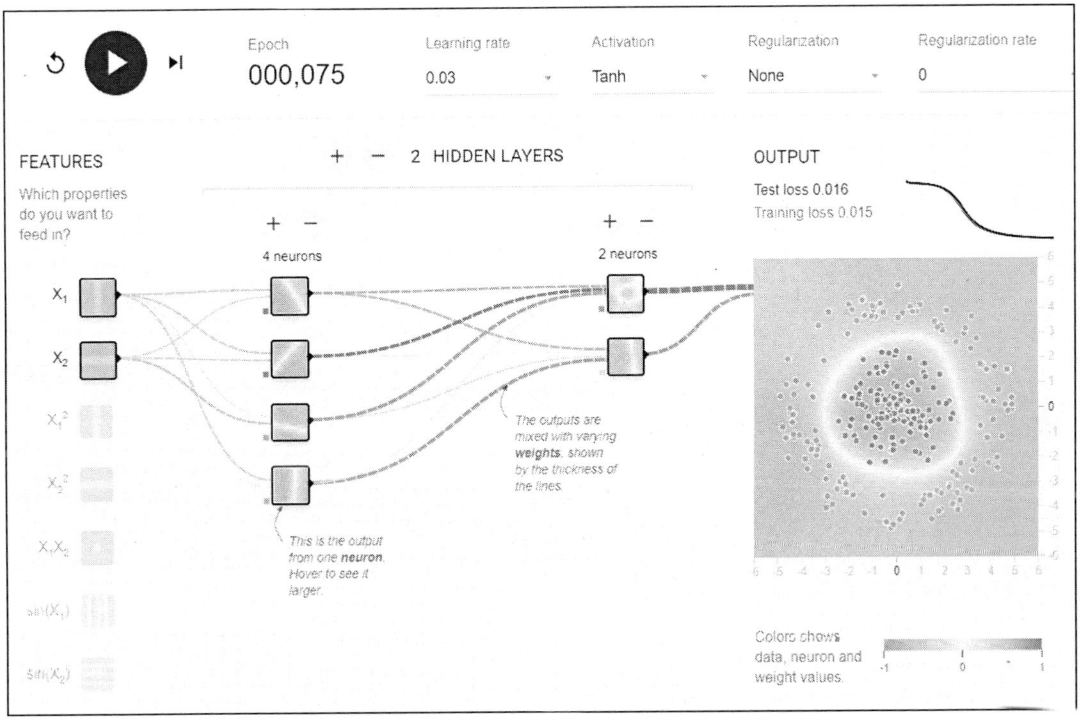

Figure 8.9: *Training with TanH activation*

We see that it took only about 70 (this may slightly vary) epochs to get to a good solution. Clearly, in this case, the TanH activation function gave us a good model much faster. It is evident that the activation function makes a huge difference in how quickly and well the model learns. This is therefore an extremely important hyper-parameter.

The example above was for a small dataset that is synthetic and made for demonstration. You could easily change the parameter and 'see' the points being classified. Unfortunately, real-world problems aren't so simple, and it is mostly not possible to visualize. Additionally, the combinations of hyper-parameters to try out can get out of hand rather quickly (as we saw in Chapter 6, *Hyper-parameter Tuning*). We therefore need to systematically tune this hyper-parameter.

Tuning the activation function

In Chapter 6, *Hyper-parameter Tuning*, for tuning classical ML algorithms, we used the handy hyper-parameter tuning utilities from sci-kit learn (GridSearchCV, RandomizedSearchCV) or similar modules (hyperband). For Neural Networks too, we have multiple libraries that help with this task. We will use **Keras Tuner** extensively for tuning our deep learning models from now on. Keras Tuner is simple to use and provides ample options for algorithms for hyper-parameter tuning for Neural Networks. It includes newer algorithms like 'hyperband' and some of the latest Bayesian algorithms. Additionally, it includes in-built tunable algorithms like HyperResNet and HyperXception, which are some great ready-to-use models for Computer Vision - more on this later in *Chapter 9, Optimizing Image Models*. The general tuning loop in the Keras tuner is depicted in *Figure 8.10*, which is the standard hyper-parameter tuning approach we saw with sci-kit learn as well:

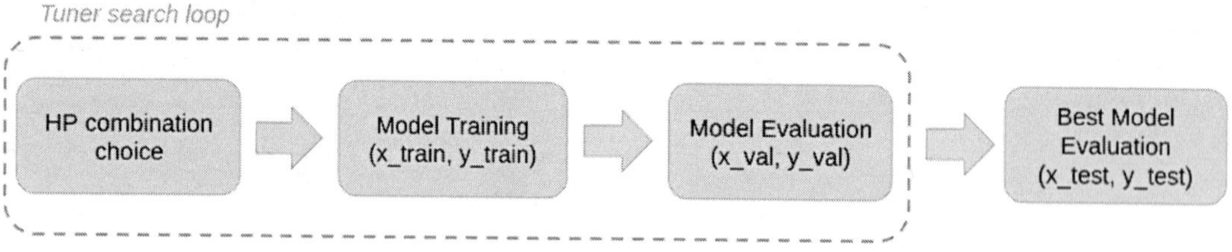

***Figure 8.10**: Hyper-parameter tuning using Keras tuner*

Note: Keras Tuner can be installed using pip by the following command: pip install keras-tuner

For an overview of the library and some very basic examples, refer to the following link: keras.io/keras_tuner

There are various tuners available in Keras. We will use some popular approaches. You are encouraged to use more types.

[Optional] For a more detailed guide on the different methods and options in the library, refer to the following link: keras.io/guides/keras_tuner/getting_started/

We will continue with the Fashion MNIST dataset in our effort to predict a product's category from its image. First, we will build a simple neural network with the same architecture that we previously used for the baseline model. This time, instead of fixing the activation function, we will perform hyper-parameter tuning to find the right activation function among Sigmoid, Tanh, ReLu, and ELu.

The functional approach of defining a neural network (vs. manually hard coding each layer) is coming in handy now. Keras Tuner also employs a functional approach, i.e., a function is the way to allow Keras Tuner to supply various hyper-parameters to Keras to create different models. Let us see the Keras Tuner in action and use it to choose the best activation function for our model. Here is a brief rundown of what we will do.

1. Define a model builder function for Keras Tuner to tweak the activation function.
2. Initialize the tuner with a search algorithm.
3. Search the hyper-parameter space using the tuner.
4. Analyze the search results.
5. Extract and evaluate the best model.

Let us begin by modifying the model-defining function suitable for the Keras Tuner.

We first define a model-building function. It takes a hyper-parameter argument (say hparams) from which you can sample hyperparameters. The hyper-parameter candidates can be provided as a list to choose from or a range of values to explore. Some hyper-parameters like activation functions are categorised and chosen from a supplied list using the **hparams.Choice** method.

As an example:

```
hparams.Choice('activation',['sigmoid','relu'])
```

This will tell Keras tuner to try out Sigmoid and ReLu as activation functions.

Whereas if you are exploring a larger range of possible values for, say, learning rates or the number of hidden units in a layer, you can use the hparams.Int method to choose from a range and a step size to try. For example:

```
hparams.Int('units', min_value=32, max_value=512, step=32)
```

For our objective, we wish to choose the best activation function. The model architecture otherwise will remain the same as before. The model building function for this is as follows:

```
def model_builder(hparams):

    model = Sequential()
    model.add(Flatten(input_shape=(28, 28)))

    hp_activation = hparams.Choice('activation',
                                   ['sigmoid', 'tanh', 'elu', 'relu'])
    model.add(Dense(units=64, activation=hp_activation))
    model.add(Dropout(0.2))
    model.add(Dense(units=10, activation='softmax'))

    model.compile(optimizer='adam',
```

```
                loss='sparse_categorical_crossentropy',

                metrics=['accuracy'])

    return model
```

Next, we will set up the tuner to perform a Random Search using the **RandomSearch** method of the Keras Tuner. Some key arguments for this method are as follows:

- **hypermodel**: A callable that takes hyper-parameters and returns a model instance (what we call "model_builder").
- **objective:** The objective that we are looking to maximize.
- **max_trials:** The number of trials or candidates to try.
- **overwrite:** Set to True; this tells the tuner to start a fresh search.
- **seed:** Similar to random seed, it uses a fixed value for reproducible results.

For our case, specify max trials as 4 and set the seed to 42. Use the following code which accomplishes this and supplies the **model_builder** function to the tuner. The tuner will determine the search space from the model builder object:

```
tuner = kt.RandomSearch(

    model_builder,

    objective='val_accuracy',

    max_trials=4,

    overwrite=True,

    seed=42)
```

The tuner is now specified. To confirm that the hyper-parameter candidates have been identified correctly, we can use the **search_space_summary** method of the tuner using the following command:

```
tuner.search_space_summary()
```

The search space gets printed as follows:

```
Search space summary
Default search space size: 1
activation (Choice)
{'default': 'sigmoid', 'conditions': [],
 'values': ['sigmoid', 'tanh', 'elu', 'relu'],
 'ordered': False}
```

Figure 8.11: *The hyper-parameter search space*

We see in the 'values' section that we have the four activation functions that we specified.

A great feature of the Keras Tuner is that we can use the regular callback and monitoring features that we have for regular Keras models. Use the EarlyStopping method, specifying a patient value of 10:

```
stop_early = EarlyStopping(monitor='val_accuracy',
                           patience=10,
                           restore_best_weights=True)
```

With the setup done, execute the search using the 'search' method of the tuner. Allow for a maximum of 25 epochs and specify a batch size of 256. Use a validation set of 20%. Use the following code:

```
tuner.search(train_images, train_labels,
             validation_split=0.2,
             epochs=25, batch_size=256,
             callbacks=[stop_early])
```

During the search process, the tuner keeps updating on the current value being tried and the best results so far. See *Figure 8.12* as an example:

```
Trial 3 Complete [00h 00m 13s]
val_accuracy: 0.8815000057220459

Best val_accuracy So Far: 0.8861666917800903
Total elapsed time: 00h 00m 39s

Search: Running Trial #4

Hyperparameter    |Value              |Best Value So Far
activation        |tanh               |relu

Epoch 1/25
188/188 [==============================] - 1s 3ms/step - los
s: 0.7196 - accuracy: 0.7555 - val_loss: 0.5030 - val_accura
cy: 0.8298
Epoch 2/25
188/188 [==============================] - 0s 2ms/step - los
s: 0.4927 - accuracy: 0.8292 - val_loss: 0.4540 - val_accura
cy: 0.8337
Epoch 3/25
188/188 [==============================] - 0s 3ms/step - los
s: 0.4459 - accuracy: 0.8422 - val_loss: 0.4183 - val_accura
cy: 0.8480
Epoch 4/25
```

***Figure 8.12**: Execution updates by the Tuner*

On completion of execution, we see the status as shown in *Figure 8.13*. It provides information on the best performance and the total time elapsed:

```
Trial 4 Complete [00h 00m 12s]
val_accuracy: 0.8801666498184204

Best val_accuracy So Far: 0.8861666917800903
Total elapsed time: 00h 00m 51s
INFO:tensorflow:Oracle triggered exit
```

***Figure 8.13:** Message on search completion*

Now that the search is complete, you must be curious to know which activation function did the best. To find out, we use the `get_best_hyperparameters` method of the tuner using the following command:

```
res = tuner.get_best_hyperparameters()[0]

res.values
```

The output is:

```
{'activation': 'relu'}
```

It looks like the ReLu activation function is the winner for this setup*.

***Note: It is important to be mindful that ReLu is the "winner for this setup". The reason for this is that with some other network structures and other hyper-parameter combinations, a different activation function may work best.**

To get a summary of the performance of all the combinations, we use the **`results_summary`** method of the tuner. Let's get the summary for our search using the following code:

```
tuner.results_summary()
```

We see the summary as follows:

```
Results summary
Results in ./untitled_project
Showing 10 best trials
Objective(name="val_accuracy", direction="max")

Trial 3 summary
Hyperparameters:
activation: relu
Score: 0.8884166479110718

Trial 0 summary
Hyperparameters:
activation: elu
Score: 0.8827499747276306

Trial 1 summary
Hyperparameters:
activation: sigmoid
Score: 0.8805000185966492

Trial 2 summary
Hyperparameters:
activation: tanh
Score: 0.8784166574478149
```

Figure 8.14: *Top hyper-parameter combinations*

While ReLu performed the best, the competition was close indeed. Elu did second best, followed by Sigmoid and finally, TanH. All these are within 1% of the leader. This should be a reminder that there is no 'general best' and the 'best' changes with the situation and setup.

Now, it is time to extract the best-trained model (the model with the best hyper-parameters and weights from the training). This can be done simply by using the get_best_models method of the tuner. We will extract the top model using the following code:

```
best_activation_model = tuner.get_best_models()[0]
```

The tuned and trained model is now available for inference. To see how the model performs on the test data, we can simply use the 'evaluate' method of the model:

```
best_activation_model.evaluate(test_images, test_labels)[1]
```

The accuracy obtained is as follows:

```
0.8816999793052673
```

While we do see an improvement from the baseline model (0.8808), the improvement is not a major one. This should not be very surprising; we saw from the tuner output that the Sigmoid was not very far away from the ReLu in performance.

Remember that in this setup, we did not tune any other hyper-parameter and we know by now (from *Chapter 6, Hyper-paramter Tuning*) that tuning multiple hyper-parameters together often helps us extract the most from the technique and the data. So, let us now turn our attention towards some other key hyper-parameters of neural networks. We look at another extremely important hyper-parameter, the learning rate.

Learning rate

The importance of the learning rate hyper-parameter has been stressed by many leading researchers. *Joshua Bengio* mentions in his 2013 paper:

If there is only time to optimize one hyper-parameter and one uses stochastic gradient descent, then this is the hyper-parameter that is worth tuning.

Why is this hyper-parameter so important?

Neural networks are trained using gradient descent. In essence, this means the weights in the neural network are changed in the direction of the gradient or in the direction where the loss function reduces the most. But how much should we move in that direction or, by how much should the current weights change? The **learning rate** controls this behavior.

A lower learning rate makes smaller changes to the weights, while a higher learning rate takes larger steps. A learning rate that is too low may take an extremely long time to converge to a good solution. Whereas a high learning rate may lead to a situation where we don't ever reach an optimum. *Figure 8.15* illustrates this theoretically. On the left side, we see that a small learning rate requires a large number of steps to reach the lowest point i.e., the optimum. On the right side, we see a situation with a high learning rate. The steps taken are so large that we may never reach the optimum and keep moving back and forth. Let us try it out and see the effect of the learning rate for ourselves.

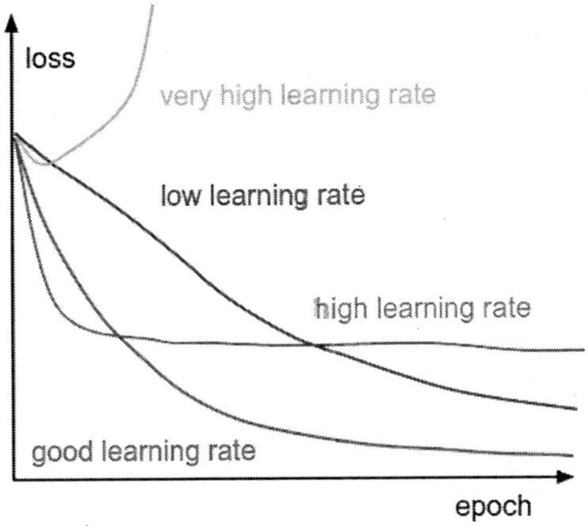

***Figure 8.15**: Learning rates and training loss*

Go back to playground.tensorflow.org and recreate the setup we had done earlier with the following architecture:

- 4 neurons in the first hidden layer
- 2 neurons in the second hidden layer
- ReLu activation function

Choose the learning rate from the dropdown to be 0.0001 and click on the Run button. You'll see that the learning happens very slowly. *Figure 8.16* shows that even after about 2,000 epochs, the model performance is poor. The model is learning, albeit extremely slowly.

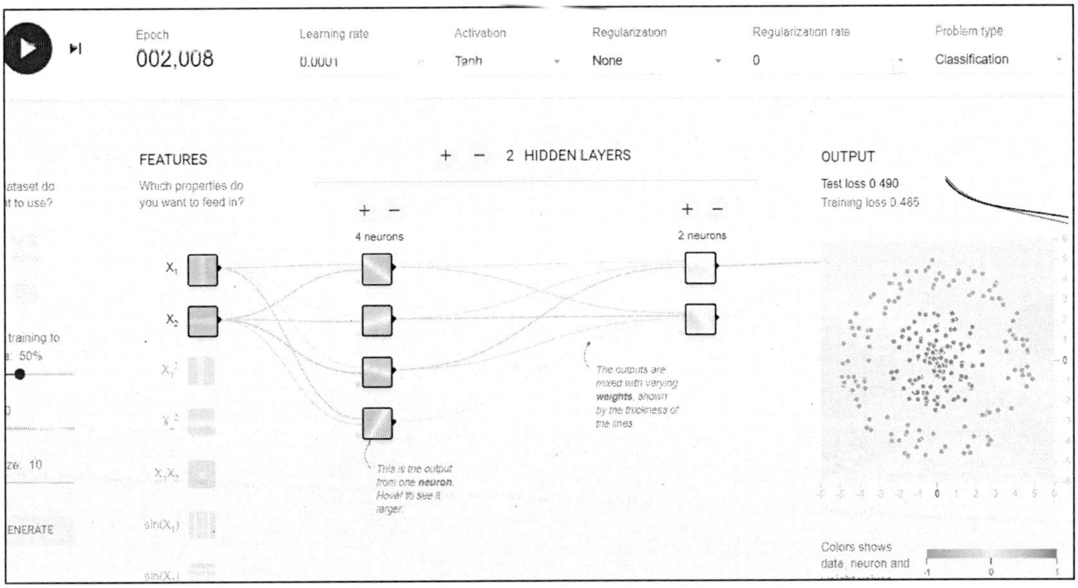

***Figure 8.16**: Training with a low learning rate*

Now, change the learning rate to a high value of 10 and start the training. What do you observe? We see that now too; the model doesn't learn well. *Figure 8.17* shows that after about 2,000 epochs, we have a very high loss showing that the model has not learnt anything at all. We learn that somewhere between 0.0001 and 10 is the optimal learning rate. We also learn that a poor learning rate can render all the predictive potential useless:

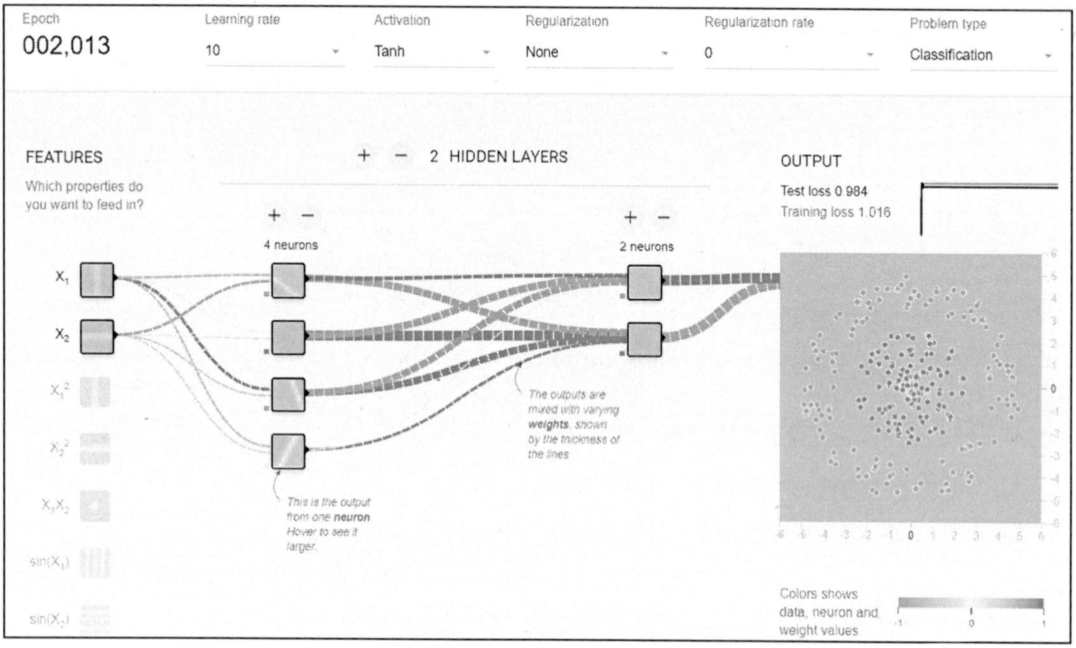

Figure 8.17: Training with a high learning rate

Task: Play around with the learning rate. What learning rate gets you the fastest convergence?

Again, this was a toy dataset, and you could really 'see' the progress and performance of the model. It is time to turn to real data and perform learning rate tuning for ourselves.

Tuning the learning rate

We will continue working on the product category classification case study. We previously tuned the activation function. Now, we will tune the learning rate as well. We need to define the hyper-parameter candidates we want to try. From tuning the activation function earlier, we saw that ReLu, ELu and TanH seemed to work well for this task. We will limit our search to these three values for the activation function. For the learning rate, practitioners usually try a wide range – from very low values (e.g. 10^-5) to relatively large values (e.g. 10), each time trying a different order of value. For our case, the values we will try are as follows:

Activation function: ReLu, ELu, TanH

Learning rate: 0.00001, 0.0001, 0.001, 0.01, 0.1

Note: In recent years, a lot of approaches have developed towards achieving a good learning rate. You may find sophisticated methods geared towards finding the right learning rate to extract some incremental performance. These methods are out of the scope of this text and present a lack of stable implementations. You could also leverage some "tribal knowledge" accumulated by practitioners and researchers. For example, 3e-4 is a value practitioners try for the Adam optimizer. This was based on a Tweet by Andrej Karpathy where he stated 3e-4 as the best value for Adam optimizer. Karpathy later qualified this as a joke, but the value stuck.

Note that the right combination of learning rate and activation may provide much better performance than tuning just one of them. We, therefore, will tune the activation function together with the learning rate. As you will see, tuning multiple hyper-parameters with Keras tuner is just as simple. Let us begin.

Define the model builder function to incorporate the combinations for the activation function and learning rate. Use the following code:

```
def model_builder(hparams):

    model = Sequential()
    model.add(Flatten(input_shape=(28, 28)))

    hp_activation = hparams.Choice('activation', ['elu', 'relu', 'tanh'])
    model.add(Dense(units=64, activation=hp_activation))
    model.add(Dropout(0.2))
    model.add(Dense(units=10, activation='softmax'))

    hp_lr = hparams.Choice('learning_rate', [1e-5, 1e-4, 1e-3, 1e-2, 0.1])
    model.compile(optimizer=tf.keras.optimizers.Adam(learning_rate=hp_lr),
                  loss='sparse_categorical_crossentropy',
                  metrics=['accuracy'])

    return model
```

Note: Training neural networks and especially hyper-parameter tuning is very resource intensive and takes a long time. From now on in this chapter, we will limit our training epochs to 25. This will help us explore more approaches quickly and conveniently. Even on a small dataset like ours, the required hyper-parameter tuning time can be in hours.

Initialize the tuner and specify max_trials as 10. Use early stopping with patience 10 and train with a batch size of 256. The following code does this:

```
Tuner = kt.RandomSearch(model_builder,
                        objective='val_accuracy',
                        max_trials=10,
                        overwrite=True,
                        seed=42)

stop_early = EarlyStopping(monitor='val_accuracy',
                           patience=10,
                           restore_best_weights=True)

tuner.search(train_images, train_labels, validation_split=0.2,
             epochs=25, batch_size=256,
             callbacks=[stop_early])
```

The search takes slightly longer this time. But once the search is complete, find out the combination of activation function and learning rate that performed the best. Use the **get_best_hyperparameters** method as follows:

```
res = tuner.get_best_hyperparameters()[0]
res.values
```

The best combination gets printed as follows:

```
{'activation': 'relu', 'learning_rate': 0.001}
```

ReLu with a learning rate of 0.001 turns out to be the best combination. But was it close? How good were the other combinations? Let us find out. Use the **results_summary** method to see the top 3 combinations, using the following code:

```
tuner.results_summary(3)
```

The top 3 combinations are printed as shown in *Figure 8.18:*

```
Results summary
Results in .\untitled_project
Showing 3 best trials
Objective(name='val_accuracy', direction='max')
Trial summary
Hyperparameters:
activation: relu
learning_rate: 0.001
Score: 0.8869166374206543
Trial summary
Hyperparameters:
activation: elu
learning_rate: 0.001
Score: 0.8817499876022339
Trial summary
Hyperparameters:
activation: relu
learning_rate: 0.01
Score: 0.875249981880188
```

Figure 8.18: *Top 3 hyper-parameter combinations*

We see that ELu with a learning rate 0.001 was close behind. Both ReLu and ELu performed well with the same learning rate of 0.001. Now, extract and evaluate the best model on the test set using the following code:

```
best_lr_model = tuner.get_best_models()[0]

best_lr_model.evaluate(test_images, test_labels)[1]
```

The output gets printed as follows:

0.8774999976158142

Notice that this is very close to the 88% we got from the ReLu model while tuning the activation function. Do you see why this is so? It turns out that the default learning rate for the Adam optimizer (that we used earlier) is 0.001. This means that when we tried ReLu, we were trying out ReLu with a 0.001 learning rate, the same combination we tried now.

We have made great progress! We have learnt how to optimize the learning rate and the activation function and we optimized the two at once. In the examples so far, we assumed a neural network architecture – a single layer with 64 neurons. We admitted earlier that this was arbitrary. Now, it is time we learn how to optimize the structure itself.

Note: The complete code can be found at the GitHub link mentioned at the beginning of the book.

Network structure

Neural networks are extremely flexible in architecture and it is you, the Data Scientist, who has to choose the right architecture. This makes the structure of the network an obvious hyper-parameter. The number of layers and the number of nodes in each layer are to be chosen every time you make a neural network.

The hidden units are the core component of the neural network. These core components are extremely simple and ineffective individually. However, it is the cooperation of these hidden units that gives the neural network its predictive power. It goes without saying that the number of hidden units in a neural network is one of the most important hyper-parameters and must be tuned. The number of layers also is an important decision. We know that in a deep network, layers build on the information and transformations from the previous layer to result in some sophisticated features that drive the performance of the neural networks. Let us now learn how to tune the structure of the neural network.

Tuning the number of hidden units

While making our simple baseline model, we rather arbitrarily chose 64 hidden units. The good news is that we can do much better and the convenient Keras Tuner package allows us to tune the number of hidden units as well. This is rather straightforward in the Keras tuner and all you need to do is provide a range of values (using **`hparams.Int`**) or a list (using **`hparams.Choice`**).

We will try a rather wide range of values – starting from 32 and ending at 512 in steps of 32. This means that we are potentially trying the values 32, 64, 96 and so on until 512. We will provide a range using the **`hparams.Int`** method.

Additionally, we know that depending on the structure of the network, the best-performing activation function may change. Therefore, we will also try both ReLu and ELu activation functions as they have been consistently performing well. The learning rate also can be tested and we will try 0.001 and 0.0001.

Define a **`model_builder`** function for Keras with the following hyper-parameter candidates:

Hidden units: 32 to 512 in steps of 32

Activation functions: ReLu and Elu

Learning rate: 0.001 and 0.0001

Use the following code:

```
def model_builder(hparams):


  model = Sequential()

  model.add(Flatten(input_shape=(28, 28)))
```

```
    hp_units = hparams.Int('units', min_value=32, max_value=512, step=32)
    hp_activation = hparams.Choice('activation', ['elu', 'relu'])
    model.add(Dense(units=hp_units, activation=hp_activation))
    model.add(Dropout(0.2))

    model.add(Dense(units=10, activation='softmax'))

    hp_lr = hparams.Choice('learning_rate', [1e-4, 1e-3])
    model.compile(optimizer=keras.optimizers.Adam(learning_rate=hp_lr),
                  loss='sparse_categorical_crossentropy',
                  metrics=['accuracy'])

    return model
```

Set the tuner to use 15 trials in a Random Search and specify the seed as 42. Use early stopping with patience 10. Start tuning with a batch size of 256 for a maximum of 25 epochs. Use the following code:

```
tuner = kt.RandomSearch(model_builder,
                        objective='val_accuracy',
                        max_trials=15,
                        overwrite=True,
                        seed=42)

stop_early = EarlyStopping(monitor='val_accuracy',
                           patience=10,
                           restore_best_weights=True)

tuner.search(train_images, train_labels, validation_split=0.2,
             epochs=25, batch_size=256,
             callbacks=[stop_early])
```

This may take a while as we are allowing more trials and have candidates with a high number of hidden units. When the tuning is complete, you should see the following message:

```
Trial 15 Complete [00h 00m 21s]
val_accuracy: 0.890500009059906

Best val_accuracy So Far: 0.8970000147819519
Total elapsed time: 00h 05m 11s
INFO:tensorflow:Oracle triggered exit
```

Figure 8.19*: Search completion message*

The search took a little longer than earlier. The best validation accuracy attained was 89.7%, which is an improvement from the accuracies we achieved so far. However, only after evaluating the model on the test data will we know its true performance. Which combination performed the best? How does it fare on the test data? Extract the best hyper-parameters using the following commands:

```
res = tuner.get_best_hyperparameters()[0]

res.values
```

```
{'units': 256, 'activation': 'relu', 'learning_rate': 0.001}
```

We see that 256 hidden units with ReLu activation and a learning rate of 0.001 performed the best. Next, extract this model and evaluate performance on the test set using the following code:

```
best_units_model = tuner.get_best_models()[0]

best_units_model.evaluate(test_images, test_labels)[1]
```

The output we get is as follows:

```
0.8897
```

We have achieved almost 89% accuracy on the test set. This is an improvement from where we started, but not by a huge margin.

Note: The complete code can be found at the GitHub link mentioned at the beginning of the book.

Tuning the number of layers

"Go wide or go deep?", is among the most common questions in defining the network architecture. How many layers should you have? Should they have the same number of hidden units? How do you decide the right combinations?

Theoretically, a single hidden layer with enough number of hidden units can be a universal function approximator. In other words, it should be able to perform well at any task. But the question is, how many are 'enough'? While the answer varies with the situation, you should not be surprised if the answer is in thousands. Training with thousands of hidden units does not seem optimal.

The other approach is going deep i.e., having more hidden layers. The benefit is that a layer can work on the transformations in the data made by the previous hidden layer, and such 'collaboration' of the layers can help create these powerful transformations in data that provide high performance with fewer neurons. Indeed, this benefit of being able to get higher performance with fewer units is a key appeal of deep neural networks. Indeed, most state-of-the-art models are deep networks with multiple layers.

How do you arrive at the right architecture? Most practitioners and experts say that there are no rules. They arrive at their architectures mostly by:

1. Intuition (through their own experience)
2. Inspiration (architecture performing well on similar tasks)
3. Trial and error

Hyper-parameter tuning, by nature, is trial and error. By now we have seen that this process can be automated. Therefore, it should be no surprise that identifying the optimal number of layers in a neural network can also be tuned. Fortunately, Keras Tuner allows us to tune the number of layers as well as the number of hidden units in each layer at the same time:

```
model = Sequential()

model.add(Flatten(input_shape=(28, 28)))


for layer in range(hparams.Int("num_layers", 1, 5)):

    model.add(

        Dense(

            units = hparams.Int("units_" + str(layer),
            min_value=32, max_value=256, step=32),

            activation="relu",

        ))
```

Optimizer

So far, we have been using the Adam optimizer. Adam stands for Adaptive momentum and is a popular choice of activation function for a couple of reasons:

- It converges faster than simple Stochastic Gradient Descent.
- It is less sensitive to other sub-optimal hyper-parameters, which means that it does well even if the other hyper-parameters have not been set well.

Adam is usually the safe first choice when building the Deep Learning model. But Adam is not the only option, as we have discussed in *Chapter 7, Optimization Algorithms*.

It is important to note that all these methods are heavily based on gradient descent, and you can think of them as modifications to the plain-vanilla gradient descent to converge faster. What this means is that if given enough time and with the right hyper-parameters, all of these should provide you with very similar results. Buy now we understand that accuracy isn't the only concern when optimizing a model. If accuracy is paramount and training time does not matter much, **Stochastic Gradient Descent (SGD)** is a good option. If faster convergence is required, at the cost of some minor loss in accuracy, then optimizers like Adagrad, Adam, Nadam, and others should be tried.

Choosing the optimal optimization algorithm, i.e., tuning this hyper-parameter, also can be performed systematically using the approach we have been using so far. Keras Tuner can be employed to tune the optimization algorithm, just like any other hyper-parameter.

Task: Continuing with the product category classification case study, use Keras Tuner to find the optimal optimization algorithm for the model. The model should have the following structure - having 1 single dense layer of 192 units with ReLu activation and 20% dropout. The candidates for the optimizer are: adam, nadam, and sgd.

Other hyper-parameters

We discussed some key parameters that in general make a significant impact on model performance. This does not mean that the other parameters are irrelevant. It just means that the hyper-parameters we discussed had a higher impact, or showed more variance in performance from case to case. Some of the remaining hyper-parameters can also help boost performance if used correctly.

Consider the dropout rate - we used 20% dropout throughout the chapter so far. It was an arbitrary choice. You could very well try optimizing the dropout rate as well. A high dropout rate would lead to high regularization and extremely slow model training. A very low dropout rate does not regularize and the deep learning model would be prone to overfitting.

Batch size is another hyper-parameter that you may want to tune. A higher batch size considers more data points together before each update and is therefore faster. A lower batch size therefore increases the training time. The effect of the batch size on performance, however, is interesting and mostly empirically understood. Reducing the batch size has the effect of regularization and helps reduce overfitting and therefore generalize better.

Coarse plus fine tuning

We have discussed this approach in detail in *Chapter 6, Hyper-parameter Tuning,* but it is worth recalling the lessons from that chapter. The coarse plus fine tuning approach refers to the idea of doing coarse tuning first to find a good 'range' of parameters to work in. Then, do a fine tuning by trying smaller variations in the hyper-parameters to find the optimal set. We saw in *Chapter 6, Hyper-parameter Tuning,* that such an approach is very practical as it helps us get to the optimal set much quicker.

This approach is particularly useful for deep neural networks because of the sheer number of hyper-parameters to tune. Performing a fine-grained tuning of all relevant parameters is impractical in most situations. Using coarse tuning on some key hyper-parameters (e.g. learning rate, activation function, number of units and layers) can provide an initial, somewhat optimized setup. This setup is a great starting point for fine tuning some other hyper-parameters that can help you get the most out of the data and the deep learning technique. This is one of our key practical tips for tuning deep neural networks. We will not share some more practical tips for tuning neural networks.

Practical tips for tuning Neural Networks

We have seen multiple times that tuning more hyper-parameters can help identify the best-performing combination that can easily be missed when tuning very few or even one at a time. A natural question is: should we always try to tune all hyper-parameters and all at once? Especially for deep learning, where we see that there are many hyper-parameters to set.

The answer is a clear no. Especially for Deep Learning models. A simple practical reason is that training Deep Learning models takes a lot of time. Trying to tune a dozen hyper-parameters at once, or even in sequence gets impractical in most situations. Indeed, in many cases, tuning several hyper-parameters may need several days more of training time. In many industry applications, there isn't enough return on the time invested in this endeavor.

Pause and ponder: Can you think of some industry applications where a 0.1% increase in accuracy/other performance metrics makes a big difference in the utility and benefit from the model? Hint: think of situations with low event rates (high class-imbalance) or applications that impact human lives.

The other, more pragmatic reason is the philosophy of parsimony, i.e., doing more with less. There is no limit to the complexity of a Deep Learning model; you can arbitrarily add a layer with a hundred more units if you want to. But do you need to? Does it give you a significant enough benefit in accuracy? Does it make your model unstable? Does the more complex model increase inference time? We have discussed such considerations before and we understand by now that accuracy is not the only criterion for judging the performance of a model.

The general guidance is - to **start simple and add complexity as you need**. This is relevant for the model optimization process as well. Start with "good defaults" for key hyper-parameters. For example, Adam is considered a safe first option for an optimizer. The learning rate of 0.001 has empirically shown to provide good performance with the Adam optimizer. Unless you have reason to suspect otherwise, Adam optimizer with a learning rate of 0.001 is a good starting point.

Pause and ponder: What are some other ways of identifying good defaults or good starting points for the hyper-parameters?

Often, there are other indications of what good starting points can be. One such indication can be a published work on a similar data and task. This applies to model architectures too. If you are working on a dataset that has been used in research before, find the paper that is closest to your research goal or task and use the architecture from the paper as your starting point.

In summary, we start simple with good defaults and add complexity only if needed.

Beyond hyper-parameters: other approaches to boost performance

In the previous sections, we learned how to optimize the many hyper-parameters to obtain the best combination - the most straightforward approach to improving model performance. But let's not limit ourselves to a single approach, when we have some other powerful approaches that can provide significant performance boosts. Let us learn some more approaches.

Regularization

The key usage of regularization is to make the model less prone to overfitting, not fit to the noise in the data and therefore generalize better to unseen data. We have already used dropout – which is a strong and direct way of regularization, but not the only way. Another extremely effective method is modifying the loss function.

The most common approach to modifying the loss function is adding a penalty term to the loss function. These are added in such a way that the higher the number of parameters and their values, the higher the penalty. A higher penalty term means the loss is higher. Since model learning is all about minimizing the loss, a higher penalty term makes higher values of parameters less desirable. Lower values of parameters get preferred and therefore the model becomes less prone to overfitting. L1 and L2 penalties are the most common approaches.

L1 penalty: a penalty term proportional to the magnitude of the weight is added to the loss

L2 penalty: a square term of the weight/parameter is added to the loss

L2 regularization puts more penalty on higher weights and therefore is a more aggressive regularization. Whether to use L1 or L2 penalty can be thought of as another hyper-parameter and can easily be tuned using Keras Tuner or a similar utility.

Beyond dropout and L1/L2 penalties, techniques like Label Smoothing (adds noise to the target values) and Stochastic depth (that drops entire blocks in the neural networks) can also be effective techniques to make the model generalize better.

More data

Models are learning patterns from data. However deep neural networks are unique in the sense that they seem to benefit more from a larger volume of data. The performance of a classical ML model may not increase merely by adding more data to it. But for deep learning models, more data means potentially more finer patterns to learn. Because they typically have a higher number of parameters, they can potentially learn finer patterns.

So, if you have maxed out on performance through hyper-parameter tuning and regularization, try to arrange for more training data for the model. The act of adding more available data may just give you that required performance boost. Even if you can't get your hands on new and unique training data, techniques like Data Augmentation can help you derive more data from the existing samples. Let us discuss that next.

Data augmentation

The case for data augmentation is most obvious in deep learning for images. Many times, it may not be feasible to get even a thousand more images to make your model better. But what if you could derive these images from existing ones?

Picture that you are making a model to classify the image as being of a cat or a dog. Naturally, you have images of various cats and dogs. But your dataset is rather small, and the model is overfitting very quickly. Also, for certain, rare breeds of dogs like the Bluetick Coonhound (*Figure 8.20*) you have just one picture. More pictures will surely help.

***Figure 8.20**: Image of a Bluetick Coonhound*

Here's where data augmentation can help. Imagine if the image were flipped horizontally, it would still show a Bluetick Coonhound. Slight rotation, a little bit of left or right shifting, shifting the image up or down – none of these will change the subject of the image and it would still be a good image of the dog. And just like that – from one image, you now have 6 images of the rare breed! This is the basic idea of data augmentation.

***Figure 8.21**: 6 images from 1 via. data augmentation*

Data augmentation works for text applications as well. For sentiment classification setup, you can increase the data size by adding variations that do not alter the sentiment. For topic modelling tasks, you can add variations that don't change the topic but make other minor changes. There are many ways for you to get creative. Just be careful and not accidentally obfuscate the characteristics of the data that are essential for the task.

In case we did not make it explicit enough, data augmentation helps you get more from your data by –

- Creating more variety in the data for the model to learn from; in many cases, it provides that much-needed variation.
- Regularizes and makes the model generalize better.

Data augmentation is an easy way of getting more out of your data. We will discuss this in more detail and perform hands-on data augmentation in Chapter 9,*Optimizing Image Models*.

Ensembles

The essence of ensemble learning is using multiple, diverse models on the same dataset and combining their predictions to create an ensemble. The ensemble model typically outperforms any of the individual models. There is no reason why the benefits of ensemble learning do not apply to deep learning methods. Indeed, with the high variance and tendency to overfit that comes with deep learning models, creating an ensemble is a great idea to get a higher-performing model that generalizes better.

Of course, considering that training deep learning models on large datasets, an ensemble consisting of multiple deep learning models may take much longer. But it could be worth the effort if you can afford it. Alternatively, you needn't restrict your ensemble to deep learning models alone. For example, a text classification model with a deep learning model, an SVM classifier and an XGBoost model may significantly outperform the individual models. Try ensembling if your situation permits, it may be well worth the effort and might just give you that extra edge.

Inject Domain knowledge through features

Even though Deep Learning promises effective, automatic feature generation, adding features based on your knowledge of the data and the domain is a good idea. Consider a situation where you are working on text classification and are aware of certain patterns that are clear indicators of a particular class. With a few lines of code, you can create a new feature that indicates the presence of this text pattern. Now whenever the model sees the class label and finds the indicator correlating strongly with it, the model will use this feature to make the classification more accurate and therefore the model performs better.

The knowledge of the domain and the data that you bring in is invaluable and injecting it will only improve the performance of the model.

Conclusion

Neural networks are extremely powerful and highly flexible in the architectures and the hyper-parameters. The data scientist must make therefore several choices carefully to get the best result from the data. We saw some key hyper-parameters in neural networks: activation function, learning rate, number of hidden units, number of layers, and optimizer. We also learned how to tune them using Keras optimizer. We also saw some practical tips for training neural networks.

Additionally, we saw that optimization of neural networks isn't limited to hyper-parameter tuning. Techniques like data augmentation and regularization can help prevent over-fitting. We learnt that creating ensembles from individual models can help obtain higher performance at the cost of additional complexity. Finally, we learnt that smart feature engineering that injects domain knowledge can be a differentiator in the value of the output.

In the next chapter, we will continue learning about optimizing deep learning models. We will focus on image models; discuss their peculiarities, and special hyper-parameters and provide practical know-how on how to get a high-performance image model.

Additional reads

For a more detailed guide on the different methods and options in the Keras Tuner library, see the following link:

https://keras.io/guides/keras_tuner/getting_started/

Andrej Karpathy's practical tips on training Neural Networks https://**karpathy.github.io/2019/04/25/recipe/.**

CHAPTER 9
Optimizing Image Models

Introduction

From facial recognition for unlocking your phone to powering self-driving cars, to object detection for video generation, the applications of image processing models are everywhere. Well-optimized image processing models make high-accuracy, real-time predictions in systems all around us (including your mobile phone) and often surpass human performance on these tasks. In the past decade, we have witnessed an increasing number of tasks being automated practically completely using machine learning/artificial intelligence. Today's data scientist needs to be versatile in handling all types of data and not be limited to tabular/ structured data. Images are now a valuable ubiquitous form of data.

It is one thing to cook up a complex, one-time, offline model as proof of concept. Creating an optimized, scalable machine learning/ artificial intelligence solution that makes near real-time predictions is a completely different ball game. In the context of image processing/ computer vision, the considerations and requirements are steep. We are generally dealing with data-hungry, complex models (for example, a deep learning model with 50 layers) with a lot of predictive power. However, we seldom have precise data for our task/ domain. Therefore, the optimization of an image processing/ computer vision solution has additional aspects that we need to be careful about.

Note: The concepts and techniques discussed in *Chapter 8, Optimizing Deep Learning Models,* all apply to image models as well. The hyper-parameter tuning techniques and hyper-parameters will be omitted in this chapter. Instead, we will focus on new aspects of model optimization that are specific to image models. We encourage you to try and apply the techniques discussed in *Chapter 8, Optimizing Deep Learning Models* to the models that we will create in this chapter.

In this chapter, we will learn all about the aforementioned aspects and learn how to create optimized solutions. Beginning with the idea of convolutional filters, we will see how this simple mathematical operation helps create powerful features for image processing tasks. It forms the backbone of most modern image-processing models. To learn how to build effective and high-performance models using the basic building blocks of convolutional neural networks, we will study the **design patterns** in various popular architectures. We will approach these neural networks as a combination of a convolutional frontend and a dense backend. From a simple convolutional neural network to the popular **Visual Geometry Group** (**VGG**) and the powerful **Residual Network** (**ResNet**) architectures, we will code these networks ourselves to maximize our practical learning.

Since we are usually dealing with complex models and low data sizes, model generalizability is an important aspect of developing solutions for image processing tasks. We will see first-hand how even a simple model can overfit very quickly. We will then learn about multiple approaches to tackle overfitting. Concretely, we will learn about various dropout approaches, the power of the extremely useful batch normalization technique, and the extremely valuable technique of data augmentation. We will have plenty of hands-on implementation of all these topics. From all our experiments and learning, we will synthesize some key guidelines for designing high-performance, optimized machine learning/ artificial intelligence solutions for image processing and computer vision.

Structure

In this chapter, we will discuss the following topics:

- Applications of image processing
- Case study: Auto image classification
- Feature detection using convolutions
- Traditional convolutional neural networks
- Parameter Regularization
    - o Spatial Dropout
    - o Batch normalization
    - o Data augmentation

- Popular architectures
    - o VGG design approach
    - o ResNet approach
- Guidelines for designing image networks

Objectives

After reading the chapter, you will get an understanding of the optimization of Deep Learning models for Image processing tasks. This chapter will begin with concepts, architectures and parameters that are unique to Image models and then demonstrate how to optimize these using TensorFlow 2.0. A case study will be used throughout the chapter for the hands-on. We will study the design of various popular model approaches and implement our own versions of VGG and ResNet models. You will also learn how to perform regularization using various approaches - dropout, data augmentation, and the powerful batch normalization technique. The chapter ends with some general guidelines for designing deep learning models for image tasks.

Applications of image processing

We listed a few popular applications of image processing in the *Introduction* section. Image models are everywhere and images as data are being increasingly used in various applications. For example, consider the application extracting image features from product images on an e-commerce platform for ranking. The attractiveness of the image and relevance of the item can be a part of the ranking system that ranks better quality products higher to increase the clicks on search results. Such systems are used by major e-commerce players and are good examples of using images as product data. An exhaustive list of such applications is not possible, especially considering the rapid rate at which we are making advances in this field. We can, however, categorize these applications into a few broad buckets.

An extremely useful application of image processing is **object detection**, that is, detecting the content/objects in the image. This could be simply classifying whether an image is that of a cat or not, or a complex application identifying the different objects in an image along with their boundaries for a self-driving car. There are broadly three types of object detection models, as illustrated in *Figure 9.1*:

***Figure 9.1**: Types of object detection models*[1]

- **Image classification:** The task is to classify whether the image belongs to one of the predetermined categories. An example application automatically identifies the product category from the item pictures users upload on an online marketplace like eBay. The labels you categorize into could be a few (for example, cat vs. dog), or even thousands (for example, the ImageNet challenge).
- **Classification with localization:** Going a step further from image classification, the task additionally involves providing a location of the object in the image. The output includes bounding boxes for the identified object, along with the probability that the object belongs to a particular class.
- **Detection:** The task is to identify the classes of the different objects present in the image. For each detected object in the image, the model classifies whether it belongs to one of the predetermined categories. Then, for each object, the model identifies its location and outputs bounding boxes. The popular **You Only Look Once (YOLO)** model is a good example. It is a deep learning-based model that divides an image into grids and calculates the probability of an object in each grid.
- **Image segmentation** is an important technique that is widely used in various applications of image processing. The task is to partition the digital image into various segments / regions. The objects in the image are identified (using labels) and each pixel in the image is assigned a label. This technique breaks down the image into components. The technique is used as a part of some of the aforementioned object detection models and is used as an input to the algorithm to produce object locations. For a self-driving car, locating any pedestrian is a critical task and image segmentation forms a vital component of the solution.

Note: Image segmentation is a whole sub-field in computer vision with a lot of ongoing research. To build perspective, we recommend reading the Wikipedia page for image segmentation, which provides a holistic overview: https://en.wikipedia.org/wiki/Image_segmentation

---

[1] *Source: https://stanford.edu/~shervine/*

We briefly look at some other prominent applications of image processing in the following list. For each application, we encourage you to explore and look for more examples.

- **Facial verification:** Whenever you unlock your phone by pointing your phone's camera to your face, you use this technology. The task is to identify whether the new face (sufficiently) matches a reference face.
- **Face recognition:** The task is to identify whether the face in the picture belongs to one of the faces in the database. A face recognition-based access in a restricted area needs to query the input face against the faces in the database and grants the user access only if there is a match.
- **Neural style transfer:** This technique modifies digital images/videos to adopt the visual style of another image. With this technique, you could make your picture look similar to the works of *Picasso* or *Klimt*. *Figure 9.2* illustrates the technique, where the image of a dog was modified to mimic the style of *Wassily Kandinsky*:

***Figure 9.2:** Neural style transfer in action*[2]

We have looked at various examples of image processing tasks and gained a high-level perspective. We are now ready to discuss the practical details and steps to create our own solutions. For this purpose, we will work on a case study throughout this chapter. Let us understand this case study next.

Case study: Auto image classification

The retail giant Azra Inc. has its popular platform Re-Fashion. The Re-Fashion platform is a marketplace for users to buy and sell used items. The items are mostly listed by individuals. Many of these individuals are not the most tech-savvy and often make mistakes in listing the item in the right product category (for example, a pair of shoes accidentally listed as a dress). Incorrect categorizations are not good for the shoppers' experience and impact the sellers' sales as the item visibility is wasted in the wrong category.

[2] *Source: https://www.tensorflow.org/tutorials/generative/style_transfer*

Azra Inc. currently employs an army of manual checkers who review thousands of listings each week. The reviewers review the image and verify if the category selected by the user matches the true category. The manual review process takes significant time and costs Azra Inc. a sizable chunk of its profits. Azra Inc. would like to reduce this cost. This problem is well suited for a machine learning/artificial intelligence solution. As the data scientist on the team, you will be taking up this challenge. Your solution will be an automatic image classification system that identifies the true category of the product, using its image. Before we start building the solution, we need to explore and understand the data well.

Note: We recommend using GPUs or TPUs if possible, for the code in this chapter. For Google Colab users, this is simply changing the Runtime type.

The first step is downloading the data to our working directory. The data is available at the GitHub link mentioned in the beginning of the book. The following command will clone the repository with the data and place a new folder titled **`clothing-dataset`** in your working directory:

```
!git clone https://github.com/alexeygrigorev/clothing-dataset-small.git
```

We need to understand the directory structure to access the files. The folder structure is shown in *Figure 9.3*. There are three folders in the main folder - **`test`**, **`train`** and **`validation`**. Each of these further contains ten folders, one for each product category/label. Opening the t-shirt folder, we see that this final level folder contains all the images for t-shirts. Likewise, the folder with the category name contains the images belonging to products in that category.

Figure 9.3: *The folder structure for the product image data*

To explore the data further, we will import some of the usual libraries using the following code:

```
import numpy as np
import matplotlib.pyplot as plt
import tensorflow as tf
from tensorflow import keras
```

Let us load one of the images from the training data into memory and view it. This will help us to better understand the format of the data. We need the **load_img** utility from Keras' inbuilt image utilities. Use the following code to load and display an image of a shoe:

```
from tensorflow.keras.preprocessing.image import load_img
path = 'clothing-dataset-small/train/shoes'
img = 'd09be031-92c0-4b14-bb7d-6d4926d3f6e2.jpg'
full_path = path + '/' + img
load_img(full_path)
```

The output image is displayed in *Figure 9.4*:

***Figure 9.4**: An image from the training data*

Let us collect the image data into a variable and understand its dimensions. We expect a matrix which we will convert into a numpy array to easily view its dimensions. Use the following code:

```
sample_img = load_img(full_path)
np.array(sample_img).shape
```

The shape gets printed as

```
(533, 400, 3)
```

The image data has three dimensions, as expected. Pixel intensity for each of the channels (Red, Blue, and Green) is present as a 533 x 400 matrix (the resolution of the image). In

Chapter 8, Optimizing Deep Learning Models, we worked with grayscale images (Fashion MNIST dataset) which could be represented in 2 dimensions. In this chapter, we will be working with color information and using all three channels of information.

Now that we understand the structure of the data folder, we can proceed to create the train and validation datasets from it. For the nested structure we have at hand, Tensorflow has an extremely handy utility called **image_dataset_from_directory**. This utility understands the folder structure and infers the labels from the names of the folders within the main folder. The data generator is useful for training larger models and dealing with larger data. It supplies data in batches to the model to perform all necessary calculations and update the parameters. In general, it is a good practice to use data generators instead of loading the entire data into memory, even if you have a small dataset. The official Tensorflow documentation has further details and examples using this utility.

Follow these steps to create the training and validation datasets:

1. First, we define the paths for the folders containing the training and the test images using the following two commands:

   ```
   train_dir = "clothing-dataset-small/train"

   val_dir = "clothing-dataset-small/validation"
   ```

2. Next, we import the **image_dataset_from_directory** utility using the following command:

   ```
   from tensorflow.keras.utils import image_dataset_from_directory
   ```

3. To the utility, we will supply the target dimensions for the images, a batch size, and the path to the folder and set a seed for reproducible results. Use the code that follows. Note that we will use an image size of 128 x 128 for all activities in this chapter. We chose this number for faster execution:

   ```
   img_dim = 128

   train_ds_gen = image_dataset_from_directory(
                        train_dir,
                        image_size = (img_dim, img_dim),
                        batch_size=32,
                        seed = 42)
   ```

The output from these steps should be as follows:

```
Found 3068 files belonging to 10 classes.
```

Similarly, we import the validation data from the validation folder using the following code:

```
val_ds_gen = image_dataset_from_directory(
                val_dir,
                image_size = (img_dim, img_dim),
                batch_size=32,
                seed = 42)
```

The output should be as follows:

```
Found 341 files belonging to 10 classes.
```

Let us print the names of the classes in the train data and store them in a variable using the following commands:

```
class_names = train_ds_gen.class_names

print(class_names)
```

The names get printed as follows:

```
['dress', 'hat', 'longsleeve', 'outwear', 'pants', 'shirt', 'shoes', 'shorts',
'skirt', 't-shirt']
```

We now have an understanding of the data format and the folder structure. Using the **image_dataset_from_directory** utility, we now have data generators for the training and the validation datasets. Let us go back to understanding some key concepts of image networks.

Feature detection using convolutions

In this section, we will briefly go over some ideas that are largely specific to image processing and are the building blocks of the convolutional neural network architecture. The first key idea is using **convolutional filters** for feature generation. In the simplest view, a convolutional filter is, well, a filter. It indicates whether a certain pattern is present in the underlying picture. This filter essentially goes over the image and compares a pattern against the pixels in the image. If the pattern (a series of numbers in the matrix) is present, the convolution operation produces a high value. The value is low if there is no pattern match. This concept is illustrated in *Figure 9.5* that follows, which represents the output from a single filter. We typically use multiple convolutional filters in a **convolutional layer** to detect more features:

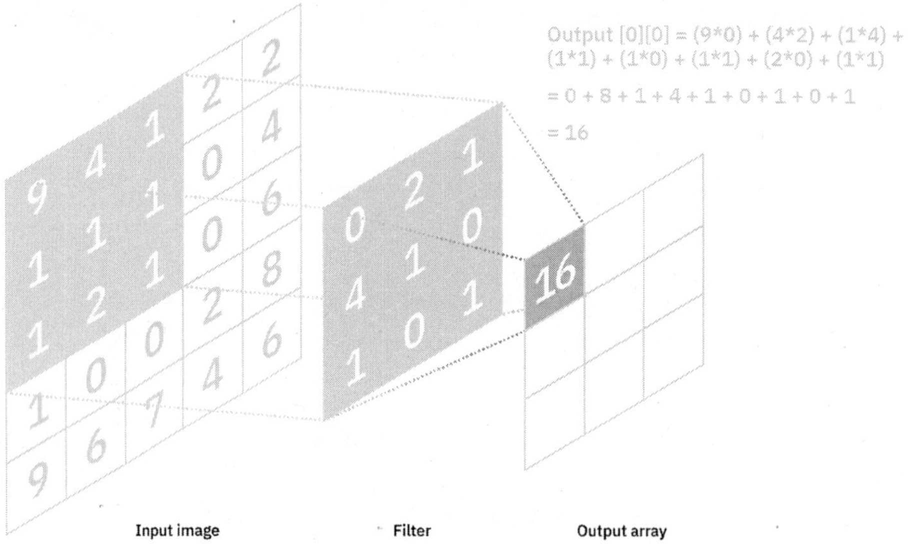

Figure 9.5: *A simple convolution layer's operation*

This simple idea is extremely powerful. When we chain multiple convolution layers, we can expect that the second layer learns combinations of feature detections from the first layer. Thus, the second layer can potentially learn more complex features. Chaining multiple layers helps us learn more and more complex features. When used in conjunction with another important idea - pooling - and applied over multiple layers, it gives the network the power to potentially detect complex patterns like entire objects (for example, a nose) in the picture.

Let us go over **pooling** next. A pooling layer is commonly inserted between successive convolution layers in a CNN. The key purpose of the pooling operation is to reduce the size of the feature vector. This helps in reducing the computation needed in the model and helps in controlling overfitting to some extent. *Figure 9.6* illustrates a simple **max pooling** operation with 2x2 filters and stride 2:

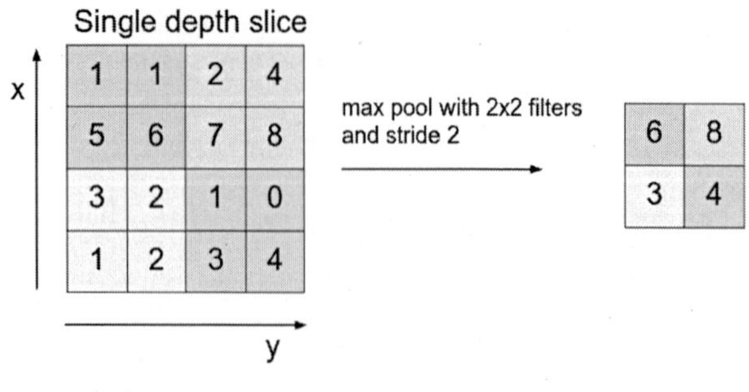

Figure 9.6: *MaxPooling with a stride*

The pooling layer uses the four values in the upper left quadrant and outputs the maximum value which is 6. Likewise, the maximum value of each quadrant is retained.

If we used an average pooling instead, it would output the average of the four values in each quadrant. The choice between average and maximum pooling is a hyperparameter. However, max pooling is increasingly becoming the more common choice. It is important to note the dimensions of the output. A 4x4 input was reduced to a 2x2 output, giving us dimensionality reduction. Note that we can use multiple filters in each pooling layer. The pooling layer operates independently on every filter output. This is illustrated in *Figure 9.7*:

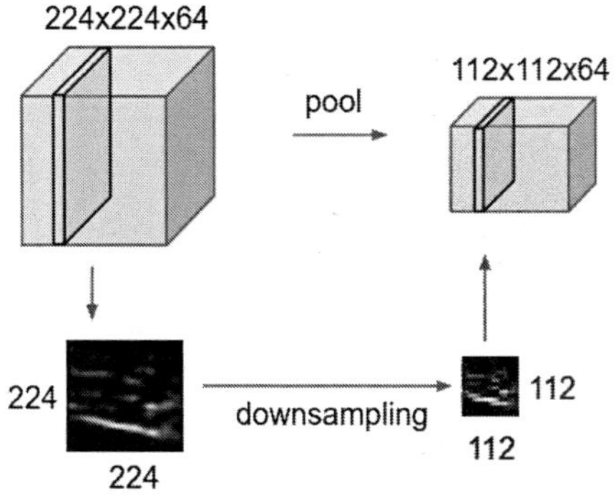

***Figure 9.7**: Pooling is downsampling*

Figure 9.7 shows how the pooling layer retains the depth of the output from the convolutional layer. The depth of the output from the convolutional layer equals the number of filters in the layer. Since the pooling layer operates on each layer independently, the output from the pooling layer has the same depth, while significantly downsampling along the height and width dimensions. If done correctly, pooling allows us to reduce dimensionality without losing significant information.

Note: To learn more details about the operationalization of these concepts and the mathematics behind them, you can refer to this excellent tutorial on the Stanford CS231 website: https://cs231n.github.io/convolutional-networks/

These two ideas and how they work together are key to understanding the effectiveness and working of convolutional neural networks. Let us now understand the architecture of the traditional convolutional neural network to make these ideas more concrete.

Traditional Convolutional Neural Networks

A convolutional neural network can be designed using three main types of layers:

- Convolutional layer,
- Pooling layer, and
- Dense layer

The convolutional layer(s) along with the pooling layers(s) form the frontend of the network. The dense layer(s) form the back of the layer. In other words, a convolutional network can be thought of as adding a convolutional frontend to a deep neural network. The idea is illustrated in *Figure 9.8*, which shows the simplest convolutional neural network:

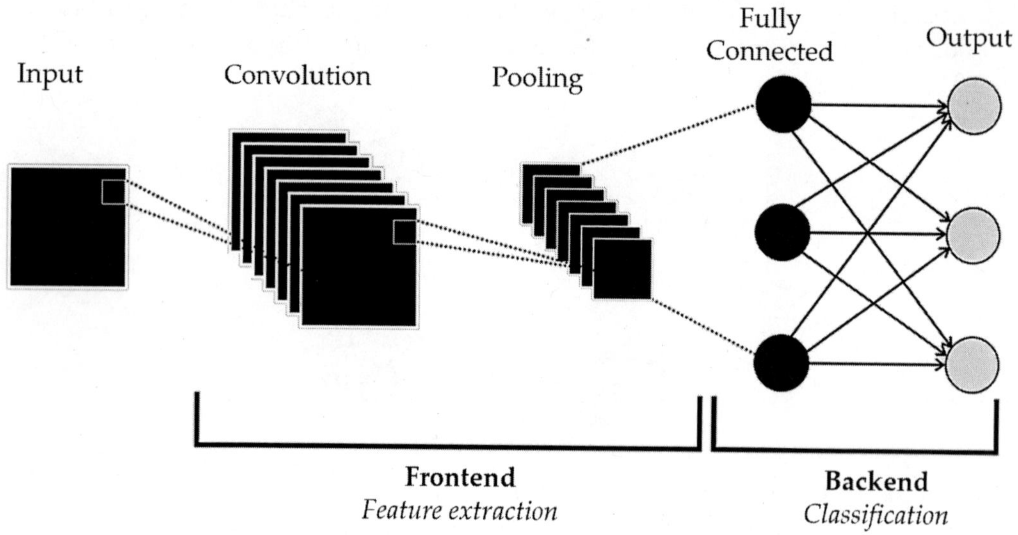

***Figure 9.8**: Traditional CNN architecture*

As denoted in *Figure 9.8*, the convolutional layers form the frontend. The purpose of this frontend is to learn powerful features and reduce the size of the feature vector. When using multiple convolutional layers, the initial layers learn very coarse features, while subsequent layers learn more and more fine features. The max pooling layers manage the size without losing information from the feature maps.

The dense layers form the classification/prediction backend. There are typically multiple, dense, fully connected layers. The output from the convolutional frontend is typically a feature vector that the backend processes to make predictions. The design is straightforward and easy to understand and implement. The hugely successful VGG class of models is a popular example of this simple approach.

For our case study, we will build a simple convolutional neural network for our image classification task. We will use a simple architecture with three convolution layers in the frontend and one dense layer (apart from the prediction layer) in the backend. The architecture is illustrated in *Figure 9.9*:

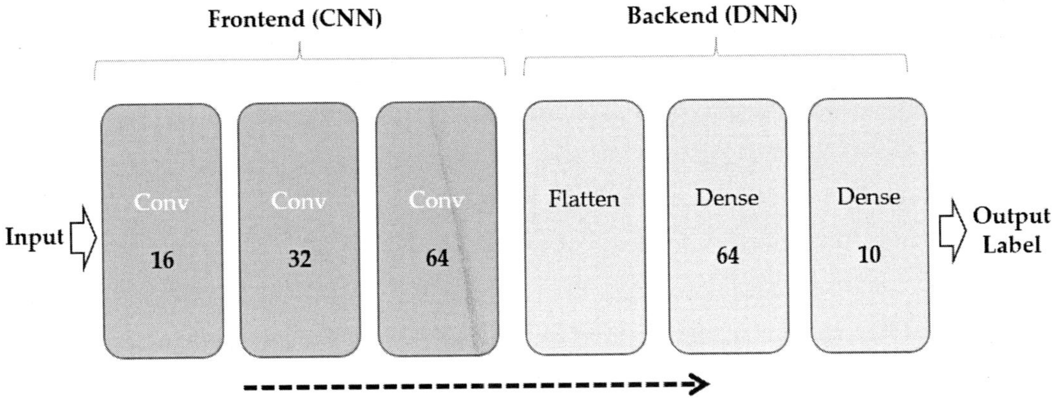

Figure 9.9: Our first, simple CNN

Let's start by creating a variable named num_classes to store the total number of classes in the dataset using the following command. This will help avoid manually entering the number of classes each time for further models:

```
num_classes = len(class_names)
```

Next, let us import the necessary utilities from Keras. We will import the Sequential model and the layers to define the architecture. Use the commands that follow:

```
from keras.models import Sequential

from keras.layers import Rescaling, Conv2D, MaxPooling2D, Flatten, Dense
```

We can now define the model architecture illustrated in *Figure 9.9*. First, let us add the Rescaling layer. This rescaling layer will ensure all pixel values are between 0 and 1 and resize all images to the same target size (128 x 128):

```
model_conv = Sequential()

model_conv.add(Rescaling(1./255, input_shape=(img_dim, img_dim, 3)))
```

Next, let us define the CNN frontend. We will use three Conv2D layers with filters of size 3. We will use ReLu activation and specify 'same' padding. The layers will contain 16, 32 and 64 filters, respectively. Each layer will be followed by a MaxPooling2D layer. Use the following code to define the frontend:

```
model_conv.add(Conv2D(16, 3, padding='same', activation='relu'))

model_conv.add(MaxPooling2D())

model_conv.add(Conv2D(32, 3, padding='same', activation='relu'))

model_conv.add(MaxPooling2D())

model_conv.add(Conv2D(64, 3, padding='same', activation='relu'))

model_conv.add(MaxPooling2D())
```

Now let us define the DNN backend. First, we use the Flatten layer to get all the features into a single vector. We follow this with a fully connected dense layer of 64 neurons with ReLu activation. The final prediction layer will be a dense layer of 10 neurons, one for each class label, with a softmax activation. We will use the code that follows:

```
model_conv.add(Flatten())
model_conv.add(Dense(64, activation='relu'))
model_conv.add(Dense(num_classes, activation='softmax'))
```

The frontend and backend are defined; we can now compile the model. We will use the Adam optimizer, which is usually a good default. We will use the **sparse_categorical_crossentropy** loss function and print out the model summary as shown in the following code:

```
model_conv.compile(optimizer='adam',
              loss='sparse_categorical_crossentropy',
              metrics=['accuracy'])
```

The summary gets printed out as shown in *Figure 9.10*:

```
Layer (type)                 Output Shape              Param #
=================================================================
rescaling (Rescaling)        (None, 128, 128, 3)       0

conv2d (Conv2D)              (None, 128, 128, 16)      448

max_pooling2d (MaxPooling2D  (None, 64, 64, 16)        0
)

conv2d_1 (Conv2D)            (None, 64, 64, 32)        4640

max_pooling2d_1 (MaxPooling  (None, 32, 32, 32)        0
2D)

conv2d_2 (Conv2D)            (None, 32, 32, 64)        18496

max_pooling2d_2 (MaxPooling  (None, 16, 16, 64)        0
2D)

flatten (Flatten)            (None, 16384)             0

dense (Dense)                (None, 64)                1048640

dense_1 (Dense)              (None, 10)                650

=================================================================
Total params: 1,072,874
Trainable params: 1,072,874
Non-trainable params: 0
```

***Figure 9.10**: Summary of the simple Convolutional model*

The summary shows about 1.07M parameters. Notice that most of these parameters come from the first dense layer. We expect (16,384 + 1) x 64 = 1,048,640 parameters, which is what we get. It should be easy to see that the 16,384 parameters in the flatten layer are simply the product of the dimensions of the final max pooling layer (16 x 16 x 64).

Now, we can fit the model on the training data generator and supply the validation data generator for validation scoring. We will train for 10 epochs. Use the following code:

```
epochs=10

history = model_conv.fit(train_ds_gen,
                         validation_data=val_ds_gen,
                         epochs=epochs)
```

The (truncated) output should look like *Figure. 9.11*:

```
6s 58ms/step - loss: 0.5064 - accuracy: 0.8282 - val_loss: 1.1151 - val_accuracy: 0.6716

6s 56ms/step - loss: 0.3328 - accuracy: 0.8843 - val_loss: 1.2322 - val_accuracy: 0.6862

5s 44ms/step - loss: 0.2126 - accuracy: 0.9316 - val_loss: 1.4145 - val_accuracy: 0.7243

4s 44ms/step - loss: 0.1215 - accuracy: 0.9651 - val_loss: 1.5533 - val_accuracy: 0.6921

6s 58ms/step - loss: 0.1174 - accuracy: 0.9661 - val_loss: 1.6795 - val_accuracy: 0.7155

4s 41ms/step - loss: 0.0903 - accuracy: 0.9716 - val_loss: 2.1751 - val_accuracy: 0.6628
```

Figure. 9.11: *Truncated output from the training*

Note: Due to randomization, the values you observe might slightly differ from ours. The pattern, however, should be consistent.

Notice that model accuracies on the training and the validation data are very different - 97% vs. 66%. This seems to be true for the last few epochs. To study this divergence better, we will plot the learning curves - the accuracy of the training and validation sets for all the epochs. Use the following code for this purpose:

```
train_acc = history.history['accuracy']

val_acc = history.history['val_accuracy']

x = np.arange(1, epochs+1)

plt.plot(x, train_acc, label="Training Accuracy")

plt.plot(x, val_acc, label="Validation Accuracy")

plt.ylim(0,1); plt.legend();

plt.show()
```

Alternatively, we can define the following function for reusability and call it using the following code:

```
def plot_perf(hist, epochs):

  train_acc = hist.history['accuracy']

  val_acc = hist.history['val_accuracy']

  x = np.arange(1, epochs+1)

  plt.plot(x, train_acc, label="Training Accuracy")
```

```
plt.plot(x, val_acc, label="Validation Accuracy")
plt.ylim(0,1); plt.legend()
plt.show()
```

Using the function, we can plot the model performance using the following single-line command. The output must be the same as using the entire code:

```
plot_perf(history, epochs)
```

The output plot should look like *Figure 9.12:*

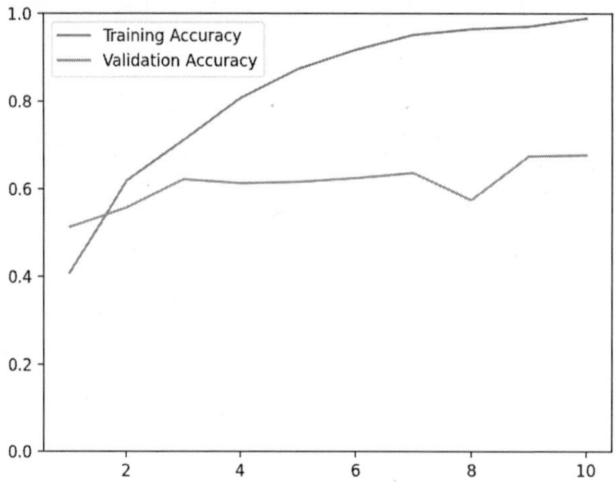

***Figure 9.12**: The Convnet overfits in a few epochs*

We can see that this is a textbook case of overfitting. The training accuracy crosses the validation accuracy very quickly and keeps increasing while the validation accuracy remains stable at around 60%. This indicates that the model is not learning any generalized pattern but is memorizing the training data.

Indeed, overfitting is a big issue for convolutional networks with multiple layers and high parameter counts. Avoiding overfitting is therefore an important aspect of building convolutional neural networks. Let us now learn and implement some ways of avoiding overfitting and improving the general performance of the model.

Parameter regularization

We have already discussed adjusting the cost function (L1 or L2 penalty) in *Chapter 5, Imbalanced Machine Learning* and *Chapter 6, Hyper-parameter Tuning*. We have been using regular, dense dropouts in the chapters so far. Now, we will learn about a version of dropout more suited for convolutional neural networks. After that, we will learn about and implement batch normalization, an extremely useful technique for building deep neural networks.

Spatial Dropout

Using a dropout is a very direct way of regularization that is extremely effective. In addition to the regular drop where some connections are simply dropped, there are many interesting approaches developed in the past few years. SpatialDropout2D is an example that is very useful for models with convolutions. It drops out entire feature maps instead of just a single weight, as illustrated in *Figure 9.13*:

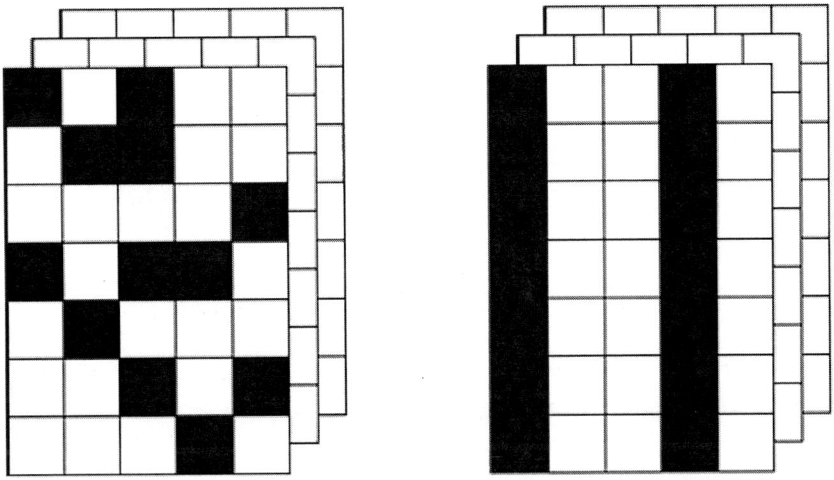

Figure. 9.13: Regular (left) vs spatial (right) dropout

Spatial dropout is a commonly used technique for convolutional neural networks. The dropout layer is commonly added right after a pooling layer. We will use spatial dropout in this chapter. However, there are some other interesting dropout techniques, not limited to those for CNNs, worth exploring:

- Gaussian dropout (injects noise to weights),
- DropConnect (zeros random weights during each forward pass),
- DropBlock (drops entire blocks in CNNs),
- Variational dropout (for recurrent networks, uses the same mask for each time step)
- Attention dropout (for transformers / attention models, drops attention units)

Note: Details about the dropout methods listed earlier in their original papers and code can be found at: https://paperswithcode.com/methods/category/regularization

These were a few prominent examples of approaches to dropout. We encourage you to explore and learn more about these approaches. Let us now see dropout in action and assess its impact on the image classification case study for Azra Inc.

Exercise 9.1: Convolution model with dropout

In this activity, we will use dropout to regularize our image model. We need two types of dropouts viz. Dropout and SpatialDropout2D. Dropout is the regular method we use for dense layers. SpatialDropout will be used to mask entire feature maps. We will use the spatial dropout layer after every pooling layer and the regular dropout after the flattening layer. Our model architecture will otherwise be the same as the previous model. Let us begin creating our model:

1. Import the dropout layers from Keras using the following command:

```
from keras.layers import Dropout, SpatialDropout2D
```

2. Instantiate a model, add the rescaling layer and the Conv2D layer, followed by MaxPooling2D. Add a SpatialDropout2D layer with 50% dropout. Use the following code:

```
model_dropout = Sequential()
model_dropout.add(Rescaling(1./255, input_shape=(img_dim, img_dim,
3)))
model_dropout.add(Conv2D(16, 3, padding='same', activation='relu'))
model_dropout.add(MaxPooling2D())
model_dropout.add(SpatialDropout2D(0.5))
```

3. To complete the frontend, add spatial dropout (50%) after the 2nd convolution layer only. Use the code that follows:

```
model_dropout.add(Conv2D(32, 3, padding='same', activation='relu'))
model_dropout.add(MaxPooling2D())
model_dropout.add(SpatialDropout2D(0.5))
model_dropout.add(Conv2D(64, 3, padding='same', activation='relu'))
model_dropout.add(MaxPooling2D())
```

4. Add a regular dropout (50%) after adding the flatten later. Add the dense layers and compile the model using the Adam optimizer and sparse categorical cross entropy as the loss function, as shown in the following code:

```
model_dropout.add(Flatten())
model_dropout.add(Dropout(0.5))
model_dropout.add(Dense(64, activation='relu'))
model_dropout.add(Dense(num_classes, activation='softmax'))
model_dropout.compile(optimizer='adam',
              loss='sparse_categorical_crossentropy',
              metrics=['accuracy'])
model_dropout.summary()
```

The (truncated) output should be as shown in *Figure 9.14*:

```
flatten_11 (Flatten)        (None, 16384)           0

dropout_5 (Dropout)         (None, 16384)           0

dense_22 (Dense)            (None, 64)              1048640

dense_23 (Dense)            (None, 10)              650

=================================================================
Total params: 1,072,874
Trainable params: 1,072,874
Non-trainable params: 0
```

***Figure 9.14**: Truncated model summary output*

From the preceding figure, we see that the number of parameters is the same as in the previous model, as expected. Let us now train the model.

5. Train the model for 10 epochs and plot the learning curves. Use the following code:

```
epochs=10
history = model_dropout.fit(
  train_ds_gen,
  validation_data=val_ds_gen,
  epochs=epochs
)
plot_perf(history, 10)
```

The learning curve is plotted as shown in *Figure 9.15*:

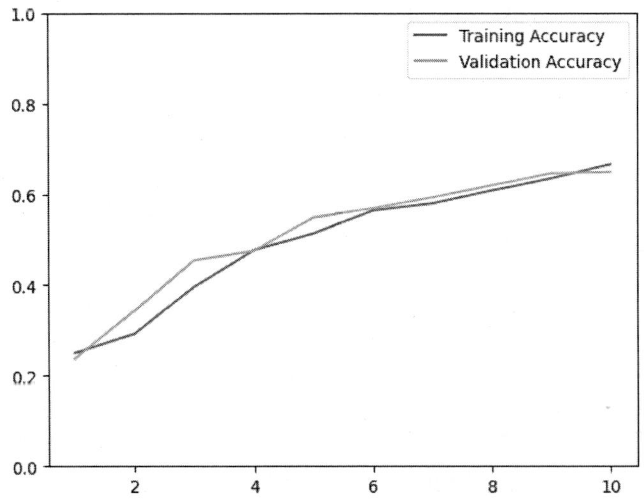

***Figure 9.15**: Learning curve for the model with dropout*

We see that both training and validation accuracies are close together and growing steadily. The training accuracy is very similar to the validation accuracy, indicating that the model is not overfitting. This exercise clearly demonstrates the power of dropout in managing overfitting. Dropout is not the only tool in our arsenal, though. Let us now look at another very important technique in the deep learning world - batch normalization.

Batch normalization

Another important and indirect way of regularization is batch normalization. It is important to note that batch normalization was originally developed to address the problem of Internal Covariate Shift that occurs in deep neural networks. The issue, briefly, is that ReLu is not zero-centered due to which the input distribution shifts over time. As a result, the deep neural network learns very slowly. Batch normalization was developed to address this issue and thus make the model learn faster.

This is how the batch normalization technique works:

Simply normalize the weights within the network for each batch. At the input of the layer, the mean and standard deviation of the batch are measured. The activations of the input are then normalized using them. As a result, we have zero mean and unit standard deviation for each batch. This is done during the training process. After the training of the model is complete, to make predictions, the mean and standard deviation of the entire training data are used.

Note: For details on Internal Covariate Shift and to understand exactly how batch normalization helps in handling it, refer to the 2015 paper on batch normalization here: https://arxiv.org/pdf/1502.03167.pdf

The primary intent of it was to address the Internal Covariate Shift issue to speed up training. However, researchers observed that batch normalization also helps in regularization, helping the model generalize better. A recent paper explains the phenomenon theoretically and is a recommended read for those interested in the mechanism. You can find the paper at: **arxiv.org/pdf/1809.00846.pdf**

Let us use batch normalization in our case study and assess if we observe any regularization. Note that we are not using it for faster convergence. However, we strongly encourage you to use batch normalization for faster convergence. You might want to use it in conjunction with other regularization techniques and try tuning the learning rate. Let us begin.

We will need the `BatchNormalization` layer and the `ReLu` layer. We will apply the batch normalization right after applying the convolutions and before the non-linearity from the `ReLu` activation kicks in. For this purpose, we need the activation applied as a separate `ReLu` layer. We will not use any dropout in this exercise and the model architecture otherwise will be the same as in the previous exercises. Let us start by importing the additional layers from Keras using the command that follows:

```
from keras.layers import BatchNormalization, ReLU
```

Start defining the frontend by adding the rescaling layer and the Conv2D layer as before. Then, add the **BatchNormalization** layer, followed by the **ReLu** layer and the **MaxPooling2D** using the following code:

```
model_norm = Sequential()
model_norm.add(Rescaling(1./255, input_shape=(img_dim, img_dim, 3)))
model_norm.add(Conv2D(16, 3, padding='same'))
model_norm.add(BatchNormalization())
model_norm.add(ReLU())
model_norm.add(MaxPooling2D())
```

Similarly, we add the remaining convolutional layers along with the batch normalization, **ReLu** activation and max pooling layers. Use the following code:

```
model_norm.add(Conv2D(32, 3, padding='same'))
model_norm.add(BatchNormalization())
model_norm.add(ReLU())
model_norm.add(MaxPooling2D())
model_norm.add(Conv2D(64, 3, padding='same'))
model_norm.add(BatchNormalization())
model_norm.add(ReLU())
model_norm.add(MaxPooling2D())
```

The frontend definition is now complete. Let us now define the DNN backend. We use the same backend as in the previous exercise.

```
model_norm.add(Flatten())
model_norm.add(Dense(64, activation='relu'))
model_norm.add(Dense(num_classes, activation='softmax'))
```

Compile the model, train for 10 epochs and plot the learning curves. Use the following code:

```
model_norm.compile(optimizer='adam',
              loss='sparse_categorical_crossentropy',
              metrics=['accuracy'])
epochs=10
history = model_norm.fit(
  train_ds_gen,
  validation_data=val_ds_gen,
  epochs=epochs
)
plot_perf(history, 10)
```

The learning curves are obtained as shown in *Figure 9.16*:

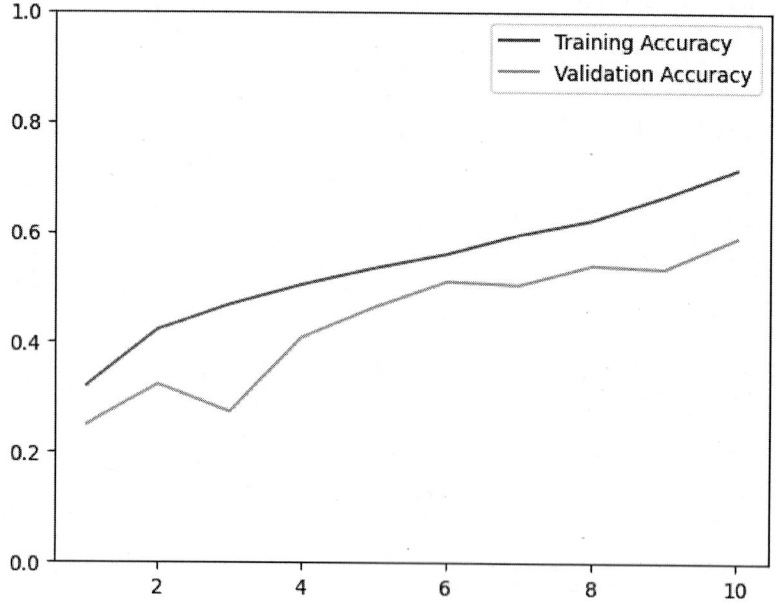

***Figure. 9.16:** Batch normalization helps with regularization*

It is important to note that batch normalization is not purely/explicitly a regularization method. Rather, the technique's regularization effect was an observation by researchers and practitioners. Batch normalization was intended to make the model learn faster. From *Figure 9.16,* we can see that the regularization effect exists, but is not as strong as dropout.

Pause and ponder: We see that there is a gap between the training and validation accuracy that appears across epochs. This behavior is not surprising. Can you explain this behavior?

Hint: Think about normalization during prediction.

Additionally, we see that the model is learning faster than the dropout model and there is still some difference between the training and validation accuracy. In practice, we should use batch normalization in conjunction with other explicit regularization methods like dropout and data augmentation. We have already learned and used the dropout technique. Let us now understand and implement an extremely powerful technique for computer vision tasks, that is, data augmentation.

Data augmentation

Data augmentation artificially enlarges the dataset. This is done by generating new images from the existing ones by applying transformations to them. Modified copies of the original image are then used as additional examples for the model to learn from. Consider the task of classification of an image as a dog or a cat. On rotation, the image still clearly represents a cat and does not change the label, as illustrated in *Figure 9.17*:

***Figure 9.17**: The label does not change on image transformation*

However, we should be extremely careful in choosing the transformation for data augmentation. The label should be invariant to the transformations. In simpler terms, the transformation should not affect the class in the label. Common transformations may lead to problems in specific situations. Consider the example *in Figure. 9.18*. In a digit recognition task, the rotation transformation can cause the label to change. 9 could become 6 and vice versa. Therefore, *we must carefully review the transformations and ensure that the label is invariant to all of them.*

***Figure 9.18**: An example where the label is not invariant to rotation*

An exhaustive list of transformations is not possible as different situations necessitate different transformations. Some of the most popular transformations are illustrated in *Figure 9.19*. For most tasks, flipping, rotation, random crop and contrast change are safer options and are types of random spatial transformation. Noise addition, color shift and information loss are types of pixel transformation.

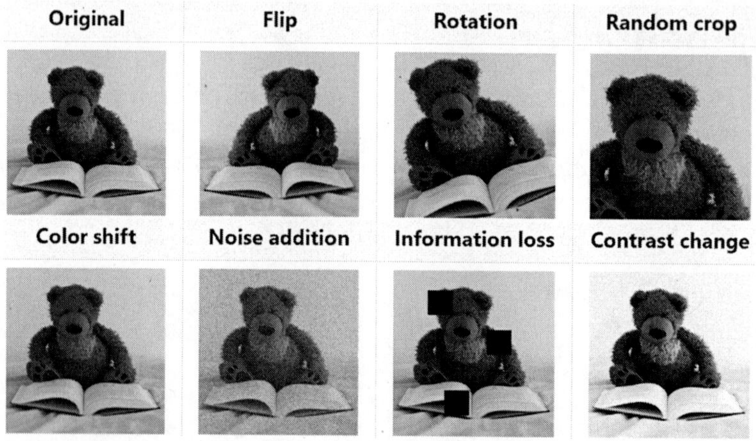

Figure 9.19: Common transformations for data augmentation[3]

We encourage you to explore some other transformation approaches, beyond the pixel transformation approaches we just learnt about. Some notable and interesting approaches are as follows:

- Feature space augmentation
- GAN-based augmentation
- Meta-learning

Let us now implement data augmentation on our own to see the kind of output these transformations can produce. Let us also see how convenient using data augmentation is with Keras. Most of the commonly used transformations are readily available as Keras layers. We will use a few different transformations from Keras. Let us start by importing the layers module from Keras:

```
from keras import layers
```

Next, we define a series/sequence of layers to perform various augmentations. This sequence can be used as a layer itself in any Keras model, as we will see in the next exercise. The transformations we will use are - random flip, random rotation, random zoom, random contrast, and Gaussian noise addition. Use the following code to define the augmentation layer:

```
data_augmentation = keras.Sequential(
  [
    layers.RandomFlip("horizontal_and_vertical",
                       input_shape=(img_dim, img_dim, 3)),
```

[3] *Source: stanford.edu/~shervine*

```
    layers.RandomRotation(0.2),
    layers.RandomZoom(0.3),
    layers.RandomContrast(0.3),
    layers.GaussianNoise(0.2)
])
```

Once defined, this layer can be applied directly to a batch of images as well. Let us take an image from the training data generator and apply various transformations to it. Let us then plot 9 different transformation combinations on the image. Use the following code:

```
for images, _ in train_ds_gen.take(1):
  for i in range(9):
    augmented_images = data_augmentation(images)
    ax = plt.subplot(3, 3, i + 1)
    plt.imshow(augmented_images[0].numpy().astype("uint8"))
    plt.axis("off")
```

The output is shown in *Figure 9.20*:

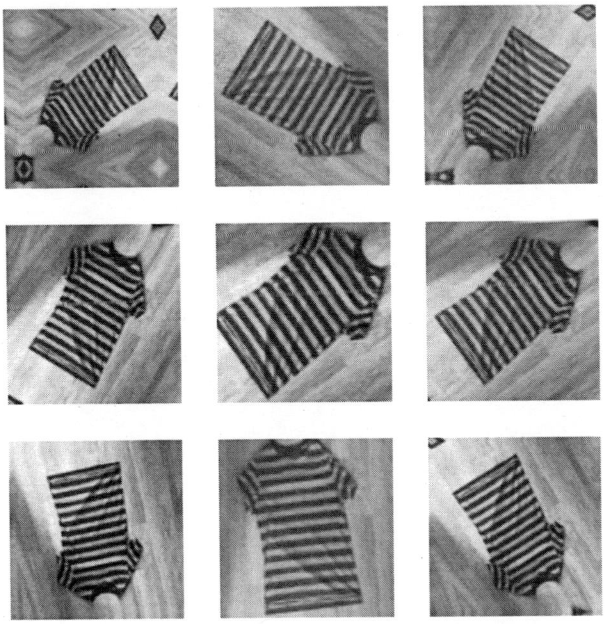

Figure 9.20: *Data augmentation derived nine images from one*

Note from *Figure 9.20* that a combination of just a few transformations gave us numerous variations of a single input image. This is extremely useful in situations where we have little data, or, for class imbalance situations where we have few examples of a particular class. We encourage you to try out more transformations that are available as Keras layers. Now that we understand how augmentation works and how to employ it using Keras, let us apply augmentation to our image classification case study for Azra Inc.

Exercise 9.2: Conv model with data augmentation

In this exercise, we will use data augmentation to improve our model for the image classification case study for Azra Inc. We will use some simple transformations for this task - horizontal flipping, random rotation (20%) and random zoom (30%). We will employ the same model architecture that we used in previous exercises. Let us begin creating our model and assessing the impact of data augmentation:

1. First, define the augmentation layer with the augmentation steps mentioned above. Use the following code:

```
data_augmentation = keras.Sequential(
  [
    layers.RandomFlip("horizontal",
                      input_shape=(img_dim, img_dim, 3)),
    layers.RandomRotation(0.2),
    layers.RandomZoom(0.3),
  ])
```

2. Instantiate a sequential model, and add the rescaling layer, followed by our data augmentation layer. Use the following code:

```
model_aug = Sequential()
model_aug.add(Rescaling(1./255, input_shape=(img_dim, img_dim, 3)))
model_aug.add(data_augmentation)
```

3. Define the remaining architecture with the convolutional and dense layers. There should be no dropout or batch normalization. This can be done using the following code:

```
model_aug.add(Conv2D(16, 3, padding='same', activation='relu'))
model_aug.add(MaxPooling2D())
model_aug.add(Conv2D(32, 3, padding='same', activation='relu'))
model_aug.add(MaxPooling2D())
model_aug.add(Conv2D(64, 3, padding='same', activation='relu'))
model_aug.add(MaxPooling2D())
model_aug.add(Flatten())
model_aug.add(Dense(64, activation='relu'))
model_aug.add(Dense(num_classes, activation='softmax'))
```

4. Compile the model and train it on the data for 20 epochs. Plot the learning curves using the code that follows:

```
model_aug.compile(optimizer='adam',
                  loss='sparse_categorical_crossentropy',
                  metrics=['accuracy'])

epochs=20
history = model_aug.fit(
  train_ds_gen,
  validation_data=val_ds_gen,
  epochs=epochs)
```

You should get the plot as shown in *Figure 9.21*:

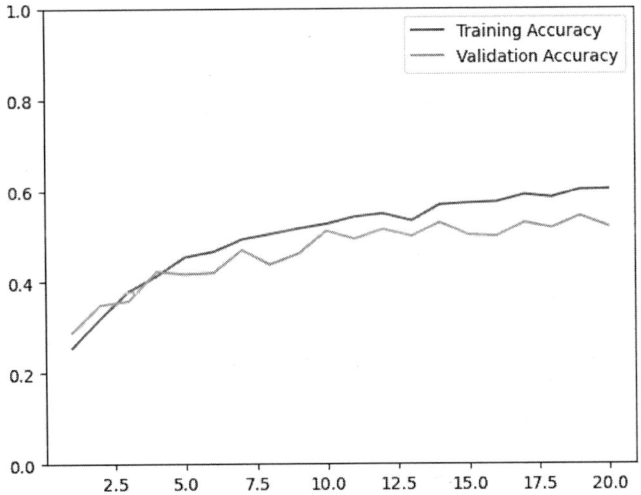

***Figure. 9.21**: Regularization using data augmentation*

The learning curves in *Figure 9.21* show a significant improvement in the model's generalizability. The training and validation accuracy curves are much closer and moving together. This means that the model is not overfitting significantly. Note that we achieved this by a simple and rather arbitrary choice of data augmentations. A well-studied and tuned approach can provide even better results. For best results, it is recommended that the regularization techniques we discussed be used in conjunction. A model that includes data augmentation, batch normalization as well dropout, with a bit of tuning, is expected to provide much better results.

This completes our discussion on regularization. We discussed three diverse approaches for this task and saw the standalone performance of each approach. We saw that these are simple to implement and can significantly improve model generalizability and help tackle overfitting. Now, let us continue our discussion on another important aspect of designing our neural network - the architecture.

Popular architectures

So far, the architecture we used in the case study was rather arbitrary. A natural question at this point would be - how do we choose this architecture? To make good decisions about the architecture, we need to first appreciate that the architecture is a system design choice. An understanding of some common design patterns employed in common architectures can be extremely useful for developing your own perspective on design.

Several architectures in the field of Convolutional Networks have gained popularity and spurred research. Some of them are as follows. These gained popularity by top performance in the **ImageNet Large Scale Visual Recognition Challenge** (**ILSVRC**), or simply the ImageNet challenge.

Note: We will skip some of the older architectures like LeNet and AlexNet

- **GoogLeNet**: This model won the ImageNet challenge in 2014. The latest Inception models are successors of the GoogLeNet model. This was the first model to develop the inception model that drastically reduced the number of parameters in the network. A significant feature of the model was the usage of average pooling at the end of the convolutional frontend. This helped reduce the number of parameters to about 4M. By contrast, other competing SOTA models had far more parameters (AlexNet had 60M+, and VGGNet had about 140M).

- **VGGNet**. The model was the runner-up in the challenge in 2014. It was a relatively deep model, consisting of 16 layers. The model was extremely simple otherwise. The success of this model demonstrated the importance of depth in neural networks for performance. We will learn about this in more detail in the section *VGG design approach*. VGGNet, however, had a high number of parameters (140M) and was therefore considered computationally very expensive then.

- **ResNet**. The 2015 challenge was won by ResNet. The key idea of ResNet was to use special 'shortcuts' in the network that allowed for data to propagate more freely to subsequent layers. The model also heavily used batch normalization. ResNet models and their derivations remained state-of-the-art for a long time. We will learn more about it in detail and create our own ResNet model.

Other than these, many more popular architectures have performed extremely well on image-processing tasks. It is recommended that you look up the latest SOTA models and try to understand their working as well. We encourage you to do so with an emphasis on understanding the design approaches employed by them to help build your own perspective on network architecture. For now, let us understand the VGG model and its design better.

VGG design approach

The VGGNet model was an extremely popular SOTA model that was the runner-up of the 2014 ILSVRC competition. The model's notable contribution was that it showed how important the depth of the architecture is for high performance. The model was rather simplistic otherwise, using small receptive fields and equal-sized convolutional layers in small blocks. The architecture is illustrated in *Figure. 9.22*:

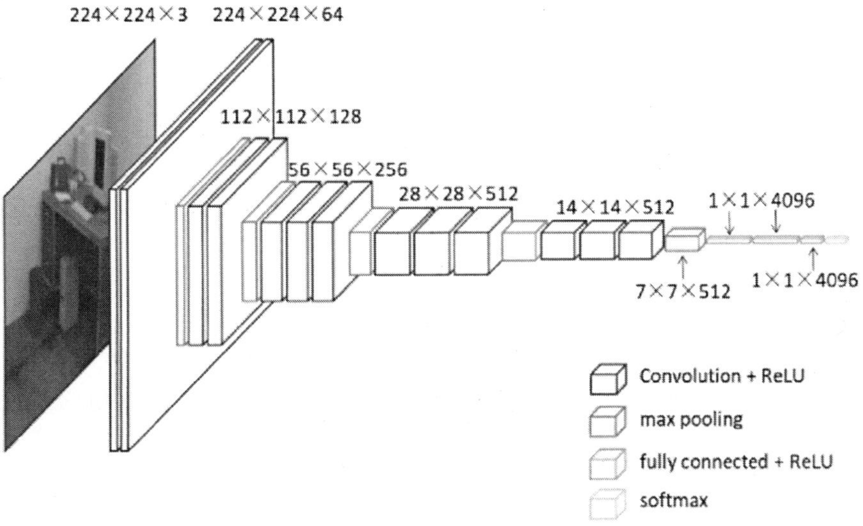

Figure. 9.22: *The VGG16 model architecture*

As we can see in *Figure 9.22*, the salient features of the VGG architecture are:

- It uses equal-sized convolutional layers in a block
- It doubles the number of filters in subsequent blocks (64, 128, 256 and then 512).
- It uses pooling at the end of a convolutional block.
- It uses a small receptive field (3x3).

Taking a simplified, frontend vs. backend perspective, the original VGG16 architecture can be represented by *Figure. 9.23*. As you can see, the number of filters in each convolutional group doubles from 64 to 512:

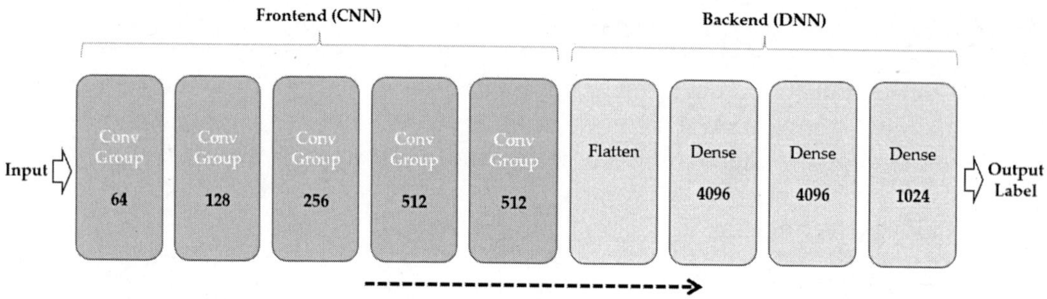

Figure 9.23: CNN Frontend and DNN backend in the VGG16 architecture

Note: We will learn how to use the original VGG16 model, trained on the ImageNet database, in *Chapter 11, Transfer Learning.*

The original VGG architecture was trained on the ImageNet database, consisting of millions of images belonging to 1,000 categories. We, however, have considerably fewer training images (just 3,068). Regardless, let us now learn how to code up our VGG16.

We will need to add about 13 convolutional layers, which need a lot of repetition. To make our code cleaner, we will use a procedure/function to create a convolutional block with a specific number of convolutional layers and filters. The filter size will be 3 x 3 in all the layers. The following code accomplishes this:

```
def conv_block(num_layers, num_filters):
  for n in range(num_layers):
    model_vgg.add(Conv2D(num_filters, (3,3),\
                    strides=(1,1), padding='same',
                    activation='relu'))
  model_vgg.add(MaxPooling2D((2,2), strides=(2,2)))
```

Note that the max pooling layer is added only at the end of the convolutional block. Also, notice that we have already specified the name of the model object as '**`model_vgg`**' in the function. This is the name of our version of the VGG16 model that we will create in the following exercise.

Exercise 9.3: Creating VGG16 from scratch

In this exercise, we will create our own version of VGG16 to help Azra Inc. automatically categorize the user-submitted product images into 10 predefined product categories. Note that the input size we use will be 128 x 128 (the original VGG16 used 224x224). Additionally, we will have 10 final labels (as opposed to 1,000 in the original model). This means that we will have significantly fewer parameters in our model (VGG16 had 140M parameters).

We will use the **conv_block** function we defined in the previous section to add convolutional blocks. Note that we will define the very first convolutional layer manually as it needs the image dimensions to be specified.

Also, we will visualize our created model using the **visualkeras** library. If you do not have it installed already, you can do so by using the following commands:

```
!pip install visualkeras

import visualkeras
```

Let us get started.

1. Instantiate a sequential model and add the first convolutional layer to it with ReLu activation using the following code:

```
model_vgg = Sequential()

model_vgg.add(Conv2D(64, (3,3), strides=(1,1), \

                    padding='same', activation='relu',

                    input_shape=(img_dim, img_dim, 3)))
```

2. Using the **conv_block** function, define the convolutional frontend with the number of blocks as illustrated in *Figure 9.23* earlier, that is, 64, 128, 256, 512 and 512.

```
conv_block(1, 64)

conv_block(2, 128)

conv_block(3, 256)

conv_block(3, 512)

conv_block(3, 512)
```

3. Define the DNN backend with a flatten layer, two dense layers of 4,096 neurons each and a prediction layer with 10 neurons and softmax activation:

```
model_vgg.add(Flatten())

model_vgg.add(Dense(4096, activation='relu'))

model_vgg.add(Dense(4096, activation='relu'))

model_vgg.add(Dense(num_classes, activation='softmax'))
```

4. Compile the model with Adam optimizer and sparse categorical entropy loss, and print out the summary using the following code:

```
model_vgg.compile(optimizer='adam',

                  loss='sparse_categorical_crossentropy',

                  metrics=['accuracy'])

model_vgg.summary()
```

The output is shown in *Figure 9.24*:

```
Layer (type)                  Output Shape              Param #
================================================================
conv2d_22 (Conv2D)            (None, 128, 128, 64)      1792

conv2d_23 (Conv2D)            (None, 128, 128, 64)      36928

max_pooling2d_16 (MaxPoolin   (None, 64, 64, 64)        0
g2D)

conv2d_24 (Conv2D)            (None, 64, 64, 128)       73856

conv2d_25 (Conv2D)            (None, 64, 64, 128)       147584

max_pooling2d_17 (MaxPoolin   (None, 32, 32, 128)       0
g2D)

conv2d_26 (Conv2D)            (None, 32, 32, 256)       295168

conv2d_27 (Conv2D)            (None, 32, 32, 256)       590080

conv2d_28 (Conv2D)            (None, 32, 32, 256)       590080

max_pooling2d_18 (MaxPoolin   (None, 16, 16, 256)       0
g2D)

conv2d_29 (Conv2D)            (None, 16, 16, 512)       1180160

conv2d_30 (Conv2D)            (None, 16, 16, 512)       2359808

conv2d_31 (Conv2D)            (None, 16, 16, 512)       2359808

max_pooling2d_19 (MaxPoolin   (None, 8, 8, 512)         0
g2D)

conv2d_32 (Conv2D)            (None, 8, 8, 512)         2359808

conv2d_33 (Conv2D)            (None, 8, 8, 512)         2359808

conv2d_34 (Conv2D)            (None, 8, 8, 512)         2359808

max_pooling2d_20 (MaxPoolin   (None, 4, 4, 512)         0
g2D)

flatten (Flatten)             (None, 8192)              0

dense (Dense)                 (None, 4096)              33558528

dense_1 (Dense)               (None, 4096)              16781312

dense_2 (Dense)               (None, 10)                40970

================================================================
Total params: 65,095,498
Trainable params: 65,095,498
Non-trainable params: 0
```

***Figure 9.24**: Summary of our VGG16 model*

5. Plot the model's frontend with the **`layered_view`** method from **`visualkeras`** using the following command:

   ```
   visualkeras.layered_view(model_vgg, legend=True, type_
   ignore=[Flatten, Dense], max_xy=300)
   ```

Note: We have excluded the flatten and dense layers to omit the dense backend.

You should get the output as shown in *Figure. 9.25*:

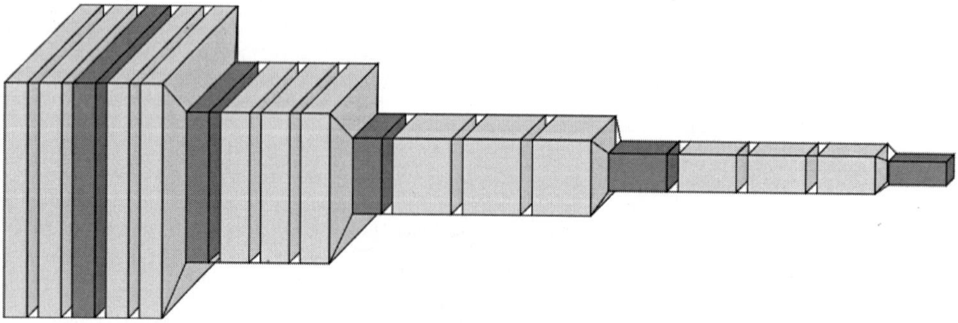

***Figure 9.25**: Our VGG16 model's frontend visualized*

The darker (red) blocks in *Figure 9.25* represent the pooling layers while the lighter color represents the convolution layers. We have 13 convolution layers in the frontend. This is a relatively deep model and was considered very deep when it was developed.

6. Train the model on the data for 20 epochs and plot the learning curves:

```
epochs=20
history = model_vgg.fit(
  train_ds_gen,
  validation_data=val_ds_gen,
  epochs=epochs
)
plot_perf(history, epochs)
```

You should get the output as shown in *Figure 9.26*:

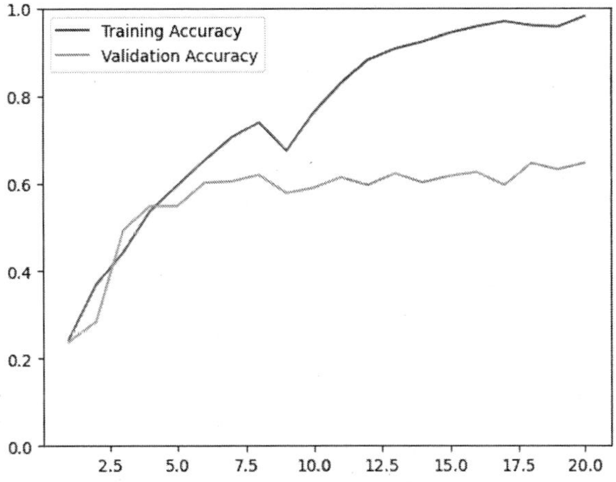

Figure. 9.26*: High overfitting in our VGG16 model*

Figure 9.26 shows that the model exhibits high overfitting to the extent of practically memorizing the training dataset. Our small dataset is easy to memorize for this complex and deep model with ~65M parameters. We encourage you to use the regularization approaches learnt earlier to improve the performance of the model. With VGG16 implemented, let us now learn another extremely interesting approach to image model architectures - the **Residual Network** (**ResNet**).

ResNet design approach

The VGG16 architecture showed that higher depth can significantly improve model performance. High depth, however, leads to issues that we have discussed due to which the model does not learn and the performance degrades. The ResNet architecture was designed to overcome this problem and to find a way for us to go deeper without performance degradation. The ResNet architecture was successful at this objective. The key element of the ResNet model is the identity link, also known as a shortcut. The idea is that the next layer sees not only the convolutional output from the present layer but also the input data, as shown in *Figure 9.27*:

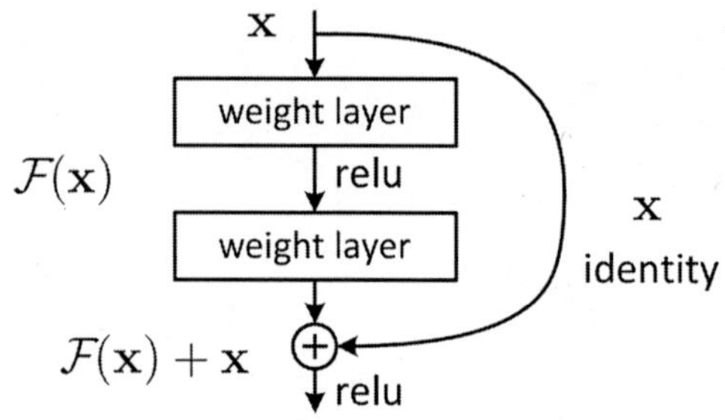

Figure 9.27: *Learning residuals*

As shown in *Figure 9.27*, the identity link is a simple concept. The two weight layers represent two convolutional layers and the entire structure in the preceding figure can be seen as a *residual block*. The input data x is not only supplied to the convolutional layers but is also copied and added (without any modification) to the output of the second convolutional layer. The last step in *Figure 9.27* denotes the operation to 'link' these values. The 'linking' operation is, essentially, simply adding the input x and the output from the second convolutional layer. This simple idea helps because now the subsequent block uses not only the previous block's output, but also the input, and can choose to propagate it if it helps the model performance. This simple trick can help us go deeper without losing relevant information.

To make the concept of the identity link more concrete, let us create our own residual block with the identity link/ shortcut. Note that the following code will use the Keras functional API. The functional API allows us to create models with non-linear topology (like our identity links). For more details and a crash course, refer to: **`keras.io/guides/functional_api/`**

```
x_shortcut = x
x = Conv2D(64, (3,3), strides=(1,1), padding='same')(x)
x = ReLu()(x)
x = Conv2D(64, (3,3), strides=(1,1), padding='same')(x)
x = ReLu()(x)
x = layers.add([x_shortcut, x])
```

The block contains two regular convolutional layers with the same number of filters of the same size. This is an important characteristic of the ResNet architecture. The final command in the preceding code uses an 'add' layer to simply add the input (to the block) to the output of the second convolutional layer. This is the part where we effectively create the link. The ResNet architecture also contains regular convolutional blocks. The key difference is the absence of the link. Now that the idea of the identity link and the various blocks in the architecture is clear, let us take a look at the full architecture of the ResNet34 model, as shown in *Figure 9.28*:

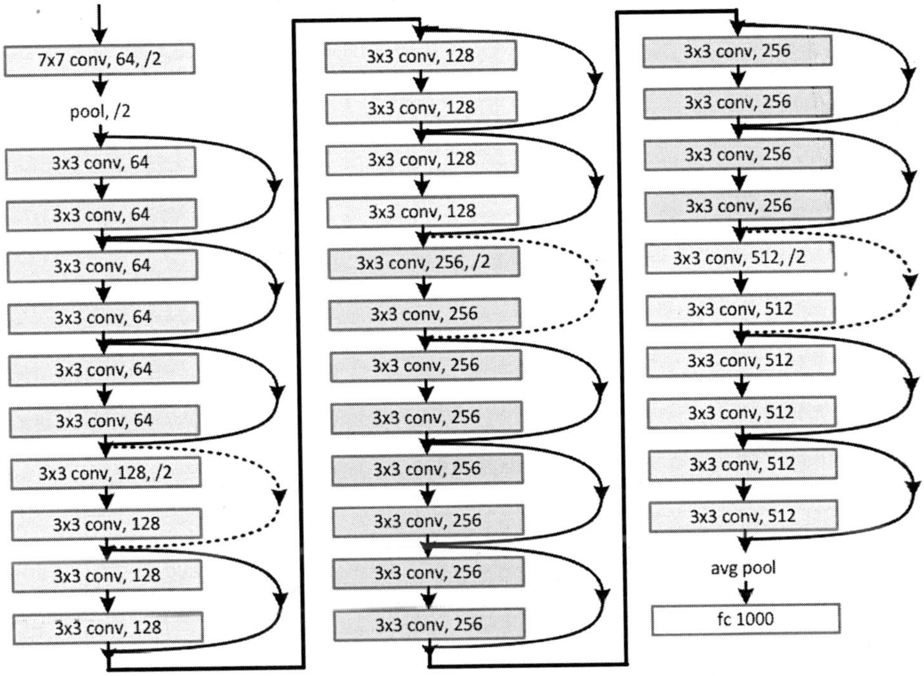

Figure 9.28: *The ResNet34 architecture with links*

The architecture in *Figure 9.28* may look complex but is rather straightforward to understand. The blocks with the solid connections between the input and the output represent residual blocks. The blocks with the dotted connections represent a regular convolutional block. As we can see from *Figure 9.28*, the architecture has a pattern where it has a regular convolutional block, followed by multiple residual blocks of the same layer size. This brings us to the salient features of the ResNet model, which are as follows:

- It uses 'shortcuts' to allow free propagation of data to subsequent layers.
- It uses the same number of convolutional layers in all the blocks.
- It heavily uses batch normalization.
- It uses a global average pooling at the final pooling stage (which significantly reduces dimensionality).
- It used only a single dense layer for the backend.

Note: The subsequent variations of the ResNet architecture brought in some more techniques (for example, bottleneck). The key ideas, however, were retained.

To complete our learning of the ResNet architecture, let us now code our own ResNet34 model from scratch. For better reusability, we define functions for creating the residual and the regular convolutional block with a specific number of filters. The following code creates the residual block:

```
def block_residual(num_filters, x):
    x_shortcut = x
    x = Conv2D(num_filters, (3,3), strides=(1,1), \
               padding='same', activation = 'relu')(x)
    x = Conv2D(num_filters, (3,3), strides=(1,1), \
               padding='same', activation = 'relu')(x)
    x = add([x_shortcut, x])
    return x
```

We also need a function for the regular convolutional block. The only difference from the previous function is the absence of the link. The following code defines the function:

```
def block_conv(num_filters, x):
    x = Conv2D(num_filters, (3,3), strides=(1,1), \
               padding='same', activation = 'relu')(x)
    x = Conv2D(num_filters, (3,3), strides=(1,1), \
               padding='same', activation = 'relu')(x)
    return x
```

With the required definitions in place, we can start defining the model architecture. First, we import the necessary utilities from Keras:

```
from keras.layers import Conv2D, MaxPool2D, Dense, GlobalAveragePooling2D
from keras.layers import add, Input
from keras import Model
```

We define the inputs using the Input layer using the following command:

```
inputs = Input(shape=(img_dim, img_dim, 3))
```

Let us now define the first convolutional layer and the max pooling layer that follows it:

```
x = Conv2D(64, (7, 7), strides=(2, 2), \
          padding='same', activation='relu')(inputs)
x = MaxPool2D(pool_size=(3, 3), strides=(2, 2), padding='same')(x)
```

Now, we can use the **block_residual** function to define residual blocks to add three residual blocks of 64 filters each using the following code:

```
x = block_residual(64, x)
x = block_residual(64, x)
x = block_residual(64, x)
```

Now use the **block_conv** function to define one regular convolutional block with 128 filters, using the following commands:

```
x = block_conv(128, x)
```

Now add three residual blocks (128 filters each), 1 convolutional block (256 filters), 5 residual blocks (256 filters), followed by 1 convolutional block (512 filters) and finally 2 residual blocks (512 filters). Use the following code:

```
x = block_residual(128, x)
x = block_residual(128, x)
x = block_residual(128, x)
x = block_conv(256, x)
x = block_residual(256, x)
x = block_residual(256, x)
x = block_residual(256, x)
x = block_residual(256, x)
x = block_residual(256, x)
x = block_conv(512, x)
x = block_residual(512, x)
```

The convolutional frontend is now complete. We now define the DNN backend. Add a GlobalAveragePooling2D layer, followed by a single dense layer with 10 neurons for prediction and complete the model definition:

```
x = GlobalAveragePooling2D()(x)
outputs = Dense(num_classes, activation = 'softmax')(x)
resnet = Model(inputs, outputs)
resnet.summary()
```

The (truncated) output is shown in *Figure 9.29*:

```
 conv2d_84 (Conv2D)            (None, 32, 32, 512)  2359808     ['conv2d_83[0][0]']

 conv2d_85 (Conv2D)            (None, 32, 32, 512)  2359808     ['conv2d_84[0][0]']

 conv2d_86 (Conv2D)            (None, 32, 32, 512)  2359808     ['conv2d_85[0][0]']

 add_10 (Add)                  (None, 32, 32, 512)  0           ['conv2d_84[0][0]',
                                                                 'conv2d_86[0][0]']

 global_average_pooling2d (Glob  (None, 512)        0           ['add_10[0][0]']
 alAveragePooling2D)

 dense_8 (Dense)               (None, 10)           5130        ['global_average_pooling2d[0][0]'
                                                                ]

==================================================================================================
Total params: 16,610,058
Trainable params: 16,610,058
Non-trainable params: 0
```

***Figure 9.29**: Truncated summary of our ResNet model*

We can visualize the full model using **visualkeras** using the following command:

```
visualkeras.layered_view(resnet, legend=True, \
                         type_ignore=[Flatten, Dense, Input])
```

You should obtain the output as shown in *Figure 9.30*:

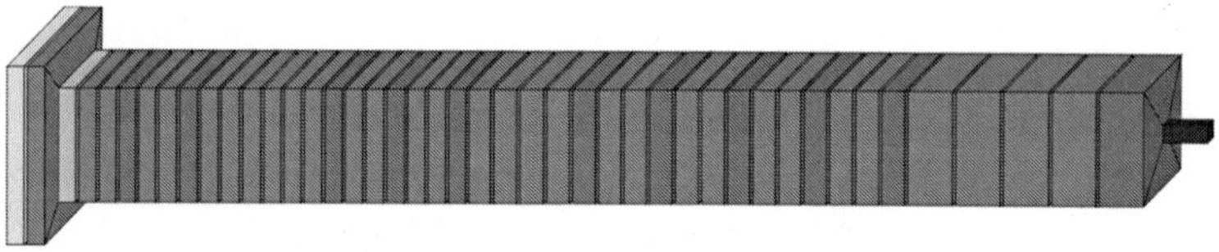

***Figure 9.30**: Our ResNet34 model visualized*

Figure 9.30 shows that our model is quite deep, consisting of 33 convolutional layers. It is important to recall that a performant model at this depth was made feasible largely because of the clever trick of the identity link. Subsequent variants of the ResNet model used more tricks to optimize the models even further (ResNet50 v2 is a good example to learn more about) while retaining this powerful core idea. Let us now summarize our learning from studying these architectures into some concrete guidelines that you can use in practice.

Guidelines for designing image models

We have discussed and implemented many ideas in this chapter. After understanding the traditional approach, the VGG approach and the ResNet approach, and the hands-on learning we did can synthesize a few guidelines for designing high-performance models.

The guidelines are as follows:

- Doubling convolutions (inspired by VGG16) in each block followed by MaxPooling helps in feature reduction.
- For deeper networks, residual networks using identity links help the model overcome various difficulties like vanishing/ exploding gradients.
- Regularization is extremely important. Use the techniques in conjunction to get good results. Data augmentation is extremely useful.
- Using batch normalization helps go deeper and with faster convergence. It also has the effect of regularization.
- GlobalAveragePooling is an effective pooling operation, worth considering for the final pooling operation.

In practice, we need to be aware that each situation and task is different and that the understanding of the data and task at hand is critical. The wise data scientist uses their experience and domain understanding to augment any general guidelines. This brings us to the end of the topic.

Conclusion

The high performance of image processing models comes largely from a simple mathematical operation - convolution. Convolutional filters are used to detect features. In progressive convolutional layers, the features learnt are increasingly sophisticated. Using convolutional layers, and pooling layers and as building blocks, we can build an excellent feature generation frontend of the convolutional network. A block of dense layers can serve as the predictive backend of the network. This frontend vs. backend view enhances our understanding and thus design of networks.

Regularization is an important step in developing deep learning models for images. We saw that even the simplest of models can overfit quickly if regularization is not used. We learnt three different techniques for implementing it. First, we saw how simple and effective it is to use dropout (both dense and spatial dropout). We then learned about the extremely useful batch normalization technique. It is not explicitly a regularization technique, but helps models learn better and has a regularization effect. Data augmentation was another useful technique that helped generate several images from a single reference and helped with training data-hungry models.

To make the design of our own deep learning model architectures better, we looked at some prominent architectures. We saw that VGG was a relatively simple approach that used repeatable convolutional blocks and achieved high performance by going deep. This approach of simply going deep, however, had limitations. We then saw how residual networks helped overcome these limitations by introducing feature reuse and identity links. The approach showed a way to build deeper models with higher performance. After all the learning and application, we looked at some guidelines for developing our own models.

With that, we have learnt how to develop high-performance image models from scratch. However, this is not the only approach to solving image problems. Sometimes, developing models from scratch may not be feasible and we need to leverage existing models/ learning. This will be the focus of *Chapter 11, Transfer Learning*, where you will learn how to use SOTA image models for your task. Let us continue our quest for mastering machine learning/ artificial intelligence models. We now look at techniques for handling another extremely common type of unstructured data, text, in the next chapter, *Chapter 10, Optimizing Text Models*.

CHAPTER 10

Optimizing Natural Language Processing Models

Introduction

Natural language data is everywhere. For a regular person, speech and text are the predominant forms of communication and information consumption. Machine learning/ artificial intelligence solutions, therefore, are practically everywhere as well. The spam classification model protects us from malicious e-mails. The news recommendation models consider the content and our preferences to rank the most relevant articles. The virtual assistant (Siri / Google) understands our commands to compose and send an email on your behalf. Your favorite translation app instantly transcribes and translates speech to text in another language as we speak. We are surrounded by machine learning/artificial intelligence models for **Natural Language Processing** (**NLP**).

ChatGPT by OpenAI is by far the most popular chatbot and one of the most successful artificial intelligence products ever. It reached 100 million users in just two months of launch. It is extremely impressive and its natural language capabilities have amazed even practitioners and researchers. The godfather of deep learning, *Geoffrey Hinton*, stated that progress in this field is much faster than expected. ChatGPT has kicked off the **Large Language Models** (**LLMs**) race where all major organizations are rushing to leverage this powerful technology.

Now, NLP is of course at the core of this rapid advancement in artificial intelligence. NLP is by no means a new field. Indeed, practitioners today benefit from linguistics work done in the 1930s. What changed in the past few years is the access to data, better computing and some innovative new models that have easily exceeded all past benchmarks. In this chapter, we learn about some keys to success in machine learning/artificial intelligence for NLP. We will learn the various considerations for handling text, learn about novel architectures for text processing, and learn how to optimize these models.

Structure

In this chapter, we will discuss the following topics:

- Key tasks in NLP
- Importance of sequence processing
    - A text classification case study
- Text pre-processing
- Text representation
    - Count-based features
    - Text embeddings
- Architectures for NLP
    - Recurrent architectures
    - Transformer architecture
- Tuning network hyper-parameters
    - Exercise 10.1 - Hyper-parameter tuning of GRU model
- Using convolutions for NLP
    - Using 1D convolutions and RNNs
- Using pre-trained embeddings
    - Benefits
    - Drawbacks
    - Exercise 10.2 - Text classification with pre-trained embeddings
    - Notable pre-trained embeddings

Objectives

In this chapter, we will learn how to optimize NLP models while handling the peculiarities of natural language data. Beginning with text pre-processing, we will further learn about text representation through embeddings and how we can create our embeddings. We will learn the two major approaches and their corresponding architectures to processing sequences, that are, recurrent architectures and transformer architecture. We will also learn hyper-parameter tuning for any chosen architecture to get the most out of the model. We will learn some more tricks to optimize our NLP model, for example, using 1D convolutions and using pre-trained embeddings. We will work on a hands-on case study to practice all these topics. By the end of the chapter, you will have all the know-how to optimize a modern NLP model.

Key tasks in NLP

NLP is concerned with helping machines make sense of natural (human) language – speech and text. NLP is not one big task, but an umbrella term for numerous smaller tasks. Machine learning/artificial intelligence models often specialize in a task and larger solutions combine these individual models. It is therefore important to understand the types of tasks in NLP. Let us look at a few salient NLP tasks:

- **Text summarization**: Provide a crisp summary of a long text without losing the salient/ key points contained in the text. An example is summarizing news articles, a thousand-word news article can be shortened into a, say, 100-word summary. This is indeed a popular application of text summarization.
- **Question answering**: Based on the input data provided, the model provides answers to the questions the user provides (as text, usually). The training data could also be a large open corpus (for example, the entire Wikipedia online encyclopedia), or maybe a sizable chunk of the internet (training data for Large Language Models like ChatGPT's base model).
- **Text generation:** Given a prompt by the user, the model creates a text. OpenAI's ChatGPT is popular for creating high-quality, human-like output given user prompts. You could ask ChatGPT to write a rap song about stubbing your toe against furniture, and it will deliver.
- **Text classification:** An extremely popular application of natural language processing is classifying text. Spam detection is a popular example, hate speech detection is another. Text deduplication, detection of plagiarism, and news topic classification are only some examples of the varied applications of text classification.
- **Translation:** As the name suggests, the task is to convert input text from one language to another target language. For example, let us assume that we visit Germany as a tourist, and we need to ask for directions. We can use a translation application to instantly figure out a well-structured, (mostly) grammatically correct question in German.
- **Text representation (encoding):** Representation is an extremely important preprocessing step for NLP tasks. A good representation that captures meaning/

other information in the text has a significant impact on the performance of the end solution. Taking the example of the Universal Sentence Encoder (by Google, based on the BERT model), you can use models to find a good general-purpose representation for text.

- **Named entity recognition (NER):** NER is the task of identifying key pieces of information in the text and classification into a set of predefined categories. A sub-task of information extraction, NER is usually concerned with identifying people, places, organizations, time expressions (and more) in the input text. When you ask Siri to book a 7 PM appointment with Maria at Chili, NER enables Siri to identify the place, person and time information contained in the command.

Note that these were only some of the popular applications of natural language processing. An exhaustive list is impractical as with each passing day, NLP is employed in more and more applications as research in the field continues to bloom. Regardless of the task, though, the nature of natural language data cannot be ignored. Let us understand this aspect better.

Importance of sequence processing

Natural language is a sequence of terms/words. Words come together in an order, with dependencies among them, to form a string of words that expresses a coherent idea. Jumbling the words can make a meaningful sentence sound gibberish. The ideal machine learning/ artificial intelligence solution, therefore, can benefit from treating text data like the sequence they are. Empirically, NLP tasks almost always benefit from processing the text as a sequence of terms/tokens. Topic models are a notable exception, where popular approaches disregard the order in the text. For the tasks listed in the previous section, we must process sequences and accommodate varying lengths of text.

Let us take a moment to reflect on how we humans process text in our minds as we read it. A simple demonstration would be in *Table 10.1*. From top to bottom, a new word is revealed in the sentence. The **text processed** in each row contains the text processed so far in that step. The **Sentiment** column captures the sentiment association with the text revealed until that step. In the first row, we only have the term **I**. The sentiment associated with it is largely neutral, as reflected in the entry in the Sentiment column. The next term revealed is **have** and the text processed sofar becomes **I have**. Now this phrase is neutral to positive, but surely not negative. With the third term being **no**, the sentence gets updated to **I have no**. The sentiment for this is negative, as you may agree. The final term revealed is **issue**. The overall sentence thus becomes, **I have no issue**. The sentiment in this statement is positive. Take a look at the following table:

Step	Text processed				Sentiment
1	I				Neutral
2	I	have			Neutral/ Positive
3	I	have	no		Negative
4	I	have	no	issue	Positive

Table 10.1: *Sentiment changes with incoming terms*

We can see in the example illustrated in *Table 10.1* that with each new term, our assessment of the sentiment contained in the statement gets updated. The arrival of the final term completely flipped our assessment from **Negative** to **Positive**. Considering the nature of speech data, it is essential to consider not only the current/latest word but also the relevant words preceding it. The key point here is that the entire sequence needs to be considered. In the upcoming sections, we will explore various neural network architectures that are well-suited for this task. However, before delving into those details, let us first familiarize ourselves with a case study that will provide concrete examples to grasp these concepts better.

A text classification case study

Azra Movie Database (**AMDb**) is an online platform for information on movies, series and other forms of entertainment content. The overall rating of the movie (based on votes) is the prominent indicator of the goodness of a movie that AMDb and other similar platforms use for ranking movies. AMDb wishes to use a new movie ranking system which uses not just the overall rating of the title, but also the sentiment in the text reviews received. For this purpose, AMDb would need to classify the sentiment in each review as positive or negative. This is a classic text classification task.

AMDb believes that the text reviews they receive are extremely similar in language and content to those received on the **Internet Movie Database** (**IMDb**). Therefore, AMDb plans to use the IMDb reviews dataset to train the model and use it to classify the sentiment of AMDb reviews. The IMDb reviews dataset contains 50,000 highly polar movie reviews along with their sentiment. A benefit of using this dataset is that it is conveniently available as a **`TensorFlow`** dataset through Keras and also available on the TensorFlow hub. Additionally, the dataset contains longer sequences (1000-word reviews are not rare) which can help us better understand the considerations in dealing with longer text. Let us begin by loading and exploring this data.

First, load the **`imdb`** module from **`TensorFlow`** datasets using the following command:

```
from tensorflow.keras.datasets import imdb
```

With this, the **`imdb`** module is loaded. We can now use this to extract the data with a specified vocabulary size (the total number of unique terms in the text). To specify a vocabulary size of 10,000 and then load the train and test data, use the following commands:

```
size_vocab = 10000
(X_train, y_train), (X_test, y_test) = imdb.load_data(num_words=size_vocab)
```

You will get the following confirmation:

```
Downloading data from https://storage.googleapis.com/tensorflow/tf-keras-datasets/imdb.npz 17464789/17464789 [==============================] - 0s 0us/step
```

The train and test data are now available in local variables for us to explore. Let us first check the number of examples in each dataset using the following command:

```
len(X_train), len(y_train)
```

The lengths get printed as follows:

```
(25000, 25000)
```

We see that there are 25,000 instances in both train and test datasets. Let us now print out a review to understand the data we are working with. Print out the 47th review (chosen because it is short), using the following command:

```
print(X_train[46])
```

The review gets printed as follows:

```
[1, 568, 65, 9, 4689, 31, 7, 4, 118, 495, 34, 4, 1300, 7, 206, 309, 1079, 8, 85, 206, 108, 568, 65, 166, 2, 5, 5811, 168, 40, 2, 4, 3410, 139, 26, 73, 2, 5, 4, 206, 139, 26, 897, 48, 162, 347, 438, 47, 101, 281, 36, 62, 766, 14, 11, 2258]
```

We do not have the raw text in the data, but a series of indices representing each term in the review. This also means that the text has already been **tokenized** and we need not perform the step. The tokens printed above are not interpretable to us. Let us decode the text. For this purpose, we can use the word index that the **imdb** module provides. Use the following command:

```
word_idx = imdb.get_word_index()
```

The mapping gets downloaded and is available as a dictionary. To check the index for a specific term, we can use it as a key. For example, to get the index for the term **text**, use the following command:

```
word_idx.get('text')
```

The index gets printed as **3001**. Likewise, we can access the index/ numeric code for the other terms in our vocabulary. To decode the review, we need to create a reverse mapping from index to term. Use the following command to do so:

```
idx_word = {id:token for token, id in word_idx.items()}
```

To confirm that this worked, let us fetch the term corresponding to the index **3001**. Use the command that follows:

```
idx_word.get(3001)
```

The output is the **text** as we expected. The mapping has been created. Now let us create a function to return the text corresponding to a series of input indices. Use the following code:

```
def showreview(inp_ids):
  return " ".join([idx_word.get(x-3,'#') for x in inp_ids])
```

The **showreview()** function can be used on any training record to show the corresponding text. For indices not found in the limited vocabulary (limited to 10,000), the function will show a **#**. Let us use it on the 47th review in the training data (the same review we saw earlier) using the following command:

```
showreview(X_train[46])
```

The output should be as follows:

 # police story is arguably one of the best works by the master of action himself compared to other action films police story makes # and stallone look like # the stunt scenes are well # and the action scenes are superb if new line cinema has any sense they would release this in theaters

We see that some of the terms have been replaced by a **#**. This is because the term was not part of the 10,000 terms in our limited vocabulary. Note that you could choose a vocabulary size of 15,000 as well. This is a hyper-parameter that you must choose. An extremely simple approach is to drop terms with a frequency lower than a threshold. The threshold could be derived from your domain understanding, or from percentiles of term frequencies. Note that the nature of the task plays an important role in this choice. A couple of papers can help you explore the topic further –

- The 2019 paper, *"How Large a Vocabulary Does Text Classification Need? A Variational Approach to Vocabulary Selection"* (Link: **https://aclanthology.org/N19-1352.pdf**) explores multiple approaches for text classification.
- For some experiments on choosing vocabulary size for machine translation, the 2020 paper, *"Finding the Optimal Vocabulary Size for Neural Machine Translation"* (Link: **https://aclanthology.org/2020.findings-emnlp.352.pdf**) is a good read.

With this, we have a fair understanding of the data we are working with. Before we proceed, we need to understand the next major step, that is, text pre-processing.

Text pre-processing

Text data can be riddled with imperfections or domain-specific nuances. As you can expect, the language and grammar of textual data found in legal documents are different from those found in tweets on Twitter. Emojis and slang are unlikely to be found in legal documents but are extremely common in social media data. What can be considered an anomaly in one domain could be a valuable feature in another. Additionally, the task at hand makes a big difference to what information we might consider important. Text pre-processing, therefore, is an extremely important step in data handling that has a significant impact on downstream model performance and therefore the success of the machine learning/artificial intelligence solution. A 2017 paper titled *On the Role of Text Preprocessing in Neural Network Architectures: An Evaluation Study on Text Categorization and Sentiment Analysis*[1] demonstrated that simple text pre-processing steps can improve/ deteriorate performance of neural network models significantly.

We reiterate that the nature of preprocessing depends on the data/domain/task at hand. As yet another example, emojis are unlikely to be relevant for topic classification. However, the emoji is an extremely important feature that can flip our understanding of the sentiment contained in the text. The main takeaway is that **there is no general, task-agnostic text preprocessing pipeline.**

However, some clean-up or preprocessing steps are commonly employed. The first important step in pre-processing text data is **tokenization**, breaking the text down into working units. If we are building a character-level model, our token would be a character. If we are working with a sentence, then that would be our token. Most commonly, we work with words as tokens. Splitting the raw input text into tokens is not a trivial task, but modern NLP utilities have extremely good performance and can mostly be directly employed without much manual fine-tuning.

Natural language typically has multiple variations of a base word. For example, the terms **ran**, **running**, and **runs** all form the base word **run**. These are examples of valid inflections that are expected and not errors. Other types of variations could be spelling errors or even abbreviations. Mapping these variations back to a base term is called **canonicalization**. Many clean-up and pre-processing steps fall under this category.

Other clean-up steps involve tasks like the removal of less valuable terms, normalizing cases, removing some special characters/ tokens and handling data/domain-specific nuances. Following are short descriptions of some of the major steps in text pre-processing:

- **Tokenization**: Splitting the raw input text into tokens that form our working units. A token can be a character, a word, a phrase, a sentence, or even a whole paragraph.
- **Case normalization**: In situations where the case of the text does not matter, case normalization is performed to get all the terms to a consistent case (lower/ upper). This ensures that **Term** is treated the same as **term** by the model (if needed). If the case matters, this step can be skipped.

---

[1] *Source: https://arxiv.org/abs/1707.01780*

- **Stemming/lemmatization:** Both stemming, and lemmatization are attempts to canonicalize text. Stemming is a rule-based method to chop off suffixes of terms to get a stem. The terms **driver, driving,** and **drive** all get mapped to **driv**. As you may have observed, the result of stemming need not be a valid English term. Lemmatization is a more sophisticated, dictionary-based method that considers the part of speech of the term to convert to the base form. **driving** and **drive** would be lemmatized to **drive**, a valid term. *Wordnet* by *Princeton University* is a great resource and a lexical database. You can find good resources here: **https://wordnet.princeton.edu/**

- **Spell correction**: Spell correction is an important task in many domains and there are various approaches for the same. While some modern text representation methods can tackle spelling variations to some extent, it is recommended that spell correction be performed. Some popular approaches are the noisy channel model and phonetic hashing. Noisy channel model is a general-purpose spell corrector, while phonetic hashing fixes spelling variations that stem from pronunciation (for example, **Dilli** vs. **Delhi**)

- **Stop word removal:** In natural language, a lot of terms are filler terms that do not add a lot of information. Often called **stop words**, these are general/functional terms like the, of, and. These might not add value to certain tasks and can be removed. We need to be careful that the notion of value depends on the task. Filler words might not be useful for topic classification but are essential for machine translation. Additionally, there are contextual stopwords that need handling. For example, in a dataset containing phone reviews, the term phone might not add a lot of value as it would be present in a large proportion of reviews. Note that you could also employ the ideas discussed in the papers referred to in the previous section to choose vocabulary size.

- **Others:** An exhaustive list of miscellaneous text pre-processing and cleanup tasks is not possible as many of these tasks are data/domain/task specific. Abbreviation handling is an example, where we need to tell the model that Television and TV refer to the same thing. Tackling domain-specific encodings is another task, where data might contain some specific codes with meaning. For example, Rx in medical text means prescription/recipe/to take. Handling special characters and emojis is another such example. Handling collocations, that is, identifying and marking that Hong Kong is one term, is another pre-processing task.

The wise data scientist considers various aspects and carefully creates a data pre-processing pipeline suited for the specific task. It is useful to have cheat sheets/guides for pre-processing, but the prudent data scientist must use them merely as guidance and be cautious at each preprocessing step. Once the cleanup is done, the next important task is representation. Let us understand this step better and how to optimize it.

Text representation

Feature engineering/data representation is one of the most important steps in machine learning/ artificial intelligence. NLP is no exception. Representation is particularly important in NLP because models can not directly interpret text and we must convert the sequence of text into a list of numbers. Our task is to convert a text term like **world** into numbers that the machine can understand that is, we need to generate features from the text. These features eventually go into the model, and we appreciate by now that garbage in is garbage out.

While there could be many creative ways to derive features from text, we discuss two fundamental and common approaches. One approach is to use count-based features, also known as, the bag of words approach. The other approach is to use embeddings. Let us understand each of these better.

Count-based features

Count-based features form one prominent approach. The idea is extremely simple. Each term in the overall text corpus gets a corresponding column. If the document in consideration contains the term, the count of the term in the document is the value in the column. Overall, there would be as many columns to represent the data, as words in the entire corpus. Often, this is several thousand. For example, if a corpus contains 10,000 unique terms, each document/row will be represented by 10,000 numbers. Among these, only the columns corresponding to terms present in the document will be non-zero. The value in the column could be the raw count, or some normalized count (**`tfidf, PM25`**).

One major drawback of this approach is the sheer number of columns needed to represent a single row (for example, 10,000) and most values will be 0. Another bigger drawback is that these features are insufficient in capturing meaning. Unless the practitioner puts in a great deal of effort, this representation will not identify that the terms **footpath** and **pavement** have similar meanings. The next approach, that is, word embeddings, tries to solve both problems and has become the dominant approach for machine learning for text.

Text embeddings

Embeddings are low-dimensional, high-density vectors. We could be working with 16 dimensional vectors, or even 500, but we rarely have vectors with higher dimensionality. Compared to 10,000, this is a big efficiency gain. These vectors can be created for each individual word, for phrases, or entire documents. In theory, a 10,000-word document can therefore be represented by a 50-dimensional vector i.e., a series of just 50 numbers. As you may expect, such compact representations make machine learning for text far more convenient and have significantly helped advance the performance of machine learning/ artificial intelligence models for NLP.

Note: Wikipedia provides a decent overview of the topic of word embeddings and good resources for further study. https://en.wikipedia.org/wiki/Word_embedding

There are various approaches to creating these vectors. For our case study and most of our discussion, we will create these embeddings from scratch while building our model for sentiment classification. Other approaches aim at creating embeddings that capture the meaning of the terms. We will revisit these in the section *Using pre-trained embeddings*. Let us now learn how we can create our own embeddings for a task.

Embedding layer in Keras

To create our own embeddings from scratch, we need to learn the representation for each term that is fit for our task. This is achieved with the help of an embedding layer in the model. In simple terms, the embedding layer is simply a lookup. That is, the layer returns the low-dimensional vector corresponding to the input term. The embeddings layer is always the first layer in any model, as it provides the numeric output that can be processed by subsequent layers in the neural network. The working of the layer is illustrated in *Figure 10.1*:

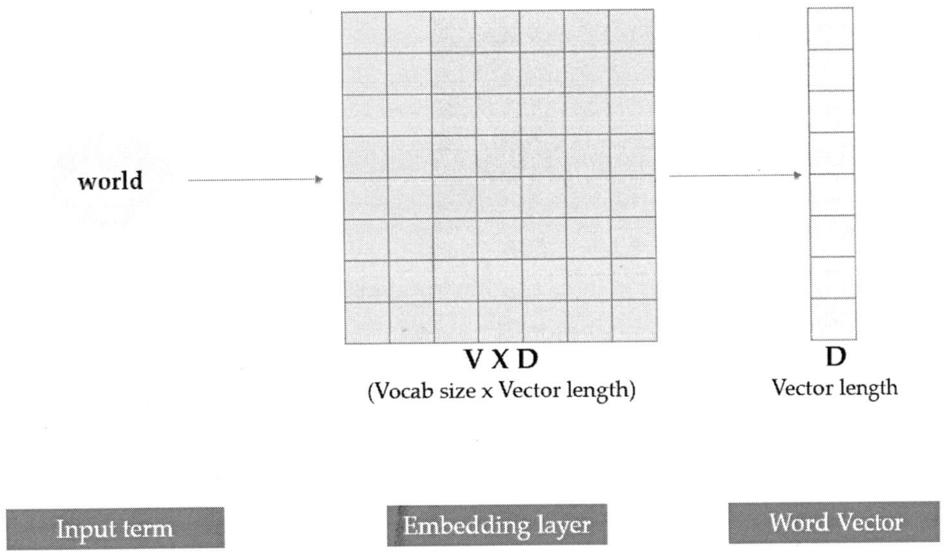

Figure 10.1: *The embedding layer*

The embedding layer can simply be a lookup table/ matrix that returns the vector corresponding to a certain term/index. These representations can be initialized randomly. When the model is trained, the layer gets trained like any other layer, and as the learning progresses, the representation for each term gets optimized for the task at hand. The embedding layer is the first layer and a regular feature of deep learning models for NLP, regardless of the architecture that follows. That brings us to the interesting topic of network architectures for NLP.

Architectures for NLP

Text data are always sequences and, in the section, *Importance of sequence processing,* we discussed that NLP tasks almost always benefit from processing the text as a sequence of terms/tokens. We repeat the example from *Table 10.1* in *Table 10.2*:

Step	Text processed				Sentiment
1	I				Neutral
2	I	have			Neutral/ Positive
3	I	have	no		Negative
4	I	have	no	issue	Positive

Table 10.2: *Sentiment changes with incoming terms*

Recall that with each new term coming in, our assessment of the sentiment contained in the statement gets updated. The arrival of the final term completely flipped our assessment from **Negative** to **Positive.** The neural network architecture for such tasks must also be capable of processing the sequence in the text and not ignoring it. There are two major approaches for this so far:

- Storing processed information and updating the assessment with each incoming term.
- Processing the entire sequence at once while considering the dependencies between the terms in the text.

Recurrent Neural Networks (**RNN**s) follow approach 1. They are designed for processing the text one token at a time storing the information received so far and updating the assessment. The transformer architecture follows approach 2. Using certain simple and clever mechanisms, the transformer architecture looks at the entire sequence while paying attention to certain parts of it and considering the dependencies between the terms in the text. We will learn about both approaches in detail in the following sections.

In the discussion around architectures for NLP, it is important to understand how we arrived at the current state-of-the-art models. NLP is not a new field, but deep learning made breakthroughs in NLP tasks only recently. It is important to understand the order of development of the models used in NLP to build perspective on the way ahead as well. Limiting ourselves to notable architectures, the chronological order of development of popular models is shown in *Figure 10.2:*

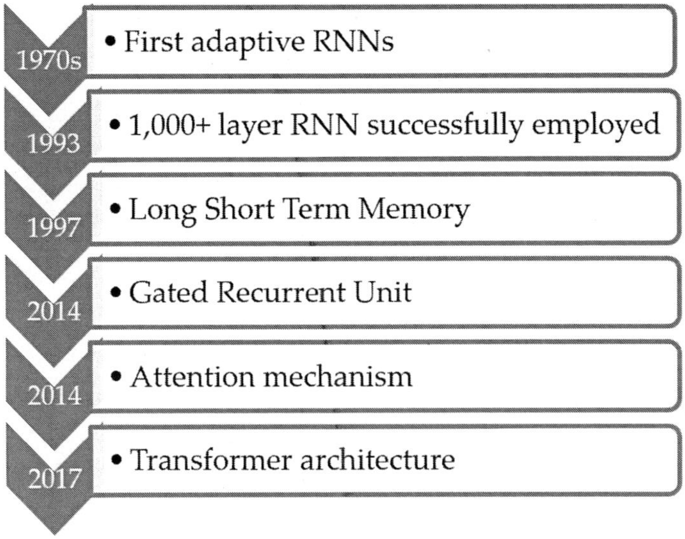

Figure 10.2: *Timeline of the development of popular architectures for text*

The first adaptive forms of RNNs were developed in the 1970s, with successful application on a deep learning task (more than 1,000 RNN layers) in 1993 bringing it into the limelight again. The **Long Short Term Memory** (**LSTM**) model was developed in 1997 to overcome some shortcomings of plain RNNs. **Gated Recurrent Units** (**GRU**s) were introduced in 2014 to simplify LSTMs without losing performance. Around the same time, RNNs were being increasingly used with attention mechanisms (introduced in 2014) to improve performance. In 2017, the transformer architecture was introduced and due to its high performance, soon became an extremely popular feature of modern NLP models. We will learn about all these variants and use them in the sentiment classification case study. While doing so, we will compare the different models on multiple aspects – complexity, size and accuracy – to explore the interplay of these factors. Let us begin by understanding recurrent architectures.

Recurrent architectures

As mentioned earlier, recurrent architectures are designed for sequence processing. The text can be fed to the neural network one term / token at a time. The new term is processed by the network, along with the information from the terms encountered so far. The new term along with the prior information is used to make a prediction. The main feature which enables such processing is a loop. RNNs have loops in them which allow the network to access some hidden information corresponding to data received in the previous step. *Figure 10.3* illustrates the idea of loops:

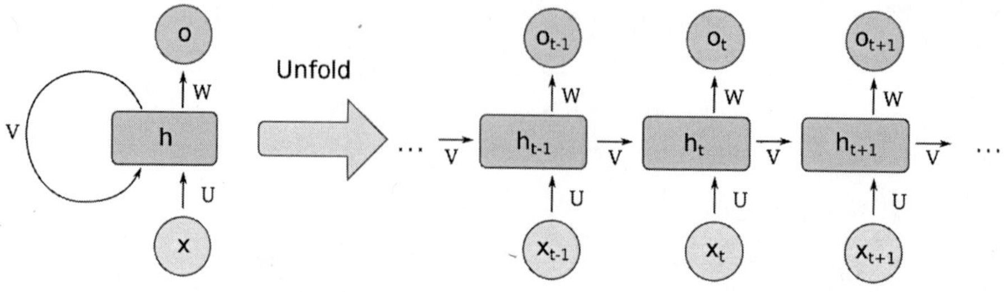

Figure 10.3: *An unfolded Recurrent Neural Network*

The Xs in the unfolded view are input tokens at different timestamps. Consider the timestamp t. The input to the hidden layers h_t is not only the new term X_t, but also the data from h_{t-1} which is the hidden state from the previous timestamp. Both of these are used to generate the output, O_t. Similarly, the next step at time t+1 will use the hidden layer data from time t. This is how recurrence occurs in an RNN.

Note: For details on the workings of the different prominent RNNs, you can refer to this tutorial. https://arxiv.org/abs/1808.03314

Figure 10.4 helps us understand the difference between the architectures of a regular feedforward neural network and a recurrent neural network. One natural difference is that the feedforward network reads the entire input data at once. The key difference in architecture is the loop, which is simply a way to copy the current hidden state and use it at the next time stamp. Note that another weight matric W_{hh} is needed for the hidden state data to be passed to the next hidden state. As you might expect, there are more parameters in the recurrent neural network due to the additional weights for the recurrent part. Take a look at the following figure:

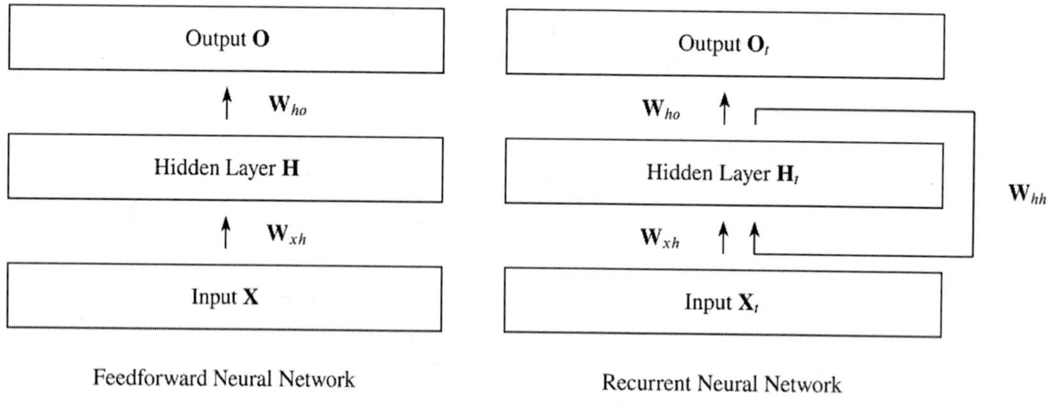

Figure 10.4: *Regular Feedforward vs. Recurrent neural network*[2]

[2]*Source: https://arxiv.org/pdf/1912.05911.pdf*

To estimate the number of parameters in a recurrent layer, we need to recall that there are two types of weights, feed-forward weights and recurrent weights. The total number of parameters would be: $(n + 1) \times m + m \times m$

Where n is the input dimension and m is the number of recurrent units.

The illustration we saw in *Figure 10.4* corresponds to the simplest, plain vanilla RNN. It forms the basis for other complex RNN variants. Let us see the simple RNN in action and see how it performs on our review sentiment classification case study.

First, we need to ensure reproducibility of the results (to the extent possible). For this, we will import **numpy** and **tensorflow** and set the seed for random number generation for both packages to 42. Use the following code to accomplish this:

```
import tensorflow as tf

import numpy as np

tf.random.set_seed(42)

np.random.seed(42)
```

With the seeds set, we can now expect largely similar runs between multiple runs and between multiple machines.

Note: Despite setting the seeds for Tensorflow and Numpy, your results might not exactly match ours. This is because there are additional sources of randomization that are hard to control. Regardless, the results you obtain should be very similar to ours.

A detail at this step is that our input sequences are still of differing lengths. That is, we have very short reviews in the data (less than 50 words) along with long reviews (more than 1,000 words). For our model to work properly, we need to fix an upper limit to the number of terms that need to be processed. For our case study, we will fix this to 200. Setting the length to 200 would require truncating longer reviews and padding shorter reviews. This can be done easily using the **pad_sequences** method in Keras. Let us import it using the following command:

```
from tensorflow.keras.preprocessing import sequence
```

Next, we use the **pad_sequence** method to get all reviews to 200 terms using the following code:

```
max_len = 200

X_train_proc = sequence.pad_sequences(X_train, max_len)

X_test_proc = sequence.pad_sequences(X_test, max_len)
```

To see if this worked, let us print the 47th review again (which was about 50 words long). Use the following command:

```
X_train_proc[46]
```

The output is as follows:

```
array([ 0, 0, 0, 0, 0, 0, 0, 0, 0, 0, 0, 0, 0, 0, 0, 0, 0, 0, 0, 0, 0, 0, 0,
0, 0, 0, 0, 0, 0, 0, 0, 0, 0, 0, 0, 0, 0, 0, 0, 0, 0, 0, 0, 0, 0, 0, 0, 0, 0,
0, 0, 0, 0, 0, 0, 0, 0, 0, 0, 0, 0, 0, 0, 0, 0, 0, 0, 0, 0, 0, 0, 0, 0, 0, 0,
0, 0, 0, 0, 0, 0, 0, 0, 0, 0, 0, 0, 0, 0, 0, 0, 0, 0, 0, 0, 0, 0, 0, 0, 0, 0,
0, 0, 0, 0, 0, 0, 0, 0, 0, 0, 0, 0, 0, 0, 0, 0, 0, 0, 0, 0, 0, 0, 0, 0, 0, 0,
0, 0, 0, 0, 0, 0, 0, 0, 0, 0, 0, 0, 0, 0, 0, 0, 0, 0, 1, 568, 65, 9, 4689,
31, 7, 4, 118, 495, 34, 4, 1300, 7, 206, 309, 1079, 8, 85, 206, 108, 568, 65,
166, 2, 5, 5811, 168, 40, 2, 4, 3410, 139, 26, 73, 2, 5, 4, 206, 139, 26,
897, 48, 162, 347, 438, 47, 101, 281, 36, 62, 766, 14, 11, 2258], dtype=int32)
```

Note that the review has been padded with 0s to get the length to 200. For longer reviews, the utility will include only the first 200 terms.

Note: For longer text, the default behavior of pad_sequences is to include the first n terms (i.e., pad on the left). To change this behavior, you can specify padding = "post" which will include the final n terms (pad on the right).

Now, from **keras**, import the **Sequential** model. Also import the **Dense, SimpleRNN, Embedding, Dropout** and **SpatialDropout1D** layers. The **SimpleRNN** layer is the implementation of the plain vanilla RNN. **The Embedding** layer creates the lookup for the token embeddings and must be the first layer in NLP models using embeddings. **SpatialDropout1D** performs the same function as a regular dropout layer. The difference is that **SpatialDropout1D** drops entire feature maps that is, vectors in our case. Use the following code:

```
from tensorflow.keras.models import Sequential
from tensorflow.keras.layers import Dense, SimpleRNN
from tensorflow.keras.layers import Embedding, Dropout, SpatialDropout1D
```

The utilities are all loaded. We can start defining the model. First, let us define the text representation part - the embedding layer. We will learn our embeddings while training. The **input_dim** argument to the embedding layer must be the size of the vocabulary. In our case, it is 10,000 (**size_vocab** variable). The **output_dim** represents the size of the resulting low-dimensional vectors. We choose a value of **32** (arbitrary at this point, we will optimize this in the section titled Tuning network hyper-parameters), meaning that we will represent each term/ token by a series of 32 numbers. Additionally, to minimize overfitting, we will use a **SpatialDropout1D** layer with a **30%** dropout rate. This can be done using the following code:

```
model_rnn = Sequential()
model_rnn.add(Embedding(input_dim=size_vocab, output_dim=32))
model_rnn.add(SpatialDropout1D(0.3))
```

Let us now add the **Simple RNN** units to the network. We will add 32 units (arbitrary choice again; we will tune this in the section titled Tuning network hyper-parameters). We will use the **SimpleRNN** layer for this. To minimize overfitting, we will use a **40%** dropout. Use the following code:

```
model_rnn.add(SimpleRNN(32))
model_rnn.add(Dropout(0.4))
```

The representation and the recurrent processing parts are now defined. We can now define the final layer for making the prediction. For our binary classification case, a single neuron with a sigmoid activation is appropriate. Add the Dense layer using the following command:

```
model_rnn.add(Dense(1, activation="sigmoid"))
```

Now, compile the model. Use the **binary_crossentory** loss function that is good for binary classification tasks. Define **adam** as the optimizer. As discussed in *Chapter 7, Parameter Optimization Algorithms,* the **Adam** optimizer is a decent choice to default to for most situations. Define **accuracy** as the metric. Print out the model summary after compilation using the following code:

```
model_rnn.compile(loss='binary_crossentropy',
                  optimizer='adam',
                  metrics=['accuracy'])
model_rnn.summary()
```

The model summary gets printed as shown in *Figure 10.5*:

```
Layer (type)                   Output Shape            Param #
=================================================================
embedding_13 (Embedding)       (None, None, 32)        320000

spatial_dropout1d_12 (Spati    (None, None, 32)        0
alDropout1D)

simple_rnn_5 (SimpleRNN)       (None, 32)              2080

dropout_13 (Dropout)           (None, 32)              0

dense_13 (Dense)               (None, 1)               33

=================================================================
Total params: 322,113
Trainable params: 322,113
Non-trainable params: 0
```

***Figure 10.5:** Summary of the plain RNN model*

Notice the total number of parameters in the model and for different layers. The embedding layer has 320,000 parameters, we have a vocabulary of 10,000 and each token would be represented by 32 numbers. The number of parameters in the recurrent layer is expected to be $(n + 1) x m + m x m$, where n is the input dimensionality and m is the number of recurrent units. Replacing the values in the formula, we get $33 x 32 + 32 x 32$, which equals 2,080. It is important to note that even for this tiny network we have more than 300k parameters, mainly coming from the embedding layer.

Now that the model is defined, we need to define the fitting process. We will use early stopping to stop training when there is no significant improvement. We will set the **`patience`** parameter to 10 to stop training after 10 epochs with no further improvement. We will set the **`restore_best_weights`** parameter to **`True`** to restore the best weights based on validation accuracy. This is done using the following command:

```
stop_early = EarlyStopping(monitor='val_accuracy', patience=10, restore_
best_weights=True)
```

We are ready to train the model. Define a validation split of **`20%`** and a batch size of **`256`**. We will train for a maximum of 20 epochs. Use the following command to start the training:

```
model_rnn.fit(X_train_proc, y_train, epochs=20, validation_split=0.2,
callbacks=[stop_early], batch_size=256)
```

The results of the last few epochs are in *Figure 10.6:*

```
· 5s 65ms/step - loss: 0.1798 - accuracy: 0.9350 - val_loss: 0.4011 - val_accuracy: 0.8606

· 4s 55ms/step - loss: 0.1510 - accuracy: 0.9475 - val_loss: 0.3649 - val_accuracy: 0.8478

· 4s 56ms/step - loss: 0.1295 - accuracy: 0.9558 - val_loss: 0.3830 - val_accuracy: 0.8554

· 5s 65ms/step - loss: 0.1309 - accuracy: 0.9544 - val_loss: 0.4185 - val_accuracy: 0.8588

· 4s 57ms/step - loss: 0.1094 - accuracy: 0.9632 - val_loss: 0.4277 - val_accuracy: 0.8506

· 5s 65ms/step - loss: 0.0916 - accuracy: 0.9700 - val_loss: 0.4946 - val_accuracy: 0.8578

· 4s 55ms/step - loss: 0.0855 - accuracy: 0.9743 - val_loss: 0.4945 - val_accuracy: 0.8562

· 4s 55ms/step - loss: 0.0700 - accuracy: 0.9790 - val_loss: 0.4935 - val_accuracy: 0.8556

· 5s 65ms/step - loss: 0.0629 - accuracy: 0.9814 - val_loss: 0.5326 - val_accuracy: 0.8514
```

Figure 10.6: *Output from final training epochs*

We see that the model obtained a validation accuracy of around 85.8%. This is a decent result for a start with no optimization at all. Let us now learn about a more complex RNN type.

Long Short Term Memory

The idea of plain RNNs is simple and works well with very short text. For longer text, however, there are a few issues. When the sequences are long, the training (that also happens over time steps) encounters issues like the vanishing gradient (the backpropagation of the error to early time steps is negligible). This made RNNs not too useful for long text and for handling long-range dependencies in the text.

LSTMs were designed to better handle the vanishing gradient problem. Instead of making all the information and error passing through all the time steps and activations, LSTMs use explicit cell states. These cell states are information that takes an expressway. The flow of information on these expressways is regulated by some gating mechanisms. The explicit cell states do not encounter any activations and therefore the vanishing gradient problem is irrelevant to them. This key difference is what allows the LSTM to model long-range dependencies.

Further reading: The Wikipedia page for LSTM provides a good overview of LSTMs and their development timeline. https://en.wikipedia.org/wiki/Long_short-term_memory For an understanding of the detailed inner workings of LSTMs, refer to this great blog: https://colah.github.io/posts/2015-08-Understanding-LSTMs/

Indeed, LSTMs are extremely powerful and have quickly replaced plain RNNs in most real-world applications. This power comes at a cost. LSTMs are far more complex owing to the additional gating mechanisms. To enable these mechanisms, LSTMs have many more parameters. By design, the LSTM cell has 4 times as many parameters as a plain RNN. Let us create our own LSTM model for the review sentiment classification case study and see if we get any improvement in the results.

We will continue using the same code notebook. The code will be very similar to the code we used for building the plain RNN model. The only difference would be in the model definition stage where we will use an LSTM layer instead of a **`SimpleRNN`** layer. To begin, import the **`LSTM`** layer from Keras using the following command:

```
from tensorflow.keras.layers import LSTM
```

Now, define the Sequential model like we did earlier. Add an embedding layer and spatial dropout (**`40%`**) using the following code:

```
model_lstm = Sequential()

model_lstm.add(Embedding(input_dim=size_vocab, output_dim=32))

model_lstm.add(SpatialDropout1D(0.4))
```

Let us now add the 32 LSTM units to the network. The result of the architecture remains the same, define the same. Use the following code:

```
model_lstm.add(LSTM(32))

model_lstm.add(Dropout(0.4))

model_lstm.add(Dense(1, activation="sigmoid"))
```

Now, compile the model using the same configuration as in the previous exercise using **`SimpleRNN`** and print out the model summary using the following code:

```
model_lstm.compile(loss='binary_crossentropy',

                   optimizer='adam',

                   metrics=['accuracy'])

model_lstm.summary()
```

The model summary is printed as follows in *Figure 10.7:*

```
Layer (type)                 Output Shape              Param #
=================================================================
embedding_1 (Embedding)      (None, None, 32)          320000

spatial_dropout1d_1 (Spatia  (None, None, 32)          0
lDropout1D)

lstm (LSTM)                  (None, 32)                8320

dropout_1 (Dropout)          (None, 32)                0

dense_1 (Dense)              (None, 1)                 33

=================================================================
Total params: 328,353
Trainable params: 328,353
Non-trainable params: 0
```

Figure 10.7: *Summary of the LSTM model*

Notice the number of parameters in the LSTM layer. As stated earlier, the LSTM cell has 4 times as many parameters as the plain RNN cell. This can be easily verified as the LSTM layer has 8,320 parameters which is exactly 4 times the parameters that the SimpleRNN layer had (2,080).

Fit the model using the same scheme as earlier and the same batch size using the following code:

```
stop_early = EarlyStopping(monitor='val_accuracy', patience=10, restore_
best_weights=True)

model_lstm.fit(X_train_proc, y_train,
        epochs=20, validation_split=0.2,
        callbacks=[stop_early], batch_size=256)
```

The training output is printed as follows in *Figure 10.8:*

```
258ms/step - loss: 0.3251 - accuracy: 0.8734 - val_loss: 0.3097 - val_accuracy: 0.8730

244ms/step - loss: 0.2371 - accuracy: 0.9135 - val_loss: 0.2924 - val_accuracy: 0.8780

236ms/step - loss: 0.1907 - accuracy: 0.9338 - val_loss: 0.2993 - val_accuracy: 0.8788

243ms/step - loss: 0.1576 - accuracy: 0.9468 - val_loss: 0.3934 - val_accuracy: 0.8730

256ms/step - loss: 0.1385 - accuracy: 0.9522 - val_loss: 0.3181 - val_accuracy: 0.8728

233ms/step - loss: 0.1164 - accuracy: 0.9624 - val_loss: 0.4183 - val_accuracy: 0.8732

267ms/step - loss: 0.0972 - accuracy: 0.9700 - val_loss: 0.3974 - val_accuracy: 0.8716

227ms/step - loss: 0.0917 - accuracy: 0.9718 - val_loss: 0.3891 - val_accuracy: 0.8706
```

Figure 10.8: *LSTM training output*

The output shows that the LSTM model quickly breached **87%** accuracy on the validation data and a couple of epochs had close to **88%** validation accuracy. This is a significant improvement over the simple RNN model. The text sequences we are dealing with are not too long. We can expect the performance difference between plain RNN and LSTMs to be larger when dealing with longer text.

The LSTM clearly has higher accuracy than the plain RNN. But we also notice that there are 4 times as many parameters and the training time was also significantly higher. This is due to the complexity of the LSTM. A lot of research went into simplifying the LSTM cell in an attempt to create a simpler version with fewer parameters without losing its predictive power. The GRU was one such prominent version coming out of this research. Let us learn more about it.

Gated recurrent units

The Gated Recurrent Unit was introduced in 2014 with the intent of simplifying the LSTM cell without losing its predictive power. In many applications, the GRUs were successful in matching LSTMs' predictive power with lower training times and fewer parameters. The main change in the GRU is the omission of the explicit cell state. Instead, in the GRU, the hidden state of the hidden layer is allowed to flow freely. A simple way to look at this is that the GRUs did to the hidden state what the LSTMs did to the explicit cell state. This movement is still regulated by gates.

As a result of these changes, GRUs still carry the major idea of LSTM, freely flowing information that does not pass through activations. Due to the gating mechanisms, GRUs have higher parameters compared to plain RNNs. Although, the GRU has **75%** of the number of parameters that the LSTM has. The GRU should therefore be able to model long-range dependencies as well with better training times.

Note: There are many more variants of RNNs other than the 3 we discussed. We encourage you to read and explore more. Some prominent examples are Independent RNNs (IndRNN), Clockwork RNNs (CW-RNN), and Time Aware LSTMs (T-LSTM).

We can easily assess the performance of the GRU model in our case study. The code for the GRU model will be like that for the **SimpleRNN** and **LSTM** models. The only change is using the GRU layer from Keras. The following code shows the model definition for the GRU model:

```
from tensorflow.keras.layers import GRU

model_gru = Sequential()

model_gru.add(Embedding(input_dim=size_vocab, output_dim=32))

model_gru.add(SpatialDropout1D(0.4))

model_gru.add(GRU(32, reset_after=False))

model_gru.add(Dropout(0.4))

model_gru.add(Dense(1, activation="sigmoid"))
```

The rest of the code remains the same. A summary of the model gives us the following result, as in *Figure 10.9*:

```
Layer (type)                 Output Shape              Param #
=================================================================
embedding_4 (Embedding)      (None, None, 32)          320000

spatial_dropout1d_4 (Spatia  (None, None, 32)          0
lDropout1D)

gru_1 (GRU)                  (None, 32)                6240

dropout_4 (Dropout)          (None, 32)                0

dense_4 (Dense)              (None, 1)                 33

=================================================================
Total params: 326,273
Trainable params: 326,273
Non-trainable params: 0
```

***Figure 10.9:** Summary of the GRU model*

The number of parameters in the **GRU** layer is 6,240. We can see that this is 3 times the number of parameters of the **SimpleRNN** layer (2,080) and 75% the number of parameters that the **LSTM** layer had (8,320). On training the model, we saw that some of the epochs gave us validation accuracy of over 87%.

Note: For brevity, we skipped the code for the complete model training and evaluation. We encourage you to create the entire model for GRUs and compare your results with ours.

In our case study, we saw that the GRU model had fewer parameters and had performance comparable to the LSTM model. Both LSTM and GRU models gave us 87%+ validation accuracy, confirming that GRUs successfully capture the power of the LSTMs while being faster to train. We still have not extracted full potential from recurrent architectures, though. Some creative uses of the RNN cells helped us get even better results. Bi-directional recurrent networks are one such idea. Let us learn about it.

Bi-directional recurrent architectures

The architectures we saw so far were predicting the next token/term based on the previous tokens/terms. In that sense they were unidirectional. In certain situations, it helps to know the terms that come after the target term. For instance, when performing named entity recognition, the terms right after the target term can be crucial for performance. The task of translation also benefits significantly from this type of **look ahead**. Bi-directional architectures allow for such a look ahead. The architecture of a bi-directional recurrent network is illustrated in *Figure 10.10:*

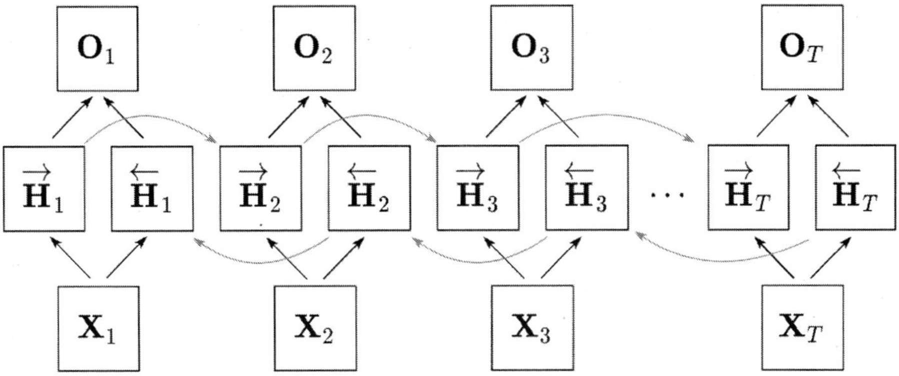

Figure 10.10: *Architecture of a bi-directional recurrent neural network*[3] *source*

The key property of bi-directional networks is an additional recurrent layer that processes the tokens in the reverse order. That is, the new hidden layer receives the last token (in the sequence) first. The bi-directional model therefore employs two RNNs in parallel, the **forward layer** and the **backward layer**. At each time step, the states of the forward and backward layers are combined to form the output.

The idea applies to all variants of RNNs. That is, you can have bi-directional networks of plain RNNs, GRUs, LSTMs or any other variant. Several tasks benefit from this architecture that permits a look ahead. Machine translation, named entity recognition, and part of speech tagging are some prominent examples. Before the transformer architecture was introduced, bi-directional RNNs (usually LSTMs) were present in state-of-the-art models. LSTMs were the most popular approach and erstwhile state-of-the-art models like `ELMO` and `ULMFiT` were based on them.

Recurrent architectures with attention

RNN architecture using an encoder and decoder needs to memorise the entire input sequence in a single hidden state. For longer text, the idea intuitively does not seem great. For different tasks, different parts of the sentence might be important. For example, for the translation use case, multiple parts of the sentence are important and need emphasis. For this purpose, the attention head was added. The attention layer gives the network access to the entire input sequence. The attention layer gives a different weightage to different parts of the input sequence, allowing it to focus on or pay attention to. It uses a second recurrent layer to selectively weight parts of the sequence.

[3]*Source: https://arxiv.org/pdf/1912.05911.pdf*

In general, attention can be taken in two sentences and aligned with them. The result of such alignment is the identification of some form of correlation or matching between the different sentences. In the general case, the attention model allows us to align the input sequence and the output sequence, identifying the parts in the input to focus on for a specific output term. To make this idea clear, let us look at a translation example in *Figure 10.11* that was part of the original paper by *Dzmitry Bahdanau, KyungHyun Cho, and Yoshua Bengio in 2015* (**https://arxiv.org/abs/1409.0473P**). Take a look at the following figure:

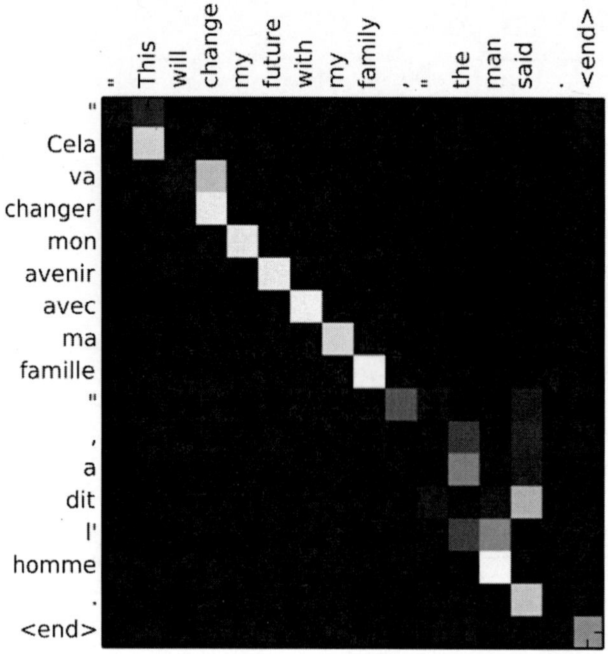

***Figure 10.11**: Alignment matrix learnt for a translation case*[4]

In *Figure 10.11,* white denotes a high correlation while black signifies a low correlation. We can see in the figure that the alignment matrix shows that the term **mon** in the input is important to the term **my** in the output. Likewise, the term **Famille** is most important for the output term **family**. It is worth noticing that for the output term **change**, the model identifies two input terms, **va** and **changer** as important. Adding attention heads to RNNs (usually LSTM with attention) was an extremely popular approach that provided the then state-of-the-art results. However, with the introduction of the transformer architecture changed this and current state-of-the-art models are largely based on the transformer architecture. Let us understand this ground-breaking development.

Transformer architecture

The RNN + attention scheme we discussed in the previous section provides high accuracy and was state-of-the-art when it became popular. The approach, however, had some

[4] *Source: https://arxiv.org/abs/1808.03314*

drawbacks. For one, training was even more time-consuming due to the attention layer. Secondly, by design, recurrent architectures are difficult to parallelize. Additionally, the long-range dependency issue was better solved, but it came at a high cost. The models were extremely complex. Attempts were made to simplify this complex architecture, and the transformer architecture resulted from it.

Note: A great and intuitive illustrated explanation of the transformer architecture can be found here: http://jalammar.github.io/illustrated-transformer/

The key features of a transformer are self-attention and positional encodings. The recurrence of RNNs is replaced by self-attention. The transformer architecture explicitly processes the entire sequence at once. This is particularly useful for tasks like translation and question answering, where capturing long-range dependencies between the terms is essential for high performance. To understand self-attention better, including the detailed workings of the components, refer to the illustrated guide here: **http://jalammar.github.io/illustrated-transformer/**

The transformer architecture is composed of encoder/decoder components. The encoder in a transformer is rather simple, a self-attention layer followed by a feed-forward layer(s). This is illustrated in *Figure 10.12*:

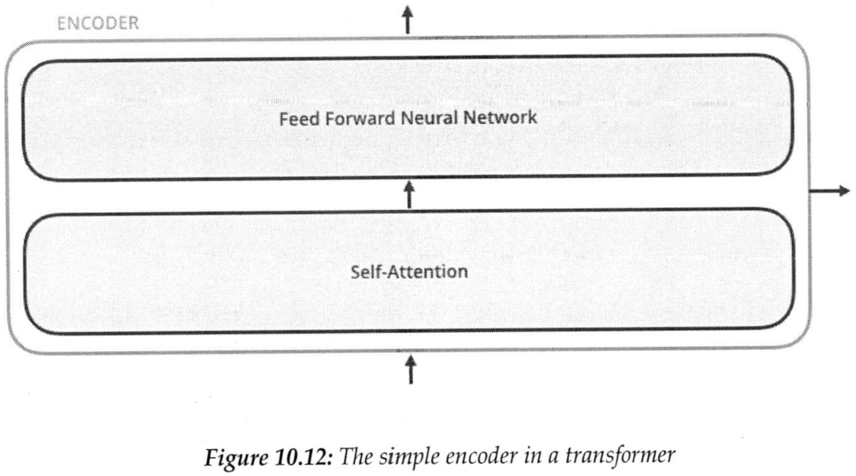

***Figure 10.12:** The simple encoder in a transformer*

Note: While self-attention was a key feature of the transformer architecture initially, the idea of the transformer doesn't need attention in the way defined earlier. Apple's Machine Learning Research team introduced the Attention Free Transformer in June 2021, which simplifies the calculation and reduces the memory complexity - resulting in a high-performant yet efficient transformer variant. Details can be found here: https://machinelearning.apple.com/research/attention-free-transformer

In Keras, a transformer block can be created using the `MultiHeadAttention` layer. The implementation is based on the paper *Attention is All You Need* (*Vaswani et al., 2017*). The layer performs 1D cross-attention over two input sequences. The arguments to the layer are listed in *Figure 10.13*. For more details on the arguments and usage examples, refer to the official documentation here: **https://keras.io/api/layers/attention_layers/multi_head_attention/**. If the `query`, `key`, and `value` are the same, self-attention is performed.

```
tf.keras.layers.MultiHeadAttention(
    num_heads,
    key_dim,
    value_dim=None,
    dropout=0.0,
    use_bias=True,
    output_shape=None,
    attention_axes=None,
    kernel_initializer="glorot_uniform",
    bias_initializer="zeros",
    kernel_regularizer=None,
    bias_regularizer=None,
    activity_regularizer=None,
    kernel_constraint=None,
    bias_constraint=None,
    **kwargs
)
```

***Figure 10.13:** Arguments to the MultiHeadAttention layer*

The functional notation needs to be used in Keras to perform self-attention (using the same inputs twice). First, we can import the layer like any other Keras layer, using the following command:

```
from tensorflow.keras.layers import MultiHeadAttention
```

The layer can then be used like any other layer (using the functional notation) as shown in the following command. Note the repeated input `(x,x)` that performs self-attention. Execute the following code:

```
x = MultiHeadAttention(
  key_dim=head_size, num_heads=num_heads) (x, x)
```

A full working example of a simple transformer in action using Keras layers can be found here: **https://keras.io/examples/timeseries/timeseries_transformer_classification/**

Note: a manual implementation of a high-performance Transformer model from scratch is tedious and requires a fair amount of fine-tuning and training. We will therefore use libraries specific to transformer models in Chapter 11, Transfer Learning, where we will employ state-of-the-art transformer models.

With this, we complete the important discussion around the various architectures for NLP. We see that we have multiple choices for architecture, each having its merits. After making a careful choice of architecture, we need to optimize its hyper-parameters to get the maximum performance from the model and the data. Let us learn how to tune the hyper-parameters for text models.

Tuning network hyper-parameters

We have seen so far that NLP tasks differ from regular machine learning/artificial intelligence tasks in two major aspects.

- First, high performance needs the right data representation, which is usually through word embeddings.
- Second, the processing of the text as a sequence requires special architectures like recurrence and attention.

Both these are usual features of modern NLP models and must therefore be optimized along with other aspects. We will learn how to tune the hyper-parameters for a text classification task. The logic can be used to tune other hyper-parameters, as we have learnt in *Chapter 8, Hyper-parameter optimization.*

We will use the GRU for our case study as it is very capable as well as fast to train.

In *Chapter 8, Hyper-parameter optimization* we have learnt how to tune hyper-parameters for deep neural networks using Keras Tuner. We will continue to use the Keras tuner for the exercises in this chapter. We recommend going through *Chapter 8, Hyper-parameter optimization* if you have not done so yet, so that the code in this section is easier to understand.

If Keras tuner is not installed already, install it using the following command:

```
!pip install keras-tuner -q
```

You should get a completion message as shown here:

```
176.1/176.1 kB 4.6 MB/s eta 0:00:00
```

Once installed, import the Keras tuner using the following command:

```
import keras_tuner as kt
```

Now we are ready to tune the hyper-parameters for a text classification model and tune text-related specifics like embedding size. Let us do so in the next exercise.

Exercise 10.1: Hyper-parameter tuning of GRU model

In this exercise, we will use hyper-parameter tuning to optimize the parameters of a GRU-based model for our text classification case study for AMDb. We will use Keras tuner for the search and use the random search approach. We will tune the size of the embedding, the number of GRU units and the activation function for the GRU cells.

We will define the parameter search space as the following:

- **Embedding size:** 16 to 64 in steps of 16
- **Number of GRU cells**: 16 to 64 in steps of 16
- **GRU Activation function**: **`ELu`**, **`ReLu`** and **`TanH`**

We will use the same network architecture that we used in *Exercise 10.3,* with the same drop-out layers and drop-out percentages. Let us begin.

Note: For illustration and quicker execution, we defined a limited search space for the parameters. To get a better result, we encourage you to try out more values for the hyperparameters.

1. Define a **`model_builder`** function for the Keras tuner with the hyper-parameter candidates defined earlier.

   Hint: Refer to *Chapter 6, Hyper-parameter tuning* for base code.

   Use the following code:

```
def model_builder(hparams):
  model = Sequential()

  hp_embedsize = hparams.Int('embedsize', min_value=16,
                              max_value=64, step=16)
  hp_units = hparams.Int('units', min_value=16,
                          max_value=64, step=16)
  hp_activation = hparams.Choice('activation',
   ['elu', 'relu', 'tanh'])

  model.add(Embedding(input_dim=size_vocab, output_dim=hp_
embedsize))
  model.add(SpatialDropout1D(0.4))
  model.add(GRU(units=hp_units, activation=hp_activation, reset_
after=False))
  model.add(Dropout(0.4))
```

```
    model.add(Dense(1, activation='sigmoid'))

    model.compile(loss='binary_crossentropy',
                  optimizer='adam',
                  metrics=['accuracy'])

    return model
```

2. Initialize a **Random Search** tuner with 10 trials using the following code:

```
tuner = kt.RandomSearch(model_builder,
                        objective='val_accuracy',
                        max_trials=10,
                        overwrite=True)
```

   The tuner is now initialized. We can now proceed to set up early stopping.

3. Now set up early stopping with a patience value of 5 and enable restoration of the best weights. Use the following code:

```
stop_early = EarlyStopping(monitor='val_accuracy',
                           patience=5, restore_best_weights=True)
```

4. Next, begin the search specifying 20 epochs and a 20% validation split. Use the following code:

```
tuner.search(train_images, train_labels,
             epochs=25, validation_split=0.2,
             callbacks=[stop_early])
```

   The search will take a while. Depending on your system configuration, this could take minutes to over an hour. Once the search is over, you should get a confirmation message similar to the following:

   Trial 10 Complete [00h 06m 12s] val_accuracy: 0.8794000148773193 Best val_accuracy So Far: 0.8809999823570251 Total elapsed time: 01h 05m 52s

   Note that because of system differences, the timing and resulting accuracy might be slightly different in your output. The differences in performance should be negligible, though. The difference in time can be significant, of course. Now. using the **get_best_hyperparameters** method of the tuner, we will print the best hyper-parameter setting identified by the tuner.

5. Use the **get_best_hyperparameters** method of the tuner to print the best hyperparameter combination.

Use the following command:

```
res = tuner.get_best_hyperparameters()[0]
res.values
```

The result gets printed as follows:

```
{'embedsize': 48, 'units': 64, 'activation': 'tanh'}
```

The best combination seems to be an embedding size of 48 with 64 GRU units and **TanH** as the activation.

6. Print the validation performance of the top 3 models using the **results_summary** method of the tuner. Use the following code:

```
tuner.results_summary(3)
```

The top three hyper-parameter combinations and their validation score get printed as shown in *Figure 10.14*:

```
Results summary
Results in ./untitled_project
Showing 3 best trials
Objective(name="val_accuracy", direction="max")

Trial 04 summary
Hyperparameters:
embedsize: 48
units: 64
activation: tanh
Score: 0.8809999823570251

Trial 05 summary
Hyperparameters:
embedsize: 48
units: 64
activation: elu
Score: 0.8795999884605408

Trial 09 summary
Hyperparameters:
embedsize: 16
units: 32
activation: relu
Score: 0.8794000148773193
```

Figure 10.14: *Top 3 hyper-parameter choices*

The best-performing model had 64 GRU units with `TanH` activation and an embedding size of 48. The validation accuracy of this model was **`88%.`** Note that the next two combinations are extremely close in their scores. The third-best model has **`87.9%`** validation accuracy. However, this model uses an embedding size of just 16 and uses 32 units (half of the top model). The third-best model is significantly simpler with practically the same performance. A data scientist seeking parsimony may choose the third model as the best one for the task.

The result we got is similar to the result we got from LSTMs earlier. We encourage you to try out more combinations and larger search spaces to maximize your chances of getting better scores. Now that we know how to tune a recurrent neural network with embeddings, let us learn a neat trick that helps with the performance and efficiency of the model. Using convolutions for NLP is not very intuitive but is extremely useful. Let us understand how that works.

Using convolutions for NLP

Convolutions are used for deep-learning image processing. As discussed in *Chapter 9, Optimizing Image Models,* there are a couple of reasons for their popularity. First, convolutions help the model learn **local features** from the image. Second, convolutions help reduce the number of parameters. The good news is that these benefits of convolutions can be obtained for NLP tasks as well, with some minor differences in how we employ the convolutions. Instead of 2D convolutions for images, we need to use 1D convolutions for text as the input is a 1D sequence of tokens. In the case of images, filters extract patches from the image to give us output features. In the case of one dimension, the filter would extract subsequences from the input sequences and give us a value for the output features.

Using convolutions also helps tackle dependencies in the data. Using multiple kernels to the same text helps in identifying dependencies among terms while extracting groups of terms. A filter size of 2 would help extract two-word combinations. Likewise, a filter of size 3 would capture relationships between trigrams/triplets of words and so on. When followed by a pooling layer, the features get further subsampled. This helps with reducing the number of features and therefore parameters in the model and as a result can lead to faster models without a significant drop in performance. The gains in efficiency are clear when working with large neural networks with multiple layers.

Let us apply 1D convolutions in conjunction with GRUs to our sentiment classification case study for AMDb and see for ourselves if the performance of the hybrid model is comparable to the models we built so far. Note that we expect the benefits from 1D convents to be apparent in larger neural networks. Our small neural network might not see the same gains but is sufficient for illustration. Let us get started.

Exercise 10.2: Using 1D convolutions and RNNs

In this exercise, we will continue working on the review sentiment classification case study for AMDb. We will use the GRU as our base recurrent cell for the model and use the same architecture as before. The embedding layer will continue to be the first layer. We will add a 1D convolution layer right after the embedding layer so that the GRU works with not just individual tokens but also data from combinations of tokens. Let us begin:

1. First, import the **Conv1D** layer from Keras using the following command:

```
from tensorflow.keras.layers import Conv1D
```

2. Initiate a sequential model, add an embedding layer with 32 as output dimension and add a **40%** spatial dropout. Use the following code:

```
model_comb = Sequential()
model_comb.add(Embedding(input_dim=size_vocab, output_dim=32))
model_comb.add(SpatialDropout1D(0.4))
```

3. Add the 1D convolution layer with 32 filters of size 2 with **relu** activation, using the following code:

```
model_comb.add(Conv1D(32, 2, activation='relu'))
```

4. Add the GRU layer with 32 cells, a 40% dropout and a single dense neuron for the prediction.

```
model_comb.add(GRU(32, reset_after=False))
model_comb.add(Dropout(0.4))
model_comb.add(Dense(1, activation="sigmoid"))
```

5. Compile the model with **binary_crossentropy** as the loss and using **Adam** optimizer. Also, set up early stopping and enable restoration of the best weights. Use the following code:

```
model_comb.compile(loss='binary_crossentropy',
                   optimizer='adam',
                   metrics=['accuracy'])
stop_early = EarlyStopping(monitor='val_accuracy',
             patience=10,
             restore_best_weights=True)
```

6. Fit the model on the train data. Specify a batch size of 256, a validation split of **20%** and 20 epochs.

```
model_comb.fit(X_train_proc, y_train,
       epochs=20, validation_split=0.2,
       callbacks=[stop_early],
       batch_size=256)
```

Some of the output records are as follows:

```
145ms/step - loss: 0.2306 - accuracy: 0.9118 - val_loss: 0.3286 - val_accuracy: 0.8656

146ms/step - loss: 0.1896 - accuracy: 0.9305 - val_loss: 0.3519 - val_accuracy: 0.8618

146ms/step - loss: 0.1714 - accuracy: 0.9391 - val_loss: 0.3394 - val_accuracy: 0.8652

145ms/step - loss: 0.1506 - accuracy: 0.9485 - val_loss: 0.3742 - val_accuracy: 0.8674

146ms/step - loss: 0.1257 - accuracy: 0.9579 - val_loss: 0.3909 - val_accuracy: 0.8656

146ms/step - loss: 0.1123 - accuracy: 0.9616 - val_loss: 0.4141 - val_accuracy: 0.8598

145ms/step - loss: 0.0943 - accuracy: 0.9687 - val_loss: 0.4166 - val_accuracy: 0.8584
```

Figure 10.15: *Training output*

We see that we have several epochs with validation scores above **86%**.

7. Evaluate the model on the unseen test data using the evaluate method.

```
model_comb.evaluate(X_test_proc, y_test)[1]
```

The output gets printed as follows:

```
782/782 [==============================] - 11s 14ms/step - loss: 0.4035 - accuracy: 0.8613

0.8613200187683105
```

The accuracy is good and comparable to the earlier models. As mentioned earlier, for bigger neural networks, the efficiency gains are very significant. Also, we did not employ any pooling for feature reduction. We therefore did not see any speed benefit. We encourage you to build a larger network for the task and employ pooling to see the benefit first-hand.

Using 1D convolutions along with recurrent neural networks is one handy trick for improving the performance of your model. We will now look at another useful trick that can be extremely handy, especially when working with smaller datasets.

Using pre-trained embeddings

Recall that in the first few sections, we stated that preprocessing and appropriate data representation are key to success in NLP tasks. For representation, we have been using low-dimensional embeddings so far for this purpose. The embeddings have been trained during the model training, meaning that the embeddings are task and model-specific. The embeddings learnt as part of the LSTM-based model would be different from those as part of the GRU-based model. Recall from the exercises that this embedding layer led to a high number of trainable parameters in the network. For 32-dimensional embeddings and a vocabulary size of 10,000, this meant 320,000 parameters. Such high parameters would contribute to overfitting as well. To effectively train such embeddings, you would generally need a lot of data and/or careful regularization.

Another alternative to training your task-specific embeddings is using **pre-trained embeddings**. This is a form of transfer learning wherein you use some pre-trained model/ feature mappings for data representation. In the simplest form, we could use ready-made term mappings (as simple as a dictionary) to simply look up the vector for a term. A more sophisticated pre-trained embedding model would give you the embedding for the entire input text. For our review sentiment classification case study, such a model would give us a single vector for any input review, regardless of its length. Both approaches have their merits and are worth trying out in your machine learning/ artificial intelligence solution.

Note: Using pre-trained embeddings is only one of the many forms of transfer learning. We will learn about transfer learning types and models in detail in Chapter 11, Transfer Learning.

Popular pretrained models are trained on billions of tokens from millions of documents. Such training would be impractical for an individual to perform. Thanks to transfer learning and the power of the open-source community, such powerful representations are available for anyone to use. Let us first understand the benefits and drawbacks of using pre-trained embeddings.

Benefits

- Benefit from transfer learning and training from high volumes of data.
- Text preprocessing effort is reduced (especially for models that allow raw text input).
- Some embedding models have fixed-size output, making the processing simpler.

Drawbacks

- Not necessarily good for your task.
- Potentially biased (especially if derived from open data, for example, chat forums).

To make the idea and the power of using pre-trained embeddings more concrete, let us use them for our case study.

We begin with installing and importing the necessary libraries, TensorFlow hub and TensorFlow datasets. The following code does this:

```
!pip install tensorflow-hub -q

!pip install tensorflow-datasets -q

import tensorflow as tf, tensorflow_hub as tfhub

import tensorflow_datasets as tfds
```

Next, we load the IMDb review data using the load function from TensorFlow datasets, specifying 80% train data and reserving 20% data for testing. Use the following command:

```
train_data, valid_data, test_data = tfds.load(name="imdb_reviews",
                    split=('train[:80%]', 'train[80%:]','test'),
                    as_supervised=True)
```

An iterator over the dataset is now ready. We can print an example review from the data using the following code:

```
train_examples_batch, _ = next(iter(train_data.batch(10)))
train_examples_batch[3]
```

The review gets printed as in *Figure 10.16*:

```
<tf.Tensor: shape=(), dtype=string, numpy=b'This is the kind of film for a snowy Sunday
afternoon when the rest of the world can go ahead with its own business as you descend into a
big arm-chair and mellow for a couple of hours. Wonderful performances from Cher and Nicolas
Cage (as always) gently row the plot along. There are no rapids to cross, no dangerous waters,
just a warm and witty paddle through New York life at its best. A family film in every sense
and one that deserves the praise it received.'>
```

Figure 10.16: *Sample raw text record from the training data*

We can see that the training data contains raw review text. The version of the dataset that we used earlier had tokenized indices. This is an important difference and a useful one. In case you want to preprocess the raw text in a customized manner, the raw text version is more useful. In our case, we wish to employ an embedding model that takes in raw text. Therefore, this raw text version is more appropriate.

We will pick an embedding model from TensorFlow Hub for our case study, as it is convenient to use in TensorFlow and Keras as a regular layer, as we will shortly see. We will use the **`Universal Sentence Encoder`** model by Google. It is a highly capable model trained on a variety of English text using a **Deep Averaging Network** (**DAN**) encoder. It outputs a vector of length 512 for any input (raw) text. The model is optimized for greater-than-word-length text. That is, the model is designed to create representations for phrases, sentences, or short paragraphs. This fits our purpose well.

Note: The Universal Sentence Encoder is a good general-purpose encoder that provides high-quality embeddings for various tasks. To learn more about USE, the official documentation on TensorFlow is a good starting point. The page also has a link to a useful demo notebook model. Refer: https://tfhub.dev/google/universal-sentence-encoder/4

There are many other pre-trained text embeddings available on the TensorFlow hub. A good alternative is **`google/nnlm-en-dim128/2`**, which outputs 128-dimensional embeddings. Smaller size embeddings may speed up the training and execution of your model but might lead to lower accuracy as fewer dimensions would capture less information. If your text contains punctuations or additional characters, you could try the model **google/nnlm-en-dim128-with-normalization/2**. This model is similar to the **nnlm** model but with additional text normalization/ preprocessing. You can explore more text embedding models on TensorFlow Hub: **https://tfhub.dev/s?module-type=text-embedding**

We are using models that output a fixed-length vector, regardless of the input text length. It is important to realize that this means that we do not need recurrence anymore as input text length becomes irrelevant. Let us try this out ourselves.

First, we will load the model into a Keras layer. The TensorFlow Hub package that we installed allows us to load models directly as a layer in Keras, that can be added to any model like any regular Keras layer. We need to specify the path and whether the layer needs to be trainable. Note that using some other model from TensorFlow Hub is as simple as changing the reference to the model. Use the following code:

```
embedding = "https://tfhub.dev/google/universal-sentence-encoder/4"

hub_layer = tfhub.KerasLayer(embedding, input_shape=[],
                             dtype=tf.string,
                             trainable=False)
```

In our case, we do not want the embedding model to be retrained, so we specified **False**. The **hub_layer** object can now be used as a standalone encoder, or like an ordinary embedding layer in a Keras model. Let us see how it encodes the example review that we saw earlier. Pass the 4th review from the **train_examples_batch** variable into the **hub_layer** as in the following command and print its shape:

```
hub_layer(train_examples_batch[3:4]).shape
```

The shape gets printed as follows:

```
TensorShape([1, 512])
```

The output confirms that we have a series of 512 numbers representing the input text. Recall that the length of the input text does not matter as the model outputs a fixed length vector for the entire input text. To see the first 10 numbers in the vector, use the following command.

```
hub_layer(train_examples_batch[3:4])[0][:10]
```

The output is as follows:

```
<tf.Tensor: shape=(10,), dtype=float32, numpy= array([-0.00274222, -0.04518872,
0.02080956, 0.03594078, -0.03814794, 0.07527251, 0.01817022, -0.02279347,
0.07460126, 0.0103387 ], dtype=float32)>
```

The first 10 numbers in the vector are printed. These do not make sense to us, but the 512 numbers together are a powerful representation that captures very well the meaning of the text. We now have the embedding layer ready and are all set to start building the model in the next exercise.

Exercise- Text classification with pre-trained embeddings

In this exercise, we will build a sentiment classification model with pre-trained embeddings. We will leverage the embedding layer we created in the previous section using TensorFlow Hub. As a result, we have a **`hub_layer`** object which can be used like a regular Keras layer. Note that we do not need recurrence due to the fixed-length output of the embedding layer. We will build a simple model with two dense layers with **`relu`** activation. Let us begin.

1. Import the required layers and utilities from Keras using the commands that follow.

   ```
   from tensorflow.keras.models import Sequential
   from tensorflow.keras.layers import Dense
   from tensorflow.keras.callbacks import EarlyStopping
   ```

2. Initialize a sequential model and add **`hub_layer`** (the embedding model) as a layer using the following code:

   ```
   model_emb = Sequential()
   model_emb.add(hub_layer)
   ```

3. Next, add two dense layers of 128 units each with **`relu`** activation and add the final dense unit for prediction. Print out the model summary. Use the following code:

   ```
   model_emb.add(Dense(128, activation='relu'))
   model_emb.add(Dense(128, activation='relu'))
   model_emb.add(Dense(1))
   model_emb.summary()
   ```

   The model summary gets printed as shown in the following figure:

```
Layer (type)                 Output Shape              Param #
=================================================================
keras_layer_4 (KerasLayer)  (None, 512)               256797824

dense_25 (Dense)             (None, 128)               65664

dense_26 (Dense)             (None, 128)               16512

dense_27 (Dense)             (None, 1)                 129

=================================================================
Total params: 256,880,129
Trainable params: 82,305
Non-trainable params: 256,797,824
```

Figure 10.17: *Summary of the model*

Notice that there are merely 82,305 trainable parameters. There are about 256 million parameters in the embedding layer (USE), but the layer is not trainable. We therefore have relatively very few parameters to train.

4. Compile the model with the **adam** optimizer and **binary_crossentropy** as the loss function. Use the following code:

```
model_emb.compile(loss='binary_crossentropy',
                  optimizer='adam',
                  metrics=['accuracy'])
```

5. Define early stopping with patience 10 and enable restoring the best weights. Use the following code:

```
stop_early = EarlyStopping(monitor='val_accuracy', patience=10,
restore_best_weights=True)
```

6. Fit the model and use the validation dataset for validation, run for 10 epochs. Use the **batch** function of the **TensorFlow** datasets to create batches of 512 instances. Execute the following code:

```
model_emb.fit(train_data.batch(512),
              epochs=10,
              validation_data = valid_data.batch(512),
              callbacks=[stop_early])
```

Partial output from the last few epochs should look like *Figure 10.18*:

```
1s/step - loss: 0.4031 - accuracy: 0.8403 - val_loss: 0.3759 - val_accuracy: 0.8392

1s/step - loss: 0.3994 - accuracy: 0.8483 - val_loss: 0.3863 - val_accuracy: 0.8394

1s/step - loss: 0.3786 - accuracy: 0.8570 - val_loss: 0.3894 - val_accuracy: 0.8484

1s/step - loss: 0.3689 - accuracy: 0.8600 - val_loss: 0.3995 - val_accuracy: 0.8514

1s/step - loss: 0.3638 - accuracy: 0.8622 - val_loss: 0.3930 - val_accuracy: 0.8538

1s/step - loss: 0.3492 - accuracy: 0.8667 - val_loss: 0.3994 - val_accuracy: 0.8576

1s/step - loss: 0.3505 - accuracy: 0.8647 - val_loss: 0.4245 - val_accuracy: 0.8598

1s/step - loss: 0.3445 - accuracy: 0.8661 - val_loss: 0.4383 - val_accuracy: 0.8526
```

Figure 10.18: *Partial output from final epochs*

We can see that we have achieved close to **86%** validation accuracy. Considering that we had very few parameters in our model (about 82k) and performed no fine-tuning, this is a good result. Also, note that **we did not use any recurrence or attention mechanism**. We encourage you to try out different hyper-parameters and improve on this result. In this exercise, we used the **Universal Sentence Encoder** model by Google, which is an embedding model. As mentioned earlier, there are various approaches to embedding and various popular models. Let us look at some other notable embeddings.

Notable pre-trained embeddings

The information that the embeddings capture depends not only on the data used for training but also on the task for which they were created. When we created our embeddings from scratch using the embedding layer for our RNN models, the vectors for the terms were getting optimized for the task at hand that is, sentiment classification. It would be incorrect to say that the embeddings we got were general-purpose embeddings, or that those embeddings captured the meaning of the terms. Those embeddings were specific for the task of sentiment classification, derived from movie review data. Fortunately for us, there have been many attempts by researchers to build more general-purpose embeddings that can be used for multiple tasks. The Universal Sentence Encoder we used in the previous exercise is one such example.

The *GloVe* project by the Stanford NLP Group is another extremely valuable project. The group trained word embeddings on billions of tokens over millions of documents and made the embeddings publicly available. Embeddings are available for different datasets Wikipedia, Common Crawl, and Twitter. Each dataset has billions of tokens. Additionally, the vectors are available in different sizes, so you can download 50-dimensional vectors or even 200-dimensional vectors. The vectors from the *GloVe* project have some impressive demos and are known to capture some very interesting regularities between words. *Figure 10.19* shows some semantic regularities captured by *GloVe* vectors. Take a look at the following figure:

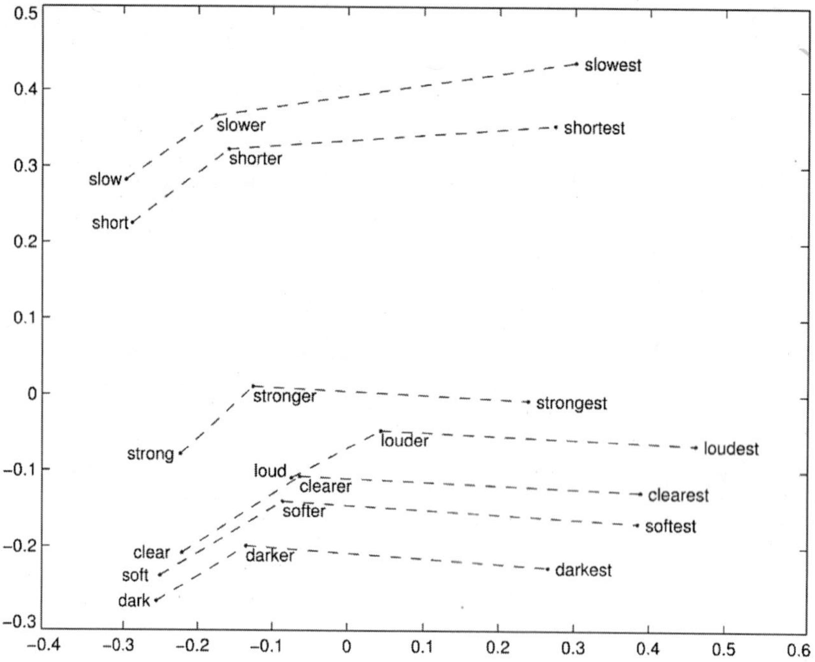

Figure 10.19: Semantic regularities captured by GloVe word vectors

Note: Read more about the GloVe project and access the different word vectors at the following link. https://nlp.stanford.edu/projects/glove/

Google Research also has publicly made available word vectors based on the word2vec algorithm and trained on the Google News dataset containing over 100 billion words. These vectors too seem to capture semantic regularities between terms. Using these word vectors, we can calculate the nearest neighbour for any target term. *Figure 10.20* shows the nearest neighbours for some test terms. We can see that the neighbours make a lot of sense and are semantically very close. Take a look at the following figure:

FRANCE	JESUS	XBOX	REDDISH	SCRATCHED	MEGABITS
AUSTRIA	GOD	AMIGA	GREENISH	NAILED	OCTETS
BELGIUM	SATI	PLAYSTATION	BLUISH	SMASHED	MB/S
GERMANY	CHRIST	MSX	PINKISH	PUNCHED	BIT/S
ITALY	SATAN	IPOD	PURPLISH	POPPED	BAUD
GREECE	KALI	SEGA	BROWNISH	CRIMPED	CARATS
SWEDEN	INDRA	PSNUMBER	GREYISH	SCRAPED	KBIT/S
NORWAY	VISHNU	HD	GRAYISH	SCREWED	MEGAHERTZ
EUROPE	ANANDA	DREAMCAST	WHITISH	SECTIONED	MEGAPIXELS
HUNGARY	PARVATI	GEFORCE	SILVERY	SLASHED	GBIT/S
SWITZERLAND	GRACE	CAPCOM	YELLOWISH	RIPPED	AMPERES

Figure 10.20: Nearest neighbours for each term's word vector

GloVe and *Word2Vec* are not the only candidates out there. The Facebook Research group used their *FastText* algorithm to train word vectors on large volumes of data in 157 languages and made it publicly available. The vectors can be downloaded following the instructions on this page: **https://github.com/facebookresearch/fastText/blob/master/docs/crawl-vectors.md**

Note: For a general, illustrated overview of embeddings and the various types of regularities and relations they capture, refer to the following link: https://colah.github.io/posts/2014-07-NLP-RNNs-Representations/

Regardless of which pre-trained embeddings we opt for, we are bound to reap the advantages of the extensive data and computing resources utilized by these organizations to develop these embeddings. These embeddings are remarkably potent, as they seem to grasp semantic patterns and possess some level of meaning, making them close to general-purpose embeddings. Armed with the capabilities of open-source models/data and the NLP model optimization techniques we have learned, you should now be well-equipped to build high-performance models.

Conclusion

We saw that natural language data has some peculiarities and a good machine learning/artificial intelligence solution must consider these. For most tasks, models must process the data as a sequence. Additionally, preprocessing is an extremely important step in NLP for which there are no generic/standard pipelines. A prudent data scientist will study the data closely and customize their approach for the task. With the pre-processing done, the representation of textual data must be done appropriately, and we learnt that embeddings/low dimensional vectors are great for most tasks.

For processing language data appropriately, we looked at two major approaches and architectures, recurrent neural networks, and the transformer architecture. While there are many variants of the RNN, the core idea remains the same. The network processes the terms one by one and maintains and updates information at each step. The transformer approach is different because it processes the entire input sequence explicitly at once, using clever mechanisms to identify the important parts of the sequence and to capture the dependencies between terms. Both these approaches provide great results, with transformer architectures now becoming the most popular approach.

We then saw ways to optimize the model architecture and hyper-parameters. Using the Keras tuner, we learnt how to tune not just regular hyper-parameters but also those about embeddings. We learnt a useful trick that 1D convolutions used along with RNNs can provide an efficiency boost without losing accuracy. Another strategy we learned and implemented was using pre-trained embeddings. Using this, we could get results similar to earlier models with very few parameters. This helped us realize the power of Transfer Learning.

Pre-trained embeddings are one of the many forms of Transfer Learning, which is the focus of the next chapter.

CHAPTER 11
Transfer Learning

Introduction

This chapter discusses the paradigm of machine learning/artificial intelligence, that is, the next driver of ML commercial success which will take artificial intelligence to the masses. The past few years have seen rapid advancements in the field of machine learning / AI. This chapter will show how you can benefit from these and utilize some of the latest **State-of-the-Art** (**SOTA**) models available in the open-source community and use them in your applications.

Structure

In this chapter, we will discuss the following topics:

- Motivation for transfer learning
- Using a SOTA image classification model
- What is transfer learning?
    - Applications of transfer learning
    - Benefits of transfer learning
    - Limitations of transfer learning
- Sources for pre-trained models

- General transfer learning workflow
- Transfer learning for images
    - o Fine-tuning a SOTA image model
- Transfer learning for text
    - o Applications of transfer learning for text
    - o Fine-tuning a SOTA NLP model

Objectives

By the end of this chapter, you will be able to appreciate and apply various forms of transfer learning. We will first understand the different types of transfer learning and see how they are helpful in modern machine learning/ artificial intelligence. We will see both the benefits and limitations of it. We will explore various sources for transfer learning modules. We will use a SOTA model out of the box for our specific task and eventually learn how to fine-tune the model for better performance. Transfer learning is slightly different for image processing and NLP tasks. By the end of the chapter, you will be able to perform both. We will use various SOTA models in the chapter and employ popular libraries for transfer learning.

Motivation for transfer learning

Let us take an example. As a data scientist at the fashion giant Azra, you want to sort various images posted by customers on popular social media platforms and identify images containing fashion items: dresses, coats, shoes, etc. This would help the organization identify trends better and anticipate demand better. This seems to be a perfect situation for a machine learning/artificial intelligence model and where you, as a data scientist, can add tremendous value. There are a couple of approaches you can take to solve this problem.

The first option is to develop your own solution from scratch. This would entail all the steps of the CRISP-DM framework, as outlined in *Chapter 1, Optimizing ML/AI Solutions.* Deep learning models would be a natural choice for this task, and you will therefore require a large number of labeled images, tens of thousands for sure. Additionally, the model needs to be complex, that is, having many layers (SOTA have more than 300 layers!). This naturally means very high training times (possibly several days/weeks) and therefore high costs. This is clearly an arduous task.

Consider another option, standing on the shoulders of giants, using a pre-trained SOTA. Pre-trained means that the model has already been trained on massive datasets and is now available to us to benefit from. What if this model was free of cost and could be used with just a few lines of code? This is exactly what transfer learning lets us do, among many other things.

In this chapter, we will first learn about transfer learning, an extremely powerful way to benefit from the hard work done by thousands of researchers and contributors in the open-source community. Using multiple case studies, we will see how transfer learning can be used in varied situations for multiple use cases: for using the models for predictions directly, for extracting features from the model, and for fine-tuning the model on a newer dataset.

Using a SOTA image classification model

First, we import the necessary modules from **Keras - EfficientNetB5** and its accompanying **`decode_predictions`** method to make sense of the predictions. Then, we load the model into memory using the **`EfficientNetV2S`** function, as shown in the following code:

```
from keras.applications.efficientnet_v2 import EfficientNetV2S, decode_predictions

model = EfficientNetV2S(weights='imagenet')
```

The model is now available to make predictions. You have the power of a SOTA model, trained on millions of images, at your command. To see if it works, let us try out an image of a fur coat. The image can be found at **https://github.com/mirzarahim2197/Optimizing-AI-and-Data-Science-Models/tree/main/Chapter11/data**

We need to import some image preprocessing utilities from Keras. Let us also import **`numpy`** for basic array manipulation, using the following code. Then, we load the image and resize it to 384x384, as the model expects:

```
from tensorflow.keras.preprocessing import image

import numpy as np

img = image.load_img("Furcoat.webp", target_size=(384, 384))

Img
```

Figure 11.1: Input image of a fur coat

The image too is now loaded into memory. As a pre-processing step, the image needs to be converted into an array of shape *1x384x384x3,* in line with the model input expectations using the following code:

```
img_array = image.img_to_array(img)

img_array = img_array.reshape((1, 384, 384, 3))
```

Now, the image can be passed to the model to get predictions. The **decode_predictions** function will provide the top 5 labels the model predicts along with their probabilities and execute the following code:

```
myresult = model.predict(img_array)

decode_predictions(myresult)
```

The output is shown in the following figure:

```
1/1 [==============================] - 0s 438ms/step
[[('n03404251', 'fur_coat', 0.9117289),
  ('n03045698', 'cloak', 0.002375166),
  ('n04325704', 'stole', 0.0013715083),
  ('n02817516', 'bearskin', 0.0010477889),
  ('n04479046', 'trench_coat', 0.0007667327)]]
```

Figure 11.2: *Top 5 classes predicted by the model*

Looking at the top 5 predictions of the model, we can see the model is very confident that the object in the image is a fur coat. The second highest probability score is a low 0.2%. Such clarity is naturally preferred, as we want the model to not be confused often.

It took just 2 lines to have a fully functional model loaded into memory, and 9 lines overall to make predictions on a user-provided image. The result was extremely good too. The model that you used is from the **EfficientNet** family; one of the best models for the task of image classification is SOTA as illustrated in the following figure:

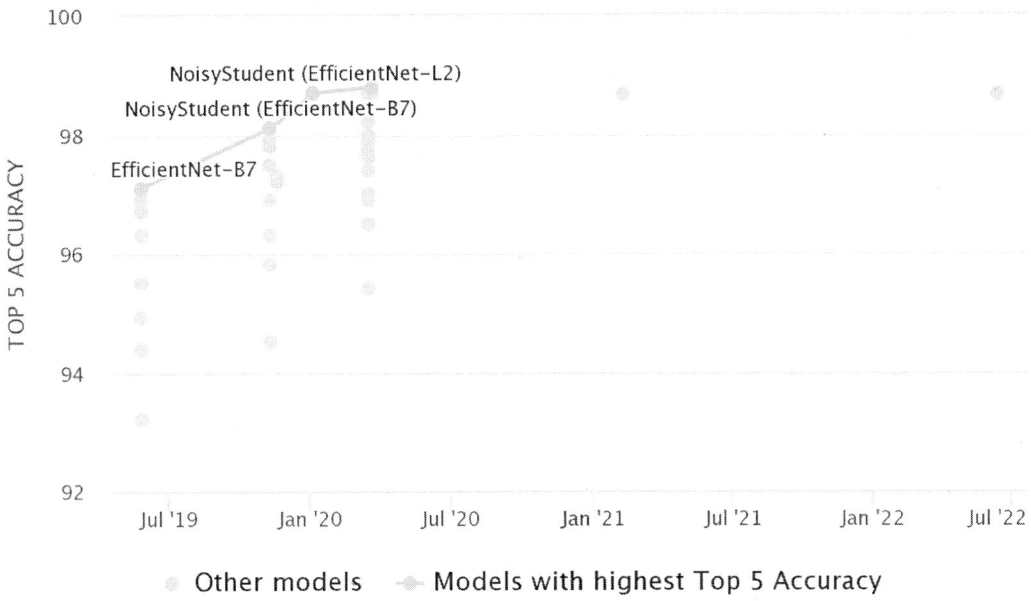

***Figure 11.3:** EfficientNet family has SOTA performance*

Note: To find out the SOTA models right now and the associated research papers, along with the code, you can refer to the following link: https://paperswithcode.com/sota/image-classification-on-imagenet?metric=Top%205%20Accuracy&tag_filter=5

The EfficientNetB5 model has 312 hidden layers and 30.6 million parameters. The base data for the model is the ImageNet database **(https://en.wikipedia.org/wiki/ImageNet)** which effectively uses more than 14 million labeled images as training data. The model was developed from late 2019 to early 2020 but is still among the highest-performing models out there. Additions to the `EfficientNet` family are continuously being developed, providing incremental prediction accuracy and memory optimization. *Figure 11.3* shows that `EfficientNet-based` models have among the highest top 5 accuracies (correct class in the top 5 predictions of the model) scores available right now. `EfficientNet` is also one of the fastest models to train and deploy, with some variations (`EfficientNetV2S` on `Keras`) being as small as 88 megabytes in size. You have a high performance, highly memory-optimized model at your disposal.

Now, consider the alternative approach; developing a comparable model from scratch. Such development would mean gathering and labeling several images, at extremely high training time and extremely high cost. Of course, deployment of such a model would be another task and the organization might end up needing multiple data science professionals and engineers for this single problem statement. Unless there are considerations against using a pre-trained model (discussed later in this chapter in the section, *Drawbacks of Transfer Learning*), this approach does not make a lot of sense.

In our example, we saw that transfer learning could save us quite some time, money and effort and is an excellent option. However, what we saw was just one of the applications of transfer learning. Let us build a holistic understanding of transfer learning, what it is? its applications, benefits, and drawbacks. Let us get started.

What is transfer learning?

The big idea here is quite simple; metaphorically, it is standing on the shoulders of giants. Not starting from scratch can have tremendous advantages. There are a couple of perspectives that will help understand the same.

The first perspective is utilizing knowledge acquired for one task to solve a related problem, and therefore going beyond the paradigm in which the learning was developed.

Somewhat like a human who knows how to drive a car, might find it easier to learn to ride a motorcycle. A person who knows how to play the guitar may learn to play the ukulele much faster. Not learning from scratch is often a great advantage. *Andrew Ng*, in his *NIPS tutorial* in 2016 stated, **After supervised learning — Transfer Learning will be the next driver of ML commercial success**.

Note: For those interested, the NeurIPS tutorial was titled Nuts and Bolts of Building AI Applications Using Deep Learning. The slides for the talk can be found at the following link: https://media.nips.cc/Conferences/2016/Slides/6203-Slides.pdf

Another actionable perspective in our context of developing machine learning / AI solutions is leveraging the contributions of others in the data science community. To make the idea more concrete, we are talking about leveraging ML / AI artefacts as follows:

- Ready to use pre-trained models, or
- Partly trained models that require some fine tuning
- Feature generation / data representation modules.

Pause and ponder: In our case study, we have used transfer learning for deep learning. Can you think of an example of transfer learning that does not involve deep learning?

Hint: Even data representation modules are Transfer Learning solutions.

The following figure shows the basic difference between traditional machine learning and Transfer Learning:

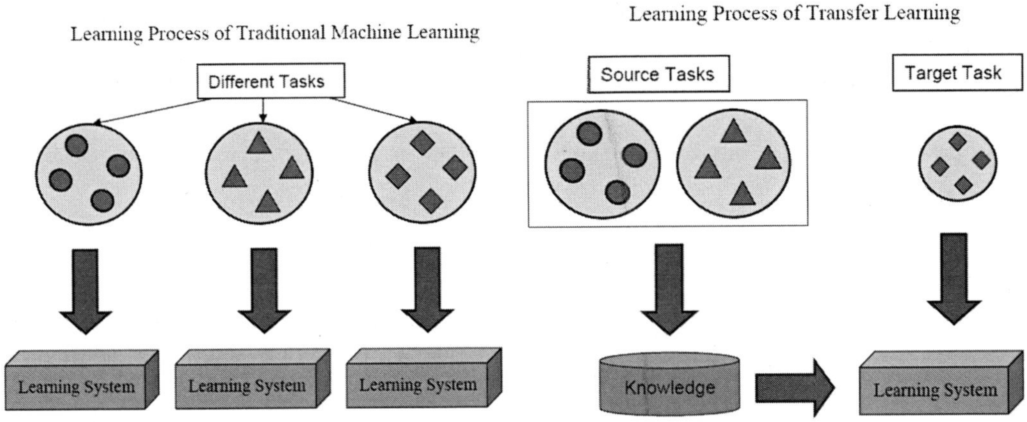

***Figure 11.4**: Traditional machine learning vs. Transfer Learning*

Figure 11.4 illustrates the difference between the learning processes of traditional machine learning vs transfer learning. In traditional machine learning, learning is focused on the data and task at hand. The patterns / knowledge learnt by the system / model are not intended to be used in another context. In contrast, the transfer learning process seeks to distil knowledge from the source task and data (typically massive datasets) into a model. It is this knowledge that we wish to leverage in another task. This target task could be different from the source task, with the data set usually being different. To understand better why this is beneficial, let us see some applications of transfer learning in the next section.

Applications of transfer learning

We understood the broad idea of transfer learning in the previous section. There are several applications of knowledge leverage. Let us understand some prominent applications and see how they benefit the field of artificial intelligence.

Ready to use pre-trained models

Revisiting the `EfficientNet` example from the previous section, we encountered one of the typical situations where Transfer Learning unlocks tremendous value. In the situation considered in the case study, it was impractical to develop a high-performance model from scratch. With transfer learning, however, we could very easily leverage a SOTA deep learning model for image classification (with 312 hidden layers and more than 30 million parameters) and get good results on our task. This was an example where we used the model **out of the box**, and we used the model for prediction without making any modifications to it.

In our case study, we did not require development to use the model and get good results. In many cases, these results are good enough for using the model. If not, these are at least good enough to form a **good baseline**, the benchmark to compare future solutions. Let us say you wish to build a highly customized model that understands the specifics of the domain data to provide better accuracy. Naturally, there is a cost to this development and justification needed, along with benchmarks that the solution must beat. If the solution you intend to create does not beat the benchmark from Transfer Learning, it is probably not a good idea to do so (as higher accuracy was the main objective).

Fine tuning models

Just because a model has been trained on millions of images, it does not mean that the model will perform extremely well on your tasks as well. Indeed, it is not always the case that the SOTA model was trained on the same task and data as your application. We need to improve on the baseline that the SOTA model provides when used out of the box. The improvement comes from fine tuning the model. While there are different approaches to fine tuning, the short explanation of fine tuning is modifications to the base model to perform better on the target data and task. We will see this in more detail later in this chapter, in the section *General Transfer Learning Workflow*.

Data representation/feature extraction

We do not always have to use the entire (sometimes huge) model. The modular nature of deep neural networks enables us to extract parts of the model that we can then employ in various situations in different ways. One common use case is to use transfer learning for getting good data representation, that is, feature extraction.

Consider the Inception model that was trained on millions of images. The initial layers of the model have undergone extensive training on millions of images to learn very powerful representations of the input images. Indeed, good data representation through great features is a key decider of the performance of the model. When dealing with small datasets, using good representations can make all the difference in model performance.

Benefits of transfer learning

There are many benefits of transfer learning. We will therefore not dwell on these points to discuss them in detail. Rather, we will see these benefits first-hand throughout this chapter through various hands-on activities. A brief overview of the benefits of transfer learning is as follows:

- **Little to no development needed to get a baseline**: Often, with minimal modifications (sometimes no modification), the base model provides a good starting point. If the source and target tasks and data are similar, then the performance of the base model can be a great baseline that you achieved with little developmental effort.

- **Increased learning speed (that is, via quicker baselines)**: Because you can arrive at a baseline quicker, the rate at which you learn what works for your problem is much higher and you can create MVPs and test your hypothesis much more quickly.
- **Access SOTA models with a few lines of code**: If pre-trained SOTA models are available freely, they would be a natural choice for transfer learning. Most of the present sources for pre-trained models make these models available to us with very minimal coding. In the section *Using a SOTA image classification model*, we got the SOTA `EfficientNetV2` model at our disposal using just 2 lines of code.
- **Create solutions with little to (almost) no labelled data**: In case the target task and data are like the base model, you can potentially use it straight away without retaining newer data. In case the task and data are slightly different, and you wish to optimize the model for your data, this can also be achieved using a few hundred data points.
- **Rich feature generation**: Using transfer learning, we can leverage feature representations from models that were trained on millions of images / billions of tokens. For problems with smaller data sizes, the features make a big difference and transfer learning lets you use the best.

Does transfer learning have any drawbacks / limitations? Let us find out in the next section.

Limitations of transfer learning

For all its benefits, transfer learning also has a few drawbacks that the wise data scientist must be aware of before using it in their next data science solution. The drawbacks are as follows:

- **Works only if source and target problems are similar enough:** It is easy to see why this is a limitation. If the model was trained on chest X-ray images, it may not be suitable for classifying if the animal in an image is a cat or a dog. Likewise, a model trained on a corpus of legal text might not be suitable for classifying the sentiments of tweets.
- **Fine tuning is complex**: There are several choices that you must make when fine tuning a model and many hyper-parameters - number of layers to freeze, positions of these layers, learning rates to retrain with and many more. Also, let us not forget that the model itself is a choice we need to make. Fine tuning can be considered more of an art than a science.
- **Prone to overfitting**: If you are using a SOTA model with a billion parameters and fine tuning it on a dataset with a few hundred records, chances are that you will overfit the data extremely quickly. The data scientist must be extremely careful while fine tuning and monitoring the training closely, using appropriate learning rates, regularization and techniques like data augmentation.

- **Propagate biases in input data**: To understand this consideration, let us consider popular NLP models. These models are trained on text in the public domain: including online discussion forums, and comments on social media. The models learn the toxicity and bias present in the data. Any user of this model will inadvertently propagate that bias into their application. Likewise, for image models, many of the images are from the public domain or curated datasets. For example, these may not represent people of all genders and skin colours adequately, making the systems perform differently and therefore induce a bias in the solution that uses such a model.

The takeaway from these points is that while transfer learning is extremely powerful and lets you truly benefit from the great advances being made by the data science community, the data scientist must be extremely careful while employing transfer learning. It comes with its own set of challenges.

Sources for pre-trained models

There are many sources currently available and practically anyone with an Internet connection can start leveraging the immense knowledge available through transfer learning. These sources / platforms have varying maturity and ease of use of the available models / data. Some notable examples are the following:

Keras Applications

For those who like the abstractions and simplicity that Keras provides, it has several pre-trained models available as **Keras Applications**. The benefit of using these applications is that they are extremely easy to load, and then they manipulate just like you would manipulate any Keras model. Keras documentation also has several, very useful examples using transfer learning and can help you quickly get up to speed.

Website: **https://keras.io/api/applications/**

Some of the current models available are shown in *Figure 11.5*.

Model	Size (MB)	Top-1 Accuracy	Top-5 Accuracy	Parameters	Depth	Time (ms) per inference step (CPU)	Time (ms) per inference step (GPU)
Xception	88	79.0%	94.5%	22.9M	81	109.4	8.1
VGG16	528	71.3%	90.1%	138.4M	16	69.5	4.2
VGG19	549	71.3%	90.0%	143.7M	19	84.8	4.4
ResNet50	98	74.9%	92.1%	25.6M	107	58.2	4.6
ResNet50V2	98	76.0%	93.0%	25.6M	103	45.6	4.4
ResNet101	171	76.4%	92.8%	44.7M	209	89.6	5.2
ResNet101V2	171	77.2%	93.8%	44.7M	205	72.7	5.4
ResNet152	232	76.6%	93.1%	60.4M	311	127.4	6.5
ResNet152V2	232	78.0%	94.2%	60.4M	307	107.5	6.6
InceptionV3	92	77.9%	93.7%	23.9M	189	42.2	6.9
InceptionResNetV2	215	80.3%	95.3%	55.9M	449	130.2	10.0
MobileNet	16	70.4%	89.5%	4.3M	55	22.6	3.4
MobileNetV2	14	71.3%	90.1%	3.5M	105	25.9	3.8

Figure 11.5: *Some models on Keras Applications*

Tensorflow Hub

For Tensorflow users, there is no dearth of models available on TensorFlow Hub - a repository of several hundred (if not in thousands already) models. These are available with minimal code, and you can easily reuse state-of-the-art models that are frequently added to the repository.

Website: **https://tfhub.dev/**

The following figure shows the Tensorflow interface:

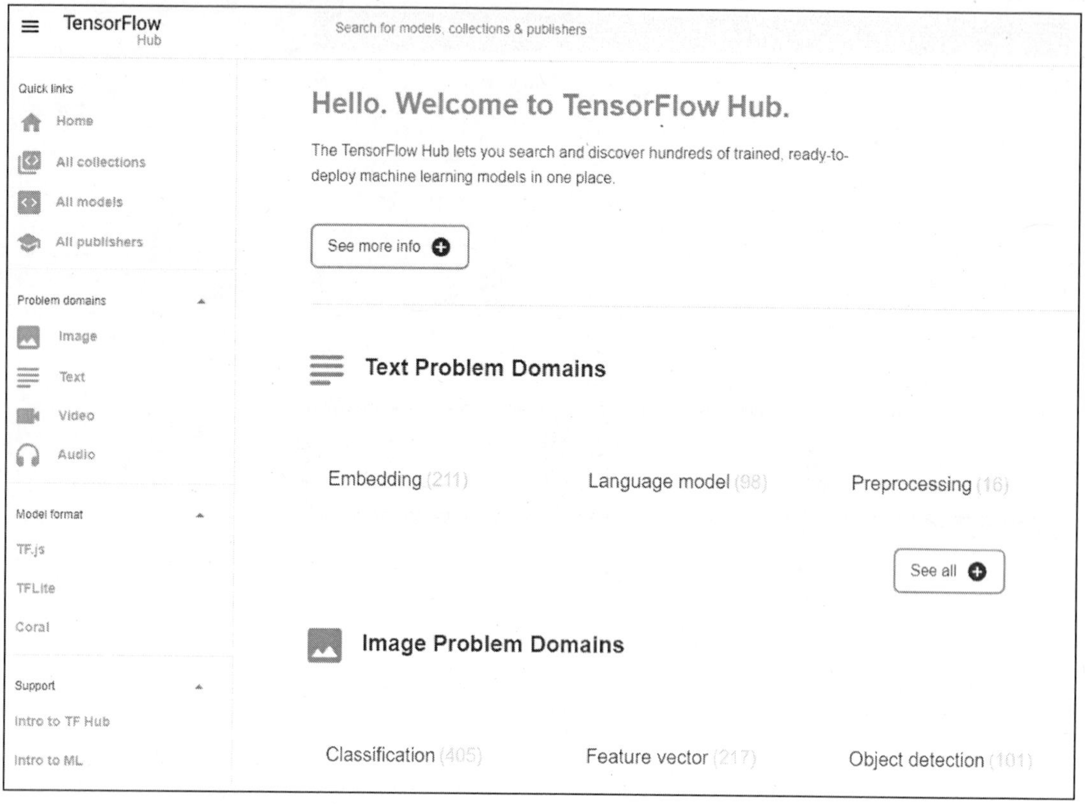

***Figure 11.6**: TensorFlow hub for hundreds of pre-trained models*

Hugging Face

Hugging Face is at present one of the most popular destinations for open-source models and transfer learning. The transformer architecture in deep learning, which took the deep learning community by storm, was first made accessible to the masses via the transformers library by Hugging Face. Now, Hugging Face is a thriving community where most SOTA models can be found. Hugging Face also has Spaces, which allows individuals / organizations to host demo applications showcasing the capabilities of their models. The platform also has several courses on deep learning. We will use Hugging Face's transformer library heavily in this chapter.

Website: **https://huggingface.co**

The following figure shows the Hugging Face interface:

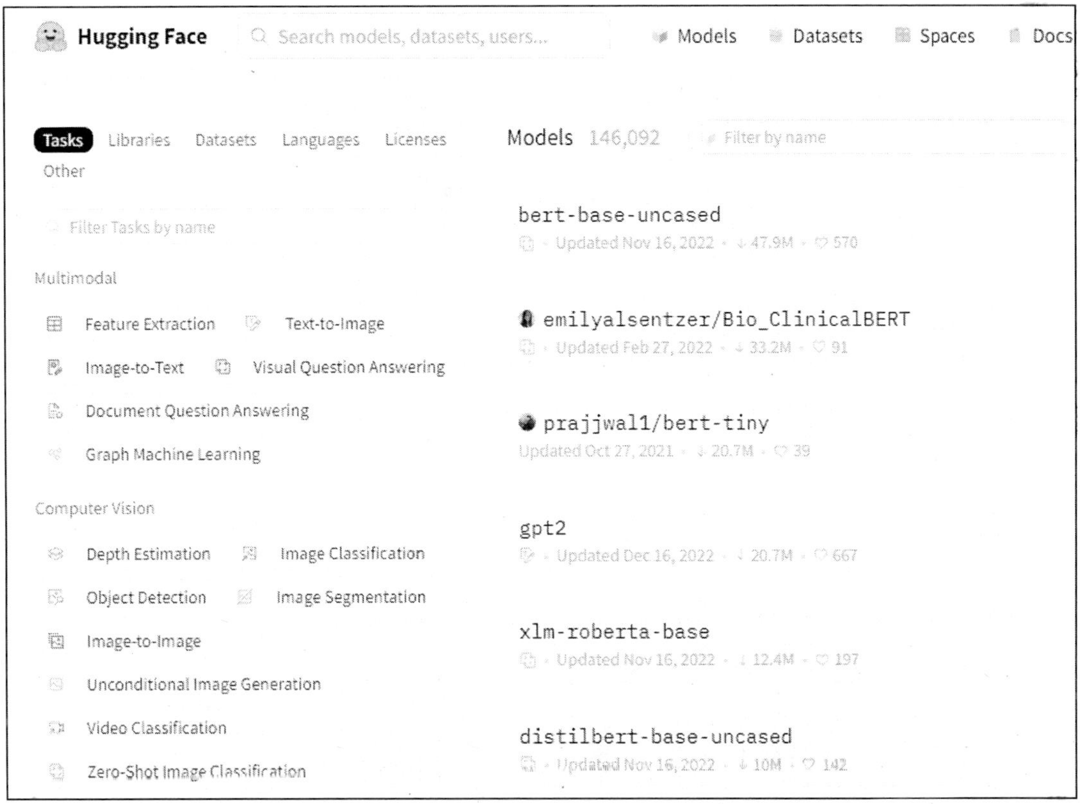

***Figure 11.7**: Models on Hugging Face*

Kaggle

Once a platform for hosting machine learning competitions, Kaggle is now one of the most popular homes for data science in general. Other than educational notebooks, courses, competitions, and kernels, Kaggle has several pre-trained models available to use in Kaggle kernels and even direct downloads.

Website: **https://www.kaggle.com/models**

The following figure shows the Kaggle interface:

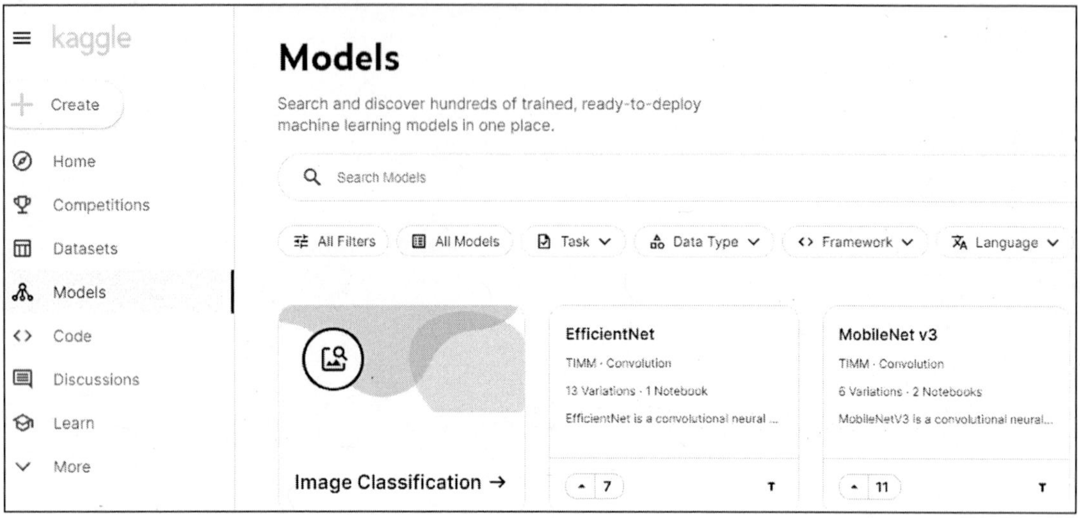

Figure 11.8: Kaggle models

GitHub

GitHub repositories have long been the source for numerous, excellent Python libraries/ packages. It is not surprising that GitHub also hosts a great many model repositories that the community can not only contribute to but also use for transfer learning by simply cloning the repository.

Website: **https://github.com/**

The following figure shows the GitHub interface:

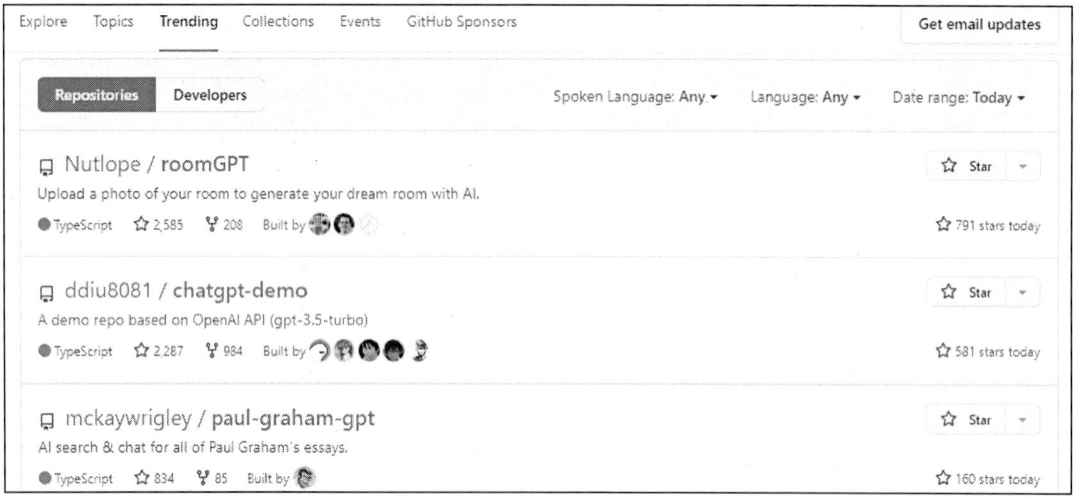

Figure 11.9: GitHub repositories

Word embeddings for text

In addition to full-fledged models for prediction/fine tuning, you can also benefit from powerful data representations. This is particularly useful for text problems, where pre-trained word embeddings can be used to represent words/ sentences/ corpora. Word embeddings are low-dimensional representations of tokens that, if trained well, can capture semantic regularities between words which can be understood as representations that capture the meaning of the term. The **Global Vectors for Word Representation (GloVe)** project by Stanford NLP group makes word vectors trained on billions of tokens available freely to everyone. Google also has their Word2Vec embeddings trained on about 100 billion tokens. Additionally, several other word embeddings are available on the Hugging Face, and Kaggle platforms, and through Python packages like Gensim, SpaCy, and many more.

Now that we know the sources for various pre-trained models, let us learn how to use them for our applications.

General transfer learning workflow

We discussed earlier that there are 3 ways we can use transfer learning: directly for prediction, feature extraction, and fine tuning. In the section *Using a SOTA image classification model*, we saw that using a pre-trained model for prediction can be achieved very simply in less than 10 lines of code. Now, let us understand the process of using transfer learning for fine tuning powerful pre-trained models to make them perform better at our task.

The process of fine tuning typically has the following steps:

1. Start with a base model with pre-trained weights loaded (for example, ImageNet weights for image models).
2. Freeze the layers that are not to be re-trained (most layers, often all).
3. Add predictive head/new final layers.
4. Train this new model on the dataset.

Depending on the size of the data and the extent of retraining you wish to do, *Step 2* can freeze varying amounts of layers. *Figure 11.10* illustrates this with the example of an image model. The diagram on the left illustrates the approach in which only the final layer(s) of the model are trained. The rest are frozen, that is, their weights will not change during training. The final layer weights, therefore, are the only trainable portions of the model which can be trained with regular learning rates. This approach makes the training extremely fast and retains most of the knowledge the earlier layers of the model contain.

The second approach (in the right diagram in *Figure 11.10*) shows another approach where we allow all the layers of the model to be trained, that is, all the weights of the model can be modified. Here, one must be extremely careful. If the learning rate is high, then we may quickly lose the knowledge of the original model and therefore lose the information derived from training over millions of images. This phenomenon is known as **catastrophic forgetting**. A sensible approach, therefore, is using a very low learning rate for the training. While this may seem like retraining of the model, this is in effect a true fine tuning of the model for the task and data at hand. The following figure shows strategies for fine tuning:

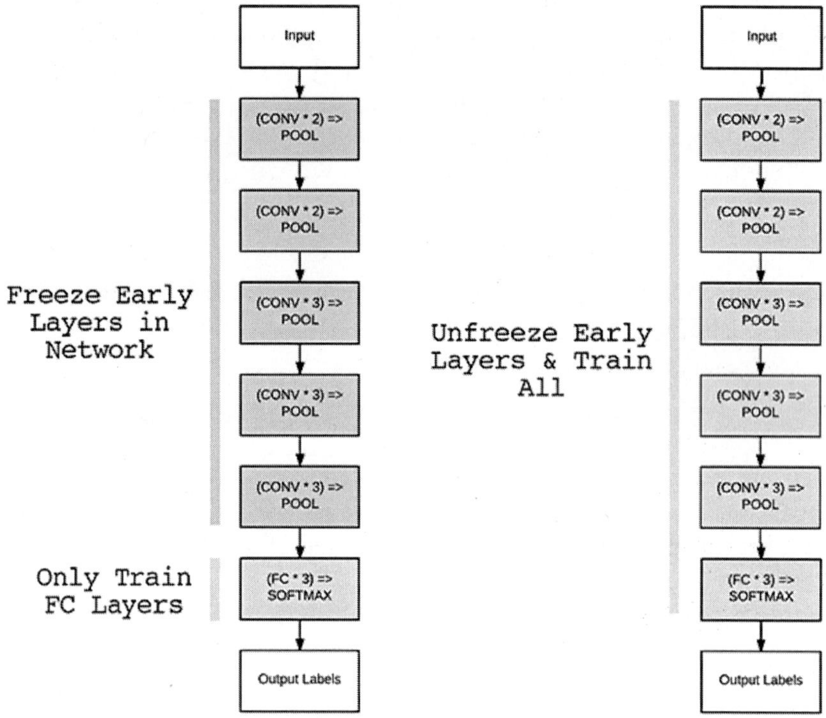

Figure 11.10: *Fine tuning strategies*

While we took an example from the image processing problem space, the principles and approaches apply to text problems as well. In the next few sections, we will see how transfer learning can be applied to both text and image problems and using a few lines of code, we will employ SOTA models ourselves.

Transfer learning for images

Transfer learning is not a new idea. The computer vision community has been practising it for several years now to learn features and even used complete pre-trained models. The adoption of transfer learning for images was significantly accelerated by the ImageNet project, which showed the importance of the quantity and quality of training data on model performance. Most SOTA models for image processing are trained on the ImageNet dataset. Let us understand the ImageNet database better.

ImageNet database

One of the most significant developments in the past couple of decades of image processing has been the development of the ImageNet project. It continues to have a significant impact on research and has contributed significantly to the advances in artificial intelligence for image tasks we see around us. The dataset was originally published in 2009. It contained 1.2 million training instances for objects from 1,000 different categories. It was one of the biggest publicly available datasets at the time. The dataset and the project have been evolving and the dataset contains about 14.2 million images (as of July 2023). The **ImageNet Large Scale Visual Recognition Challenge** (**ILSVRC**) is based on the ImageNet dataset and has been instrumental in advancing deep learning and computer vision research.

Note: You can learn more about the ImageNet project here: https://www.image-net.org/index.php

The rich ImageNet dataset, publicly available for free, is an excellent resource for training and testing models. Over time, the ImageNet dataset became a go-to resource for research and development. One of the key insights that greatly accelerated transfer learning was that weights trained on the ImageNet dataset could be used for other tasks. Consequently, most SOTA have been trained, in some way or the other, on the ImageNet dataset. These models, with ImageNet training weights, can be further fine-tuned for the specific task. To understand better if we can use the SOTA model out of the box or need to fine tune, we need to understand a few considerations. Let us do so in the following section.

Choosing a Transfer Learning approach

The best case for fine tuning is when the data and task on which the model was trained are the same as or similar to your application. In such a situation, it may be possible to use the model directly. This means that we do not perform any fine tuning and use the model as we did in the section *Using a SOTA image classification model*. However, such alignment between our task and the model is rare.

For example, your task is to separate images of fashion articles into shirts/ trousers/ shoes etc. Models trained on Fashion MNIST, or similar datasets (that use full colour images) are great candidates for the task. It might happen that the original model was trained to identify, say, 20 item categories. While you need to identify just 5. In this situation, using a pre-trained model and modifying the final dense layer (that makes the prediction) to adjust for the number of classes might be a good starting point. The idea is that the many layers of the pre-trained model have learnt some great feature representations that you can use to get high performance yourself. The following table shows a choice of transfer learning approach:

Size of New Dataset	**Large**	Train the model from scratch	Fine tune
	Small	Use higher-level features from the pre-trained model. Learn low-level features from data.	Chances of overfitting. Train simple classifiers using features from the pre-trained model.
		Low	High
		Similarity to Original Dataset	

***Table 11.1**: Choice of transfer learning approach*

In yet another, much more common, situation, you might not find a pre-trained model that matches your task and data well. For example, your task could be to identify the species of the flower from the image, but you might not find any pre-trained model for this task. However, models trained on the `imagenet` database can identify a thousand categories of objects in images and a flower is one of them. This is a situation where you might need to fine tune a pre-trained model. If you have little training data, fine tuning might be a good option. However, if you have a fair amount of labelled data, then training a model from scratch may be a better option. The four situations - based on the size of your dataset and similarity with the data for the pre-trained model - and the action in each case are listed in *Table 11.1*. Whether the features learnt by the pre-trained model can be useful for your task is a key consideration in this choice.

Fine tuning approaches

From *Table 11.1* we can understand fine-tuning approaches but it is rather a simplification. There are various other choices as follows:

- Unfreeze and train only the final prediction layer.
- Unfreeze and train all fully connected layers, using features from convolution layers.
- Replace final layers with custom layers; train only those (freeze the remaining layers).
- Unfreeze and train (very low learning rate) all layers.

Again, as discussed in the previous section, the choice depends on the data at hand and the data scientist's judgement on what knowledge from the pre-trained model can be transferred to the task at hand.

In general, freezing certain layers, i.e., making them untrainable is a usual step in transfer learning. Including or excluding the top/final predictive layer of the model is also a standard choice we must make. The model class in Keras/TensorFlow makes such configurations convenient. Let us see how these can be done.

Let us import the **EfficientNetB5** pre-trained model again using Keras Applications by executing the following code:

```
from keras.applications.efficientnet import EfficientNetB5

model_base = EfficientNetB5(weights='imagenet',

                            include_top=False,

                            pooling='avg')
```

With this, we have the **base model** in memory. The difference this time is that we do not have the prediction layer (by setting **include_top** to **False**) and will need to specify our own. This allows us to use the model on a task with categories different from the original dataset.

Note: Another change in the code that you might notice is specifying avg to the pooling parameter. This parameter defines the output format (agrees with the final convolutional layer). If set to None, the output would be a 4D tensor. If we apply an average pooling, as in the preceding code, the output of the model would be a 2D tensor. Be mindful that the pooling is done across width and height, thereby reducing two dimensions from the input. If you add any layers to the model, you need to be mindful of the output dimensions.

A (truncated) summary of this model is shown in *Figure 11.11*:

```
 top_bn (BatchNormalization)     (None, None, None,    8192        ['top_conv[0][0]']
                                 2048)

 top_activation (Activation)     (None, None, None,    0           ['top_bn[0][0]']
                                 2048)

 avg_pool (GlobalAveragePooling  (None, 2048)          0           ['top_activation[0][0]']
 2D)

==================================================================================================
Total params: 28,513,527
Trainable params: 28,340,784
Non-trainable params: 172,743
```

***Figure 11.11**: Trainable parameters in the model*

Note that most parameters in the default state are trainable. If you wish to train all these layers and parameters, you only need to add the final layers and fit the model on the data. Of course, you will be training **all the layers and all parameters** of the model. If we wish to make the base model completely non-trainable, that is, freeze all the layers imported, we can do so with the following command:

```
model_base.trainable = False
```

The truncated summary of this model is shown in *Figure 11.12:*

```
top_bn (BatchNormalization)     (None, None, None,    8192        ['top_conv[0][0]']
                                2048)

top_activation (Activation)     (None, None, None,    0           ['top_bn[0][0]']
                                2048)

==================================================================================
Total params: 28,513,527
Trainable params: 0
Non-trainable params: 28,513,527
```

Figure 11.12*: Non-trainable parameters on freezing the model*

The single command freezes all the layers in the base model. As shown in *Figure 11.14*. We can see that the number of trainable parameters is exactly 0 and the total parameters match the non-trainable parameters. In this setup, you are using freezing the base model and will mostly add some final predictive layers that you need to train.

We can also freeze/unfreeze specific layers in the model. The Keras model class makes the layers iterable, so we could loop over them and take action. The following commands make all but the last 5 layers of the base model trainable. Execute the following code:

```
model_base.trainable = True

for layer in model_base.layers[:-5]:

  layer.trainable = False
```

A (truncated) summary of the model is shown in *Figure 11.13*. We have about 1 million trainable parameters. These belong to the final 5 layers that we froze. You can try changing the number of layers to freeze and verify that the number of trainable parameters changes correspondingly.

```
top_conv (Conv2D)               (None, None, None,    1048576     ['block7c_add[0][0]']
                                2048)

top_bn (BatchNormalization)     (None, None, None,    8192        ['top_conv[0][0]']
                                2048)

top_activation (Activation)     (None, None, None,    0           ['top_bn[0][0]']
                                2048)

==================================================================================
Total params: 28,513,527
Trainable params: 1,052,672
Non-trainable params: 27,460,855
```

Figure 11.13*: Trainable parameters after freezing the final 5 layers*

Note: The number of layers to freeze is a choice and is therefore another hyper-parameter. The data scientist must therefore be careful in making this choice. As discussed in multiple earlier chapters, while some parts of hyper-parameter optimization can be automated, a good understanding of the data and the task at hand is essential for maximizing the performance of the model.

Now that we understand how we can freeze/unfreeze parts of the model, we have learned how to make our base model. To this base model, we would need to add our layers and train on new data. Let us learn to do so in the next section.

Fine tuning a SOTA image model

Our case study for this learning would be the task of classifying images, our model would identify if the scene contained in it is rural or urban. In modern automobiles with smart features, identifying traffic signs is an important task. A common application is to detect and inform the user about a changing speed limit by detecting the appropriate traffic sign. The signs, their frequency and nature can differ between rural and urban settings (for example, city speed limits are usually lower). Identifying whether the user is in a rural/urban setting is therefore an important task. We will use a small, curated dataset of urban and rural images and fine tune a SOTA model on it.

Some sample images from the data are shown in *Figure 11.14:*

***Figure 11.14:** Sample images from the data*

The top row in *Figure 11.16* contains samples of rural images in the data, while the bottom row contains images of urban settings. You might already identify from these sample images that there are significant differences between the two classes. Although, it is not straightforward to articulate the differences and it is therefore not a trivial task for the model either. We need to employ a complex model that has learnt some excellent feature representations that we can leverage.

Let us define our approach to solving this problem. The approach that we will follow, to fine tune a SOTA image model is as follows:

1. Start with a base model with pre-trained weights loaded (**`ImageNet`** weights).
2. Make all layers trainable (we will train with a very low learning rate).
3. Add predictive head/new final layers.
4. Train this new model on the dataset.

We will use the **`EfficientNetB5`** model from Keras Applications. The model is SOTA which has 30.6 million parameters and a depth of 312. The model has been trained on ImageNet and therefore has learnt features on training on millions of images. We will use most layers of this model and take advantage of the extensive knowledge contained in them. But first, let us load and prepare the dataset for modelling.

Note: For the following steps, make sure that the file rural_urban.zip has been added to your working directory.

First, let us unzip the dataset in our working directory. This can be done very simply, using the following command:

```
!unzip "rural_urban.zip"
```

This should create two additional folders in the working directory. The **`train`** and **`val`** folders further contain one folder each for rural and urban images. Note that if you are not using Google Colab, the appearance could be different and the **`sample_data`** folder could be missing. The structure is shown in *Figure. 11.15:*

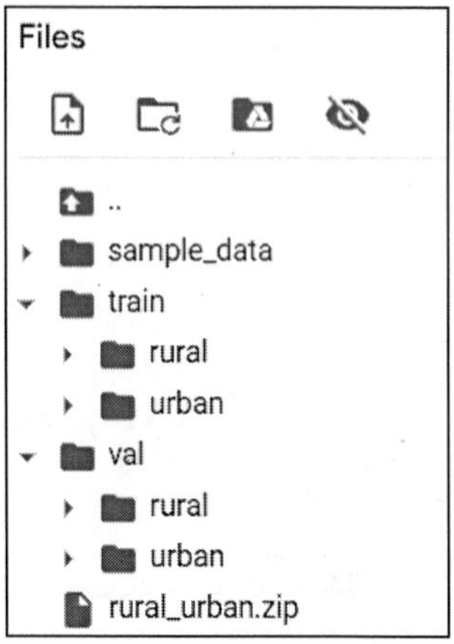

***Figure 11.15**: Folder structure on unzipping*

This structure is a common way of organizing image data and Keras has a utility that lets us load data from directories conveniently. Let us import the utility using the following command:

```
import keras

from keras.utils import image_dataset_from_directory as load_images
```

load_images can now be used to read directly from directories. We have separate folders for training and validation. To create a dataset generator for the training images, we can use the following code:

```
train_ds = load_images(

  "train",

  seed=42,

  image_size=(224, 224),

  label_mode='categorical',

  batch_size=12)
```

The output of the command is:

Found 72 files belonging to 2 classes

We specified a seed 42 so that the batches generated are consistent and created 6 batches from the data. We have a total of just 72 images, so our dataset is small. The image size is 224 x 224. Next, create a generator for the validation images using the following code:

```
val_ds = load_images(

  "val",

  seed=42,

  image_size=(224, 224),

  label_mode='categorical',

  batch_size=20)
```

The output should be as follows:

Found 20 files belonging to 2 classes

With the dataset generators for train and validation at hand, we can load and start configuring the model. Let us begin by loading the model, excluding the predictive top and specify the input size as 224 x 224 using the following code:

```
from keras.applications.efficientnet import EfficientNetB5, decode_predictions

model_base = EfficientNetB5(weights='imagenet',
```

```
                                include_top=False,
                                pooling='avg',
                                input_shape=(224,224,3))
```

The model is now instantiated as we desired. The next step is to make sure all layers of the model are trainable. We do so, using the following command:

```
model_base.trainable = True
```

The base model is ready. Now, we must make our modifications. We will keep it simple and add only one dense layer with 32 neurons and a dense layer with 2 classes for the prediction. Note that this is a choice, and you could add more layers as well. Let us see the following code:

```
from keras.models import Sequential
from keras.layers import Dense, Dropout


model_upd = Sequential()
model_upd.add(model_base)
model_upd.add(Dense(32,activation='relu'))
model_upd.add(Dense(2,activation='softmax'))
```

The model architecture has now been defined. The summary of the model is shown in *Figure 11.16*:

```
Model: "sequential"
_________________________________________________________________
 Layer (type)                Output Shape              Param #
=================================================================
 efficientnetb5 (Functional)  (None, 2048)             28513527

 dense (Dense)               (None, 32)                65568

 dense_1 (Dense)             (None, 2)                 66

=================================================================
Total params: 28,579,161
Trainable params: 28,406,418
Non-trainable params: 172,743
```

***Figure 11.16**: Summary of our model*

Note the number of trainable and non-trainable parameters in *Figure 11.17*. Most of the layers are trainable. *Figure 11.17* also confirms that the base model (**efficientnetb5)** has been incorporated into the new model architecture. Let us now specify the optimizer and compile the model using the following code. We will use a very low learning rate of **3e-5.** Execute the following code:

```
optimizer = keras.optimizers.Adam(learning_rate=3e-5)

model_upd.compile(loss='categorical_crossentropy',

                  optimizer=optimizer,

                  metrics=['accuracy'])
```

Now, we fit the model on the train data for 15 epochs using the following code:

```
history = model_upd.fit(train_ds,

                        epochs=5,

                        validation_data=val_ds,

                        validation_steps=1,

                        verbose=1)
```

To assess the model performance on the validation data, let us plot the learning curve using the following code:

```
import matplotlib.pyplot as plt

plt.plot(history.history['val_accuracy'])

plt.title("Validation accuracy")

plt.show()
```

The output should be similar to that shown in *Figure 11.17:*

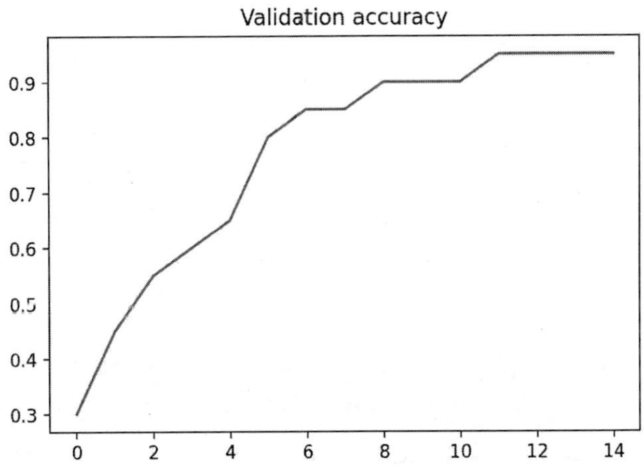

Figure 11.17: *Validation accuracy over the training*

We can see in *Figure 11.19* that towards the end we got 95% accuracy on the validation data. This can be considered a pretty good result considering the small size of our data and that it took us only a few minutes to arrive at this result.

The case study above is a good summary of the learnings on transfer learning for images. Note that there were several choices that we needed to make during the process. We also discussed the various considerations in making these choices. We used the SOTA **`EfficientNetB5`** model (30 million parameters, depth 312) and fine-tuned it for our task in a few minutes. We got a very impressive result that highlights the power of transfer learning and how easy it is to use SOTA models for anyone. Now, let us turn our attention towards transfer learning for text, an extremely exciting space with rapid developments taking place every week.

Transfer learning for text

Like it is for computer vision/ image processing tasks, transfer learning is a boon for text/ NLP tasks as well. The applications of transfer learning are as follows:

- Prediction using pre-trained models
- Feature extraction
- Fine tuning

As with considerations for image use cases, we need to be mindful of the task at hand and the data we have. We discussed the various tasks in Natural Language Processing in *Chapter 10, Optimizing NLP Models*. Let us understand how transfer learning can benefit NLP tasks.

Applications of transfer learning for text

Recent developments in Transformer models (models using the transformer architecture) have enabled machines to outperform humans on many (if not most) NLP tasks. As the open-source model becomes more prominent, most of the state-of-the-art models on these tasks are now available to the public to use via transfer learning.

Hugging Face is a leading organization in the open-source movement and it makes most of the SOTA models easily available in Python. More on this in the next section. **SpaCy** is another great package that provides models for many tasks available via a simple API. **Stanford NLP** is another notable example of some great NLP research work available to the community. Let us see how these can be used for the three main applications of transfer learning.

Prediction using pre-trained models

For most of the NLP tasks listed in the previous section, you could easily find stable implementations of SOTA models via the **`transformers`** library by Hugging Face. As we will see in the next section, these are available through a simple-to-use API and Hugging Face is therefore great for beginners. SpaCy also has a clean and simple-to-use API and high-performance models available for multiple NLP tasks.

Feature extraction

Word embeddings are an extremely popular way of representing the meaning in the text. The Stanford NLP group has made available pre-trained word vectors trained on massive datasets (for example, embeddings from 27 billion tokens from Twitter tweets). Similarly, Facebook created **`FastText`** embeddings that are available to all. Google's **Universal Sentence Encoder** (**USE**; available on TensorFlow hub) is a relatively recent model (based on the BERT transformer model) that helps generate powerful representations for sentences. Hugging Face also has made available various other transformer models which you can employ for feature extraction.

Note: To learn more about word embeddings and the amazing ways in which they capture meaning, and to learn about GloVe Product by Stanford NLP, visit https://nlp.stanford.edu/projects/glove/

Fine tuning

Hugging Face is a notable example that allows easy fine tuning of most models available for most tasks. Tuning can be done using **`Tensorflow`** (or even Keras), **`PyTorch`** and **`Flax`** conveniently using only a few lines of code. The process is very similar to that for image models.

Let us now see for ourselves how we can leverage transfer learning for text using Hugging Face's solutions.

Hugging face for transfer learning

At the time of writing this chapter, Hugging Face is one of the most popular organizations in the open-source community. The **`transformers`** library by Hugging Face is the most popular NLP library in Python. It allows you to build, train and deploy state-of-the-art models via a clean API that is simple to use and perfect for beginners. They can be credited with making transformer models widely accessible to the masses. In recent times, most SOTA models became available on Hugging Face shortly after being published. This can also be attributed to the fact that more than 5,000 organizations actively use their solutions, and their research teams readily make the latest models available on the Hugging Face platform. Let us now familiarize ourselves with the extremely popular and powerful **`transformers`** library from Hugging Face.

Note: To learn more about Hugging Face, visit their website (https://huggingface.co). The site contains details on the many models available on the platform, some great documentation on using the Transformers library, and some great courses on deep learning.

To access the models made available by Hugging Face, you need to install the **`transformers`** library in Python. Using the pip command makes it simple as shown in the following code snippet:

```
!pip install transformers
```

There could be differences depending on the existing packages on your system. If you are using Google Colab, the output should not be very different. The output should be like the image in *Figure 11.18*:

```
!pip install transformers

Looking in indexes: https://pypi.org/simple, https://us-python.pkg.dev/colab-wheels/public/simple/
Collecting transformers
  Downloading transformers-4.26.1-py3-none-any.whl (6.3 MB)
     ━━━━━━━━━━━━━━━━━━━━━━━━━━━━━━━━━━━━━━━━ 6.3/6.3 MB 96.8 MB/s eta 0:00:00
Requirement already satisfied: pyyaml>=5.1 in /usr/local/lib/python3.8/dist-packages (from transformers) (6.0)
Requirement already satisfied: requests in /usr/local/lib/python3.8/dist-packages (from transformers) (2.25.1)
Collecting tokenizers!=0.11.3,<0.14,>=0.11.1
  Downloading tokenizers-0.13.2-cp38-cp38-manylinux_2_17_x86_64.manylinux2014_x86_64.whl (7.6 MB)
     ━━━━━━━━━━━━━━━━━━━━━━━━━━━━━━━━━━━━━━━━ 7.6/7.6 MB 112.6 MB/s eta 0:00:00
Requirement already satisfied: tqdm>=4.27 in /usr/local/lib/python3.8/dist-packages (from transformers) (4.64.1)
Requirement already satisfied: filelock in /usr/local/lib/python3.8/dist-packages (from transformers) (3.9.0)
Requirement already satisfied: packaging>=20.0 in /usr/local/lib/python3.8/dist-packages (from transformers) (23.0)
Requirement already satisfied: numpy>=1.17 in /usr/local/lib/python3.8/dist-packages (from transformers) (1.22.4)
Collecting huggingface-hub<1.0,>=0.11.0
  Downloading huggingface_hub-0.12.1-py3-none-any.whl (190 kB)
```

Figure 11.18: *Transformers library installation*

Hugging Face also provides access to several datasets to benchmark various NLP tasks. To access them, install the datasets library using the following command:

```
!pip install datasets
```

On successful execution, you would have access to all the models available on Hugging Face and all the datasets. Using the transformers library is straightforward with the use of **pipelines**.

Pipelines are a straightforward way to use existing models for inference/prediction. You could also build your own NLP pipelines with ease. These are essentially abstractions (objects that have various methods available for various NLP tasks). The way to use the pipeline varies slightly with the task and the API is therefore very general purpose. The way to use a pipeline for, say, text classification is like the usage for text summarization. The Transformers library smartly performs the background actions needed without complicating the usage.

Pipelines perform the following steps:

- **Preprocessing:** A tokenizer takes the raw input text, breaks it down, and maps it to token (IDs).
- **Model application:** A model (usually pre-trained) is used to make predictions from the inputs.
- Some (optional) post-processing on the model's output, modifying it to suit the requirements of the specific task.

To gain a better understanding, let us create our initial sentiment analysis pipeline. We will observe how Hugging Face simplifies the process of utilizing the most up-to-date transformer models. We initiate by importing the pipeline module with the given command:

```
from transformers import pipeline
```

For instantiating a pipeline, the task must be specified. For a sentiment analysis task, we must specify **`sentiment-analysis`** as an argument to the call, as shown in the following command:

```
classifier = pipeline("sentiment-analysis")
```

The library would download the model and required utilities, as seen in the following figure:

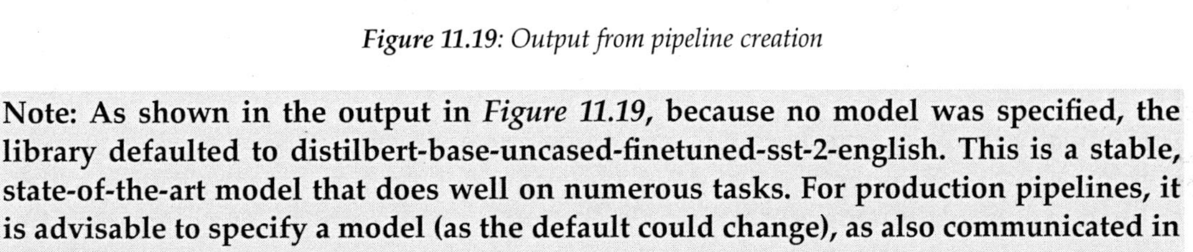

***Figure 11.19**: Output from pipeline creation*

Note: As shown in the output in *Figure 11.19*, because no model was specified, the library defaulted to distilbert-base-uncased-finetuned-sst-2-english. This is a stable, state-of-the-art model that does well on numerous tasks. For production pipelines, it is advisable to specify a model (as the default could change), as also communicated in the output.

With the given two lines of code, you now have a powerful SOTA model for sentiment analysis loaded in memory and ready to apply to any input text. Let us go ahead and try it out on a simple input text, as shown in the following command:

```
res = classifier("No good acting or great story in this movie.")
res
```

The output gets printed as follows:

```
[{'label': 'NEGATIVE', 'score': 0.9997885823249817}]
```

The model predicts the sentiment in the text to be negative, with a high level of confidence (0.99978 probability). Despite the highly positive individual phrases like **good acting** and a **great story**, the model identified that the **no** at the beginning of the sentence negates all the positive phrases. Go ahead, and try out a few other input sentences to assess for yourself if the predictions are good.

This is simple, we use a SOTA model for sentiment analysis on arbitrary input data with just a couple of lines of code. This example should reiterate the power of Transfer Learning for text. In the next sections, we will see some examples of using the transformer library for various NLP tasks.

Sentiment analysis

In the previous section, we saw an example of a sentiment classification task. For simplicity, we used the default model and only one sentence as input to the model. However, the transformers library allows us to choose the model to employ in the pipeline. For example, if you are working on Tweets and wish to use the Twitter `RoBERTa` model for this purpose, choosing the model for the pipeline is as simple as using the following command:

```
classifier = pipeline("sentiment-analysis",
                      "cardiffnlp/twitter-roberta-base-sentiment")
```

Note: The exact reference to use for the model is available on the model's page on the Hugging Face site: https://huggingface.co/cardiffnlp/twitter-roberta-base-sentiment. To get a full list of the models available, check out the Hugging Face website at the following link: https://huggingface.co/models.

Additionally, we are not restricted to providing just a single input string. We can easily provide a list of strings and the pipeline would provide the output corresponding to each of them in a list. Additionally, data can also be provided in batches (using generators) to the pipeline. Let us try out this Twitter data-trained model on a few different input texts in the next exercise.

Exercise 11.1: RoBERTa for tweet sentiment classification

In this exercise, we will use the Twitter `RoBERTa` model for classifying the sentiment of a few input tweets. The `roBERTa-base` model was trained on approximately 58M tweets for the purpose of sentiment analysis. We therefore expect this model to handle some non-standard language usage and some usual features of tweets (hashtags, smileys for example). Let us perform the following steps.

1. Begin by importing the pipeline from the transformers library and instantiating a pipeline using the Twitter **RoBERTa** model. Make sure to use the model reference we used in the previous section. Use the following code:

   ```
   from transformers import pipeline
   classifier = pipeline("sentiment-analysis",
                         "cardiffnlp/twitter-roberta-base-sentiment")
   ```

2. Create a list that contains a few simple sentences that contain smileys, as shown in the following command:

   ```
   input_tweets = ['Love the mountains! :D #blessed',
                   'Super supper wid besties xoxo #livingitup',
                   'Dis is it. Njoy it to the fullest #YOLO :D'
                   ]
   ```

3. Run the tweets by the classifier and print the output, as shown in the following code snippet:

   ```
   res = classifier(input_tweets)
   res
   ```

   The following output is printed:

   ```
   [{'label': 'LABEL_2', 'score': 0.988944411277771},
    {'label': 'LABEL_2', 'score': 0.9282486438751221},
    {'label': 'LABEL_2', 'score': 0.9688595533370972}]
   ```

All three tweets were correctly labeled as having positive sentiment, with high confidence. We must appreciate that creating a model from scratch that can handle such non-standard text would require a lot of effort. With the **transformers** library, we have a solution with just a few lines.

Text generation

Another popular task in NLP is text generation. In a common form of text generation, the user provides some initial text that provides the necessary context for the model. The model then generates a specified number of sequences with a specified length. **GPT-3, GPT-4, and ChatGPT** are popular examples of models that have been trained in a semi-supervised manner and are SOTA for text generation.

With the **Transformers** library, a pipeline for text generation is extremely simple to use. Let us try it out ourselves. We first create a pipeline and specify **text-generation** as the task in the following command:

```
generator = pipeline("text-generation")
```

You should get the output with the details of the download progress as shown in the following figure:

```
No model was supplied, defaulted to gpt2 and revision 6c0e608 (https://huggingface.co/gpt2).
Using a pipeline without specifying a model name and revision in production is not recommended.
Downloading (…)lve/main/config.json: 100%          665/665 [00:00<00:00, 8.34kB/s]
Downloading (…)"pytorch_model.bin";: 100%          548M/548M [00:02<00:00, 238MB/s]
Downloading (…)neration_config.json: 100%          124/124 [00:00<00:00, 2.43kB/s]
Downloading (…)olve/main/vocab.json: 100%          1.04M/1.04M [00:00<00:00, 16.9MB/s]
Downloading (…)olve/main/merges.txt: 100%          456k/456k [00:00<00:00, 5.65MB/s]
Downloading (…)/main/tokenizer.json: 100%          1.36M/1.36M [00:00<00:00, 18.1MB/s]
```

***Figure 11.20**: Output from initializing the text-generation pipeline*

Note that the library defaulted to using **GPT2**, as no model was specified. **GPT2** is good for our purpose. Now, we simply need to provide the initial text, the maximum length of the output string, and the number of sequences to return. Take a look at the following command:

```
res = generator("A father's love for his daughter",
                max_length=30,
                num_return_sequences=3)
```

The output is shown in the following figure:

```
[{'generated_text': "A father's love for his daughter, Aja (Jodie Foster) is so
strong that he has to deal with having his entire life ruined"},
 {'generated_text': "A father's love for his daughter began early in life, he has
not seen his daughter since she was 8 years old. Now he has lost his"},
 {'generated_text': "A father's love for his daughter has been tested and
tested.\n\nA father's love for his daughter has been tested and tested.\n\n"}]
```

***Figure 11.21**: Output of text generator*

The output in *Figure 11.21* contains the three responses from the model. All three sentences are grammatically correct and individually coherent. The first output is interesting as it seems to be inspired by a movie review/synopsis. This gives some indication of the kind of patterns and data that the model was trained on. Let us now look at another important task in NLP: Zero Shot Classification.

Zero-shot classification

In a general machine learning context, Zero-shot Learning is when the model can predict the class without any prior training data. In the context of NLP, Zero-shot classification would allow making predictions without any prior training. The user provides only the input text and the choice of labels. Conceptually, this is possible when the model understands the labels and the input text in the same way. Let us create a simple pipeline for Zero-shot classification using the following code:

```
classifier = pipeline("zero-shot-classification")
```

The output is shown in the following figure:

```
No model was supplied, defaulted to facebook/bart-large-mnli and revision c626438 (http
Using a pipeline without specifying a model name and revision in production is not reco

Downloading (…)lve/main/config.json:            1.15k/1.15k [00:00<00:00,
100%                                            10.4kB/s]

Downloading (…)"pytorch_model.bin";:            1.63G/1.63G [00:19<00:00,
100%                                            81.5MB/s]
```

***Figure 11.22**: (Truncated) output from pipeline creation*

The library chose the **`BART Large`** model by Facebook, more details about the model can be found at the following link: **https://huggingface.co/docs/transformers/model_doc/bart.**

Now, let us create the input corpus (the sentences that the model must map correctly to a candidate label). We must also create a list containing the candidate variables the model must choose from. Use the following code:

```
inp_corpus = ["The family will meet at my uncles place'",

              "A CEO must be organised.",

              "My niece is super annoying."]

labels = ["business", "politics", "family"]
```

The labels we provided were: **`business`**, **`politics`** and **`family`**. If the model works fine, no sentence should be mapped to **`politics`**. Next, we use the pipeline similarly. This time, the pipeline needs an additional input, the **`candidate_labels`**. Use the following code to make the predictions and print:

```
res = classifier(inp_corpus,

                 candidate_labels = labels)

res
```

The output is shown in the following figure:

```
[{'sequence': "The family will meet at my uncles place'",
  'labels': ['family', 'business', 'politics'],
  'scores': [0.9936457276344299, 0.0033247247338294983, 0.003029499901458621]},
 {'sequence': 'A CEO must be organised.',
  'labels': ['business', 'politics', 'family'],
  'scores': [0.9443104863166809, 0.03410574793815613, 0.021583713591098785]},
 {'sequence': 'My niece is super annoying.',
  'labels': ['family', 'business', 'politics'],
  'scores': [0.995790421962738, 0.0021097641438245773, 0.0020998634863364484]}]
```

Figure 11.23: *Output from Zero shot classification pipeline*

Figure 11.23 shows that the model pipeline output contains, for each input, the top labels, and their associated scores. The most probable is listed first. Sentences 1 and 3 were mapped to **`family`** with extremely high scores. Sentence 2 was mapped to **`business`** as we expected. Now, let us look at another extremely important application of NLP, translation.

Translation

Translation between languages using the **`Hugging Face transformers`** library has very similar usage with its pipeline module. Note that for the translation task we must have a source and a target language. The model for the pipeline is also chosen accordingly. For example, if we are to translate text from English to French, the model in the pipeline must be an English-to-French model. Let us create our own simple pipeline for this task.

Create a pipeline with **`translation_en_to_fr`** as the task, as in the following code:

```
en_to_fr = pipeline("translation_en_to_fr")
```

The output is shown in the following figure:

```
No model was supplied, defaulted to t5-base and revision 686f1db (https://huggingfa
Using a pipeline without specifying a model name and revision in production is not
Downloading (…)lve/main/config.json: 100%            1.21k/1.21k |
Downloading (…)"pytorch_model.bin";: 100%            892M/892M
Downloading (…)neration_config.json: 100%            147/147 [00:
```

Figure 11.24: *Output from pipeline creation*

Note that as no model was specified, **`T5`** was chosen. **`T5`** is a powerful translation model trained on a very large corpus. More details can be found at: **https://huggingface.co/t5-base**

With the pipeline ready, translating is as simple as supplying the source language text to the pipeline. Use the following code:

```
text_en = "Aiza is moving to London"

text_fr = en_to_fr(text_en)

text_fr
```

The output is given here:

```
[{'translation_text': 'Aiza déménage à Londres'}]
```

The resulting translation is indeed the standard translation one would expect. Yet again, a SOTA model like **T5**, trained on several billion tokens, could be employed easily with very few lines of code.

Fine tuning a SOTA NLP model

By now we have seen how easy it is to use pre-trained models from Hugging Face for various NLP tasks. But sometimes we need to fine tune the model to work better on our domain/data. The **transformers** library enables you to perform fine tuning with ease using a couple of utilities and support for **TensorFlow**, **PyTorch** and **JAX**.

The key steps in the process would be:

1. Import the dataset to fine tune on.
2. Import the preprocessing utility (tokenizer) for the task.
3. Choose and load the pre-trained model designed for the task.
4. Compile the model with necessary settings (optimizer, loss etc.).
5. Fit the model.

The initial decision involves selecting the appropriate tokenizer, which is responsible for dividing the input text string into a sequence of tokens for the model to handle. It is crucial to choose a tokenizer that aligns with the specific task at hand. For instance, when dealing with Twitter tweets, it is advisable to utilize tokenizers trained on Twitter data or similar social media datasets. In the following section, we will explore the usage of a tokenizer and its application.

We will use the tokenizer from **BERT**, the popular transformer model that showed great success in language modelling and next sequence prediction tasks. The tokenizer from the **BERT** model can also be used with other models. In our case, we will use the **BERT** case model for tokenizing. Let us begin by importing the **AutoTokenizer** utility from the **transformers** library. Execute the following code:

```
from transformers import AutoTokenizer
```

Using the **AutoTokenizer** utility, we can load the tokenizer from the **BERT** case model, using the following command:

```
tokenizer = AutoTokenizer.from_pretrained("bert-base-cased")
```

The tokenizer is ready to process input text. It can take in iterables and can return **numpy** tensors that can be then used in **TensorFlow** or **PyTorch**.

Note: The tokenizer must be agreeable with the final model that you intend to use. For example, if you wish to use a BERT cased model for fine tuning/prediction, a Twitter RoBERTa-based tokenizer is not a good choice.

The second choice you must make is that of the pre-trained model you wish to fine tune. **HuggingFace** has a large list of models available. You must identify the one suitable for your task and compatible with the tokenizer you chose. For loading a model for text, a frequently used utility is **TFAutoModelForSequenceClassification** from the **transformers** library. This is a generic model class that can be used to get a specific model. It returns a model object that you can use in **TensorFlow** or **Keras**, using the following code:

```
from transformers import TFAutoModelForSequenceClassification as TFA
```

To load a specific pre-trained model, all you need to do is use the following command, where **model_name** needs to be replaced by the name of the model you wish to load. Use the following code:

```
model = TFA.from_pretrained("model_name")
```

With this command and the previous one, you now have a trainable SOTA model at your disposal to make predictions or fine tune. This can be used like any other **TensorFlow/Keras** model. To fine tune this, you can compile the model, supply the dataset and fit the model using a very low learning rate. Note that depending on the dataset size, training settings and the extent of fine tuning, the fine-tuning activity can take a very small or very large amount of time.

Exercise 11.2: Fine tuning a BERT model

In this exercise, we will fine tune the **BERT** cased model (that was trained on a large amount of text in the public domain), on an NLP task in the **General Language Understanding Evaluation(GLUE)** dataset. It consists of data for 9 NLP tasks around natural language understanding/ modelling. The GLUE benchmark format is model agnostic, therefore many different types of models can be benchmarked and compared.

Note: More information on GLUE benchmarking, detailed descriptions of the tasks involved, some starter code, datasets and a leaderboard with the best-performing models on GLUE tasks can be found at https://gluebenchmark.com/

We will fine tune the **BERT** model for the **Corpus of Linguistic Acceptability (CoLA)** task. The task is to classify if a provided input sentence in English is grammatically correct. It consists of 10,657 sentences along with an annotation indicating if they are grammatically correct. More details on the dataset can be found at **https://nyu-mll.github.io/CoLA/**.

Follow the given steps:

1. Begin by importing the data for the CoLA task from the GLUE dataset. We use the **load_dataset** method from the **datasets** library. Use the following code:

```
from datasets import load_dataset
dataset = load_dataset("glue", "cola")
```

The (truncated) output is given in the following code:

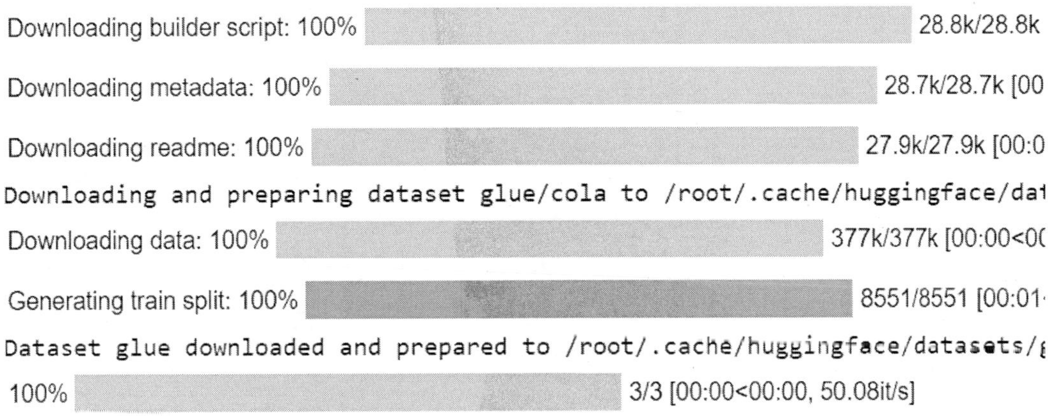

Figure 11.25: GLUE dataset downloaded and prepared

2. Extract the training subset. Print the contents of the **train_ds** variable. Use the following code:

```
train_ds = dataset["train"]
train_ds
```

The output is shown here:

```
Dataset({
    features: ['sentence', 'label', 'idx'],
    num_rows: 8551
})
```

The output shows that the dataset has 8,551 sentences for training and a label.

3. Print 5 sentences and their corresponding labels to examine the data, using the following code:

```
train_ds['sentence'][40:45], train_ds['label'][40:45]
```

The output is shown here:

```
(['They caused him to become angry by making him.',
  'They caused him to become president by making him.',
  'They made him to exhaustion.',
  'They made him into a monster.',
  'The trolley rumbled through the tunnel.'],
 [0, 0, 0, 1, 1])
```

As you can see, the first three sentences are not grammatically correct, and the corresponding labels confirm this.

4. Use the **AutoTokenizer** utility from the transformers library and load the tokenizer from the **bert-base-cased** model. Use the following code:

```
from transformers import AutoTokenizer
tokenizer = AutoTokenizer.from_pretrained("bert-base-cased")
```

5. Convert it into a dictionary for ease of processing. Apply this tokenizer to generate training tokens using the following command:

```
train_tokens = tokenizer(dataset["sentence"], \
                         return_tensors="np", \
                         padding=True)
train_tokens = dict(train_tokens)
```

6. The labels are currently in a list, copy them into a numpy array using the following code:

```
import numpy as np
labels = np.array(train_ds["label"])
```

The training data is now ready to be supplied to a model.

7. Next, import **TFAAutoModelForSequenceClassification** and import our target model that is, **bert-base-cased** using the following code:

```
from transformers import TFAutoModelForSequenceClassification
as TFA
model = TFA.from_pretrained("bert-base-cased")
```

8. Import the **Adam** optimizer from **Keras** and compile our **BERT** model with a low learning rate of **3e-5**, as shown in the following code:

```
from tensorflow.keras.optimizers import Adam
model.compile(optimizer=Adam(3e-5))
```

The model and data are now ready. We can start the training process.

9. Fit the model for 3 epochs using the following code. Use a 20% validation split:

```
history = model.fit(train_tokens, labels, \
                    epochs=3, \
                    validation_split=0.2, \
                    verbose=2)
```

The training should take a few minutes. The output is shown in the following figure:

```
Epoch 1/3
214/214 - 143s - loss: 0.3233 - accuracy: 0.8652 - val_loss: 0.4199 - val_accuracy: 0.8317
Epoch 2/3
214/214 - 76s - loss: 0.1765 - accuracy: 0.9344 - val_loss: 0.4663 - val_accuracy: 0.8358
Epoch 3/3
214/214 - 76s - loss: 0.1221 - accuracy: 0.9564 - val_loss: 0.5287 - val_accuracy: 0.8369
```

Figure 11.26: *Training output*

In a short span of three epochs and a minimal training time, we accomplished an accuracy of approximately 84% on a sequence classification task. This outcome was achieved with minimal coding on our part, without the need to delve into the intricate details of the SOTA model's implementation.

Note: We used just 3 epochs for pedagogical reasons. Please feel free to train for more epochs to get a better result. Of course, that needs more time and computation.

In this exercise, we demonstrated the simplicity of fine-tuning a cutting-edge NLP model using just a few lines of code. Thanks to the abstraction provided by `HuggingFace's` transformer library, we can easily accomplish this without having to handle the intricate implementation details of the model. This level of convenience enables anyone to effectively leverage SOTA models in their applications.

In the previous sections, around transfer learning for text, we saw that with the advent of transformer models, it is remarkably easy to utilize SOTA models with just a few lines of code. Excellent packages like the `transformers` library by `HuggingFace` abstract the details and enable anyone to start using SOTA models in their applications.

Conclusion

In this chapter, we learned about transfer learning - a powerful way to benefit from the latest advances in the field of artificial intelligence and machine learning. We saw that transfer learning can be used in three ways - prediction, feature extraction, and fine tuning. While there are numerous benefits, we also acknowledge that transfer learning has its limitations that the data scientist must be aware of while employing it.

We saw a general transfer learning process, including one that fine tunes a SOTA model for a different target task. For image problems, we used `Keras` which lets us conveniently and quickly use SOTA models (`Keras` Applications) with minimum coding. We also saw that we could make several choices around this fine tuning easily using `Keras` and we could fine tune the model, using all the utilities, just like we would train any `Keras` model.

Finally, we learnt and practised transfer learning for NLP on various tasks. We saw that the transformers library by Hugging Face is a great way to access various SOTA models for NLP. We used many of the SOTA transformer models for different tasks. We also fine-tuned a BERT model for an NLP task, getting good performance with just a few epochs of training.

You now know not only how to create your own end-to-end models from scratch but also how to benefit from the rapid advances in the field of machine learning and artificial intelligence by using transfer learning effectively.

Join our book's Discord space

Join the book's Discord Workspace for Latest updates, Offers, Tech happenings around the world, New Release and Sessions with the Authors:

https://discord.bpbonline.com

Index